Five Centuries of Civil Procedure

Legal History Library

VOLUME 76

The titles published in this series are listed at *brill.com/lhl*

Five Centuries of Civil Procedure

The Polish Experience in a European Context (16th to 21st Centuries)

Edited by

Andrzej Dziadzio
Franciszek Longchamps de Bérier

BRILL | NIJHOFF

LEIDEN | BOSTON

This publication was funded by the Faculty of Law and Administration of the Jagiellonian University granted within the Priority Research Area Heritage under the program "Excellence Initiative—Research University" at the Jagiellonian University in Kraków.

Cover illustration: (Left) Title page of the statute of King Sigismund I. 1524. Krakow: National Museum in Krakow, Princes Czartoryski Library. 29 III Cim. (Middle) Text on a column of the Supreme Court of Poland in Warsaw. Photograph by Franciszek Longchamps de Bérier. (Right) Coat of arms of the Polish Crown printed in the statute of King Sigismund I. 1524. Krakow: National Museum in Krakow, Princes Czartoryski Library. 29 III Cim.

Library of Congress Cataloging-in-Publication Data

Names: Dziadzio, Andrzej editor | Longchamps de Bérier, Franciszek editor
Title: Five centuries of civil procedure : the Polish experience in a European context (16th to 21st centuries) / edited by Andrzej Dziadzio and Franciszek Longchamps de Bérier.
Description: Leiden ; Boston : Brill Academic Publishers, Inc, 2025. | Series: Legal History Library ; volume 76 | Includes bibliographical references and index.
Identifiers: LCCN 2025029964 | ISBN 9789004736665 hardback | ISBN 9789004736672 epub
Subjects: LCSH: Civil procedure--Poland | Civil procedure--Poland--History | International and municipal law--Poland | Civil law--Poland | Law reform--Poland | Civil procedure--European Union countries | LCGFT: Law commentaries
Classification: LCC KKP1710 .F57 2025 | DDC 347.438/05--DC23/ENG/20250825
LC record available at https://lccn.loc.gov/2025029964

Typeface for the Latin, Greek, and Cyrillic scripts: "Brill". See and download: brill.com/brill-typeface.

ISSN 1874-1793
ISBN 978-90-04-73666-5 (hardback)
ISBN 978-90-04-73667-2 (e-book)
DOI 10.1163/9789004736672

This book is printed on acid-free paper and produced in a sustainable manner.

Contents

Tables

Contributors

Grzegorz J. Blicharz
Associate Professor of Roman Law and Director of the Centre for Law and Religious Freedom at the Department of Roman Law, Faculty of Law and Administration, Jagiellonian University in Kraków, Poland

Andrzej Dziadzio
Professor of Law and Head of the Department of Common History of the State and the Law, Faculty of Law and Administration, Jagiellonian University in Kraków, Poland

Radosław Flejszar
Professor of Civil Procedure and Head of the Department of Civil Procedure, Faculty of Law and Administration, Jagiellonian University in Kraków, Poland

Krzysztof Fokt
Associate Professor of Legal History at the Laboratory of Source Editions, Faculty of Law and Administration, Jagiellonian University in Kraków, Poland

Kacper Górski
Assistant Professor of Legal History at the Department of History of Polish Law, Faculty of Law and Administration, Jagiellonian University in Kraków, Poland

Jan Halberda
Associate Professor of Common History of the State and the Law at the Department of Common History of the State and the Law, Faculty of Law and Administration, Jagiellonian University in Kraków, Poland

Vincent R. Johnson
Distinguished Professor at the St. Mary's University School of Law for Global and International Law, San Antonio, Texas, USA

Izabela Lewandowska-Malec
Professor of Legal History and Head of the Department of History of Polish Law, Faculty of Law and Administration, Jagiellonian University in Kraków, Poland

Martin Löhnig
Professor at the Faculty of Law, University of Regensburg, Germany

Franciszek Longchamps de Bérier
Professor of Law and Head of the Department of Roman Law, Faculty of Law and Administration, Jagiellonian University in Kraków, and Visiting Professor, University of Warsaw, Poland

Dorota Malec
Professor of Law and Head of the Department of the History of Administration and Law on Religious Denominations, Faculty of Law and Administration, Jagiellonian University in Kraków, Poland

Maciej Mikuła
Professor of Legal History at the Department of Ecclesiastical Law and Law on Religious Denominations, Faculty of Law and Administration, Jagiellonian University in Kraków, Poland

Andrzej Olaś
Professor of Civil Procedure at the Department of Civil Procedure, Faculty of Law and Administration, Jagiellonian University in Kraków, Poland

Grzegorz Smyk
Professor of Legal History and Head of the Department of History of the State and the Law, Faculty of Law and Administration, Maria Curie-Skłodowska University in Lublin, Poland

Kamila Staudigl-Ciechowicz
Assistant Professor of Legal and Constitutional History at the Department of Legal and Constitutional History, Faculty of Law, University of Vienna, Austria

Abdoul Yatera
Lecturer at the University of Paris Nanterre and attaché temporaire d'enseignement et de recherche (ATER), Université Paris—Panthéon-Assas, France

Introduction: The Monograph and Its Purpose

Andrzej Dziadzio and Franciszek Longchamps de Bérier

Half a millennium is a beautiful and unique jubilee. It is committed to presenting and assessing the development of Polish civil procedure. The first codification of court proceedings in the form of the so-called *Formula processus* was made in Poland in 1523. Its entry into force 500 years ago prompts contemporary jurists to undertake a careful analysis of the transformation of civil procedure in the European country against the historical background of the development of modern legal orders in Europe. The monograph being presented to readers is the result of the work of a research group established at the Jagiellonian University in Kraków. This group consists not only of Polish historical and modern jurists and scholars specializing in civil procedure and private law. The authors attempt to reconstruct European heritage in the field of legal institutions of civil procedure. They are inspired by the book *European Traditions in Civil Procedure* edited by C.H. van Rhee (Intersentia 2005). Yet, they are interested in the impact of this Polish and European heritage on the currently applicable legal regulations. They try to determine to what extent this heritage is noticeable in the contemporary legal system and to what extent it is appreciated by courts and legal doctrine.

Until now there has been no study of the history of civil procedure in Polish territories made on such a large scale as in the presented monograph. The formal structure of the book organizes the entire discussion on developing civil procedure in terms of content and chronology, bringing closer the phases of the development of Polish civil process: from the Procedural Roman-Canonical law to contemporary procedural systems. Each chapter contains a synthesis of the research that each author has carried out. The chapters are arranged in such a way that they complement each other in order to create a compact, concise and coherent picture of possible changes in the law of civil procedure.

The history of civil litigation in Polish lands was divided, beginning in the 16th century, into three periods. They are marked by two clear caesuras: the loss of independence by the Polish-Lithuanian Commonwealth in 1795, and then its regaining by Poland in 1918. The chronological order required that the chapters of the monograph be arranged in a way that would show the state of procedural legislation for historically distinguished periods: the Polish-Lithuanian state (1569–1795), Poland under three partitions (1795–

 | DOI:10.1163/9789004736672_002

1918) and Polish statehood after 1918, i.e., the Second Republic (1918–39), Poland under communist rule (1944–89) and finally the Third Republic.

The three parts show the originality and specificity of the Polish civil process—both for the Old Polish period and especially for its evolution in the 20th century. The description of the shape of foreign court procedures that were in force on Polish territories, namely French (1806), Russian (1864), German (1877) and Austrian (1895), is, in turn, a starting point for the analysis of the codification works on the creation of Poland's own Code of Civil Procedure. This codification took place in 1930. The new Code of Civil Procedure entered into force in 1933. When the current 1964 Code of Civil Procedure is amended several times each year, the 1933 code developed by the Codification Commission in work the Second Republic set the course for future changes in civil procedure. This is because it provided a clear reference point for later procedural regulations. To some extent, the 1933 code became an antimodel for the 1964 codification, because socialist law of the 1960s found a predilection for the concept of so-called material truth, which justified the admissibility of the court's activity in, for example, seeking evidence. The 1933 code became a source of positive paradigms for numerous amendments of the 1964 code in the democratic state of law after 1989 as a marker of accepted and cultivated legal tradition.

The 1523 codification is of particular importance for the entire history of court proceedings in the former Poland. This codification regulated civil procedure before the courts of the nobility, which applied land law—largely customary and uncodified. Judicial law in the Polish-Lithuanian Commonwealth until its fall in 1795 was social strata-specific. Therefore, each social stratum, i.e., the clergy, nobility, bourgeoisie and peasantry used separate regulations for their civil proceedings. The Roman-Canonical process shaped the legal proceedings before Church courts. Procedural law, codified in 1523, in the form of the so-called *Formula processus*, defined the rules for adjudicating disputes between the nobility. Standards of judicial procedure based on the sources of German law—*Sachsenspiegel, Weichbild* of Magdeburg or *Constitutio Criminalis Carolina*—impacted the course of trials before urban and rural courts. Therefore, the first part of the monograph consists of chapters whose authors analyze the peculiarities of procedural law in Poland from the 16th to the 18th centuries against the background of the two systems of procedural law dominant at that time: the Roman-Canonical process and the common German civil process. Thus, it becomes clear that canon law and broadly understood German law shaped the civil procedure of both land and urban court in the former Poland.

The adoption of the institution of appeals in 1523 is a classic example of the influence of canon law on land and urban trials. On the other hand, the catalog of means of evidence in the Polish territories had features similar to the regulations adopted in German law. Thus, the peculiarities of Polish civil process of the modern era are confronted in the monograph with the principles and development of Procedural Roman-Canonical law and the regulations known from the common German trial. All this made it possible to highlight the distinctiveness and originality of Polish civil procedure.

The separation of administrative and judicial powers was a characteristic feature of the French Napoleonic procedure, the principles of which shaped the civil (but also criminal) procedure in central and eastern Europe in the 19th century. This separation as a principle turned out to be characteristic also of the judiciary of the Polish-Lithuanian Commonwealth. The impact of the principle was evident not only in Polish lands during the period of Napoleon's domination in Europe, when the French procedure was introduced, among others, in the Duchy of Warsaw in 18109, but the principle also influenced the shape of court proceedings after the fall of the German First Reich in 1806. Therefore, the second part of the monograph consists of chapters presenting the French model of civil procedure and its preponderance in Europe of the 19th century, including in Russia, under whose influence the law in Polish territories remained. In this part, the authors of the chapters try to show the process of the implementation of Napoleonic civil procedure on Polish lands in the 19th century, as well as its application on the example of the jurisprudence of the courts of the Free City of Kraków (1815–46). The French model of civil procedure also had to be taken into account when presenting the works that led to the creation of the Polish Code of Civil Procedure in 1930. These works showed the importance of regulations adopted in foreign legislation, i.e., in Austrian, German and Russian law. The experience drawn from the use of these civil procedures on Polish lands until 1918 led to the formation of Poland's own model of civil procedure for the 20th century.

For a fuller understanding of this model, it was necessary also to review the directions of the development of French civil procedure in the 20th and 21st centuries. Within the European Union this constitutes special background for the changes in contemporary Polish civil procedure. This type of finalizing historical analyses and thus marking the challenges of modern times as a result of confronting the evolution of French civil procedure with the reforms of Polish civil process is dictated by the question of what has remained of the European tradition of procedural law to this day. What legal solutions prove to be universal, always maintaining their undeniable value?

The monograph is accompanied by an appendix—a text analyzing the transformation of the English judicial process. It provides evidence of a significant dissimilarity of this process when compared to civil procedures on the continent. The rationale for presenting English law while analyzing the judicial proceedings of the Polish-Lithuanian Commonwealth became the similarities in the development of these legal systems. This is because in both of them at least three procedural principles have survived in modern times. These are the principle of orality, the principle of openness and the principle of immediacy, which is of direct examination of evidence by the judge. By contrast, in continental western Europe, the medieval complaint process was replaced by the inquisitorial process in criminal cases and by the Procedural Roman-Canonical law in civil cases. Not insignificant for the different line of development of procedural law in England and the Polish-Lithuanian Commonwealth was the fact that in both countries the influence of Roman law and the *ius commune* on the legal system was negligible. The procedures of the two jurisdictions, located at opposite ends of Europe, were still based mainly on customary law rather than statutory law. The political models of the two kingdoms also proved to be different when absolutist monarchies were taking shape in continental Europe.

Polish civil procedure since *Formula processus* onward has been characterized by a tendency to shorten and partially deformalize civil proceedings. This is the right direction, because *simplicitas est legibus amica* ("simplicity is a friend to the laws"). These are obviously not the only values and features that constitute the spirit of Polish civil procedure. This is why there are many presented and discussed in the following pages.

CHAPTER 1

Procedural Roman-Canonical Law in European and Polish Legal Culture

Franciszek Longchamps de Bérier

Formula processus is the name given to the codification of Polish procedural law which was successfully completed in 1523 and resembled in its very essence the textbooks of ecclesiastical procedural law of the time, which are well known in legal literature to this day, the so-called *ordines iudiciarii*.[1] It is not without reason that Wiesław Litewski titled his 1999 fundamental, two-volume work on Roman-Canonical civil procedure *Der römisch-kanonische Zivilprozess nach den älteren ordines iudiciarii*. In this book the famous scholar from Krakow, a professor of Roman law, made a complete and very interesting synthesis of civil procedure, presenting it according to the ancient *ordines iudiciarii*. As he explained at the beginning of this work, according to the tradition of the *ordines iudiciarii* civil proceedings were proceedings that had the aim of establishing and realizing private rights that were in dispute. In a broader sense, this category also included voluntary, non-adversarial proceedings. All civil proceedings were heard either by a state court (broadly understood) or by an ecclesiastical court, which distinguished such proceedings from both self-help and arbitration proceedings.[2]

Judicial procedures in force from the Middle Ages until the 18th century (at least in most Western and also some Central European countries) had their origin in solutions developed in the Middle Ages themselves in Italian cities as well as in the practice of ecclesiastical courts. In this way, from the late 11th to the early 13th centuries, court procedures were formed whose principles, institutions and paradigms were substantively derived from two distinct sources, i.e., from the private law judicial procedure used in ancient Roman law and from canon law. Due to its origin in these two roots, we refer to the classical ecclesiastical process as Procedural Roman-Canonical law.[3]

1 Wacław Uruszczak, *Historia państwa i prawa polskiego 966–1975*, Warszawa, 2021, 183.

2 Wiesław Litewski, *Der römisch-kanonische Zivilprozess nach den älteren ordines iudiciarii*, 2 Vols., Kraków, 1999, 48.

3 See Arthur Engelmann, *A History of Continental Civil Procedure*, Robert Wyness Millar (trans.), Boston, 1927, 455.

 | DOI:10.1163/9789004736672_003

The means by which this happened is explained by Hartmann and Pennington: "By the end of the thirteenth century, court procedure on the continent in both secular and ecclesiastical courts shared many characteristics. As the jurists of the *Ius commune* began to excavate the norms of procedure from Justinian's great codification and then expound them in the classroom and in their writings, they shaped the structure of the courts not only in ecclesiastical courts but in secular courts as well."[4] Because of the many jurisdictions in which the one and same Roman-Canonical process was used, it necessarily became extremely diverse in specific application. The manner in which it was understood and organized, as well as verified on an ongoing basis, was by referring to the source, i.e., to the *cognitio* procedure, the process used to protect rights in Roman private law. This type of Roman process was the only one to be found in the compilation of the law which had been made between 528 and 534 under the auspices of Emperor Justinian. Justinian's compilation consisted of three parts: the *Digest* as a collection of the intellectual inheritance of Roman jurisprudence; the *Code* as a collection of imperial constitutions; and a student textbook called *Institutions*. At the time when *Formula processus* was written, this compilation was already well known, published in print and constantly commented on by contemporary jurists. Besides, the reading and interpretation of the various parts of Justinian's compilation have been the basis of the curriculum of legal studies since the establishment of universities in Europe, and perhaps even before the first one was founded in Bologna in 1088.

If, after the fall of Rome, there was any administration in the territory of Italy that was operating as stably as it was able to, giving some sense of security and creating a chance to resolve the legal conflicts that naturally arise in society, then it was the Church administration. At this time, the hierarchical structure of the Church was becoming stronger, both in the areas of the former empire and also beyond its borders. And ecclesiastical administration possessed a feature which has not always been observable to written history: importantly, it effectively reached down to the very bottom of society. The only comprehensive reference for the pragmatics of procedures used by this administration was that provided by Roman law: *Ecclesia vivit lege Romana*. Moreover, it was still late antiquity when the Roman Empire allowed the introduction of episcopal courts—*episcopalis audientia*.[5] Until then, the republican process had relied on the activity of private judges "as civil litigation was regarded as essen-

4 Wilfried Hartmann and Kenneth Pennington, "Preface", in *The History of Courts and Procedure in Medieval Canon Law*, Wilfried Hartmann, Kenneth Pennington (eds.), Washington, D.C., 2016, vii.

5 CTh. 1,27,1 Constantine (318); Nov. Val. 35; N. 123,21 Justinian (546).

tially private arbitration."[6] In the era of the *cognitio* procedure, however, individual bishops became private judges to whom any of the faithful could turn to settle virtually any dispute, including those concerning private rights. And we may note that when bishops gathered together for synods they also turned to the regulations of the Roman process, for example, in 411 during the well-known meeting with supporters of Donatism in Carthage.[7]

It is a well-known fact that the Roman Empire adopted Christianity as its state religion. From the perspective of the medieval question of the permissibility of using ancient Roman law, however, far more important than this fact were the legal reforms undertaken in the years 528–534 by Justinian, the last Roman emperor whose native language was Latin. In ordering a compilation of existing law, making great efforts to collect the entire legal and jurisprudential heritage, he in this way gave full authorization to all the previous pagan Roman law that was collected. But most importantly, by promulgating his compilation this Catholic ruler handed down Roman law to posterity in the Church. Henceforth, this legal heritage could not be considered pagan, and as a consequence Roman regulations and legal solutions were readily available for everyone to take advantage of. This is what happened successfully in the Middle Ages. And from that period, Roman law was passed on to subsequent eras.

The process of basing the entire European legal tradition on Roman law was spurred on further in the ninth century, particularly under the influence of the collection (which was in fact forged) of *Decretales Pseudo-Isidorianae*.[8] It is as a result of this well-attested fact that there is not the slightest doubt that the Canonical process from the end of the 12th century as known today was based on the reception of Justinian's compilation, i.e., on the *cognitio* procedure.

We may note, in addition, that the second part of Gratian's *Decretum*—a 12th-century collection concerning, among other things, judicial proceedings—contains not a small number of norms taken from Roman law. Some of these were taken over from the above-mentioned pseudo-Isidorian sources, but Gratian also made much use of Justinian's compilation itself.[9] As we know, the *Digest* was read not only by learned lawyers and legal scholars but was in

6 Andrew Borkowski, *Textbook on Roman Law*, London, 1997, 66.

7 Artur Steinwenter, "Eine kirchliche Quelle des nachklassischen Zivilprozesses", in *Acta Congressus Iuridici Internationalis*, vol. 2, Rome, 1935, 123–144.

8 Albert Gauthier, *Roman Law and Its Contribution to the Development of Canon Law*, Ottawa, 1996, 92.

9 Antoni Dębiński, *Church and Roman Law*, Lublin, 2010, 148.

fact widely used and of great subsequent influence.[10] "*Ordines iudiciorum* of that time containing a description of the process, regardless of their authorship by canonists or legists, were basically created in compliance with the Roman sources. Moreover, a large number of the titles of Book Two and Five of *Decretals* by Gregory IX, in which the pope revised the ecclesiastical civil and penal process in the 13th century, was taken from Book Three, Four and Seven of the Justinian Code."[11]

As to the Roman component of the Procedural Roman-Canonical law, this comes from the *cognitio* procedure, i.e., *cognitio extra ordinem*. This is how Roman law scholars refer to the historically latest type of civil procedure in ancient Rome. From this Latin term they name it the *cognitio* procedure, although every procedure in Rome, especially civil, was, in fact, *cognitio* —'an investigation', i.e., a consideration of a case brought before a Praetor or Emperor. *Cognitio extra ordinem* literally means extraordinary procedure, i.e., consideration beyond (the established) order. The 'order' referred to was the earlier, republican process which is nowadays called the formulary system. This lost its importance with the beginning of the principate, but only in the middle of the fourth century was it definitively replaced by a new order, no longer based on the authority of the Praetor but on the power of the Emperor. And as Justinian's compilation had the opportunity to know of only one type of private law litigation—the *cognitio* procedure—so only this type was handed down to posterity as 'the Roman civil process'.

In early Roman classical law, *cognitio extra ordinem* did not constitute a true system of procedural law, and the Romans did not have a unified vision or concept of this imperial type of private law process. As soon as the first emperor, Augustus, gained power, he used the *cognitio* procedure skillfully to resolve private disputes arising between citizens as well as to create new legal solutions. The first procedure in the nature of *cognitio extra ordinem* appeared in 15 BC or 4 AD and concerned testamentary bequests called *fideicommissa* (in English, sometimes called 'trusts' due to their fiduciary nature). It should be noted that, correctly speaking, the procedural protection granted by the emperor actually created the *fideicommissa* as a new, autonomous legal institution, a new type of testamentary bequest. It seems quite plausible that, in fact, during the first decades—even centuries—of the principate, several imperial procedures were created separately one after another, not as a single *cognitio extra ordinem* but as numerous *cognitiones extra ordinem*. These

10 Franciszek Longchamps de Bérier, "Possesso e proprietà nel pensiero di san Tommaso", *Revue Internationale des Droits de l'Antiquité* 52 (2005), 251–252.

11 Dębiński, *Church and Roman Law*, 148–149.

coexisted with each other in parallel before merging into a homogeneous 'Roman process' which replaced the older, formalistic procedural solutions. This was not, however, just a matter of replacing the formulary system. After all, it should be remembered that, as late as the 2nd century AD, remaining in force before the centumviral court was the very oldest of Roman processes, i.e., the archaic process called the *legis actiones*, the actions-at-law, which dated back to the era of the Twelve Tables of 451–50 BC.

Aware of the many historical and social changes they had gone through and of the diversity afforded by the three types of Roman legal process, the Romans abandoned the two republican types of process and deliberately shaped their latest imperial process to be a mature, functional and flexible system, one that was capacious and universal, able to provide effective protection of the private rights of individuals. These desirable qualities were not denied to the *cognitio extra ordinem* by future centuries and indeed by the entire European legal tradition, which adopted the Roman *cognitio* procedure as a model and source of inspiration, as a useful *tertium comparationis*, and, above all, as the basis for teaching law at university faculties up to and including the 18th century.

Research on the sources of Roman law have revealed that it was governed by certain principles. It was the procedural law theory of the 19th century which first established abstractly formulated principles in this regard,[12] enabling a better presentation of the Roman regulations that were subsequently in force in various historical epochs or which influenced the adoption of other legal solutions. Hence, we can see that, as one instance, in the law of medieval Europe detailed Roman institutions and solutions, especially those of a procedural or extraordinary nature, again found effective applications—sometimes completely new applications. There is one at least of these which must be mentioned as an example, i.e., *restitutio in integrum*—a reinstatement into the former legal position—which had a truly staggering career, unequaled by that of any other Roman legal regulation:[13] originally just an extraordinary measure (*auxilium*) granted by a Roman magistrate, a Praetor, when the Canonical procedure appeared, however, it became an exceedingly important remedy.[14]

12 Günther Wesener, "Prozeßmaximen", in *Handwörterbuch zur deutschen Rechtsgeschichte*, Dieter Werkmüller (ed.), vol. 4, Berlin, 1990, 55.

13 Władysław Bojarski, "*In integrum restitutio* w prawie rzymskim", *Roczniki Teologiczno-Kanoniczne* 10 (1963), 4, 15–26; Władysław Bojarski, "*Restitutio in integrum* od wyroków w Kodeksie justyniańskim i w Kodeksie Jana Pawła II", in *'Plenitudo legis dilectio'. Księga pamiątkowa dedykowana prof. dr. hab. Bronisławowi W. Zubertowi OFM z okazji 65. rocznicy urodzin*, Antoni Dębiński, Elżbieta Szczot (eds.), Lublin, 2000, 49–58.

14 Richard H. Helmholz, *The Spirit of Classical Canon Law*, Athens, London, 1996, 88–115.

Principles are, by their nature, timeless. Because of this, we can use them to understand the Roman-Canonical process—the *Formula processus*—itself. In this way, they allow us to draw on the jurisprudential experiences of the past as manifestations of concrete solutions to social problems arising from the need to protect private rights. Thus old solutions become instructive examples, but, of more importance practically, they can also provide serious inspiration. It was due to the influence of the Procedural Roman-Canonical law that the Polish codification of the civil process of 1523 became easier, more accessible and more effective for the protection of private rights than previous Polish regulations. We should add that principles emerge as a description of adopted norms, which means that the norms are reflected in them, which in turn means that the principles also constitute a summary and synthesis of the legal regulations in force at a particular time and place. Moreover, the principles interact with each other, determining the spectrum of possible legal solutions (a fact which is best seen in the case of procedural principles).[15] And the fact that principles clash brings them up to date: it determines which specific regulation is applicable in a given place and time.[16] The law is a realization of values, which find expression in it. And if we ask, how are values different from principles, then it would seem that values establish or designate goals, while principles are the paths to these goals.

Procedural principles are primarily directives for efficient action which serve to realize the values that should be reflected in the law at a given moment in history, because, according to the directions of legal policy adopted at any given moment, they are what lie behind the legal regulations introduced by a legislator. With regard to Roman procedural principles, they clearly demonstrate the extraordinarily high functionality of the Roman procedural devices themselves but also allow for a better understanding of the entirety of those procedural norms that subsequently drew on the traditions of Roman law. Regardless of the variety or richness of its forms and local manifestations, its local uses and adaptations, the classical ecclesiastical process known as the Roman-Canonical procedure was always characterized by three fundamental distinguishing principles: the dispositive principle, the adversarial principle and the principle of written proceedings.[17] These prin-

15 Franciszek Longchamps de Bérier, "Evolution of Roman law", in *Research Handbook on Legal Evolution*, W. Załuski, S. Bourgeois-Gironde, A. Dyrda (eds.), Cheltenham, Northampton, MA, 2024, 161 and 165.

16 Franciszek Longchamps de Bérier, *Law of Succession. Roman Legal Framework and Comparative Law Perspective*, Warszawa, 2011, 52–53.

17 Dębiński, *Church and Roman Law*, 149.

ciples are never, however, absolute, as is proven by the jurisprudential experience of Roman law.

Of these three types of Roman process, the most primordial principle of all was the dispositive principle. This is because this principle resulted directly from the fundamental principle of complaint and was its logical continuation. In Rome, in order to start a trial, one would approach a Praetor (or an imperial judge, in the *cognitio* procedure) with a request that he be willing to grant a measure of protection—*actio*. The Praetor did not adjudicate the dispute,[18] but rather, after examining the issue, he would allow the case to proceed in an *ius civile* action, that is, as regards a private litigation, what was referred to as *iudicia privata*. In criminal actions, however, i.e., in *iudicia publica*, it was the Roman magistrate himself who decided the issue (and also imposed the punishment).

This is how the Roman criminal process was shaped, in contradistinction to the civil process or *ordo iudiciorum privatorum*. As mentioned before, each of the *iudicia privata* used in the *ordo* was called an *actio*, which in colloquial language meant 'action' but in law was understood rather as a proceeding based on a statute. The principle of complaint meant that without applying for an *actio*, i.e., without the plaintiff's initiative, a civil trial could not begin. Similarly, a criminal trial could not begin without the filing of an accusation—*accusatio*. The Romans "thought in terms of remedies rather than of rights, of forms of actions rather than of causes of action."[19] Therefore, they were characterized by claim-and-remedies thinking, as well, of course, as their experience and, it must be said, love of judicial process. According to their legal understanding, if there was no appropriate *actio* legal protection was excluded, i.e., the trial could not proceed. This remained true for received Roman law in Europe, which, although it did not adopt the Roman understanding of *actio*, did adopt the dispositive principle.

This dispositive principle, which is broader than the principle of complaint, requires that the parties to the proceedings themselves dispose of the subject matter of the proceedings and the means or remedies used therein. It is the parties to the proceedings who first and foremost draw the boundaries of the protection sought. Both in Rome and in the Roman-Canonical process, and also today, the court cannot go beyond the party's request or decide above the party's demand. This was expressed in the saying *ne eat iudex ultra petita*

18 Franciszek Longchamps de Bérier, "The praetor as a promoter of *bonum commune*", *Legal Roots: The International Journal of Roman Law, Legal History and Comparative Law* 3 (2014), 220–222.

19 Barry Nicholas, *An Introduction to Roman Law*, Oxford, 1962, 20.

partium, formulated in the Middle Ages but based on Roman sources,[20] and which should be translated as follows: "let the judge not go beyond the pleadings of the parties."

However, the dispositive principle means not only the initiation of a given stage of the proceedings, as the mere principle of complaint would imply, but also the possibility of concluding a settlement at every stage of the proceedings. In private types of process in ancient Rome, it was mandatory that such a settlement be recognized by the court as a matter of unconditional respect for the will of the parties. The dispositive principle was also expressed in the right to file procedural objections—*exceptiones*. Hence, in modern civil litigation, it is emphasized, following the third-century jurist Ulpian, that by choosing to raise a procedural objection, the defendant becomes the plaintiff to the extent determined by the content of that objection—*reus in exceptione actor est*.[21] Another expression of the dispositive principle is the possibility of the defendant's acknowledgment of the claim. And equally true is the idea that "no one is forced to defend things against his will"—*invitus nemo rem cogitur defendere*.[22] Everyone is free to waive legal protection if they wish, an idea which we tend to associate with the statement, often repeated and not only in the legal context, that *volenti non fit iniuria*.[23] This principle, developed by canon law, that "to the willing person comes no injury", came to penetrate English common law and became entrenched in the *ius commune*, becoming an antonomasia of the plain dispositive principle.

On the other hand, in ancient Rome acting *ex officio*—and so with the full force of the official principle, which was in opposition to the dispositive principle—was actually possible only in the construction of the *cognitio* procedure. Even then, however, the Roman court could not initiate proceedings on its own, a fact which is expressed in a maxim derived from the constitution of Emperor Diocletian: *invitus agere vel accusare nemo cogitur*—"no one can be compelled to sue or accuse against his own will."[24] From the sources of Roman law comes yet another silver-tongued phrase concerning this question, a phrase which is often repeated because it so perfectly and simply captures the essence of the matter: *nemo iudex sine actore*: "there is no judge without a plaintiff." However, there is also in this respect a relevant sentence from the jurist Cervidius Scaevola, which, first in Rome and then later through the

20 See D. 10,3,18 Javolenus, *Letters*, Book 2.

21 D. 44,1,1 Ulpian, *Edict*, Book 4.

22 D. 50,17,156 pr. Ulpian, *Edict*, Book 70; see D. 9,4,33 Pomponius, *Sabinus*, Book 14.

23 See D. 47,10,1,5 Ulpian, *Edict*, Book 56.

24 C. 3,7,1 Diocletian and Maximian (284).

centuries of the adoption and transmission of the Roman legal tradition in Europe, has remained a resounding encouragement to take care of the procedural protection of one's own rights, but which could also be taken to be an eternal invitation to the vigilant to engage in litigious activity:[25] *ius civile vigilantibus scriptum est*—"civil law is written for those who guard their rights."[26]

Linked to the dispositive principle is the adversarial principle, or principle of party control. Both the adversarial principle and the principle of contestability were well known to the Roman process. This happened, in the first place, because the Roman process always had an adversarial form: the proceedings consisted of appearances by two opposing parties. The adversarial principle as a procedural principle expresses the requirement of the parties to the proceedings to prepare the procedural material themselves. The opposing model, brought about by the investigative or inquisitorial principle, only found a chance to make an enduring appearance with medieval law. Both principles—the adversarial and the inquisitorial—concern who collects the factual and evidentiary material to be used in the proceedings. If this is done by a court, then it is the inquisitorial system that is at work. Both of these principles open a range of possible legal solutions, those actually chosen depending on the decisions of a legislator. It is the legislator who must decide to what extent the court can and is allowed to be actively involved in the determinations pending before it and what authority the court has to remain active without exposing itself to accusations of bias. Of course, in a civil trial it is easier to maintain a model in which the principle of contestability dominates.

The main practical rationale for the investigative or inquisitorial principle should this be: 'the adversarial principle', which has been highly persuasive to various legislators throughout centuries of history, is that it is the parties themselves who best know the entire situation giving rise to the dispute. Moreover, each party has a vested interest in clarifying the circumstances that speak in their own favor. The parties must always cite facts in the form of assertions and must prove what they rely on—in accordance with the maxim *ei incumbit probatio qui dicit non qui negat*.[27] The requirement that "the burden of proof lies upon the person who asserts but not who denies"

25 Wojciech Dajczak and Tomasz Giaro and Franciszek Longchamps de Bérier, *Prawo rzymskie. U podstaw prawa prywatnego*, Warszawa, 2018, 168–170.

26 D. 42,8,24 Scaevola, *Questions Publicly Discussed*, Sole Book. See Franciszek Longchamps de Bérier, "*Nec stultis solere succurri*", in *Au-delà des frontières. Mélanges de droit romain offerts à Witold Wołodkiewicz*, M. Zabłocka, et al. (eds.), vol. 1, Varsovie, 2000, 469–475.

27 D. 22,3,2 Paul, *Edict*, Book 69.

seems to be an obvious requirement of procedural justice, an expression of *aequitas* and preservation of fairness. This requirement is sometimes formulated in the words: *negativa non sunt probanda*, which means that there is no obligation to prove the so-called negative facts. It is also emphasized, following the Roman emperors Diocletian and Maximian, that denial is not evidence—*negantis probatio nulla est*.[28] Guided by the maxim "the burden of proof lies upon the person who asserts but not who denies" as expressing fairness, the Procedural Roman-Canonical law developed precise rules regarding the burden of proof—*onus probandi*. In this ecclesiastical process, unlike in any type of Roman process, the hearing of evidence was based on the so-called legal theory of proof.[29] In contrast, the Roman trial was invariably characterized by a free evaluation of adduced evidence, which remained the timeless ideal of all procedures, not just those intended to protect private rights.

Since the plaintiff was the one obliged to prove—*actori incumbit probatio*—he should always be better prepared for the trial. The maxim expressing this thought—*actor venire debet instructior quam reus*—was formulated by glossators on the basis of Emperor Constantine the Great's constitution from 314.[30] In this formulation, it was sufficient for the defendant to stop at denial (though this was not always the case). This may also be seen to be an expression of procedural justice and a manifestation of the anthropological constant, the apogee of which is the presumption of innocence (mainly important in criminal law). In many cases, the defendant's passive attitude would be sufficient to give him victory in the dispute: he would win despite the fact that he did not adduce any evidence.

Of course, the defendant's situation would change if he himself decided to bring procedural charges or objections—*exceptiones*. Exceptions contained statements made by the defendant which effectively, i.e., if proven by the person raising the objection, blocked the other party's claim. If the defendant brought *exceptiones*, a particular result of the dispositive principle would be that that *reus in exceptione actor est*: the defendant in bringing a procedural objection takes the role of plaintiff. The system of exceptions, from which the entire European legal tradition drew, came from the earlier types of Roman process.

From Roman times to the present day, all procedural charges can be divided into two kinds: peremptory (*peremptoriae*: nullifying) or dilatory (*dilato-*

28 See C. 4,19,23 Diocletian and Maximian (294).

29 Dębiński, *Church and Roman Law*, 149; see Knut Wolfgang Nörr, *Romanisch-kanonisches Prozessrecht. Erkenntnisverfahren erster Instanz 'in civilibus'*, Berlin, Heidelberg, 2012, 127–130.

30 C. 3,12,2 Constantine (321).

riae: postponing).[31] The former type retain their force at all times, an example being *exceptio doli*, i.e., the objection of deceit as a dishonest act calculated to cause harm to another, as also acting contrary to a statute (*contra legem*) or litigating again for the same thing in Roman *actiones in personam*, which *actiones* were characteristic of Roman contract law. The latter type—dilatory objections—curtail, though only for a certain period of time, the possibility of pursuing one's claim, as when, for example, the parties have entered into an agreement not to bring a lawsuit for five years (a *pactum de non petendo*): in such a case, the postponement was protected precisely by a dilatory objection —*exceptio pacti de non petendo*.

The dispositive principle held out the possibility of a more categorical solution: the defendant's acceptance of the claim against him. For from the dispositive principle, as also from the principle of complaint as the opposite of the inquisitorial principle, it seems to follow directly that "no one is forced to defend things against his will"—*invitus nemo rem cogitur defendere*.[32] Besides, already in the ritual modes recognized by statute—the *legis actiones*, that is, in the oldest Roman republican process—such a solution was summed up in the simple words, *confessus pro iudicato habetur:* "the person who accepts the claim is considered to have been adjudicated."[33] In fact, for one to admit liability was regarded as if judgment had indeed been pronounced against him. Acceptance of the claim immediately opened the way for enforcement, which was an obvious manifestation of the principle of procedural economy, which requires speed and simplicity of proceedings. This principle applies not only to the construction of the legal regulation but also to the practice of the proceedings themselves, in which the parties should take actions and decisions and cite facts and evidence without delay, while the court should ensure that the proceedings are not unnecessarily prolonged and arrive at decisions as quickly as possible, provided that doing so does not pose any risk of detriment to the proper and complete explanation of the matter.

Due to its adoption of the legal theory of evidence, in the Roman-Canonical trial the defendant's confession gained the status of the acme of evidence. In the Roman republican trial, the acceptance of a claim was not subject to judicial review, whereas in the imperial process, i.e., the *cognitio* procedure, much more depended on a judge. It is clear from our knowledge and understanding of the Roman legal tradition in Europe that it is advantageous for the court to

31 G. 4,120–125. See Nörr, *Romanisch-kanonisches Prozessrecht*, 42–45.

32 D. 50,17,156 pr. Ulpian, *Edict*, Book 70; see D. 9,4,33 Pomponius, *Sabinus*, Book 14.

33 D. 42,2,3 Paul, *Plautius*, Book 9; see T. 3,1; D. 42,1,51 Paul, *Handbook*, Book 2; C. 7,59,1 Caracalla (211).

have the opportunity to assess the significance of adduced evidence, such as the acceptance of a claim or a confession by the accused. The same applies to the settlement agreement entered into by the parties. The above issues seem to concern not so much the implementation of procedural justice itself as the requirements posed by a sense of justice with regard to the legal transactions of the actual participants themselves.

The issue of the meaning and weight of individual evidence also brings up the matter summarized in the famous saying *quod non est in actis, non est in mundo*—"what is not in the files is not in the world." This saying is undoubtedly of Roman origin, but it seems to have been formulated only in the Middle Ages with regard to the principles of written evidence.[34] The saying indicates the requirement to produce everything in written form, which was another principle of the Procedural Roman-Canonical law. However, this principle is in competition with the principle of the orality of court proceedings, which was characteristic of ancient Rome and its entire *ius civile*, for the significance of this ancient principle lies in the fact that the parties to the proceedings can freely, using their own words, present their personal position in the proceedings. In ancient Rome, the only occasion on which writing was signaled in the proceedings was the requirement to prepare a set of words or *formula* which constituted a pleading in the second type of republican process. It was from this requirement that this type of process took the name we use for it today: 'the formulary procedure'. By contrast, the *cognitio* procedure had many more written elements, and this imperial process, moreover, even under the principate, lacked both formalism and orality.

The number of written procedural elements used in *cognitio extra ordinem* increased with the bureaucratization of the empire. In the first place, a summons was written and this summons to court was official. The *cognitio* procedure was not divided into two phases like the republican types of process, and so from the very beginning the proceedings could proceed without the participation of the other party.

Also in written form was the response to the summons. *Litis contestatio*—that is, the moment of joinder of issue—actually took place after both parties had presented their positions in the form of *narratio* and *contradictio*, but *litis contestatio* did not result, as in the republican process, in the consummation

34 Mauro Cappelletti, *Procédure orale et procédure écrite*, Milano, 1971, 42; Günther Wesener, "Prozeßmaximen", 55–57; Mario Ascheri, *The Laws of Late Medieval Italy (1000–1500). Foundations for a European Legal System*, Leiden, Boston, 2013, 128, 228, footnote 125. See Gerald Strauss, *Law, Resistance, and the State. The Opposition to Roman Law in Reformation Germany*, Princeton, NJ, 2014, 125.

of the litigation power. Therefore, the joinder of issue occurred with less rigid consequences than before. In the imperial process, the consummation effect was transferred to the end of the proceedings, i.e., to the moment of issuing the judgment. Other effects, such as interruption of the usucapion period, were transferred to the beginning, that is, to the initiation phase of the process. And this solution was passed on to the entire tradition of Roman law in Europe. Therefore—what may come as a surprise—the Roman-Canonical trial was in fact divided into two phases.

Although this was in fact the case in both Roman republican types of process, in the Middle Ages this fact was completely unknown. Besides, the nature of these two phases in the later Roman-Canonical process was quite different. While in Rome they had been held successively before first a Praetor and then a private judge (*iudex*), in the Roman-Canonical process both phases took place before the same court. Therefore, in the case of the Roman-Canonical trial it is better to speak of two procedural stages. The first began with the *citatio*—i.e., the filing of a lawsuit by the plaintiff, accompanied by a written complaint or *libellus actionis*.[35] The judge examined the correctness of the complaint in terms of form and then officially sued the other party, who at this point was allowed to file a letter containing arguments and defenses and procedural objections. The plaintiff could prepare a reply to the defendant's letter, to which the defendant was in turn allowed to respond—obviously also in writing. The *cognitio* procedure, and consequently the Procedural Roman-Canonical law, here benefited from the idea, developed by the republican formulary system, of multiplying at the very outset of the proceedings all arguments to one another, submitting them in writing in the form of *replicatio, duplicatio*, *triplicatio*, etc.[36] Only after the defendant's clear denial of the plaintiff's claims was established did *litis contestatio* occur, thus opening up the second stage of the trial, which served to evaluate the evidence and resolve the dispute.[37] Adjudication could—as in the Roman *cognitio extra ordinem*—require the delivery of the thing, i.e., the handing over of the object in dispute. This was not the case in the Republican process, and this was not the only significant dissimilarity, a more important difference being that in the Republican process, due to the structure of the trial and its two phases, an appeal was impossible.

35 Katarzyna Sójka-Zielińska, *Historia prawa*, Warszawa, 2015, 179.

36 We know this today thanks to the testimony of the jurist Gaius from the second century, G. 4,127–129.

37 Nörr, *Romanisch-kanonisches Prozessrecht*, 116–122.

The appeal as a means of challenging a judgment was developed only through the *cognitio* procedure. The *cognitio* procedure passed it on to European procedural law, which adopted the Roman legal tradition. The appeal turned out to be an outstanding achievement, because it served the rule of law and, above all, an overseeing of the actions of the court and judges. In imperial Rome, where, in a single-phase *cognitio* procedure, the judge acted on behalf of the emperor or provincial governor, any legal course of action was possible. In theory, the judge, in issuing a sentence, decided the case definitively, but as a consequence of the hierarchy of offices of the imperial administration there naturally developed an instance course. This became more apparent under Diocletian, with his multilevel division of the empire. The *praefecti praetorio*, who administered the four prefectures of the empire with the rank of *illustres*, were demoted from the level of central administration to the more modest role of the highest organs of territorial administration; the vicars at the head of the dioceses held the rank of *spectabiles*; and finally, the provinces were administered by governors with the title of *clarissimi*: from their procedural decisions one could appeal to the diocesan board, to the prefectures and, finally, to the emperor himself; appeals from the prefectures, however, could only be made by way of grace, since they were decided directly in the name of the emperor (*vice sacra*).[38]

At the same time, in imperial Rome an issue was recognized that required a decision with regard to each new procedure in which appeal was possible, i.e., the means of challenging judicial sentences, according to the means that the Romans had developed. This issue was the possible limitation of the instance mode to only one or two. Of course, when using the possibility of appeal and transferring the process to a higher instance, the dispositive principle applied—at least one of the parties should take appropriate action, expressing their reservations about the decision received and their expectations regarding the judgment by the higher instance. Therefore, unless an appeal was actually filed, there was no possibility of initiating the appeal proceedings.

Initially, it was only from the imperial provinces that appeals were made to the emperor, that is, only from those provinces created during the principate, but later they also came from the senate provinces that had been established in the Republican era. In order to appeal against a judgment that had been passed, the appeal was originally submitted to the minutes orally, then also in writing. The appeal, of course, was not subject to the ban on retrial—*bis de eadem re agi non potest*.[39] However, an appeal was characterized by suspen-

38 Dajczak and Giaro and Longchamps de Bérier, *Prawo rzymskie*, 85.

39 G. 4,107.

sive effect, which meant suspension of execution and, therefore, of the finality of the existing judgment. Today, in the case of an appeal against a judgment, we talk about the devolutive character of the appeal, which simply means transferring the consideration of the case to a higher instance, as known from the Roman imperial process. In such situations, the question always arises about the scope of the cognizance of a higher court. What is known, however, about the situation in Rome is that in an appeal the case was considered on its merits, and thus the entire proceedings were practically conducted anew. Within the same proceeding, as a rule, only entirely new claims were inadmissible, while new assertions, allegations and evidence were permitted. Until the times of Justinian, the general rule was a prohibition against adjudicating less favorably for the appellant—*reformatio in peius iudici appellato non licet*.[40] It was not until 530 that the emperor explicitly allowed a change for the worse in the situation of the appellant—*lex ampliorem*[41]—an outcome which was, in fact, well known in the Middle Ages.

The Roman-Canonical process that was part of the practice of the universal Church was, of course, also used in Poland, and the jurisprudential framework and general principles of this system, as well as numerous specific formulations of it, permeated through many routes into the various secular laws known in our country in the Middle Ages.[42] In this way, they also significantly influenced the Polish procedural codification of 1523. When we talk about 'codification' on this occasion, it should be noted at the very beginning that we do not mean implementation of the Enlightenment postulates of the codification movement, which were the clarity, conciseness, uniformity and universal comprehensibility of a set of regulations that were to be the basic and binding normative source in a given field.

Through the code, as a group of stereotypical, objectified, and somehow autonomous sets of thought, the Enlightenment movement wished to guarantee the stability of the law, anticipate all possible controversies, and prevent arbitrariness of adjudication and the autonomous action of the administrative authorities. However, it is also traditional to refer to as 'codification' collections of laws that are earlier than the concept of codification developed during the Enlightenment. The historical argument suggests that such codifications

40 See D. 49,1,1 pr. Ulpian, *Appeals*, Book 1.

41 C. 7,62,39,2a Justinian (530).

42 Rafał Wojciechowski, "Wyrokowanie w postępowaniu arbitrażowym według nauki procesu rzymsko-kanonicznego XIII–XIV wieku", *Studia z Dziejów Państwa i Prawa Polskiego* 12 (2009), 53–66.

belong to a different codification paradigm—in fact, to the very same paradigm that characterized the Roman codifications known to us from antiquity. This paradigm was simply a matter of comprehensive and stable regulations, accessible to all and easy to learn. In these terms, perhaps even the Twelve Tables should be considered a codification. Certainly the work of Julian was a codification, i.e., of the second-century jurist who, at the request of Emperor Hadrian, collected and consolidated the provisions of the edicts of Roman magistrates. Julian's *edictum perpetuum*—the Praetor's Edict—edited in this way, was then adopted by the Roman senate as a unified and uniform resolution—*senatus consultum*—with the force of generally applicable law.[43]

The private collections of constitutions of the Roman emperors were called *Codex Gregorianus* and *Codex Hermogenianus* in late antiquity.[44] Historically, the Theodosian Code of 438 and the afore-mentioned Justinian Code[45] as directly succeeding codes were prepared at the express orders of their eponymous emperors. They are official collections because, thanks to imperial power, they gave the force of binding law to the previous constitutions that were included in them but only in the versions of the texts as presented in these new codes.

All these codifications, and the paradigms behind them, are manifestations of the perspicacity of reason, expressions of human skill and intelligence, coming into actual being thanks to the political will of legislators. Codification is always expected to bring order and ensure relative stability. Lawyers associate with it in the hope of being able to control all regulations and ensure the predictability of judges' actions. This does, of course, imply a lack of confidence in judicial preparation, free judgment, experience and life wisdom. The legal theory of evidence as an expression of the desire to keep the judge within bounds is the best example we have of this attitude in Procedural Roman-Canonical law.[46] Much, of course, depends on *who* becomes a judge: whether it is a lawyer or if there are any requirements regarding education and preparation; whether one becomes a judge, for example, only at the culmination of a legal career, or, on the contrary, very young people are allowed to be appointed to the bench. Codifiers have always

43 Henryk Kupiszewski, *Prawo rzymskie a współczesność*, Kraków, 2013, 112, footnote 32.

44 Franciszek Longchamps de Bérier, "Hermogenianus and the Fundaments of Legal Anthropology", *Studia et Documenta Historiae et Iuris* 87 (2021), 59–60 and 63–64.

45 Dajczak and Giaro and Longchamps de Bérier, *Prawo rzymskie*, 89–92.

46 Engelmann, *A History of Continental Civil Procedure*, 447.

treated judges with suspicion, making numerous attempts and using various methods to limit their freedom.[47]

In Poland, codifiers began their activities in 1523 by collecting procedural law. The year 1523 belongs to the period known in Polish history as the Jagiellonian Golden Age and it was during the reign of King Sigismund I that the codification was created.[48] This codification, called *Formula processus*, consists of 111 articles, edited in Latin like the Roman codifications.[49] However, it differed significantly from its Roman predecessors in being extremely concise and, indeed, single-themed. And it also possessed a much more important difference in that, unlike the Roman codifications but typical of Roman law and in particular well known to the Praetor's Edict, structurally it was divided into two parts. The first part, articles 1-75, contains procedural norms. The second part, articles 76-111,[50] are almost exclusively pattern formulas: articles 76-86 are "formulas of various legal acts, the object of which was primarily landed property, such as bequests of sale, annuity (*wyderkaf*), exchange, donation, life annuity of spouses, pledge, money loan", while articles 87-111 are almost exclusively inscriptions as well as all kinds of lawsuits and summons.[51] The activity of Praetors and of Roman jurisprudence boiled down to the interpretation of applicable law for the arrangement of forms of legal action and procedural formulas. The entire Roman preclassical jurisprudence is sometimes called 'cautelary' from the word *cautelae* and the verb *cavere*, referring to the drafting of agreements (*sponsiones*, *mancipationes*) and last wills, which the jurists composed upon the request of private individuals.[52] In fact, the entire codification of 1523 is usually called by two very Roman-sounding words which come from its longer Latin title, two words which accurately reflect the nature of this Polish codification; they are: *formula* and *processus*.

---

47 *Dekodyfikacja prawa prywatnego w europejskiej tradycji prawnej*, Franciszek Longchamps de Bérier (ed.), Kraków, 2019, 9–15 and 230–231.

48 Anna Karabowicz, "Anna Jagiellon (1523–1596)", in *Law and Christianity in Poland. The Legacy of the Great Jurists*, Franciszek Longchamps de Bérier, Rafael Domingo (eds.), London, New York, 2023, 79–93.

49 Translation of the codification into Polish and English in *500 lat 'Formula processus'. Kodyfikacja polskiej procedury sądowej z 1523 roku*, Warszawa, 2023.

50 Stanisław Kutrzeba, *Dawne polskie prawo sądowe w zarysie*, Lwów, Warszawa, Kraków, 1927, 61.

51 Wacław Uruszczak, "*Formula processus iudiciarii*. Kodyfikacja polskiej procedury sądowej z 1523 r.", in *Źródła i współczesność polskiej procedury sądowej. 500-lecie konstytucji 'Formula processus'*, Tomasz Szanciło (ed.), Warszawa, 2024, 13; see also Zbigniew Naworski, "*Formula processus*. Geneza, treść, dzieje, znaczenie", *Prawo i Więź* 3 (2023), 210.

52 Adolf Berger, *Encyclopedic Dictionary of Roman Law*, Philadelphia, 1953, 385.

CHAPTER 2

Formula Processus (1523): The Landmark of Polish Land Procedural Law

Kacper Górski

1 Introduction

The year 2023 marks the 500th anniversary of the *Formula processus* Act (hereinafter referred to also as the Formula of Proceedings, or the act).[1] In 1523 Polish general Diet (or the Sejm) passed an act that contained provisions governing land law process, i.e., proceedings before land law courts in the Kingdom of Poland.[2] This was one of the most important acts on judicial law enacted by the Sejm in the first half of the 16th century in order to deal with the problems faced by the justice system. The literature on this subject is surprisingly poor, though.[3]

The *Formula processus* is even sometimes referred to as a codification of land procedural law. But is this claim justified? In order to answer this question, I will present and analyse the origins of the Formula of Proceedings against the background of earlier endeavours (2), and the structure of the act itself (3). Then I will outline the course of judicial proceedings in its light (4). Finally, I will try to assess the Formula of Proceedings in terms of the objectives guiding its drafters (5), and I will draw conclusions (6).

---

1 Full name: *Formula processus iudiciarii, terrarum Cracoviensis, Sandomiriensis, Lublinensis, Russiae, Belzensis et Podoliae, quam deinceps ab omnibus dignitariis, praefectis, iudicibus, subiudicibus et aliis officialibus nostris et terrestribus ac castrensibus generaliterque ab omnibus subditis nostris terrarum praedictarum volumus et decernimus in omnibus iudiciis et actibus iuridicis scribendisque dicis seu citationibus firmiter observari. Volumina Constitutionum*, Part 1: 1493–1549, vol. 1: 1493–1526, Stanisław Grodziski, Irena Dwornicka, Wacław Uruszczak (eds.), Warszawa, 1996, 392, https://iura.uj.edu.pl/dlibra/publication/3011 (access 30.09.2023).

2 For more on land law process and land law courts, see the beginning of the section 4.

3 As regards non-Polish studies, see Witold Maisel, "*Formula processus iudiciarii*—code polonais de procédure civile de 1523", *Právněhistorické studie* 19 (1975), 211–227, and Wacław Uruszczak, "Essais de codification de droit polonais dans la première moitié du XVIe siécle", *Revue historique de droit français et étranger* 59/3 (1981), 419–430. In terms of papers written in Polish one should definitely see Wacław Uruszczak, *Próba kodyfikacji prawa polskiego w pierwszej połowie XVI wieku*, Warszawa, 1979, 71–106.

DOI:10.1163/9789004736672_004

2 Origins[4]

One of the major challenges at the dawn of the modern era in the Kingdom of Poland was the standardisation of law. The legal system of the time was characterised by particularism. It had both an estate and a territorial dimension. The former meant that the estates (nobility, clergy or burghers) were governed by their own laws. It was inherent in the estate society and was not considered a problem whatsoever. The latter was apparent in the law of the noble estate, the so-called land law (*ius terrestre*). It consisted of the fact that the law was not uniform throughout the country. In other words, the laws in force in the realm differed from one territory to another. Why? Because the land law was essentially customary law, which was the source of most of the norms that are nowadays classified as belonging to civil, criminal or procedural law. Of course, it was amended and supplemented by statutory laws, i.e., acts passed by the king or (since the beginning of 16th century) by the Diet, which were usually destined for the entire country. Furthermore, customary laws were scripted and edited. If formally approved by the king, they acquired a status tantamount to statutory law. Nonetheless, the majority of rules remained customary and unwritten.[5]

Another challenge faced by the then elites was the codification of land law. It did not, obviously, stand for drafting a code of law comparable to those produced in the age of codification (late 18th to 19th centuries).[6] In the dis-

4 For the depiction different from presented below, see Maisel, "*Formula processus iudiciarii*", 212–215.

5 For a general overview of sources of law in medieval and early modern Poland in English, see Anna Karabowicz, "Custom and Statute: A Brief History of Their Coexistence in Poland", *Krakowskie Studia z Historii Państwa i Prawa* 7/1 (2014), 111–131. According to Uruszczak, half of 16th century marks the shift of the Polish jurisprudence's view on the relationship between customary and statutory law. From that moment on, both could be presumably treated as equal sources of law. More on this problematic issue, see Wacław Uruszczak, "Zwyczaj a ustawa w staropolskiej myśli prawniczej", in *Z historii państwa, prawa, miast i Polonii. Prace ofiarowane Profesorowi Władysławowi Ćwikowi w czterdziestolecie jego pracy twórczej*, Józef Ciągwa, Tomasz Opas (eds.), Rzeszów, 1998, 263–279. This statement is based upon works of Polish lawyers of the time. An in-depth study of the then court practice would definitely help to verify it.

6 The expression was used by Jan Peter Schmidt. The modern codifications were characterised by completeness, or comprehensiveness within a given area of the law, internal coherence and a systematic nature. Reinhard Zimmermann, "Codification. The Civilian Experience Reconsidered on the Eve of a Common European Sales Law", *European Review of Contract Law* 8/4 (2012), 371–373. Of course, the literature on this subject is rich, see also Jan Peter Schmidt, "Codification", 2012, https://max-eup2012.mpipriv.de/index.php/Codification (access 29.09.2023), and the studies cited therein. In Polish, see, for example,

cussed period the preparation of a code meant above all that the norms of the law in force were gathered in one written compilation which, upon assent of the competent power, was thus an official source of law and, therefore, the legal text was recognised authentic. Such a concept of an early modern code of law was coined by Wacław Uruszczak, an eminent Jagiellonian University professor and legal scholar, according to whom a code in the early modern period, especially in the Renaissance, should have been defined as 'a written collection of laws (a book of laws), which conveyed the content of legal norms and covered a whole or the substantial part of the legal system of a given state, and it has been recognised by legislative act (*ex lege*) or by custom (*ex consuetudine*) as a valid source of law or learning about the law'. Such a collection could be compiled chronologically, alphabetically or systematically.[7] Clearly, preparing such a code could have been easier if the laws had been already standardised.

Finally, the improvement of the law (*reformatio iurium*). What drew the attention was undoubtedly the judicial and enforcement proceedings before land law courts. The procedure was widely considered too long and overly complicated.[8] This was an issue that could be addressed while standardisation and codification efforts were made.

The tool that significantly increased the possibilities with regard to standardisation and codification of law was, of course, printing. The invention helped to disseminate legal texts throughout the realm, something that had hitherto only been possible through manuscripts. It was also much more reli-

---

Katarzyna Sójka-Zielińska, *Wielkie kodyfikacje cywilne. Historia i współczesność,* Warszawa, 2009.

7 Wacław Uruszczak, "Europejskie kodeksy prawa doby renesansu", *Czasopismo Prawno-Historyczne* 40/1 (1988), 62–63. For more on the definition, see there 59–63. These issues were also discussed in French: Wacław Uruszczak, "Les codes de droit en Europe à l'époque de la Renaissance", *Acta Poloniae Historica* 62 (1990), 91–133, and Wacław Uruszczak, "La typologie de codes de droit parus en Pologne à l'époque de la Renaissance", in *Historia Integra. Księga Pamiątkowa ofiarowana Prof. Stanisławowi Salmonowiczowi w siedemdziesięciolecie urodzin*, Danuta Janicka, Ryszard Łaszewski (eds.), Toruń, 2001, 285–302.

8 On the proposals, including the ambiguity of the expression *reformatio iurium* in the first decades of the 16th century, see Wacław Uruszczak, *Próba kodyfikacji*, 80–91. Selected issues concerning the proceedings before land law courts were recently discussed in English by Łukasz Gołaszewski, "The Procedure at the Noble Courts of the Kingdom of Poland at the Turn of the 16th Century: The Ups and Downs", *Beiträge zur Rechtsgeschichte Österreichs* 10/2 (2020), 186–193, although he focused primarily on the turn of 16th century, and Adam Moniuszko, "Principles of Polish civil procedure in the early modern period: Remarks on law and legal practice", in *Justice and Judicial Process. Evolution and Development in the History of Law*, Javier Belda Iniesta (ed.), Murcia, 2021, 441–453.

able, since it ensured the uniformity of copies of a given legal text and largely removed the problem of errors made by scribes.

Tangible effect of this revolution in Poland came first with the *Syntagmata*, a printed collection of medieval Polish land law (1487–1488), and almost two decades later with the Łaski Statute.[9] The latter was prepared at the request of the Radom Sejm of 1505 by the then chancellor of the Crown, Jan Łaski, and printed in 1506. Since it had been formally approved by the king, Alexander Jagiellon (1501–1506), it enjoyed the status of an official book of laws. Acts contained therein thus had the value of authentic legal texts. The statute included, inter alia, royal legislation (privileges, edicts, statutes), mainly from the 14th and 15th centuries, first Sejm legislation from the late 15th and early 16th centuries, sources of municipal law (Sachsenspiegel and the Magdeburg Weichbildrecht), international treaties and, what interests us most, collections of customary laws. In terms of land law, two such acts can be found there, namely: *Consuetudines terrae Cracoviensis* (Customs of the land of Kraków)[10] and *Processus iuris* (Procedure of Law).[11] In the next paragraph I will focus on the latter.

As the name suggests, provisions of the Procedure of Law concerned court proceedings. The aim of the editor, who was presumably Jan Łaski himself, was to organise customary procedural law for the purposes of judicial practice.[12] In the first provision it was even plainly called 'an instruction' (*instructio*) addressed to judges who applied the law. However, it was by no means a complete collection. The provisions basically concerned three issues regarding judicial proceedings: (1) Postponement of a court date (*terminus*) by means of *dillatio* (Polish: *dylacja*) in ordinary proceedings (nos. 2–6); (2) Enforcement of judgments by the adjudicating court (nos. 7–16); (3) The

9 Full title: *Commune incliti Regni Poloniae privilegium constitutionum et indultuum publicitus decretorum approbatorumque*. For an extensive description, see Wacław Uruszczak, "*Commune incliti Poloniae Regni privilegium constitutionum et indultuum*. O tytule i mocy prawnej Statutu Łaskiego z 1506 roku", in *Prace poświęcone pamięci Adama Uruszczaka*, Jan Halberda, Michał Hosowicz, Anna Karabowicz (eds.), Kraków, 2006, 115–135.

10 *Volumina Constitutionum*, Part 1: 1493–1549, vol. 1: 1493–1526, 156–162, https://iura.uj.edu.pl/dlibra/publication/3147/edition/2386 (access 30.09.2023).

11 *Volumina Constitutionum*, Part 1: 1493–1549, vol. 1: 1493–1526, 165–170, https://iura.uj.edu.pl/dlibra/publication/3149/edition/2388 (access 30.09.2023). On the contents of the Łaski Statute, see Wacław Uruszczak "*Commune incliti Poloniae Regni privilegium constitutionum et indultuum*", 123–127, 132–135.

12 [...] *per quam instructi essent iudices ad servandum rectum et conformem ordinem in terminis conservandis et processu iudiciario et praesertim circa executiones iudicatorum.* See *Volumina Constitutionum*, Part 1: 1493–1549, vol. 1: 1493–1526, 165.

subsequent stages of enforcement proceedings, which were the responsibility of a captain (Latin: *capitaneus*; Polish: *starosta*) and his subordinate officials (nos. 17–26).

As claimed by Stanisław Kutrzeba, the main part of the Procedure of Law was based on customary laws of the land of Kraków, and it was to be regarded as the model of procedure.[13] Proceeding according to these rules was officially encouraged by the king, who enjoyed the status of ultimate legislative power at the time, which was to eventually lead to these provisions becoming binding law:

> And although His Royal Majesty described private customs of some lands, yet His Majesty, by way of counsel, exhorts all his subjects to keep and observe this instruction [i.e., the Procedure of Law—KG] perpetually in all the lands [of the realm, so] it becomes the law and custom.[14]

This did not yet mean the abolition of particular customary laws, though. Some of them were even included in the Procedure of Law, albeit to a limited extent.[15] However, their status was clearly diminished, since they were referred to as 'private customs' (*consuetudines privatae*). Finally, it is noteworthy that the Łaski Statute also included the king's recommendation that the particular customary laws of other lands and territories of the realm, approved and edited by the monarch, should be entered in (hand)writing onto 12 blank pages, following the Customs of the land of Kraków in the issued copies of the statute.[16]

The Procedure of the Law and the entire Łaski Statute clearly showed a desire to standardise procedural law across the realm, whether by writing

13 These were provisions: nos. 2–26. Stanisław Kutrzeba, *Historja źródeł dawnego prawa polskiego*, vol. 1, Lwów, 1925–1926, 106.

14 Translated by the author. Original text in *Volumina Constitutionum*, Part 1: 1493–1549, vol. 1: 1493–1526, 170, https://iura.uj.edu.pl/dlibra/publication/3149/edition/2388 (access 30.09.2023): *Et licet eadem Maiestas Regia aliquarum terrarum privatas descripsit consuetudines tamen sua Maiestas per modum consilii, subditos hortatur universos, ut eam teneant et observent instructionem ubique terrarum aevoque diuturniori continuatam approbabit lex ac consuetudo.*

15 These were provisions: nos. 27–30, 31–32 (norms concerning postponement of proceedings in two particular laws), as well as nos. 16 and 30 (enforcement proceedings in another particular law). Unfortunately, it was not indicated from which land or territory the customs described originated.

16 *Volumina Constitutionum*, Part 1: 1493–1549, vol. 1: 1493–1526, 162, https://iura.uj.edu.pl/dlibra/publication/3147/edition/2386 (access 30.09.2023).

down customary law or by indicating the *model* norms. As it turned out, these measures were not sufficient to achieve this goal, and in the following years the initiative was taken by the general Diet.

From the beginning of the 16th century the Sejm was involved in efforts to standardise, codify and reform the law. After all, it was not only a forum for political clashes but also an institution responsible for lawmaking. The foundation of its legislative power was the constitution (i.e., a statute) adopted by the Radom Sejm in 1505, commonly known as *Nihil Novi*.[17] It laid down the rule that every act that concerned the universally binding law (Latin: *ius commune*;[18] Polish: *prawo pospolite*), required the consent of senators and deputies deliberating together with the king at the Sejm. This undoubtedly applied to the judicial land law. The efforts of the Diet intensified in the second decade of 16th century. The Sejm of 1511 called for the customary procedural law of the lands of the realm to be collected and edited by lawyers (*iuris periti*). In doing so, it referred to the royal order contained in the Łaski Statute that was discussed above. The issue was also raised at later assemblies.[19] However, it was not until 1519 that a significant decision was made. During the Sejm held in Piotrków, a commission was appointed, chaired by Andrzej Tęczyński, Palatine of Lublin. It was instructed to standardise and codify (that is, to edit) customary laws (with special attention to court proceedings), as well as to correct and improve statutory law. To facilitate the achievement of the first goal, the palatines were instructed to write down particular customary laws.[20] At the next Sejm, held in Bydgoszcz in 1520, further deputies were coopted to the commission. The order addressed to the palatines was also renewed.[21] The

17 *Volumina Constitutionum*, Part 1: 1493–1549, vol. 1: 1493–1526, 138, https://iura.uj.edu.pl/dlibra/publication/3143/edition/2382 (access 30.09.2023). On the meaning and influence of the Nihil Novi act in English see Wacław Uruszczak, "The *Nihil novi* Statute and the General *Seym* of Radom in 1505", in *Separation of Powers and Parliamentarism: The Past and the Present: Law, Doctrine, Practice*, Wacław Uruszczak, Kazimierz Baran, Anna Karabowicz (eds.), Warszawa, 2007, 39–46.

18 The expression *ius commune* was a synonym for *ius terrestre*—land law, i.e., the law of noble estate. By no means was it the 'Western' *ius commune* which principally did not play any role in the Polish legal system.

19 Uruszczak, *Próba kodyfikacji*, 75–91.

20 Uruszczak, *Próba kodyfikacji*, 100–101; *Volumina Constitutionum*, Part 1: 1493–1549, vol. 1: 1493–1526, 306–307, https://iura.uj.edu.pl/dlibra/publication/3218/edition/2457 (access 30.09.2023).

21 Uruszczak, *Próba kodyfikacji*, 102; *Volumina Constitutionum*, Part 1: 1493–1549, vol. 1: 1493–1526, 349, https://iura.uj.edu.pl/dlibra/publication/3236/edition/2475 (access 30.09.2023).

commission completed its work in 1523, when it presented the draft at the general Diet.[22]

The Sejm, which King Sigismund I convened in Piotrków, lasted from 24 October to 17 December 1523. The deliberations were, according to accounts, very turbulent, although unfortunately little is known about their course. Finally, the draft, entitled *Formula processus*, was accepted only by representatives of the palatinates of Lesser Poland and Ruthenia, while deputies from Greater Poland refused approval.[23] The adopted Formula of Proceedings was published in 1524 in an official collection of laws, the so-called Statute of Sigismund I, which was the official collection of Sejm legislation (so-called constitutions) from 1507 to 1523.[24] Unfortunately, no earlier drafts are known; therefore the first known version of the act comes from the official edition from 1524. This is how the Formula of Proceedings came into force.

3 The Structure of the Formula of Proceedings

Formula processus, as its name suggests, was intended to regulate proceedings before land law courts. It consisted of 111 provisions.[25] Among them, four groups can be distinguished:[26]

(1) The first group (nos. 1–41) contained rules in the matter of ordinary proceedings. They concerned, firstly, a written complaint, namely its form (nos. 1–6) and the manner of its service (nos. 10–11); secondly, rules regarding evidence (nos. 7–9). The subsequent provisions were devoted to proceedings themselves. Virtually all of them concerned, however, actions taken in the absence of one of the parties. Thus, the act regulated almost exclusively default proceedings, commonly re-

22 Uruszczak, *Próba kodyfikacji*, 102–105.

23 Uruszczak, *Próba kodyfikacji*, 104–105; *Corpus Iuris Polonici*, s. I., vol. 4/1: 1523–1534, Oswald Balzer (ed.), Cracoviae, 1910, 47.

24 Kutrzeba, *Historja źródeł*, vol. 1, 239–240. Further description in Oswald Balzer, *Przyczynki do historyi źródeł prawa polskiego*, in *Rozprawy Wydziału historyczno-filozoficznego Akademii Umiejętności*, vol. 46, Kraków, 1903, 11–24.

25 In this and the following section, the numbers in brackets refer to the numbering used in the edition *Volumina Constitutionum*, Part 1: 1493–1549, vol. 1: 1493–1526, 392–407, https://www.iura.uj.edu.pl/dlibra/publication/3252/edition/2491 (access 30.09.2023). In the original print from 1524 the articles were not numbered.

26 Both Balzer and Maisel divided the Formula into two parts, which basically correspond to groups 1–2 and 3–4, as depicted below. *Corpus Iuris Polonici*, s. I., vol. 4/1: 1523–1534, 48; Maisel, "*Formula processus iudiciarii*", 216–217.

ferred to as contumacious proceedings (*in contumaciam*), while so-called apparent proceedings (*ex controversiis*), that is, the trial, were largely left to customary laws and earlier legislation. The act focused on selected issues, in particular the postponement of court date due to illness and the consequences of the contumacy (see below). Further provisions described the course of enforcement proceedings, starting with *terminus concitatus* (Polish: *termin przypowieszczony*, see Section 4), through the successive stages of enforcement against land estate to the partial regulation of enforcement against the person of the defendant.

In the part devoted to default proceedings, one can find isolated provisions containing important procedural principles: equality of the parties (no. 18),[27] the compulsory appearance of the plaintiff on every court date (no. 18), the right to court (no. 19) and the fundamental rule governing the jurisdiction of the courts which established a land court (*iudicium terrestre*) as the primary jurisdiction in civil cases, regardless of the amount of the claim (no. 19).[28]

The first part was concluded by several provisions of general significance. The first provided for a sanction to be imposed on a captain who would neglect his enforcement duties (no. 36). The second regulated the activity of a castrensial (i.e., captain's) office (*officium castrense*) as the competent jurisdiction for offenders caught in the act (*in recenti crimine*) and for enforcement actions (no. 38). Finally, the last three provisions introduced the appeal, which was to be the primary ordinary remedy (nos. 39–41; see below in more detail).

(II) In the subsequent, second group of provisions, the Formula of Proceedings regulated (in more or less detailed way) certain special proceedings, namely: for the redemption (buying back) of dower land property from a widow (*redemptio bonorum reformatoriorum*—nos. 42–43),[29] for fugitive peasants (*pro kmethonibus fugitivis*—no. 53) and for the demarcation of land estates (*pro graniciebus*—nos. 54–70). Similarly to

27 Albeit expressed casuistically, with reference to the rights of the parties regarding postponements.

28 Civil cases were all cases in which the subject matter of the claim expressed in the petition was not criminal punishment (that is, on the life, honour or entire property of the defendant). By this, the act primarily meant cases for money, damage (to real property), injury (to a person) and property: *pro quacunque summa pecuniae vel iniuria haereditaria et personali aut bonis quibuscunque.*

29 Including two provisions on the protection of widow's dower land property against enforcement (nos. 44–45).

the first group, most of these provisions concerned actions in default of one of the parties. In addition, it also included provisions on the actions of court notaries, namely fees they collected and the consequences of their refusal to act (nos. 46–52), as well as the list of the dates of the land court sessions, but only for Ruthenia (nos. 71–72), two formulas for the entries of the adjournment of the court date on the initiative of the judge and both parties (nos. 73–74) and finally a provision for the loss of the copy of complaint by the plaintiff (no. 75).[30]

(III) The third group was devoted to noncontentious proceedings. It contained ten formulas for noncontentious entries relating to land estates, namely: sale (nos. 77–79), establishment of redeemable annuity (rent) to a clergyman (no. 80), exchange (no. 81), donation (no. 82), establishment of annuity (*advitalitium*) between spouses (no. 83),[31] antichresis (nos. 84–85),[32] and lease (no. 86). These were preceded by a provision on capacity for legal acts (no. 76).

(IV) Finally, the final, fourth group contained twenty-four formulas of complaints (nos. 87–111).[33]

---

30 On the probable reasons, see footnote 53.

31 The *advitalitium* (or *advitalitas*) was the marital agreement that intended to establish the right of usufruct of land estate in case of the passing of one of the spouses.

32 An antichresis was the pledge with a lien over land estate and the right of the pledgee to usufruct until the repayment of the debt. The income from the estate did not, however, reduce the principal amount, unless stipulated otherwise.

33 These were complaints for: debt inscribed in court records (*pro debito inscripto*) or ordinary debt (*pro debito non inscripto*), felling of an ordinary tree (*pro excisione gaii aut silvae vel mericae*) or a fruit tree (*pro arboribus fructiferis*), vulneration (*pro vulneribus*), homicide (*pro capite occiso*), right of proximity (*pro propinquitate*), division of land estate (*pro divisione*), redemption of pledged land estate (*pro redimendis bonis obligatoriis*), a fugitive peasant (*pro kmethone profugo sive quovis alio subdito*), guarantee (*pro cautione fideiussoria*), the seizure of hay or grain (*pro receptione feni aut frumentorum*) or the destruction of crops (*pro conculcatione et depastione frumentorum*), the seizure of cattle (*a kmethone sive alio quovis subdito*), the demarcation of land estate (*granicierum*), the failure to administer justice to a subject (*pro non administrandae iustitiae*), as well as: three formulas of renewed court summons (*adcitatio*, usually called *concitatio* in the act; Polish: *przypozew*), general formulas for the second summons (*post condemnationem in poena contumaciae*), and for third summons (*concitatio*; Polish: *przypowiast*) in both contumacious (*concitatio post condemnationem in lucro*) and apparent proceedings (*concitatio post latam sententiam pro re decreta*), the petition before succamerarius' court (Polish: *sąd podkomorski*; *ex officio succamerarii ad campum*), and an *ad querelam* complaint before the captain's court.

4 The Course of Ordinary Judicial Proceedings[34]

The Formula of Proceedings governed a land law process, that is, proceedings before courts that applied land law. The act referred essentially to procedure before a land court (*iudicium terrestre*), which it established, as already mentioned above, as the primary court of first instance in civil cases (no. 19). These provisions were to be applied also before other land law courts and offices, such as a castrensial court and office, succamerarius' court, court *in colloquio* (Polish: *sąd wiecowy*) and royal courts (including the Sejm court). A crucial feature of land law process was that these rules governed the course of both civil and criminal cases.[35] In other words, the proceedings were uniform, and it was not by any means proper to limit them to civil procedure.[36]

In the light of the Formula of Proceedings, the primary way of initiating proceedings was a written complaint (*citatio literalis*). In essence, the citation constituted an extensive summons served on the defendant to appear in court. In its first provisions, the act relaxed formalism regarding its structure and content. Fines for formal defects in the petition were abolished, and convalidation of certain mistakes was allowed upon payment of a fee by the plaintiff (nos. 1–6).[37] The complaint was issued by the court and served by the bailiff (*ministerialis*; Polish: *woźny sądowy*), who should do so at least one week before the scheduled court date (nos. 10–11).

---

34 For major detailed studies on land law process, see Oswald Balzer, *Przewód sądowy polski w zarysie (wykład uniwersytecki)*, Lwów, 1935; Stanisław Kutrzeba, *Dawne polskie prawo sądowe w zarysie*, Lwów, Warszawa, Kraków, 1927; Józef Rafacz *Dawny proces polski*, Warszawa, 1925; Marian Mikołajczyk, *Na drodze do powstania procesu mieszanego. Zmiany w polskim procesie karnym w latach 1764–1794*, Katowice, 1991; and recently Adam Moniuszko, *Mazowieckie sądy ziemskie (1588–1648). Organizacja—funkcjonowanie—postępowanie*, Warszawa, 2013.

35 On the distinction between civil and criminal cases, see footnote 28.

36 Therefore, Maisel is obviously wrong when he says that 'although it does not appear in the title [the Formula processus] only relate to civil procedure' ('Quoique cela n'apparaisse pas dans le titre, elle [i.e., La Formula processus] n'a trait qu'à la procédure civile'), Maisel, "*Formula processus iudiciarii*", 218.

37 However, irrespective of the removal of the fines, the principal effect of the failure to ensure the right form of the complaint was to release the defendant from the suit (with the right to sue again on the same matter). A provision of Formula of Proceedings made it even possible to avoid this effect by paying a fee (12 *groszy*), but only in the case of faults concerning: title, designation of the plaintiff or defendant, and seal. See *Volumina Constitutionum*, Part 1: 1493–1549, vol. 1: 1493–1526, 157, https://iura.uj.edu.pl/dlibra/publication/3147/edition/2386 (access 30.09.2023) (*Consuetudines terrae Cracoviensis*, no. 10).

A court date (*terminus*) was nothing else than the determination of a date and place of appearance for the parties, that is, the plaintiff (*actor*) and the defendant (*citatus, reus*). However, the consequences of their default (or contumacy) differed in this regard. For the plaintiff, each date was final, or peremptory (*terminus peremptorius*), which meant that failure to appear before the court resulted in losing the case (*condemnatio in lucro*). The Formula of Proceedings illustrated this rule with a maxim: *actores semper habent terminos peremptorios*. For the defendant, as a rule, only the second term was final. Failure to attend the first one meant only the imposition of a fine (the so-called *poena contumaciae*), which, however, was abolished shortly thereafter.[38] Thus, the defendant was actually able to miss the first date (the so-called ordinary date) without further consequences. Only the second contumacy resulted in losing the case (nos. 12, 20).

As indicated above, the Formula of Proceedings extensively regulated the possibility of the postponement of a court date at the request of either party through the so-called *dillatio* (Polish: *dylacja*). Particularly, much space was devoted to postponement due to illness. Unlike other *dillationes* (for example, to gather evidence—no. 18), it was essentially an excuse for absence from the appointed date. The rights of the parties differed in this regard. Both parties enjoyed the right to excuse their contumacy by serious illness (*vera infirmitas*). The indisposed party should then send a messenger (*nuntius*) to the court, who was to inform the judge of the reason for default. On the next date, the party had to confirm under oath (*mettertius*, that is, with two witnesses) that his reason was indeed a serious illness (nos. 12–18). Moreover, *dillatio* on these grounds could be used only once by each party in order to curb the protraction of proceedings (no. 17). In addition, the defendant could also justify his absence by a slight illness (*simplex infirmitas*), but this only applied to the ordinary date and thus only meant avoiding the fine that was discussed earlier (*poena contumaciae*).

As mentioned above, the Formula of Proceedings only vaguely regulated procedure in the presence of both parties (the so-called apparent proceedings—*ex controversiis*). It stipulated, inter alia, the right of both parties to submit evidence, raise objections, make requests for the postponement of the proceedings and the possibility of responding to them (nos. 7, 9), and it introduced into a land trial the institution of an appeal (*appellatio*) as a primary remedy. In principle, each party who disagreed with the judgment could

38 This occurred on the basis of the royal judgment of 1537. Uruszczak was the first to draw attention to this fact in Wacław Uruszczak, *Korektura praw z 1532 roku. Studium historycznoprawne*, vol. 1, Kraków, 1990–1991, 152.

appeal to a higher instance, a court *in colloquio*, or, if the colloquium would not be held, to the Sejm court. The proceedings could even be three-instance, as a party could still appeal against the judgment of the colloquium to the royal court (usually the Sejm court), since it was the monarch who was the supreme judge of the realm (*iurium omnium regni dominus superior*). One of the conditions for the acceptance of the appeal was that the appellant pay a deposit, the so-called *kocz*, the amount of which was set by the Formula of Proceedings at three *grzywnas*. The acceptance of the appeal was decided by the court which issued the judgment. If the decision was favourable, it issued to both parties an extract from the court books containing the hitherto course of the case (nos. 39–41).[39]

If the defendant failed to attend the peremptory date, he or she lost the case by default (*condemnatio in lucro*). Nevertheless, one more summons should have been issued and served by means of the so-called *concitatio* (Polish: *przypowiast*). This was usually the third date in the course of the case. The so-called *terminus concitatus* (Polish: *termin przypowieszczony*) was a kind of bridge between the lawsuit and the enforcement proceedings. It gave the hitherto absent defendant the opportunity to satisfy the plaintiff's claim without further consequences or to raise ignorance of the proceedings (*ignorantia processus*). If the defendant did not appear on this date, the so-called *astitio termini concitati* occurred and the enforcement proceedings began (nos. 21–24).

If the defendant was present during proceedings before the court and did not comply with the judgment, or if he or she lost the case by default and did not appear at the *terminus concitatus*, the adjudicating court commenced enforcement.[40] As a rule, the subject of execution was immovable property, or land estate (*bona*). Subsequent actions were aimed at forcing the defeated party (*iure victus*) to satisfy the judgment by taking away his land property and handing it over to the victor. From a legal point of view, the plaintiff thus became a pledgee who collected the profits from the property he or she received. The income was supposed to cover the sum owed to the plaintiff by the defendant, as long as it was not paid in full (*ad extenuationem*).[41]

The first stage of the enforcement proceedings belonged to the adjudicating court. It assigned a bailiff (*ministerialis*), whose task was to formally

39 If the appellant was successful, the *kocz* was returned; if the appellate court upheld the judgment, the amount went to the other party.

40 In the first case, the defendant was additionally charged with a fine of 14 *grzywnas* (no. 25).

41 For more details see Balzer, *Przewód sądowy polski*, 265–270.

transfer the possession of a given estate by means of *intromissio*.[42] This consisted of acquiring the peaceful possession (*pacifica possessio*) of the estate so that the plaintiff could collect income from it and enjoy possessory protection (no. 26). If the defendant did not allow *intromissio*, the case was remitted to the castrensial office (*officium castrense*), that is, the office of the captain, a royal official who was responsible for enforcement actions in the area under his jurisdiction (nos. 25–27). Further stages of execution belonged to the captain and his castrensial officials. A special writ of summons—the so-called *innotescentia*—was issued, by means of which the defendant was ordered to appear before the castrensial office under pain of imposition of a threefold deposit (*vadium triplicatum*) and the assignment of the bailiff (first court date in enforcement proceedings). If the defendant refused *intromissio* for the second time, he was summoned again before the castrensial office. The aforementioned deposit was adjudicated, and the bailiff and the castrensial official (usually the vice-gerent) were assigned to carry out *rumatio*, that is, the actual deprivation of the possession, and subsequent introduction into the possession, of given property (second court date). The third refusal gave rise to an action before the castrensial court (*iudicium castrense*), i.e., before the captain himself, with a claim for the imposition of banishment on the defeated party (*citatio ad banniendum*—third court date). His or her contumacy meant being sentenced to banishment by default, resulting in the loss of legal and judicial capacity, as well as the right of the captain to summon the local nobility to stand in arms and assist in carrying out the ultimate *rumatio* (nos. 27–31, 34).

To a limited extent, the Formula of Proceedings regulated the enforcement against the person of the defendant. The provisions indicated cases in which the captain, as the official responsible for the enforcement, should capture the defeated party and place him or her in the tower (prison). This was possible when he or she: (1) was sentenced to banishment (no. 35),[43] (2) did not own land estates subject to the enforcement proceedings (no. 33). There was virtually no regulation in the Formula of Proceedings concerning enforcement against movable property.

42 The presented procedure was shorter if the adjudicating court was a castrensial court or office. In such a case, in addition to the first assignment of the bailiff, a three-fold deposit was imposed at once, an action usually taken by the castrensial office in the next stage of enforcement proceedings (no. 37).

43 It could have been the defendant himself or a person who assisted him or her, for example, by refusing *intromissio* and *rumatio* on his or her behalf. Such an action was considered unlawful, and the perpetrator could be sued before a castrensial court, with a claim to impose banishment (no. 32).

5 The Significance and Assessment of Formula of Proceedings

The editors of the Formula of Proceedings were guided by three objectives: to standardise procedure before land law courts across the realm,[44] to codify it and to simplify and shorten the proceedings.[45] The work on the act was thus a continuation of endeavours already undertaken from the turn of the century.

As already mentioned, representatives of the Greater Poland palatinates refused approval of the Formula Proceedings in 1523. As a result, the Formula became binding law only in Lesser Poland and Ruthenia, i.e., in the palatinates of Kraków, Sandomierz, Lublin, Ruthenia, Bełz and Podolia. Only later was it adopted by the palatinates of Inowrocław and Brześć (1526–38),[46] as well as Łęczyca (1552).[47] Finally, thirty years after its enactment, in 1553, King Sigismund II Augustus, at the request of the deputies, also granted the new law to the remaining lands of Greater Poland, i.e., presumably the palatinates of Poznań, Kalisz, Sieradz, Płock and Rawa.[48] Polish law, including the Formula of Proceedings, was also in force in the palatinates of Podlachia (1569)[49] and Masovia (1576) that were incorporated into the Crown.[50]

---

44 In addition to the above-mentioned documents concerning the activities of the 1519/1520 commission, see, for example, the heading of the Formula of Proceedings, in which all courts of the realm were obliged to observe the new rules: *Formula processus iudiciarii* [...] *quam deinceps ab omnibus* [...] *volumus et decernimus in omnibus iudiciis et actibus iuridicis scribendisque dicis seu citationibus firmiter observari* (*Volumina Constitutionum*, Part 1: 1493–1549, vol. 1: 1493–1526, 392), or the preamble of the Statute of Sigismund I (1524), where the king emphasised that one way of proceeding before the court had been established: [...] *Adiecimus praeterea Formulam processus iudiciarii, in compendium et modum unum per iurisperitos iussu nostro reductam* [*redactam*], *ac per nos et consiliarios nostros approbatam et observari decretam* [...] (*Corpus Iuris Polonici*, s. I., vol. 4/1: 1523–1534, 89).

45 In the preamble cited in footnote 44 the king mentioned, inter alia, less difficulties and ambiguities in terms of the lawsuit, and the quicker and more facile *route to justice* (*facilior et celerior via iustitiae*), *Corpus Iuris Polonici*, s. I., vol. 4/1: 1523–1534, 89–90. The easier and more comprehensible *route to justice* (*planior via ad iustitiam*) as well as convenience (*commodum*) of the subjects were referred to in the act for the land of the Inowrocław nobility of 1526, too (see footnote 46).

46 *Corpus Iuris Polonici*, s. I., vol. 4/1: 1523–1534, 196–198, *Volumina Constitutionum*, Part 1: 1493–1549, vol. 2: 1527–1549, Stanisław Grodziski, Irena Dwornicka, Wacław Uruszczak (eds.), Warszawa, 2000, 188 (1538), https://iura.uj.edu.pl/dlibra/publication/3011 (access 30.09.2023).

47 Under the royal mandate of 25 May 1552. Józef Rafacz, "Formuła procesowa w Łęczyckiem", in *Księga pamiątkowa ku czci Władysława Abrahama*, vol. 2, Lwów, 1931, 1–4.

48 *Volumina Constitutionum*, Part 2: 1550–1609, vol. 1: 1550–1585, Stanisław Grodziski, Irena Dwornicka, Wacław Uruszczak (eds.), Warszawa, 2005, 54.

49 *Volumina Constitutionum*, Part 2: 1550–1609, vol. 1: 1550–1585, 218.

50 *Volumina Constitutionum*, Part 2: 1550–1609, vol. 1: 1550–1585, 373–374.

However, there was never a complete standardisation of land procedural law across the entire Kingdom of Poland. Two parts of the realm remained under its own laws. Firstly, in Royal Prussia (i.e., the palatinates of Pomerania, Chełmno and Malbork) the proceedings were codified in the so-called Prussian Correction (*Ius terrestre nobilitatis Prussiae correctum*) of 1598. Secondly, the palatinates of Volhynia, Bracław and Kijów (Kyiv) incorporated to the Crown in 1569 (or the so-called Ukrainian palatinates), kept the Lithuanian law codified in the Second Statute of Lithuania of 1566. It should also not be forgotten that the scope of the Formula of Proceedings (as discussed below) meant that, to the extent not regulated therein, the already binding law (both statutory and customary, universal and particular) remained in force, and thus could vary in certain lands and territories of the realm. *Formula processus* was therefore an act which only partially standardised land procedural law, in terms of both territory and subject matter.

It is much more difficult to answer the question as to whether the Formula of Proceedings was a codification of the procedural law. It was undoubtedly a body of provisions on the procedure before land law courts and offices, designed to disseminate to courts, offices and all citizens the procedural rules and formulas in a uniform, standardised form. Of course, it was an official source of law, and the legal text therein was authentic. In this regard it meets the definition presented in Section 2. Nevertheless, it was far from being a procedural law code for two reasons. Firstly, it only partially covered court proceedings, governing selected aspects of them in more or less detail, such as the form of a complaint, default proceedings (especially postponements), enforcement proceedings, certain special proceedings or, finally, the formulas for contentious and noncontentious entries. As a matter of fact, numerous institutions or even entire stages of proceedings were omitted.[51] Moreover, it seems that this was intentional—it was not the goal of the commission responsible for the draft to cover the whole of land procedural law, even if a significant part of the provisions were to be norms already in force, subject only to editing. Secondly, the attempt to prepare the act in a systematic arrangement was not entirely successful. Apparently, the editors divided the collection into two parts: dedicated to court proceedings (1, 2) and containing formulas for contentious and noncontentious entries (3, 4).[52] Evidently, in the first part, they also tried to arrange the rules according to the course of proceedings, starting with a complaint and ending with an appeal,

51 Maisel reached a similar conclusion in Maisel, "*Formula processus iudiciarii*", 218.

52 These were the two parts distinguished by both Balzer and Maisel, as mentioned in footnote 26.

which, however, was only partially successful. In several places one can find provisions or even groups of provisions that were not logically connected to the preceding or following ones.[53] In addition, the headings for groups of provisions were used selectively and without a central idea.[54] Therefore, the Formula of Proceedings can be regarded as merely a substitute for a full-fledged code of land procedural law.

The editors of the Formula of Proceedings noticeably focused on provisions which reduced formalism (especially in terms of written complaints), as well as shortening and simplifying default and enforcement proceedings, in particular regarding actions taken without the presence of the defendant. The results of their efforts should be viewed positively, especially if we compare them to the course of the proceedings as visible in the Procedure of Law of 1506. They succeeded (at least theoretically) in limiting the possibilities for the participants of proceedings (especially defendants) to protract procedure before the judge, which was then one of the major problems of the land law justice system. This was accomplished, inter alia, by reducing the number of available postponements (*dillationes*) due to illness, as well as limiting the number of stages of enforcement proceedings.[55]

In his study, Uruszczak claimed that the Formula of Proceedings showed a resemblance to medieval *ordines iudiciarii*—tracts that described the Romano-canonical procedure.[56] This analogy seems to be not necessarily accurate, especially due to different origin, legal status and incompleteness of the *Formula processus*. However, as Uruszczak noted, it is indeed riveting that the editors included the formulas of entries in the act, which was an element often introduced in the medieval *ordines*. Maybe an inspiration really came from canonists' works? In conclusion, one should definitely

53 More detailed observations were made in *Corpus Iuris Polonici*, s. 1., vol. 4/1: 1523–1534, 48–49. Balzer believed that some of the provisions were not present in the original draft of the Formula, and they were probably added during the deliberations at the Diet. This assumption was repeated in Maisel, "*Formula processus iudiciarii*", 216–217.

54 This lack of consequence was also pointed out by Maisel, "*Formula processus iudiciarii*", 217.

55 More detailed analysis was conducted by Maisel, "*Formula processus iudiciarii*", 219–223, although it requires thorough verification. In general Maisel assessed the act positively, despite its deficiencies. Maisel, "*Formula processus iudiciarii*", 225–226.

56 Uruszczak, *Próba kodyfikacji*, 106. On the origins and development of *ordines iudiciarii*, see, for instance, Kenneth Pennington, "The Jurisprudence of Procedure", in *The History of Courts and Procedure in Medieval Canon Law*, Wilfried Hartmann, Kenneth Pennington (eds.),Washington, D.C., 2016, 125–131, 143–153, and the studies cited therein, especially Linda Fowler-Magerl, *Ordines iudiciarii and libelli de ordine iudiciorum (from the middle of the twelfth to the end of the fifteenth century)*, Turnhout, 1994.

agree with Uruszczak, that the question of the influences of canon law, the procedural rules in particular, on Polish land law process demands in-depth studies.

6 Conclusions

The aim of the initiatives undertaken at the end of the 15th and the beginning of the 16th centuries was to provide a uniform printed text of the law in force in the Kingdom of Poland, and to have customary particular laws drawn up, edited and promulgated under the royal privilege, following the example of the Customs of the land of Kraków included in the Łaski Statute of 1506. Only the first of these tasks was accomplished. The *Syntagmata*, and above all the Łaski Statute, were instrumental in the dissemination of a uniform text of the most important legislative acts across the realm. The foundation for further standardisation of the law was thus laid. Both collections were codes befitting their time.

In the following decade, efforts to standardise, codify and improve the law continued. These resulted in the passing of the Formula of Proceedings at the Piotrków Sejm in 1523—an act governing land law courts proceedings. Even though it did not become the only and complete code of procedural law in the Kingdom of Poland, it undoubtedly formed the foundation of standardised proceedings in land law courts on the territory of the Crown (excluding the area of Royal Prussia and the so-called Ukrainian palatinates). It was a procedure that was: (1) uniform for civil and criminal cases; (2) adversarial, disposal and contradictory, conducted orally and in public; (3) in which the subject of civil enforcement was, as a rule, land estate, the enforcement proceedings were initially conducted by the adjudicating court, and the following stages belonged to the enforcement authorities, that is, a captain and his officials.[57]

What is worth emphasising is the continuity of standardisation and codification efforts in the field of judicial proceedings in the first decades of the 16th century. The provisions of the Procedure of Law—the collection of customary land procedural law of 1506—established a course of proceedings which, according to the king's urging, provided a model for the courts of other lands of the realm. However, being just a royal recommendation, these norms did not *ipso iure* abolish other particular laws. This was to be achieved through

57 Principles of Polish court procedure were recently briefly discussed by Moniuszko, "Principles of Polish Civil Procedure", 371–379.

practice, i.e., the application of new rules. The Procedure of Law was a forerunner. A further step was taken by the Formula of Proceedings, which, as an act of the Sejm, should supersede customs contrary to its provisions. In this respect, the *Formula processus* played a greater role in the history of court proceedings in pre-partition Poland than did the *Processus iuris*.

The aforementioned continuity can also be seen in the subject of regulation. Editors of both discussed landmarks of land procedural law focused on institutions which, in their opinion, were behind the greatest problem of the justice system of the time, i.e., the protracted nature of proceedings. It is not without reason that both the *Processus iuris* and *Formula processus* devoted most space (regarding ordinary procedure) to postponements of proceedings due to illness and to enforcement proceedings. In the 16th century one more attempt to codify and unify judicial law was taken. However, the much more extensive draft of the so-called Correction of Laws (*Correctura statutorum et consuetudinum regni Poloniae*) of 1532 ultimately failed to gain the approval of the general Diet.[58] It is worth noting, however, that the course of court procedure as regulated in the Correction of Laws was based on the Formula of Proceedings.[59] Unfortunately, despite the efforts, the idea of a full codification of land law was not achieved until the end of the existence of the Polish-Lithuanian Commonwealth (1795). Consequently, the Formula of Proceedings remained one of the main sources of rules governing proceedings before courts and offices applying land law, although later legislation, in particular laws passed at the Sejm, amended and supplemented it.

58 Uruszczak, *Próba kodyfikacji*, 115–251. The Correction of Laws covered not only procedural law but other areas of law as well, including the political system, civil law and criminal law. For an extensive study of this draft, see Uruszczak, *Korektura praw*, 2 vols.

59 The editors presumably exploited the final text, that is, the one included in the Statute of Sigismund I. According to Uruszczak, 95% of the content of the Formula of Proceedings was utilised. Uruszczak, *Korektura praw*, vol. 1, 19, 123.

CHAPTER 3

Procedure before a Land Court in Civil Cases in the Polish-Lithuanian Commonwealth at the Turn of the 17th Century

Izabela Lewandowska-Malec

In the times of the Polish-Lithuanian Commonwealth, procedure before a land court was uniform, with certain differences in criminal cases. Thus, civil procedure was not known in the strict sense at that time; hence, the issue discussed in this chapter is *procedure in civil cases*. Due to the need to limit the length of the chapter, selected issues are presented of the then procedure before a land court as a lower court and, after the introduction of the appeal, a court of first instance.

It should be added that considerable legal and territorial particularism prevailed during the period presented. A discussion of the procedures applied in individual regions of the vast country is not possible within the framework of this publication. Therefore, the author has focused on procedural issues occurring in the Crown of the Kingdom of Poland as part of the Polish-Lithuanian Commonwealth—a Polish-Lithuanian community established in 1569 by the union concluded in Lublin.

1 Sources of Land Procedural Law

Identifying the sources of land procedural law from the Old Polish period is a very difficult task. Despite the adoption by the Sejm in 1523 of a codification of procedural law under the name *Formula Processus*, its validity was extended successively over the next 30 years on the territory of the Kingdom.[1] The provisions of the Statutes of Casimir the Great from the 14th century, legislative acts of subsequent rulers, parliamentary constitutions and even references to customary law, continued to be applied in court practice as well. Jan Łączyński, a late-16th-century lawyer, even argued that procedural law was based

1 See *Volumina Constitutionum*, Part 1: 1493–1549, vol. 1: 1493–1526, Stanisław Grodziski, Irena Dwornicka, Wacław Uruszczak (eds.), Warszawa, 1996, footnote 8, 387.

 | DOI:10.1163/9789004736672_005

more on custom and practice than on statutory law.[2] The procedural matter was in fact not covered comprehensively, without gaps, in a single legal act. *Formula Processus* contained mainly specimens of petitions to courts and various legal acts; as far as procedural law was concerned, it only made some changes to shorten trials and the enforcement of judgements, and provided for the possibility of an ordinary remedy; the act did not include issues concerning the evidentiary proceedings.[3] It certainly did not regulate the entirety of judicial proceedings. This state of affairs was confirmed by the observation made by Grzegorz Czaradzki—a respected jurist and scribe in the royal chancellery of King Sigismund III Vasa: "It must be understood that what the statutes do not expressly discuss, or the constitutions do not notice, include almost every powiat district *quod capita, tot sententia*."[4]

An example that illustrates this problem is the constitution of the Cracow Sejm of 1543 under the title: "On incompatible and self-contradictory statutes." The legislator attempted to put the state of the law in order by confirming the "minor statute" (*pośledni statut*) and revoking all other provisions concerning proceedings before land, castle and commissioners' courts.[5] The people of those times must have known which of these statutes was the last[6] and which regulations ceased to be in force, but for us contemporaries it is unclear whether it was Łaski's Statute,[7] *Formula Processus* or some other act, or perhaps this "minor" act, is the Constitution of 1543, for the first time written in Polish, especially as it contains provisions on commissioner's courts in border

2 Jan Łączyński, "Kompendium Sądów Króla Jegomości prawem koronnym na dwie części rozdzielone", in Zygmunt Kolankowski, *Zapomniany prawnik XVI wieku Jan Łączyński i jego 'Kompendium Sądów Króla Jegomości'. Studium z dziejów literatury prawniczej*, Toruń, 1960, 81.

3 Łukasz Gołaszewski, *Konflikty o dziesięciny w dawnej Rzeczypospolitej. Aspekty prawne i społeczne na przykładzie parafii Kobylin na przełomie XVI–XVII wieku*, Warszawa, 2021304, https://www.wpia.uw.edu.pl/uploads/media/60827be9c66e6/konflikty-o-dziesieciny-w-dawnej-rzeczypospolitej-aspekty-prawne-i-spoleczne-na-przykladzie-parafii-kobylin-na-przelomie-xvi-xvii-wieku.pdf?v1%E2%80%A6 (access 3.05.2023).

4 Grzegorz Czaradzki, *Proces sądowny polski prawa koronnego*, Anna Marcol (prep.), Maciej Mikuła (ed.), 12, https://www.iura.uj.edu.pl/dlibra/publication/3061/edition/2304/content?ref=desc&q=dygesta (3.05.2023).

5 See 1543, 20 "according to the … minor statute all things are to be judged …, having ignored earlier statutes made by the court, and contrary to this minor statute." *Volumina Constitutionum*, Part 1: 1493–1549, vol. 1: 1493–1526, 250.

6 For the etymology of the word *pośledni*, see https://sjp.pwn.pl/poradnia/haslo/posledni-i-ostatni;11590.html (access 3.05.2023).

7 *Commune incliti Poloniae Regni privilegium constitutionum et indultuum publicitus decretorum approbatorumque*, Jan Łaski (ed.), Kraków, 1506.

cases and on certain matters before land and castle courts. However, it was still not a comprehensive regulation. In the Cracow edition of the constitution of this Sejm, the editors noted that it was valid temporarily, for one year until the next Sejm, and for this reason it failed to reach official publication.[8] The duration of this law, however, is not fully explained because as far as these conflicting statutes are concerned the Constitution indicates that in cases heard before these courts, this statute will apply until new legislation is enacted.[9] The binding force of this Constitution was extended by a royal privilege in 1550 at the Sejm in Piotrków.[10] If, therefore, the provisions of the 1543 Constitution were included in Januszowski's collection (translated into Latin) at the beginning of the 17th century, this means that its provisions continued to be applied.

The legislator's wish was not ultimately fulfilled, as in the following decades up to the end of the Polish-Lithuanian Commonwealth a land trial was regulated by numerous royal statutes and Sejm constitutions. If we add to this the fact that the mentioned provisions did not apply to the entire territory of the state, because in Lithuania the provisions of the Lithuanian statutes were applied, and even in the Crown there were distinctions in Mazovia. Moreover, in the individual lands of this Duchy—different despite the adoption *in genere* of Polish law in 1576—it gives us a picture of a complicated mosaic of particular laws.[11]

The disorderly nature of procedural law, the lack of a uniform, compact, official codification and the weakness of the legislative technique of the time

---

8 See *Volumina Constitutionum*, Part 1: 1493–1549, vol. 2: 1527–1549, Stanisław Grodziski, Irena Dwornicka, Wacław Uruszczak (eds.), Warszawa, 2000, 32, 242–243 footnote 8, see also 262.

9 *Ten statut aż do tego czasu trwać ma, iż na którym inszem sejmie walnym z pany radami swymi i z posły ziemskimi co lepszego postanowić będziem móc*—"This statute shall remain in force until a new law is passed by the Sejm in the presence of the king, senators and deputies," *Volumina Constitutionum*, Part 1: 1493–1549, vol. 2: 1527–1549, 250.

10 See 1550, 48; *Volumina Constitutionum*, Part 2: 1550–1609, vol. 1: 1550–1585, Stanisław Grodziski, Irena Dwornicka, Wacław Uruszczak (eds.), Warszawa, 2005, 27.

11 See 1553, *Porządek sądów ziem mazowieckich*; *Volumina Constitutionum*, Part 2: 1550–1609, vol. 1: 1550–1585, 52–53; 1565, 84. Shortening court proceedings in Mazovia, *Volumina Constitutionum*, Part 2: 1550–1609, vol. 1: 1550–1585, 175–176; 1567, 1565, 36. Shortening court proceedings, *Volumina Constitutionum*, Part 2: 1550–1609, vol. 1: 1550–1585, 204; 1576, 21. *Prawa polskiego przyjęcie przez Mazowsze*, *Volumina Constitutionum*, Part 2: 1550–1609, vol. 1: 1550–1585, 373–74; the customs of the Mazovian voivodeship from the old statute, conforming to Crown law, taken out and left at the General Sejm in Toruń, anno domini 1576 *Volumina Constitutionum*, Part 2: 1550–1609, vol. 1: 1550–1585, 381–392; see Adam Moniuszko, *Mazowieckie sądy ziemskie (1588–1648). Organizacja—funkcjonowanie—postępowanie*, Warszawa, 2013, 24–25.

resulted in the necessity to make use of the private codification works by Polish legal scholars of the time and studies by practicing lawyers. From the late 16th and early 17th centuries, these include *Kompendium sądów Króla Jegomości* (1594) by Jan Łączyński; *Statuta, prawa i konstytucje koronne* (Cracow 1600), by Jan Januszowski; *Processus iudiciarius Regni Poloniae* (Zamość 1601) by Tomasz Drezner; Teodor Zawacki's *Formula processus* (Cracow 1602), *Processus iudiciarius Regni Poloniae* (Warsaw 1612) and *Compendium, to jest krótkie zebranie wszytkich a wszytkich praw, statutów i konstytucji koronnych aż do roku 1613 inclusive* (Cracow 1614); and Grzegorz Czaradzki's *Proces sądowny polski prawa koronnego* (Poznań 1614).[12]

2 Court

The Statutes of Casimir the Great already contained indications of the obligation to judge disputes fairly on the basis of common law in order to preserve the uniformity of rulings.[13] A judge had a duty to make judgments without taking into account the wealth of the defendant.[14] Court sessions were supposed to take place from early morning to midday, because after lunch, when the judges but also the parties have eaten and drunk, they did not fulfil their duties properly.[15] The literature of the time emphasized that the courts were "the basis of true freedom, as they protect society and ensure public peace."[16]

Land judges were obliged to hold court sessions, and therefore their postponement or rescheduling was forbidden on pain of punishment, unless the parties unanimously requested a postponement of the hearing. The constitution of the Cracow Sejm of 1543 included a provision that a judge could only be excused for incapacity, which, if it occurred, he should have sworn at the next court sitting.[17]

12 Wojciech Witkowski, "XVIII-wieczny zbiór formuł prawnych Grodu Lubelskiego", *Rocznik Lubelski* 16 (1976) 143; Czaradzki drew extensively on Łączyński's work, but also on Drezner's, rewriting certain passages, Kolankowski, *Zapomniany prawnik*, 52–59.

13 Kazimierz Władysław Wójcicki, *Statuta polskie króla Kazimierza w Wiślicy złożone*, Warszawa, 1847, 28.

14 *Nie ważąc sobie person bogatego ani ubogiego*—"not distinguishing between rich and poor persons", Wójcicki, *Statuta polskie*, 11.

15 *Od zarania aż do dziewiątej godziny, to jest południa*—"from early morning until midday", Wójcicki, *Statuta polskie*, 10.

16 Krystyna Bukowska, *Tomasz Drezner 1560–1616*, Warszawa, 1960, 162.

17 *Volumina Constitutionum*, Part 1: 1493–1549, vol. 2: 1527–1549, 248.

3 Parties to Proceedings and Their Attorneys

In Polish land law, the principle adopted from the Roman-canonical procedure was applied, contained in the maxim: *actor sequitur forum rei.*[18] This *actor* was the plaintiff, otherwise known as the *pierca*, while the *reus* was the defendant—the *sąpierz*. The plaintiff sued before the court which had local jurisdiction over the defendant nobleman, and therefore, in principle, in the district in which the defendant resided.[19] This was at the same time the location of his immovable property, as the nobleman's manor house, where he and his family and servants stayed, was located there. If the plaintiff broke this rule and sued his opponent in the court of another powiat district he, according to the Statute of Jan Olbracht of 1496, paid a fine.[20] Likewise, the filing of a lawsuit in a court without subject matter jurisdiction was also punishable, as confirmed by King Sigismund II Augustus in 1550.[21]

The judicial districts were called "powiats"[22]—they were established in such a way that a land court went to a given voivodeship, or land, to certain towns and judged disputes originating in the adjacent area.[23] The location of the courts was of paramount importance; if a judge tried in a place other than the agreed location, he risked a complaint called a *nagana*.[24] The idea

18 *Gdyż powodowa strona wszędy ma iść za prawem pozwanego, do którego przynależy*—"For the plaintiff is everywhere to follow the law of the defendant to which it belongs", Jan Januszowski, *Statuta, prawa i konstytucje*, Kraków, 1600, 515.

19 Stanisław Płaza, *Historia prawa polskiego na tle porównawczym*, vol. 1, Kraków, 1997, 441.

20 37, *Volumina Constitutionum*, Part 1: 1493–1549, vol. 1: 1493–1526, 68; see Januszowski, *Statuta, prawa i konstytucje*, 545.

21 41, *Volumina Constitutionum*, Part 2: 1550–1609, vol. 1: 1550–1585, 27; see Januszowski, *Statuta, prawa i konstytucje*, 545–546.

22 In the 16th-century translation of the Statute of Wiślica, published by Wójcicki, this name of the judicial territorial unit was in use; see Wójcicki, *Statuta polskie*, 10.

23 Edyta Ścibor, "Staropolskie księgi sądowe z zasobów Narodowego Archiwum Państwowego Białorusi w Mińsku w Bibliotece Cyfrowej Wojewódzkiej Biblioteki Publicznej im. Hieronima Łopacińskiego w Lublinie. Historia, zawartość, charakter zbioru", *Bibliotekarz Lubelski* 64 (2021), 38; Januszowski, *Statuta, prawa i konstytucje*, 515.

24 *Sędzie mają sądy polecone, wzięli byli sobie w obyczaj miejsca, jacy gdzie ku sądzeniu wybierając, a to strony uciążając, przeto, aby każdy sędzia wiedział, gdzie ma sądzić, chcemy, aby pan Krakowski we trzech miejscach, to jest w Krakowie, w Andrzejowie i Wiślicy sądził. Pakniąliby to inaczej uczynił, tedy od niego może być odezwano, jako nie od prawego sędziego. To też ustawiamy o panu Sandomierskim*—"Judges are to judge in the places agreed upon, and if they were to judge elsewhere, oppressing a party, we resolve that Cracow judges are to judge in Cracow, Andrzejów and Wiślica. If a judge were to fail to judge in the designated places he could be held liable as an unlawful judge. This is also what we decide about Sandomierz judges", Wójcicki, *Statuta polskie*, 11–12.

behind this provision was to preserve legal certainty and the efficiency of the judiciary.

However, there were exceptions to the rule described in the second to preceding paragraph. Under Polish law, the defendant, as Wacław Uruszczak assumed, could not submit a counterclaim in the court of "his powiat district."[25] However, this issue may be questionable, as the Latin version in Januszowski's collection refers only to "German law courts", whereas the translation refers to "any other" courts. The prohibition of bringing a counterclaim exclusively before the courts of German law was pointed out by Romuald Hube.[26] However, attention should be paid to the content of the provision of the Statute of Wiślica, which clearly stated that the legislation of the last Piast applied to landowners.[27] The practice of the time allowed for the application of the provisions *per analogiam*, and the creative efforts of scribes and printers were also permissible. Moreover, more than two centuries passed between the promulgation of the statutes in the 14th century and their citation by Januszowski at the dawn of the 17th century; practice may have deviated from the literal initial wording of this provision. It is therefore very possible that this norm was indeed also applied in Polish law courts.

As a general rule, from the known beginnings of procedure, litigants should have appeared in person before the court.[28] Over time, however, they could appoint their own representatives, with the result that in civil disputes the presence of the plaintiff and the defendant was not required; this may have led to the *pierca* being referred to as the plaintiff's attorney and the *sąpierz* as the defendant's representative.[29] A court representative was also called a prosecutor, attorney or *prolokutor*. A *prolokutor* provided assistance to the party present at the trial, while a representative could act for the party absent on his behalf. The researcher of this issue, Józef Rafacz, assumed that in the Polish procedure, unlike in western Europe, no distinction was made between these functions.[30] However, it may be that *prolokutors* preceded prosecutors chronologically and the terms were then used interchangeably.

25 Wacław Uruszczak, *Historia państwa i prawa polskiego*, Kraków, 2013, 273.

26 Romuald Hube, *Prawo polskie w 14-tym wieku. Ustawodawstwo Kazimierza Wielkiego*, Warszawa, 1881, 152.

27 *Aby układy i statuta ... wszyscy ziemianie dzierżeli*—"so that agreements and statutes ... are followed by all landowners", Wójcicki, *Statuta polskie*, 6.

28 Józef Rafacz, *Zastępcy stron w dawnym procesie polskim*, Kraków, 1923, 7 [55].

29 Hube, *Prawo polskie*, 15 [63]–16 [64]; see Józef Rafacz, *Dawny proces polski*, Warszawa, 1925, 95.

30 Rafacz, *Prawo polskie*, 19 [67]–23 [71].

The right to establish representation, initially allowed only for persons endowed with a royal privilege, was extended to the whole population.[31] This provision did not derive directly from the Statutes of Casimir the Great themselves; it was added by an *ekstrawagant*, i.e., a later royal act.[32] However, the plaintiff or defendant could still appear before the court in person on their own behalf. The 1543 Constitution of the Cracow Sejm emphasized that a party acting without his own representative must be heard "so that justice may be done to everyone"; in such a situation the court disregarded the defendant's errors and waived the application of procedural formalism. This provision, in Latin translation, was included in Januszowski's collection.[33] The parties appointed their advocates orally before the court, in writing, by an act of the court clerk written down in the presence of witnesses[34] or, in some cases, the appointment of a representative could take place at the place of residence of the litigant. The latter case concerned women, due to the belief at the time of the "weakness of the female gender."[35] A woman appearing as the plaintiff or the defendant had the right to establish her representative at the place of residence in the presence of a court clerk and the adversary in the case.[36] Representatives were also provided for in the Statutes of Nieszawa, issued by Casimir Jagiellon in 1454, for a party who was poor or unable to cope with a case and asked the court for legal assistance.[37]

4 A Petition to a Court and Its Delivery

A petition was defined by Teodor Zawacki as *ad iudicis conspectum legitima vocatio*.[38] In the times in question it was in written form, but not always. It

31 *Aby w sądach naszego Królestwa kożdy człowiek kożdegokolwiek stanu mógł mieć swego prokuratora albo przepowiadacza*—"so that in the courts of our kingdom every person of any estate may have their own prosecutor or representative", Januszowski, *Statuta, prawa i konstytucje*, 516.

32 Hube, *Prawo polskie*, 158.

33 *Omnis qui procuratore careret, poterit suam causam coram iudicio exponere, vel controversiam et definitionem sui facere, sepositis atque reiectis in partem, captiunculis poenarum, quas captiones iudex permittere non debet, nisi hoc custodire ut iustitia unicuique ministretur*, Januszowski, *Statuta, prawa i* konstytucje, 518.

34 Hube, *Prawo polskie*, 157–158, cited the example of Jolanta as the superior of St. Andrew's monastery establishing attorneys in this way in the case with Bishop Bodzanta.

35 See Wacław Uruszczak, *Korektura praw z 1532 roku. Studium historycznoprawne*, vol. 1, Warszawa, Kraków, 1990, 127.

36 Wójcicki, *Statuta polskie*, 9; see Januszowski, *Statuta, prawa i konstytucje*, 518.

37 Januszowski, *Statuta, prawa i konstytucje*, 518.

38 Teodor Zawacki, *Processus iudiciarius Regni Poloniae*, Kraków, 1612, 46.

happened in certain cases—Czaradzki enumerated that a "verbal petition" was used in a *rok nadworny* (*tactus terminus*) in criminal cases before the royal and Sejm court as well as the Tribunal, but also in other courts "for a fresh crime." In this way people were sued for a special, accelerated trial date called *rok licowy* (*facionatus terminus*), when the perpetrator was caught with the object of the offence, as well as when he was caught in the act of committing the offence (*reales seu violentae citationes*).[39]

Usually, however, a written petition was drafted as the first procedural writ in the case, initiating court proceedings. Petitions were known to be either criminal or civil—the difference being the inclusion or omission of financial claims; hence a trial involving a criminal offence could also be classified as civil.[40] The fee for a petition brought before a land court[41] was not limited as to amount—it was a court of general jurisdiction.[42] A petition should have included: (1) a judge, (2) the plaintiff and the defendant, (3) the claim, indicating the circumstances of the case (time and place) and the fee, (4) the date and place of appearance before the court.[43]

According to the 1543 constitution, a petition should have been written in Polish. However, this provision was not applied, and even in Januszowski's collection there was a misrepresentation in the Latin translation of this provision, as the term *citationes in acta Polonicae vel Latinae inscribantur* was used.[44] Due to the developed legal terminology, the spread of Latin in society[45] and romanization through canon law, petitions were still written in Latin.[46] *Formula Processus* simplified the content of a petition and also made it somewhat less formal. The description of the competent court and the effects of formal defects were reduced. In the case of such defects in a petition, such as failure to indicate the title or the names of the plaintiff or the defendant, or even the affixing of a false seal to a petition, the plaintiff

39 Czaradzki, *Proces sądowny polski*, 26–27, see 1578, 45. About the *licowny rok*, see *Volumina Constitutionum*, Part 2: 1550–1609, vol. 1: 1550–1585, 414.

40 Łączyński, *Kompendium Sądów*, 90.

41 *Civilis, ad lucrandum rem, in qua damna et taxa ponitur*, see Tomasz Drezner, *Processus iudiciarius Regni Poloniae*, Zamość, 1601, 10.

42 *Formula Processus*, 19; *Volumina Constitutionum*, Part 1: 1493–1549, vol. 1: 1493–1526, 393.

43 Czaradzki, *Proces sądowny polski*, 27, and the same Drezner, *Processus iudiciarius*, 10. See Łączyński, *Kompendium Sądów*, 90; Zawacki, *Processus iudiciarius*, 50.

44 *Volumina Constitutionum*, Part 1: 1493–1549, vol. 2: 1527–1549, 254; Januszowski, *Statuta, prawa i konstytucje*, 527.

45 Łączyński, *Kompendium Sądów*, 82.

46 Irena Szczepankowska, *Język prawny I Rzeczypospolitej w 'Zbiorze praw sądowych' Andrzeja Zamoyskiego*, vol. 1: *Pojęcia prawne*, Białystok, 2004, 22–24.

incurred a fine, and when the petition was corrected the case was given a further course of action.[47] This was not a novelty, because as early as 1505 Alexander I approved the "Customs of the Cracow Land" included in Łaski's Statute, which provided for similar legal solutions.[48] The wording of the petition should have specified the demand, i.e., the claim that the plaintiff was seeking to enforce. If the claim was not sufficiently clear to the defendant it should have been clarified by the plaintiff in the oral complaint he presented at the hearing.[49]

In 1543, prosecutors were obliged under oath not to allow their clients to believe that a trial was worthwhile or to undertake a case that clearly had no foundation. This provision was intended to counteract litigiousness in the court. In addition, it obliged attorneys to indicate in the petition the amount of compensation appropriate to the damage, the extent of which could be proven. Breach of these rules may have even resulted in a ban on practicing the profession.[50]

Attacks on the defendant, damaging his honor, were not allowed in the petition; in Casimir Jagiellon's Nowy Korczyn Statute of 1451 the judges were given the right to punish the author of the petition.[51] During the reign of Sigismund I, a decree was issued in Cracow in 1537, in the dispute between Strzałkowski and Kołaczkowski. in which the king's judgment, "which had the force of a statute", forbade prosecutors and all other persons from any estate to bring defamatory petitions (*citationes calumniatoriae*) to court under penalty of imprisonment for a week for the prosecutor or a party.[52] However, the enforcement of these regulations was problematic due to the lack of indication of the court competent to hear the case of such slander—in 1550, at the Sejm in Piotrków, Zygmunt II August issued a privilege approving the laws of the Kingdom, with new solutions for their enforcement. From then on the court with jurisdiction over petitions containing defamatory content was to be the court where the petition was filed, with the possibility of an appeal to

47 *Formula Processus*, 5; *Volumina Constitutionum*, Part 1: 1493–1549, vol. 1: 1493–1526, 392.

48 10, *Volumina Constitutionum*, Part 1: 1493–1549, vol. 1: 1493–1526, 157, see footnote 1, 156; Januszowski, *Statuta, prawa i konstytucje*, 527.

49 *Formula Processus*, 3–4, *Volumina Constitutionum*, Part 1: 1493–1549, vol. 1: 1493–1526, 392.

50 1543, 25: *Szacunki pieniężne, które o krzywdy albo o szkody albo na pozwie kładą, mają być tak miarkowane ważne, jako szkoda jest ważna, aby stąd dowodniej a z świadki ludzie nie byli obciążeni*—"Advocates of choice, who are hired by the plaintiffs, are supposed to limit the amount of compensation in petitions so as not to oppress anyone", *Volumina Constitutionum*, Part 1: 1493–1549, vol. 2: 1527–1549, 251.

51 Januszowski, *Statuta, prawa i konstytucje*, 529–530.

52 Januszowski, *Statuta, prawa i konstytucje*, 529; Łączyński, *Kompendium Sądów*, 90.

the royal court.[53] Despite clear rules on the subject the phenomenon was evidently spreading, since the proposals for procedural reform called for a ban on defamatory petitions.[54]

Where two petitions were filed by a plaintiff in one case, the second one was dismissed. If the subject matter of the proceedings was the same in two petitions from different plaintiffs, however, the proceedings were not initiated until the dispute first pending had been resolved. In the matters described above, customary law continued to apply.[55]

An extremely important procedural act was the delivery of the petition, which was carried out by a court usher (*ministerialis*).[56] Failure to deliver it resulted in the defendant's right to refuse to appear before the court, which was inferred from the "Customs of the Cracow land" (*Consvetudines Terrae Cracoviensis*), contained in the Łaski's Statute and reprinted in Januszowski's collection.[57]

The delivery of the petition to a settled nobleman took place at his estate, and this was done because one was sued from property, usually any property, belonging to the defendant in order to effectively enforce the expected judgment.[58] The form of delivery developed much earlier and was recorded in the Statute of Wiślica. The usher should have gone to the defendant's estate, stood at the gate of his house, struck the gate with a cane and verbally sued him, stating the subject matter of the case.[59] Subsequently, the issue of delivery was regulated in *Formula Processus*: the delivery of the petition was done by the so-called "aying" of the petition, which did not require personal delivery to the defendant. The usher, with the participation of a nobleman nominated by the plaintiff, would either sue the landlord in his manor, "laying" the petition there, or hand it over to his peasant.[60] If the estate was unoccupied (abandoned) the usher put the petition in wood and drove it into the ground,

53 1550, 32, *Volumina Constitutionum*, Part 2: 1550–1609, vol. 1: 1550–1585, 26.

54 Adam Moniuszko, "Postulaty zmian w ziemskim procesie koronnym a próba jego reformy na przełomie XVI i XVII wieku", *Zeszyty Prawnicze UKSW* 5/1 (2005), 163–164.

55 *Commune incliti Poloniae Regni privilegium constitutionum et indultuum publicitus decretorum approbatorumque*, 122v; see Januszowski, *Statuta, prawa i konstytucje*, 530; see also 24, *Volumina Constitutionum*, Part 1: 1493–1549, vol. 1: 1493–1526, 159.

56 Court clerk known in sources from the 13th century onwards; see Zygfryd Romaszewski, *Woźny sądowy*, Warszawa, 2008, 4.

57 *Commune incliti Poloniae Regni privilegium constitutionum et indultuum publicitus decretorum approbatorumque*, 121; compare Januszowski, *Statuta, prawa i konstytucje*, 531; see also *Volumina Constitutionum*, Part 1: 1493–1549, vol. 1: 1493–1526, 156–162.

58 Adam Moniuszko, *Mazowieckie sądy ziemskie*, 219.

59 Wójcicki, *Statuta polskie*, 12.

60 *Formula Processus*, 10; *Volumina Constitutionum*, Part 1: 1493–1549, vol. 1: 1493–1526, 393.

announcing the accomplishment of this action in a neighboring village or parish.[61] "Against an unsettled person", the petition was announced either in the parish of his place of birth or where he had previously owned property or resided. It also could be delivered personally to him.[62] The usher gave an account of the delivery, i.e., the "laying" of the petition, which was entered in the land books, from which a copy was issued.[63]

A petition was drawn up in two copies with the same content, often on a single document, which was then cut up as proof of its authenticity. It could happen that a party lost or misplaced the petition before entering into a dispute on its substance. If this problem affected the plaintiff, he could, at no extra charge, file a new petition, even of different content, but the fee had to be correct. After *litis contestatio* this was also possible, unless the petition was entered in a complaint called *żałoba*. Then the case was deemed to be pending, even if the defendant had filed his petition against that plaintiff in the meantime. If the petition had been lost by the defendant, then the plaintiff, having expressed his *żałoba*, should have lent this document to him so that the defendant could prepare a reply to the petition. This provision, contained in the *Formula processus*, applied to Ruthenian lands, but it is to be believed that it later applied universally.[64]

5 Dates (*roki*) of Sessions of Land Courts

A land court met for two to four sessions per year, depending on the voivodeship.[65] These sessions were referred to as *roki*. Initially, their dates had to be announced four weeks in advance, because if anyone was initiating a case before the court they should notify the defendant of this act (deliver the petition) three weeks before the session, so the defendant could prepare to present his position, unless the case was for a small debt, in which case he was

---

61 *Formula Processus*, 11; *Volumina Constitutionum*, Part 1: 1493–1549, vol. 1: 1493–1526, 393.

62 *W parafii, gdzie miał kiedy osiadłość albo się rodził, albo gdzie przemieszkiwa: może też w ręce temu samemu oddać*—"in the parish where he used to live or was born or where he resides: it may also be handed over to him", Czaradzki, *Proces sądowny*, 27.

63 *Formula Processus*, 10; *Volumina Constitutionum*, Part 1: 1493–1549, vol. 1: 1493–1526, 393; see Łączyński, *Kompendium Sądów*, 86.

64 Januszowski, *Statuta, prawa i konstytucje*, 531; *Formula Processus*, 75; *Volumina Constitutionum*, Part 1: 1493–1549, vol. 1: 1493–1526, 400; see Uruszczak, *Korektura praw*, 132, 134.

65 1565, 7–35, *Volumina Constitutionum*, Part 2: 1550–1609, vol. 1: 1550–1585, 163–165. Subsequent adjustments to the dates were collected by Januszowski, *Statuta, prawa i konstytucje*, 461–469; see Płaza, *Historia prawa*, 536; Uruszczak, *Historia państwa*, 259.

obliged to answer "the following day."[66] Subsequently, these terms varied depending on the type of court and case.[67]

The 1423 Warka Statute of Władysław Jagiełło regulated the consequences of the parties' failure to appear by introducing the concept of the final date (*rok zawity*), the consequence of which was that the plaintiff lost the trial if he was not present. From earliest times, the first term was peremptory for the plaintiff—he lost the case unless the defendant was present in court, in which case he had to pay a fine.[68] If the defendant failed to appear on either the first or second date he paid a fine; for him, the third term was final.[69] This regulation was amended in *Formula Processus* in order to accelerate proceedings. It was still mandatory for the plaintiff to appear at the first term on pain of losing the trial, and he was not excused by an ordinary illness; *a contrario*, it had to be a bedridden, genuine illness.[70] The defendant had to appear on the first date at the plaintiff's request and, if he did not excuse himself, he paid a penalty (*poena contumatiae*), known as *niestanne*.[71] However, he was allowed to argue that he had an ordinary illness (*dilatio simplicis infirmitatis*), while in the second term that he had a bedridden illness (*dilatio verae infirmitatis*), confirmed by three witnesses—landowners from the same powiat district.[72]

The postponements of the trial date were referred to as *dylacje*.[73] They played a very important role in proceedings, for the second date became final and the defendant's absence resulted in losing the case and a default judgment. Apart from the excuse of illness, there were also other reasons for postponing a hearing. These included the so-called "for greater" (*dilatio pro*

66 Wójcicki, *Statuta polskie*, 13.

67 Łączyński, *Kompendium Sądów*, 86.

68 See Wójcicki, *Statuta polskie*, 18.

69 *Si citatus parere non curaverit vel contempserit, quo quolibet termino, videlicet primo et secundo, octo scotos solvere teneatur; et in tertio termino, si non comparuert, casam perdet, et ab actione cadet. Si vero actor in primo termino non comparuerit* [*nec per se*] *nec per nuntium, causam amittet cum poena septem marcarum.* Published in *Starodawne prawa polskiego pomniki poprzedzone wywodem historyczno krytycznym tak zwanego Prawodawstwa Wiślickiego Kazimierza Wielkiego w tekście ze starych rękopism krytycznie dobranym*, Antoni Zygmunt Helcel (ed.), Kraków, 1856, 313.

70 *Formula Processus*, 1; *Volumina Constitutionum*, Part 1: 1493–1549, vol. 1: 1493–1526, 393.

71 *Pozwany ... upuścił to sobie dopuszczeniem kontumacyjej*—"the defendant ... failed to appear at the trial date, leading to him being fined"; Łączyński, *Kompendium Sądów*, 87; Drezner, *Processus iudiciarius*, 13.

72 *Formula Processus*, 13–17; *Volumina Constitutionum*, Part 1: 1493–1549, vol. 1: 1493–1526, 393, by custom, however, this *dylacja* was not permitted *ad recipiendas pecunias de bonis obligatis*, Zawacki, *Processus iudiciarius*, 93.

73 List of *dylacjas*, Zawacki, *Processus iudiciarius*, 90–91.

maiori).[74] The "Customs of the Cracow Land" included in the Statute of Łaski and still in use during the period in question, provided that a defendant could obtain a *dylacja* in a given case if he had a trial in another court with a higher tax. However, at the subsequent term he had to prove this fact with a type of certificate on pain of losing the case "for lesser."[75] If a party had contractually agreed to the first term as peremptory, it could only be postponed on the basis of an oath-certified "genuine illness."[76] The 1588 Constitution also restricted the use of *dylacja ad munimenta simplicia*, i.e., a postponement in order to submit private documents to the court.[77]

The defendant's objection (*ekscepcja*),[78] causing a postponement of the hearing, was treated as an auxiliary case called *akcesoryjna*, which ended with the issuing of a decision, called *sententia interlocutoria*. In such a situation a party had no recourse—the *sentientia interlocutoria* was then unappealable.[79]

6 Procedural Steps

The plaintiff's claim was reiterated in a complaint filed directly before the court. The claim could not be amended to prevent the defendant from being misled. This was already provided for by the Statutes of Casimir the Great.[80]

The defendant was given the right to consider the plaintiff's complaint, allowing time for consultation with his friends or legal representative, after which he presented his response to the complaint. If the defendant's objection was such that the plaintiff was losing the main case, this stage of the proceedings, treated as an *accesorium*, ended in a final judgment (*sententia definitiva*). This type of objection included the objection of limitation (*praescriptio*). As early as in the Statutes of Casimir the Great it was stipulated that if the owner of real estate remained inactive towards the possessor who had leased his property for three years and three months, he would lose it by acquisitive

74 Drezner, *Processus iudiciarius Regni Poloniae*, 23.

75 Januszowski, *Statuta, prawa i konstytucje*, 549.

76 *Commune incliti Poloniae Regni privilegium constitutionum et indultuum publicitus decretorum approbatorumque*, 122; Januszowski, *Statuta, prawa i konstytucje*, 549.

77 *Volumina Constitutionum*, Part 2: 1550–1609, vol. 2: 1587–1609, Stanisław Grodziski (ed.), Warszawa, 2008, 81, text partially incompatible with Januszowski, *Statuta, prawa i konstytucje*, 549; see Moniuszko, *Mazowieckie sądy ziemskie*, 258–259.

78 *Exceptio est quae intentionem actoris excludit*, Drezner, *Processus iudiciarius*, 24.

79 1543, 17, Accesoria; *Volumina Constitutionum*, Part 1: 1493–1549, vol. 2: 1527–1549, 249.

80 Wójcicki, *Statuta polskie*, 13.

prescription.[81] The passage of time was then identical to the statute of limitations. It was also considered to be a long-established custom that, when a plaintiff did not support a commenced case for one year and six months (*fatalia iuris*) he lost the trial.[82] Usually, however, the defendant had allegations of a lesser caliber at his disposal, which at least allowed him to prolong the proceedings; these should have been presented in a strict order, but recent research indicates that in practice no rigid rules were applied.[83] The effect of the defendant's position of requesting the dismissal of the claim was *litis contestatio* ("entering into a dispute").

There was a maximum of three exchanges of positions between the litigants: the petition and the defendant's reply,[84] possibly followed by the plaintiff's reply and the defendant's surrejoinder, the plaintiff's triplicate and the defendant's quadruplicate.[85] In order to speed up the proceedings, a rule of statute of repose was introduced, as memoranda or protests filed at a later date were disregarded unless the court agreed to their submission.[86]

Before passing the judgment, as *Formula Processus* stated, the judge would ask the parties for evidence to support their litigation position.[87] The rules of evidence, embodied in the rule of proximity to proof, were highly complex at the time. As a rule, the defendant had the right to present evidence, but there were numerous exceptions to this rule. The most common means of proof was the oath, while official documents and inspection became particularly prominent.[88]

81 Januszowski, *Statuta, prawa i konstytucje*, 550.

82 Januszowski, *Statuta, prawa i konstytucje*, 552; see 1587–1588, 27, O znoszeniu pozwów, *Volumina Constitutionum*, Part 2: 1550–1609, vol. 2: 1587–1609, 70.

83 Gołaszewski, *Konflikty o* dziesięciny, 254–363.

84 See 1496, 21, [*De controversiis et responsis*], *Volumina Constitutionum*, Part 1: 1493–1549, vol. 1: 1493–1526, 64.

85 *Volumina Constitutionum*, Part 1: 1493–1549, vol. 2: 1527–1549, 254; *Procede, potem responde, za ostatnim directe responde; za czym już in principali litem contestari musi* —"*procede*, then *responde* and *directe responde* after the last one, after that it must be *in principali litem contestari*", Łączyński, *Kompendium Sądów*, 83.

86 *Formula Processus*, 8; *Volumina Constitutionum*, Part 1: 1493–1549, vol. 1: 1493–1526, 392.

87 *Formula Processus*, 7; *Volumina Constitutionum*, Part 1: 1493–1549, vol. 1: 1493–1526, 392.

88 *Dowody trojakie bywają, albo listowne albo przez przysięgę, albo przez strony bądź świadków przyznanie*—"there are three types of evidence, either by letter or oath, or by the parties or witnesses admitting them", Łączyński, *Kompendium Sądów*, 101–102. Zawacki, *Processus iudiciarius*, 112, included among the evidence the sources of law on which the judgment is based; for more see Gołaszewski, *Konflikty o dziesięciny*, 365–374; Moniuszko, *Mazowieckie sądy ziemskie*, 264–280.

The judge could postpone the pronouncement of the judgment ("decree") in order to consider the case, but only once. As can be seen from the wording of the 1543 Constitution, there were abuses in this case caused by a misinterpretation of the provision of *Formula Processus*; namely, as the court was obliged to invite the parties to present their final procedural position before pronouncing judgment, the plaintiff or defendant attempted to supplement the procedural material. This led to a prolongation of the proceedings, as the judge in such a case could again set a time limit to consider the case ("deliberation"); this situation could be repeated several times. It was therefore decided that a change in a party's position could irrevocably take place on the final date before deliberation was ordered.[89]

The introduction of an appeal against a judgment in the judiciary of the nobility[90] by virtue of *Formula Processus* does not dispel all doubts about the application of remedies. The aforementioned constitution of 1543 contained the provision that if an auxiliary case led to a decision with regard to the "main thing", a party to the trial could first bring a motion ("moving the judge")[91] to a court in *colloquio* (*sąd wiecowy*), and only then bring an appeal to the Sejm.[92] The courts of both successive instances then decided the main case. The filing of an appeal was associated with the obligation to pay a fee

89 1543, 17, Accesoria; *Volumina Constitutionum*, Part 1: 1493–1549, vol. 2: 1527–1549, 249.

90 *Appellatio est ab inferioris iudicis sententia, ad superiorem cui lege ea iurisdictio est data, motio*, Drezner, *Processus iudiciarius*, 27; almost identical in Zawacki, *Processus iudiciarius*, 112, but with an explanation: *appellatio est iurisdictionis inferioris iudicis per legittimam invocationem superioris, hic in eodem iudicio factam, suspensio.*

91 *Apelacyja od mocyjej w tym jest różna, iż za apelacyją sama strona dekretu broni, za którą wynidzie, dla czego też ad prosequendam appellationem samę stronę przypozywają ..., a z mocyją sędzia albo urzędnik ruszony przedtem był powinien przy stronie bronić sentencyjej swojej, dawając przyczyny słuszności jej*—"An appeal differs from a motion in that, if one party appeals, the judgment appealed against is defended by the other party to the proceedings, whereas in the case of a motion, the judgment is defended by the party together with the judge who made the judgment," Łączyński, *Kompendium Sądów*, 93. Zawacki, *Processus iudiciarius*, 113, made an attempt to distinguish between an appeal and motion: *motio autem est iudicis redargutio ad quam reguiritur, ut iudex eam suscipiat. Terminusque illi per ministerialem asignatur: ut personaliter in superiori iudicio compareat.*

92 Similarly in the Constitution of the 1556–1557: *Aby tym prędsza odprawa sprawiedliwości szła, żaden sąd ani urząd nie ma dopuścić apelacyjej ani ruszenia ab accesorio, chyba iż by takowe było, które by niosło zysk albo stratę*—"In order that the faster administration of justice may take place, no court or authority shall allow any appeal or motion *ab accesorio*, unless it is for profit or loss," *Volumina Constitutionum*, Part 2: 1550–1609, vol. 1: 1550–1585, 76, confirmation 1587–88, 59, De accessoriis, *Volumina Constitutionum*, Part 2: 1550–1609, vol. 2: 1587–1609, 80.

called *kocz*. If it was brought and confirmed by an entry in the books it was not paid again in a Sejm court. Ultimately, the *kocz* went to the one who won the case.[93] It follows from the above that the proceedings could be of three instances. This was also confirmed by the privilege of Sigismund II Augustus in 1550, although in this act an appeal against a court in *colloquio* was already called an appeal, but at the same time it was confirmed that "from colloquia an appeal to the Sejm is to be."[94] However, if the verdict of the village court was "agreed", which could mean both unanimity of the judges and agreement of the parties, the appeal was not allowed to go before the king at a Sejm, in accordance with the provision of the 1553 Constitution.[95] A change in the organization of the judiciary took place in 1578 in the Crown, and in 1581 in Lithuania, as the Crown and Lithuanian tribunals became courts of second instance; courts *in colloquio* were abolished. As a rule, a trial became a two-step process. However, there was still confusion between an appeal and a motion in studies of the period, due to the judge's individual responsibility for the judgment, although this happened less and less frequently with the passing of time.[96]

7 Conclusion

Land courts have declined over time. The reasons why they convened less frequently than they should have were court recesses due to: obstructions of statutory or customary law, all public conventions, warfare, interregnums, epidemics, illnesses or deaths of members of the judiciary and conflicts between them, as well as church holidays.[97] Łukasz Gołaszewski, when examining cases in the Bielsko Land, also drew attention to an interesting phenomenon—that the defendants did not appear for hearings before the land courts, and judgments were made in default. The plaintiff, wishing to enforce a decree favorable to him, would submit to the rigors of the enforcement proceedings, conducted in the castle court. More often than not, the defendant only started to act in the last phase of these proceedings, when the plaintiff sued him with a special petition called an *innotestencja* to a castle court. At that time, the

93 *Volumina Constitutionum*, Part 1: 1493–1549, vol. 1: 1493–1526, 249.

94 1550, 19, *Volumina Constitutionum*, Part 2: 1550–1609, vol. 1: 1550–1585, 25.

95 1553, *Volumina Constitutionum*, Part 2: 1550–1609, vol. 1: 1550–1585, 51.

96 Bukowska, *Tomasz Drezner*, 188–189.

97 Łączyński, *Kompendium Sądów*, 99; Drezner, *Processus iudiciarius*, 22; Bukowska, *Tomasz Drezner*, 172; see Gołaszewski, *Konflikty o dziesięciny*, 143–159.

defendant claimed that he knew nothing about the plaintiff's claim and his petition. The castle court was obliged to investigate all of the defendant's objections; hence, in practice, the case started from the beginning and was heard in the castle court, bypassing the land court.[98]

98 Gołaszewski, *Konflikty o dziesięciny*, 301–304, 396, 430–431, 434–434.

CHAPTER 4

Reform of the Procedure of Polish Municipal Law: *Processus Iuris Cracoviensis in Civilibus* of 1544

Maciej Mikuła

The mosaic of legal orders in the states of Europe at the end of the Middle Ages and the early modern period was the result of the fusion of two phenomena: the principles of legal personality and territorial particularism. Respectively, they were the ability of certain social groups to use their own law and the fact that different legal solutions were applied to the same social groups in different territories of the same state. Also, the diversity of law in Polish cities was a consequence of the progressive isolation of social states and the legal closure of the bourgeois state, which finally occurred at the end of the 15th century,[1] on the one hand, and of the complex history of the Kingdom of Poland, whose borders evolved significantly between the 13th and 16th centuries, on the other hand. In the 13th century, the legal solutions of the so-called German law were adopted because of their usefulness.[2] In the southern and central parts of the country, the regulations of Magdeburg law (*Ius Magdeburgense*) and Środa law (*Ius Novoforense*) were selectively adopted. The latter was a variant of Magdeburg law and was almost completely replaced in later centuries by its very evolved prototype. In the north, on the other hand, the state of the Teutonic Order developed after 1226. The pattern of Magdeburg law was creatively developed with the prominent jurisprudence of the higher court in Chełmno (1230). For this reason, the law thus emerging was referred to as Chełmno law (*ius Culmense*). It was applied not only in the cities of the Teutonic State, but also in Mazovia in central Poland. The defeat of the Order State by the Kingdom of Poland eventually led to the incorporation of part of its lands, includ-

1 See Henryk Samsonowicz, "Relacje międzystanowe w Polsce w XV wieku", in *Społeczeństwo Polski średniowiecznej*, vol. 2, Stefan K. Kuczyński (ed.), Warsaw, 1982, 244–265; Henryk Samsonowicz, "Problem stanów w Polsce średniowiecznej", *Przegląd Historyczny* 80/4 (1989), 743–751.

2 For a review of the literature on the subject, see Wieland Carls and Katalin Gönczi, "Forschungsüberblick", in Inge Bily, Wieland Carls, Katalin Gönczi, *Sächsisch-magdeburgisches Recht in Polen. Untersuchungen zur Geschichte des Rechts und seiner Sprache*, Berlin, 2011, 39–67; Heiner Lück, "Aspects of the Transfer of the Saxon-Magdeburg Law to Central and Eastern Europe", *Rechtsgeschichte—Legal History* 22 (2014), 79–89.

 | DOI:10.1163/9789004736672_006

ing Gdańsk Pomerania (1466), into the Kingdom of Poland, as a result of which the number of cities governed by Chełmno law in the Kingdom of Poland was greatly expanded.[3] Naturally, the wealth of legal solutions was also influenced by legal practice, petrifying local customary law[4] and legislation within individual cities. The latter consisted of both statutes enacted by municipal bodies and statutes granted by city owners—the king, the nobility, and ecclesiastical institutions.[5]

The processes of law diversification were countered by efforts to unify and also reform it. Efforts to preserve the uniformity of jurisprudence within the two basic legal orders—Magdeburg law and Chełmno law—were undertaken by higher courts, including the aforementioned Chełmno court, the Higher Court of German Law at Wawel Royal Castle in Cracow and other higher courts.[6] This occurred both as a result of the handling of appeals and the issuance of instructions to legal inquiries. It is worth noting that the court in Cracow was established by King Casimir the Great (1333–1370) in 1356 in order to eliminate the practice of turning directly to Magdeburg for instructions, among other reasons.[7] This phenomenon continued well into the 15th century. Similarly, by the way, in the Kingdom of Bohemia, where the custom of turning to Magdeburg for legal instructions was not effectively stopped until 1549. Another way of unifying the law was to borrow statutes enacted in model cities. For the cities of the Kingdom of Poland founded under Magdeburg law, such a model was undoubtedly the capital Krakow.[8] This has been proven both by research on private law and guild legislation.[9]

---

3 Only a few Pomeranian towns in the Kingdom of Poland were governed by Lübeck law. Krystyna Kamińska, *Lokacje miast na prawie Magdeburskim na ziemii polskich do 1370 r. Studium historyczno-prawne*, Toruń, 1990, 109.

4 Grzegorz M. Kowalski wrote that a custom played a primary role among the sources of municipal law: Grzegorz M. Kowalski, *Zwyczaj i prawo zwyczajowe w doktrynie prawa i praktyce sądów miejskich karnych w Polsce XVI–XVIII w.*, Kraków, 2013, 167.

5 Stanisław Kutrzeba, "Autonomia miast i władza ustawodawcza panów miast w dawnej Rzeczpospolitej", in *Księga ku czci Oswalda Balzera*, vol. 2, Lwów, 1925, 93.

6 Ludwik Łysiak, "Höhere Gerichte des deutsche Rechts in Polen im XVI.–XVI. Jahrhundert", in *Rechtsbehelfe, Beweis und Stellung des Richters im Spätmittelalter*, Wolfgang Sellert (ed.), Köln, 1985, 21–33.

7 Ludwik Łysiak, *Ius supremum Maydeburgese castri Cracoviensis 1356–1794. Organisation, Tätigkeit und Stellung des Krakauer Oberhofs in der Rechtsprechung Altpolens*, Frankfurt am Main, 1990, 15–25.

8 Maciej Mikuła, *Prawodawstwo króla i sejmu dla małopolskich miast królewskich (1386–1572). Studium z dziejów rządów prawa w Polsce*, Kraków, 2014, 281, footnote 214.

9 Maciej Mikuła, "Das Krakauer Zunftrecht Im 16. Jahrhundert: Auf Der Suche Nach Einem Universellen Regulierungsmuster", in *Krakau—Nürnberg—Prag: Stadt Und Handwerk in*

However, it was the success of the idea of a uniform code of laws for cities that may have represented a breakthrough in diversity. The European movement of writing down local customs and codification aspirations was also familiar to urban legal culture in the Kingdom of Poland in the 16th century.[10] Unfortunately, this action was only partially successful. The codification drafts of Chełmno law, although they did not acquire the attribute of an official source of law, constituted an orderly collection of at least some of the regulations. In the second half of the 16th century, the so-called revisions of the Chełmno law—Lidzbarska I (1552–1554), Lidzbarska II (1566), Nowomiejska (1580), and Toruńska (1594)—were created in succession. The extensive use of the last three in legal practice is not in doubt.[11] Not even Polish drafts developed under Magdeburg law came close to this success. The first of these, Maciej Śliwnicki's so-called *Sigismundina* of 1523, survives in manuscript form. It was supposed to be a comprehensive codification of law for cities, compiled using the sources of the European *ius commune*. And it was this that was responsible for the failure of the entire project. The extent of the use of canon law and Roman law was unacceptable in Polish cities, where the primary sources were Saxo-Magdeburg law, local legislation, and customary law; the *ius commune* could at most be a subsidiary source of law.[12] This was in fact the case, since Master Raimundus' *Summa legum brevis, levis et utilis*, a handbook of Roman-canon law, was printed in the official law collection of 1506, the so-called Statute of Jan Łaski.[13]

Der Vorindustriellen Zeit, Olga Fejtová, Antonia Landois, Zdzislaw Noga (eds.), Praha, 2022, 15–39.

10 Witold Maisel, "Kodyfikacje prawa miejskiego w dawnej Polsce", in *Dzieje kodyfikacji prawa. Materiały na konferencję historyków prawa w Karpaczu*, Poznań, 1974, 93–126; Witold Maisel, "Kodyfikacje statutów miejskich w dawnej Polsce", *Studia Źródłoznawcze* 22 (1977), 151–166.

11 More about revisions of the Chełmno law, see Danuta Janicka, *Prawo karne w trzech rewizjach prawa chełmińskiego z XVI wieku*, Toruń, 1992.

12 Compare Jarosław Reszczyński, *Sądownictwo i proces w kodyfikacji Macieja Śliwnickiego z 1523 roku: o wpływach prawa rzymskiego i praw obcych na myśl prawną polskiego Odrodzenia*, Kraków, 2008, 58–60.

13 *Commune incliti Poloniae Regni privilegium constitutionum et indultuum publicitus decretorum approbatorumque cum nonnullis iuribus tam divinis quam humanis per serenissimum principem et dominum dominum Alexandrum, Dei gratia Regem Poloniae, magnum ducem Lithwanie, Russie, Prussieque dominum et haeredem etc. Non tamen in illud privilegium sed motu proprio regio serenitatis sue p[er] adhortationem p[ro] instructione Regnicolarum, proque Regni eiusdem, ac iusticie statu feliciter dirigendis eidem privilegio annexis et ascriptis*, (Cracoviae, MDVI). See Wacław Uruszczak, "*Commune incliti Poloniae Regni privilegium constitutionum et indultuum*: O tytule i mocy prawnej Statutu

The practical failure of Maciej Sliwnicki's project, which was not used in practice even in ecclesiastical localities remaining in the hands of the Archbishopric of Gniezno, could prompt the scribe of the Cracow city chancellery, Mikołaj Jaskier (1504–1539), to develop a new translation of works of Saxo-Magdeburg law: Saxon Mirror (*Iuris provincialis quod Speculum Saxonum vulgo nuncupatus libri tres…*, ed. 1535, 1602), Magdeburg Weichbild (*Iuris Municipalis Maideburgensis Liber vulgo Weichbild nuncupatus…*, ed. 1535, 1602), and an alphabetical, hash-tag lecture on issues of Saxo-Magdeburg law (*Promptuarium Iuris Provincialis Saxonici, quod Speculum Saxonum vocatur…*, ed. 1535).[14] The publication of Jaskier's works was a significant event. It was not a literal translation of the German sources, but a compilation and adaptation. Among other things, Jaskier made use of an earlier edition in Poland of the *Ius municipale* and the Saxon Mirror in the Statute of Jan Łaski, and he drew on Cracow legislation. In addition, unlike the 1506 manuscripts and editions that were widespread in the Kingdom of Poland, this edition was provided with a *glossa* containing numerous references to Roman law and canon law.[15] Nevertheless, Jaskier's work could not replace a uniform codification. Suffice it to mention the anachronism of numerous regulations of procedural law, in which a court duel was still repeatedly mentioned.

The shortcomings of the codification were resolved by the Cracow city council. On February 6, 1539, it appointed a special commission to arrange a draft codification of proceedings.[16] As will become apparent, it was a draft that, in its content, went well beyond procedural issues and included numerous provisions of civil law—especially inheritance and matrimonial property law. Significantly, one of the two surviving manuscripts used a title that indi-

Łaskiego z 1506 roku", in *Prace poświęcone pamięci Adama Uruszczaka*, Jan Halberda, Michał Hosowicz, Anna Karabowicz (eds.), Zakamycze, 2006, 126.

14 Compare Zygfryd Rymaszewski, *Łacińskie teksty Landrechtu Zwierciadła Saskiego w Polsce. Jaskier—tekst główny i noty marginesowe*, Łódź, 1985, 5–6. A biography of Jaskier, see inter alia Heiner Lück, "Jaskier Mikołaj", in *Handwörterbuch zur deutschen Rechtsgeschichte*, vol. 2, Berlin, 2012, 1355–1356. A short new report on Jaskiers' works, see Wieland Carls, "Rechtsquellen Sächsisch-magdeburgischen Rechts", in *Sächsisch-magdeburgisches Recht in Polen. Untersuchungen zur Geschichte des Rechts und seiner Sprache*, Inge Bily, Wieland Carls, Katalin Gönczi (eds.), vol. 2, Berlin, 2011, 104–105.

15 In the literature, it has been conjectured that the *glossa* could be known in the Kingdom of Poland, but this view needs to be better substantiated. See Jarosław Reszczyński, *Sądownictwo i proces*, 32, footnote 30.

16 *Prawa, przywileje i statuta miasta Krakowa (1507–1795)*, Franciszek Piekosiński (ed.), Kraków, 1885, 75.

cated that the codification was based on legal practice in Cracow.[17] This is an important clue, although determining the extent to which the draft's provisions are consistent with practice still requires further research. Nevertheless, the surviving draft provides a valuable starting point for the study of the practice of procedural law, and at the same time provides material to better understand the urban legal culture of the Kingdom of Poland. So far, this draft has not been the subject of in-depth study[18] and for this reason and because of its cognitive value, it is the main source of this article.

1 Work on the 1544/1546 Cracow Draft

The legislative committee was composed of influential townspeople. Cracow Councilman Jan Morsztyn the Elder (1481–1541) was listed first in the resolution establishing the commission, so one can guess that he acted as chairman of the work. He belonged to the city's elite.[19] Also listed was the influential goldsmith, Councilman Jan Zimmerman (ca. 1470–1539). Another prominent figure was Councilman Justus Ludwik Decius (ca. 1485–1545), a patrician of Cracow and secretary to King Sigismund I (1506–1548). One gets the impression that he closed the group of prominent and influential members of the commission. Next, the resolution mentions the physician Wojciech Kraina (ca. 1485–1559), who was also part of the city council. Further on, we learn about Councilman Wacław Chodorowski (–1551?). We know that he graduated from the Faculty of Law at the University of Cracow.[20] This circumstance makes it possible that he may have played an important role in the work on the draft, especially since he was part of another commission, appointed in 1546 to improve the original draft. The first commission also included the councilman, merchant, and financier Jan Schilling (–1542), Councilman Bar-

17 *Processus iuris ciuilis consuetudinem Cracouiensium olim per consules vrbis eiusdem in gratia suorum ciuium consriptus et aeditus.*

18 Introductory remarks were included in the introduction to the first edition of the printed draft by Jan K.H.S. Rzesiński (*Proces cywilny krakowski przez rajców miasta w roku 1544 za panowania Zygmunta I napisany*, Jan H.S. Rzesiński (ed.), Kraków, 1840, lv–lvi. The draft was also mentioned in a review article by the eminent expert on the Polish legal historical sources Stanisław Kutrzeba, "Autonomia miast", 95, a few remarks; see also Maciej Mikuła, *Prawodawstwo króla i sejmu*, 247–248, 265–266. For the purposes of this chapter, I use the edition of Franciszek Piekosiński, *Prawa, przywileje i statuty*, 109.

19 Bogdan Kasprzyk, "Jan Morsztyn starszy", in *Poczet sołtysów, wójtów, burmistrzów i prezydentów miasta Krakowa (1228–2010)*, Bogdan Kasprzyk (ed.), Kraków, 2010, 432.

20 Bogdan Kasprzyk, "Wacław Chodorowski", in *Poczet sołtysów*, 449.

tholomew Kromer (1500–1563), and the lawyer Councilman Andrzej Vogelweder (–1543).[21] In addition, the resolution mentions the *wójt* (*advocatus*) of Cracow (chairman of the jury court), who was then Jerzy Morsztyn, elected to the post in 1538. How the committee's work may have proceeded allows one to imagine the final passage of the resolution. It mentioned that the above list of persons was not a closed list, and if they could not all gather, it was enough for four members to attend the meetings.[22]

According to the findings of Franciszek Piekosiński, the commission worked until 1544. The draft was submitted to the city council and presented to the king. However, Piekosiński doubted that it was permanently approved by the king.[23] It is worth mentioning that approval was necessary under Magdeburg law, since any new regulation or one that modified existing regulations required the approval of the city owner. As it turns out, the lack of consent of the city's citizens (commoners) meant that the draft was unsuccessful and the king revoked the approval privilege, obliging the councilors to acquaint the city's citizens with the draft. The date for the presentation of the draft was set for December 29, 1544, eventually February 25, 1545.[24] The rejection of the draft is part of the disputes, typical of royal cities in the Jagiellonian era, between the urban elite concentrated in the council, which was striving for oligarchic rule, and representatives of the commoners. Regardless of the political reasons, substantive comments on the draft were made by the citizens.

According to Piekosiński, after the consultations ended on August 2, 1546, a new commission was appointed to draft a new version of the *Processus iuris*.[25] It is assumed that the comments made on one of the two surviving manuscripts of the draft were probably the result of the new commission's work.[26] It consisted of the following councilors: merchant Piotr Tanigel (–1548),[27] the aforementioned lawyer Wacław Chodorowski, bachelor of law Erazm Wunzam (–1555),[28] craftsman and merchant Bartholomew Ha-

21 Bogdan Kasprzyk, "Andrzej Fogelweder starszy", in *Poczet sołtysów*, 458.

22 Zdzisław Noga, *Krakowska rada miejska w XVI wieku. Studium o elicie władzy*, Kraków, 2003, 24, 57–58.

23 *Prawa, przywileje i statuty*, 180.

24 *Prawa, przywileje i statuty*, 181.

25 *De processu iuris reformando. Prawa, przywileje i statuty*, 124.

26 *Prawa, przywileje i statuty*, 181.

27 Bogdan Kasprzyk, "Piotr Tanigel", in *Poczet sołtysów*, 436.

28 Erasmus Wunzam should not be confused with Erazm of Cracow, Doctor of Decretals and Rector of the University of Cracow. See Maciej Mikuła, "Erazm z Krakowa", in *Profesorowie Wydziału Prawa Uniwersytetu Jagiellońskiego*, vol. 1: 1364–1780, Wacław Uruszczak (ed.), Kraków, 2015, 54–55.

bicht (–1572),[29] and goldsmith Stanislaw Straus (–1556).[30] As in the 1539 resolution, the possibility was left open for other people to join, but councilors were explicitly mentioned. So far, it has not been possible to establish any details of the work of the two committees. The appearance of lawyer Wacław Chodorowski is significant. I hypothesize that he was the main rapporteur of the original draft and also joined the second committee as an expert experienced in legislative work.

2 Scope and Structure of Codification

While Maciej Śliwnicki's project was intended to be a very broad codification of the law, the Cracow codification was not planned as a complete code. However, as we will see, in addition to strictly procedural regulations, it also contained a set of provisions that we would undoubtedly classify today as substantive civil law, such as testamentary inheritance. The rules on litigation would have applied not only to civil cases, but also partially to criminal cases. Thus, one can speak of the heterogeneous scope of the Cracow draft.

The provisions of the draft regulated proceedings before the municipal courts of Cracow: the ordinary municipal court (*iudicium civile* and *iudicium ordinare*) and the municipal "senate". Originally, the city's judicial body was the hereditary *wójt* (*advocatus hereditarius*), who judged together with the bench (*scamna*). In addition, three times a year the so-called "burgrave grand courts" were held along with the city owner. The term "senatus" refers to the city council, which was the second judicial and administrative body besides the city bench in cities under Magdeburg law in the Kingdom of Poland. The division of powers between the council and the bench was originally specified in the Magdeburg *Weichbild* (*Ius municipale Magdeburgense*), indicating that the council had jurisdiction over issues of crafts and trade and could enforce municipal resolutions.[31] However, depending on the locality, the practice of municipal bodies holding courts and the city owner actually participating varied greatly.[32] Cracow is an excellent example of a city where

29 Bogdan Kasprzyk, "Bartłomiej Habicht", in *Poczet sołtysów*, 468.

30 Bogdan Kasprzyk, "Stanisław Straus zwany Struś" [Stanisław Staus named Struś], in *Poczet sołtysów*, 465.

31 Articles 1-3. See the edition in the database "IURA. Sources of Law from the Past", https://iura.uj.edu.pl/dlibra/publication/46#structure (access 30.11.2023).

32 Marian Mikołajczyk, *Proces kryminalny w miastach Małopolski XVI–XVIII wieku*, Katowice, 2013, chapter 1.

the scope of judicial powers of the city council was significantly expanded. Suffice it to mention that as early as the 14th century, the council could adjudicate criminal cases.[33] The division into cases tried by either the council or the bench also determined the course of instances. The scheme presented below, applying to the 16th century, did not constitute a principle that was absolutely observed in all royal cities, let alone private cities—noble and ecclesiastical—where the variants of appeal paths were much more extensive and varied. According to the model presented here, appeals against the verdicts of the city bench were directed to the Higher Court of German Law in Wawel and further to the Court of the Six Cities, as the royal court of last resort. Meanwhile, appeals from the city council were directed to the so-called Assessor's Court, a royal court established in the 16th century to replace ad hoc royal courts consisting of commissioners. Such commissioners' courts are still mentioned in the draft under discussion.

The codification established the general rule that all matters of litigation were within the jurisdiction of the ordinary municipal court, except for those that were expressly assigned to the jurisdiction of the "senate", such as merchant, artisan and guild matters; punishment for falsifying weights and measures; adjudication of riots and tumults; inheritance divisions and property demarcations; matters relating to the erection and repair of buildings; "servitudes" (*servitus*); care of minors; care of the poor, including hospitals; contracts of commission, leases, and resulting damages; repair of roads; matters between masters and servants, including servants' wages; and bequests and obligations testified before the council. Despite the seemingly exhaustive list, one item introduced a significant break: matters in which a dispute would arise before the council (*item si qui coram senatu litem contestati fuerint*). As one may assume, this referred to situations in which the parties unanimously decided to proceed with the case before the city council. It is worth noting that the council and the bench adjudicated disputes, but also settled non-contentious matters before them. The entries in the city books of records regarding legal actions and obligations entered into before the council were mentioned explicitly. The handling of both categories of cases is reflected in the provisions of the draft.

The source's publisher identified 37 chapters of the draft, which are divided into 220 paragraphs. For the first 14 chapters, the source does not specify *Caput/Capitulum*. Only for the subsequent ones is the original chapter numbering included. One can see a certain intention of the authors in this. The first

33 Michał Patkaniowski, *Krakowska rada miejska w średnich wiekach*, Kraków, 1934, 58–60; Marcin Starzyński, *Krakowska rada miejska w średniowieczu*, Kraków, 2010, 106.

part is regulations that take into account the diversity of municipal courts. In addition to the regulations devoted to the jurisdiction of the council court, it contains provisions specifying how to verify whether a case falls within the council court's jurisdiction. This part includes rules for appealing to the royal court and covering the litigation costs of higher courts. The principle of *ne bis in idem* was expressed, and the principle that the resumption of proceedings is an exception that must be provided for by Magdeburg law was adopted. The sanction of eight florins for groundless suing of the council before the king was also specified. The regulations devoted to proceedings before the council were followed by another set devoted to litigation before the city bench, including: (a) trials in the absence of the defendant, (b) trials with the defendant present, (c) trials when a defendant was arrested. They specified not only the rules for filing and answering a lawsuit, but also for filing appeals to the Wawel Higher Court and the Court of the Six Cities. Separate regulations governed the burgrave grand court, in which the burgrave was replaced by a mayor (simultaneously elected from among the councilors). The last chapter of this section contained regulations devoted to the guest court.

The next section, which also consists of fourteen chapters, contains detailed regulations on the various stages of litigation. Here, there are regulations on lawsuits, attorneys at law, *exceptions* (*exceptiones*), evidence, security (*gwar/satisdatio/warenda*), court *feriae*, judgments, appeals and enforcement of judgments. Thus, while the arrangement of the first part was dictated by the type of court, the next part is ordered by the successive stages of litigation.

I propose to separate the third part as well. The last nine chapters contain provisions on special proceedings: the sale of real estate, the making of a will, the establishment of a dowry, the appointment of attorneys, letters of administration, the redemption of property by right of proximity, proceedings for the registration of legal actions before an improper authority, proceedings involving women acting alone, and on the rights of widows to use property that would have fallen to a deceased child. In these chapters, numerous regulations of private substantive law mention provisions devoted to wills. It is noteworthy that a set of regulations devoted to non-contentious proceedings was included in the partial codification of land law of 1523, *Formula processus iudiciarii*.[34]

As can be seen, the authors of the codification were successful in organizing the material as clearly as possible. The layout was not changed in the course of

34 Wacław Uruszczak et al., *Formula processus iudiciarii. Kodyfikacja polskiej procedury sądowej z 1523 roku*, Białystok, 2023.

the work of the second commission. It prepared comments on dozens of articles.

3 Legislative Technique

The failure of Maciej Śliwnicki's project was a sufficient warning not to overlook the regulations of Saxo-Magdeburg law and local legislation used in practice in the codification work. As a working hypothesis, I assume that it was quite different in the Cracow case: it was based on the regulations already in use in the city, though subjected to analysis, improvement, and modification, nonetheless. This has already been confirmed by the previously published partial analysis, confirming that the commission reaches back to the city statute of 1530, to the regulation of wills and other matters.[35]

The reference to the regulations of Saxo-Magdeburg law is also undeniable. § 66 specified the dates of the Great Burgrave Courts of St. Agatha, St. John, and St. Paul the Martyrs, and the octave of St. Martin. Similarly, the Saxon Mirror and the Magdeburg *Weichbild* (*Ius municipale Magdeburgense*), in the 1535 Latin translation by Mikołaj Jaskier, provides the same.[36] This provision was also present in the *Weichbild* in the earlier 1506 Silesian-Małopolska compilation.[37] Naturally, one can assume that the members of the commission had no reason to go back to the earlier edition, since the newer one from a few years prior was considered valid by the king. However, this was not the case. It turns out that in Jaskier's edition, the legal definition of a guest is very general. It is one whose household is a full day's journey from the court.[38] Meanwhile, the Cracow draft precisely specifies that it is 11 miles. The 1506 text also has a precise definition, though the distance was to be 12 miles. Research into the texts of Magdeburg law in Poland has shown that a precise definition of this distance was found only in the Cracow version of the Silesian-Małopolska compilation of the Magdeburg *Weichbild*, with 12 miles

35 Maciej Mikuła, "Testamentary Regulations in 16th-Century Cracow", in *Právno-Historické Trendy a Výhľady* vol. 6, Adriana Švecová, Ingrid Lanczová, Adrián Gajarský (eds.), Trnava, 2021, 107–121.

36 Mikołaj Jaskier, *Iuris Provincialis quo Speculum Saxonum vulgo nuncupatur libri tres...*, Cracoviae, 1535, liber I art II, liber III art LXI; Mikołaj Jaskier, *Iuris Municipalis Maideburgensis Liber vulgo Weichbild nuncupatus...*, Cracoviae, 1535, art XLV.

37 §5 of *Ius municipale Magdeburgense*, edition: "IURA. Sources of Law form the Past" https://iura.uj.edu.pl/dlibra/publication/1227/edition/580/content?ref=struct (access 30.11.2023).

38 Mikołaj Jaskier, *Iuris Municipalis*, Article 46.

TABLE 4.1 Sources for the definition of 'guest' in the Cracow draft

Cracow draft (1544)	**National Library manuscript shelfmark 12607 III**[a]	***Ius municipale Magdeburgense* (1506)**	***Ius municipale Magdeburgense* (1535)**
§76. Hospitem autem eum intelligi volumus, qui vltra vndecim milliarium spacium incolatum habet, ceteros omnes propinquiores pro vicinis reputare conueniens est.	[fol. 29ra] Ille dicitur esse hospes, qui ultra xi miliaria extra iudicium habuerit mansionem.	[fol. CLXXVIII] Ille debet esse hospes, qui ultra XII miliaria extra iudicium suum domicilium habet.	[fol. XL *verso*] Hospes tamen iurare tenetur, quod sit alienigena, et ita remote domicilium habeat, quod una die ad iudicium venire non possit.

a Edition in "IURA. Sources of Law from the Past" https://iura.uj.edu.pl/dlibra/publication/4360/edition/3418/content?ref=struct (access 30.11.2023).

appearing only in the Statute of Jan Łaski. From here, it is a simple conclusion that the members of the commission used a different text of Magdeburg law than Jaskier's 1535 edition, the most recent for them, and that it was not (or not exclusively) the Statute of Jan Łaski, but a manuscript text.

Research on the influence of canon law and Roman law on Polish municipal law has not yet been completed, so any general assessment—especially one stating a broad reception of European *ius commune*—should be considered premature. Nevertheless, it is possible to point to regulations whose origin in *ius commune* has been confirmed. One of them is the regulation of *exceptions* (*excepciones*). Below, I include the relevant provision from the draft:

> § 99. Exceptiones autem quaedam sunt peremptoriae, quaedam dilatoriae, quaedam fori declinatoriae, quaedam indifferentes.

Wacław Uruszczak's research on the Correction of Rights, a 1532 draft codification of the law of the land (*ius terrestre*), showed that it included dilatory (postponing in time), peremptory (nullifying a dispute), and declinatory (pointing to the wrong court) *excepciones*.[39] In addition, the Correction of Rights indicates that peremptory *exceptions* are divided into those that can be brought before and after the formation of a dispute and those that can only be brought before the *litis contestatio* (*exceptiones de re iudicata, transacta et finita*). The three types of exceptions mentioned in the Correction of Rights are also found in the Cracow draft. This would be a trace of the creators of the codification referring back to the law of the land and would require further verification.

Note that the draft distinguished yet another type by additionally introducing the category of "indifferent" (*indifferentes*). This indifference did not consist only in the possibility of filing before or after *listis contestatio*, as provided for in the Correction of Rights; it was explicitly stated that it could be filed even after the proceedings had ended, if it turned out that the party in the case was a heretic or an outlaw or had been excommunicated. Under a different name, this category appeared in a manual of canonical process by Grzegorz of Szamotuły, a professor at the Faculty of Law in Cracow (first edition 1524).[40] He explained that three types of *exceptions* are known in canon law: dilatory, peremptory, and irregular (*anomala*). The last category included those that can be brought before and after a dispute has been established, such as when an excommunicated person was a party. In a similar vein, the issue was presented by Johannes Cervus Tucholiensis. He was a lecturer at the Faculty of Theology at the University of Cracow, superior of the cathedral school in Lwów, and author of the widely read textbook on municipal law, *Farraginis actionum* (published in 1540).[41] It is not excluded that he followed Grzegorz of Szamotuły's textbook.

Naturally, Grzegorz of Szamotuły drew on studies by eminent experts in canon law when writing his textbook. Nevertheless, a comparative analysis

---

39 Wacław Uruszczak, *Korektura praw z 1532 roku. Studium historycznoprawne*, vol. 1, Warszawa, Kraków, 1990, 140. Provision C. 271 reads: *In omnibus iudiciis regni nostri exceptiones omnes dilatoriae et declinatoriae ante litis contestationem, peremptoriae vero ante et post litis contestionem indifferenter fieri et proponi possint. Exceptis tamen peremptoriis exceptionibus de re iudicata, transacta et finite, quae de sui natura, ante litiscontestationem propositae, ipsam impediunt et retardant.* In *Correctura statutorum et consuetudinum Regni Poloniae anno MDXXXII decreto, publico per Nicolaum Taszycki, Bernardum Macieiowski, Georgium Myszkowski, Benedictum Izdbieński, Albertum Palicki et Nicolaum Koczanowski confecta, et conventione generali Regni anno MDXXXIV, proposita opera*, Michaelis Bobrzyński (ed.), vol. 3, Kraków, 1874, 73.

40 Grzegorz of Szamotuły, *Processus iuris brevior Joannis Andreae.... pro tirunculis resolutus*, Cracoviae, 1537, fol. 16 recto–18 recto.

41 Władysław Bojarski and Zbigniew Naworski, *Jan Jelonek Cereus z Tucholi i jego twórczość prawnicza. Ustrój sądów i prawo procesowe*, Toruń, 1993, 109.

TABLE 4.2 A comparison of passages about exceptions in the Cracow draft and *Processus Iuris Brevior* by Grzegorz of Szamotuły

Draft of 1544	Grzegorz of Szamotuły
§ 98 Exceptio est actoris exclusio vel est quaedam defenssio, qua reus intendit se deffendere *causam allegans, vt non respondeat ad obiecta actoris.*	Exceptio est actoris exclusio. Et est quedam defensio per quam reus intendit se defendere.
§ 99. Exceptiones autem quaedam sunt peremptoriae, quaedam dilatoriae, *quaedam fori declinatoriae,* quaedam *indifferentes.*	Exceptionum autem quedam est dilatoria, quaedam perem[fol. 16v] ptoria et quedam *anomala.*

indicates that the committee members were following the Polish textbook and not, for instance, Guillaume Durand's study (Grzegorz's lecture was considerably narrower than Durand's treatise).[42] The summary in the Table 4.2 confirms language similarities.

In conclusion, it can be noted that the commission drew on various sources when preparing the provisions on exceptions. A clear division into dilatory, declinatory, and peremptory exceptions occurred in the Correction of Rights of 1532. In turn, the fourth category, "indifferent", is close to that of "irregular" in the work of Durand, the textbooks of Grzegorz of Szamotuły, and Johannes Cervus Tucholiensis. The use of canon law sources in the drafting work was unquestionable. On the other hand, whether the writers were familiar with the draft of the Land Law, rejected by the Polish Sejm in 1534, remains for the time being a hypothesis that needs to be tested in further research.

In the discussion so far, it was mentioned only in passing that the second commission proposed amendments to dozens of provisions. One of these was §103, dedicated to the exegesis of "indifferent" *exceptiones*. The category of heretics was examined. It was considered that the charge of heresy did not nullify a complaint, but withheld it, and that it had to be proven that someone remained a heretic. It is not excluded that this was a voice that was part of the

42 Guillaume Durand, *Speculum iudiciale, cum Inventario Berengarii Fredoli et cum additionibus Ioannis Andreae et Baldi de Ubaldis*, part 1.1–2, Venezia, 1488, [337] https://www.dbc.wroc.pl/dlibra/doccontent?id=36523 (access 30.11.2023).

discussions of the era of the religious reformation. It is not impossible that this amendment was intended to safeguard the rights of dissenters.

4 Conclusions

The fact that the draft probably did not enter into force can be read as a painful legislative failure. However, it did not mean that the committee's work was completely in vain. The Cracow draft of 1544/1546 (in addition to a handbook of municipal procedural law by Bartholomew Groicki, 1519/1534–1605)[43] is both a starting point for research into legal practice and a testament to the considerable legislative artistry of its authors. In a clear layout, they enclosed 220 paragraphs regulating the entirety of litigation and non-litigation in civil cases, selected substantive regulations, and provisions that were also relevant to the criminal process. Previous research shows that the authors drew on municipal resolutions, such as the Cracow Statute of 1530, sources of Saxo-Magdeburg law in the edition by Mikołaj Jaskier, and Magdeburg law in earlier editions—such as the Magdeburg *Weichbild* in the Cracow version of the Silesian-Małopolska compilation. Canon law was also an important source, which was probably accessed through textbooks. It may also be, although this requires further research, that the members of the commission did not shy away from sources of land law, such as the 1532 Correction of Rights. The Cracow draft was a very successful codification of the Renaissance era. Unfortunately, like the aforementioned 1532 Correction of Rights, it did not come into effect. In both cases, however, the main source of failure was not substantive objections, but a lack of political consensus.[44]

43 Bartłomiej Groicki, *Porządek sądów prawa magdeburskiego*, Kraków, 1559.

44 The research for this publication has been supported by a grant from the Priority Research Area Heritage under the Strategic Programme Excellence Initiative at Jagiellonian University.

CHAPTER 5

Procedural Law in Village Statutes in the Crown of the Kingdom of Poland (15th–18th Centuries)

Krzysztof Fokt

"As in everything there are its ways, so in this mode of judgment there is a certain procedure and an order of reaching the end of justice, which is nothing else than a just and lawful ordination, according to which the differences of cases are being recognised and quickly discerned with good and just sagacity": with these words, in 1614, the Polish landlaw lawyer Grzegorz Czaradzki described legal procedure.[1] In this definition, procedure is a means of obtaining desired ethical goals with the help of a judicial instance. The procedure thus understood did not, in fact, require a written form. The necessity to codify it, in order to refine specific concepts or introduce some new institutions, was primarily acknowledged in contexts where substantial properties were disputed, multiple jurisdictions converged, and representatives of estates with the ability to invoke group privileges—such as the nobility, the clergy and burghers—convened within legal proceedings. It is not surprising, therefore, that at the end of the 15th century and in the 16th century numerous undertakings were made to codify Polish land and municipal law;[2] one of these was *Formula processus*, the 500th anniversary of which we were celebrating in the year 2023.

1 Grzegorz Czaradzki, *Proces sądowny polski prawa koronnego. Teraz nowo wydany przez Grzegorza Czaradzkiego Kancelarii Koronnej pisarza*, Poznań, 1614, Anna Marcol, Maciej Mikuła (eds.), Kraków, 2022, 9 https://iura.uj.edu.pl/dlibra/publication/3061 (access 31.05.2023).

2 See Jarosław Reszczyński, *Sądownictwo i proces w kodyfikacji Macieja Śliwnickiego z 1523 roku*, Kraków, 2008, 25–27. The Polish codification effort under the third generation of Jagellons was an element of the third wave of codification of law in Europe, identified by Armin Wolf, *Gesetzgebung in Europa 1100–1500: Zur Entstehung der Territorialstaaten*, München, 1996, 48–49.

 | DOI:10.1163/9789004736672_007

1 Procedural Law in Rural "Micro-codifications": Introductory Discussion

The codification movement could not extend to rural law, which during this period was increasingly defined as particularistic (manorial).[3] Nevertheless, rural law did not develop in isolation from other phenomena occurring in the Kingdom of Poland in the late Middle Ages and early modern period. Thus, on its grounds too, specific micro-codifications appeared in the form of so-called village statutes. They covered the areas of individual demesnes, which ranged in size from a part of a village to several or even several dozen villages, but usually—as was the case with rural court books—a single village or a compact group of landed estates. In this text I would like to consider the questions of what place procedural law provisions occupied in village statutes, the motivation for their appearance, as well as what legal-formal issues were not regulated by these acts and why.

The earliest known acts of rural legislation date back to the beginning of the 15th century, but the surge of rural legislation, taking on increasingly complex forms, began in the second half of the 16th century and continued steadily, weakening only during the difficult times of the Northern Wars in the mid-17th and early 18th centuries. An important phenomenon in the development of rural legislation was the emergence of Olendrian settlements in the northern and western parts of the Crown, and with them elaborate bylaws (in Polish, *wilkierze*), often written down when villages were founded. Laws for villages were issued either by the village communities themselves or by the landowners (the king, the nobility, church institutions and towns). The communities passed their resolutions (eventually sometimes called *wilkierze*, just as the town statutes) while the landlords issued ordinances. Despite this important formal difference, in practice it was not easy to distinguish between acts from one group and the other. This problem is not at all unique to Poland.[4] Moreover, from the point of view of territorial authority, it was the owner of the village in question and not the village community who was endowed with judicial immunity. Consequently, even if the peasants themselves

3 Ludwik Łysiak, "Prawo i zwyczaj w praktyce sądów wiejskich XV–XVIII wieku", *Czasopismo Prawno-Historyczne* 34/2 (1982), 8–9.

4 Cf., e.g., Warren O. Ault, "Village By-Laws by Common Consent", *Speculum* 29/2 (1954), 380–394; Hannes Obermair, "Soziale Produktion von Recht? Das Weistum des Gerichts Salurn in Südtirol von 1403", *Concilium medii aevii* 4 (2001), 183–185; Wolfgang Wüst, "Village Policing—Early Modern Systems of Order in the Countryside", *Advances in Social Sciences Research Journal* 9[8] (2022), 178–179.

enacted a law, its practical effectiveness depended on its approval by the demesne, which also had the power to decide on matters of greater importance. Thus, even when the landowner's approval was not mentioned in a particular piece of legislation it cannot be ruled out that it was implicit. In view of this, in this text I will discuss—following in principle the definition by Stanisław Kutrzeba[5]—all legal acts regulating relations within a peasant community, regardless of the form in which they were enacted and promulgated (lawmaking judgments, ordinances, resolutions of village communities and even economic instructions, if they contained norms concerning relations within a village community). The subject of my interest here will be village statutes from the lands of the Crown of the Kingdom of Poland, now belonging to Poland and Ukraine. A considerable number of them were published in print, and these are the ones I will mainly take into account in this chapter; however, it should be remembered that there is still an unspecified number of unpublished village statutes concealed in archives.

In this study, my focus will not extend to the provisions within village statutes related to administrative, police and constitutional matters (such as the regulation of temporary suspect detentions, the establishment of village authorities and the remuneration of officials). Instead, my attention will be directed towards the laws involving the community's organs (such as the village assembly, village office, village mayor, councillors and jurors) and at least potentially related to court proceedings. In doing so I include not only those provisions that directly concerned the course of a trial or the activities, formulas and rituals associated with it, but also those relating to evidentiary and enforcement proceedings, as well as those rules of order that were designed to ensure the proper and efficient conduct of court proceedings concerning appearance, dignity of office, behaviour before the court, time and place of sessions, etc. An overview of the issues covered can be found in Tables 5.1 and 5.2, divided into issues concerning the organisation and ritualisation of court sessions (Table 5.1) and the course of the trial (Table 5.2). The reader will find detailed contextual and bibliographical data on village statutes cited in Tables 5.1 and 5.2 and the text of the article in Table 5.3.

At least in villages founded under so-called German law, whether in its Magdeburg variant in southern Poland or its Chełmno variant in the north, there were autonomous village court institutions from the High Middle Ages, where court proceedings were conducted without direct supervision of the landlords, even if the hereditary mayors (Pol. *sołtysi*, Ger. *Schulzen*) were sys-

---

5 Stanisław Kutrzeba, *Historja źródeł dawnego prawa polskiego*, vol. 2, Lwów, 1926, 323–324.

tematically replaced as chairmen of these courts by advocates/voigts (Pol. *wójtowie*), appointed by landowners. Also in villages that did not have officially granted autonomy in terms of jurisdiction, the lower courts were rarely exercised by the landowners themselves, but more often by persons of lower status delegated by them for this purpose: voigts or stewards. The procedural rules in such courts certainly varied considerably over the vast and heterogeneous area of the Crown, but in general the proceedings were characterised by certain features, e.g., the oral and public character and the adjudication based primarily on the ethical insight of the jury rather than on the provisions of written law.[6] Formally enacted statutes were not necessarily required in order to judge efficiently in this manner, because even without them the village courts had something to refer to: not only to custom but also to principles drawn from Church teaching, or finally to legal systems more universal than rural law: urban, land and even Roman legal orders.[7] In spite of this, village statutes were being issued, with a particular surge from the second half of the 16th century onwards. In the northwestern part of the Crown, this situation was to some extent enhanced by the development of Olendrian (originally Dutch) settlement, which was based on contracts between landowners and settlers. The increase in the number of village statutes was certainly also influenced by the growing tendency to rationalise the rural economy.

In addition, at least in some demesnes, the level of juridification of social life was increasing as early as in the 16th and 17th centuries. The wealthy Prussian cities with extensive chancelleries were at the forefront in this respect, which was particularly reflected in the very long and detailed statute for Toruń's urban villages (1605), but also, for example, in the statutes of Gdańsk for Pruszcz (1595) and the Gdańsk Fens (1598), of Elbląg for the village of Ellerwald (1623) and of Chełmno for the village of Rozgarty (1632). A high level of complexity and juridification is also shown by some acts issued by ecclesiastical institutions in Royal Prussia already before the mid-17th century, e.g., by the Pelplin monastery for the village of Hoppenbruch (1621) or by St. Bridget's Monastery in Gdańsk for the village of Siedlce (1637). These acts, often expanded even to a two-tier structure (chapter/article or title/point), placed

6 See Józef Rafacz, *Ustrój wsi samorządnej małopolskiej w XVIII wieku*, Lublin, 1922, 350–368; Zbigniew Zdrójkowski, "Postępowanie procesowe w sądach wiejskich", in *Historia państwa i prawa Polski*, Juliusz Bardach (ed.), vol. 2, Warszawa, 1966; Ryszard Łaszewski, *Wymiar sprawiedliwości we wsiach województwa chełmińskiego w XVII i XVIII wieku*, Toruń, 1974, 43–90; Stanisław Grodziski, "Kultura prawna wsi polskiej w świetle wiejskich ksiąg sądowych", in *Chłopi, naród, kultura*, t. 4: *Kultura i oświata wsi*, Andrzej Meissner (ed.), Rzeszów, 1996, 82–85.

7 Łaszewski, *Wymiar sprawiedliwości*, 182–183, footnote 7; Łysiak, "Prawo i zwyczaj", 10–13.

considerable emphasis on procedural issues, including those outside the proper *processus iuris*. Provisions of this kind often appeared in these statutes accessorily, as a supplement to substantive legal provisions on potentially controversial matters such as the guardianship of orphan's goods or partitions, and transfers of the possession of immovable property. They indicated what requirements had to be met when performing certain legal acts (drawing up an inventory of orphan's goods when taking custody, notifying the mayor of the intention to transfer the ownership of a farm, etc.).

2 Incompleteness of Codification of Procedural Law in Rural Statutes and Its Causes

The essential core of procedural law provisions contained in village statutes—by no means only in the most elaborate ones—concerned matters that were, at least potentially, directly related to court proceedings. Due to the layout of individual statutes, which does not reflect the modern division between substantive and formal law, provisions of this kind are often scattered across different parts of these texts. Often, however, most of the procedural provisions were gathered in one place, usually in the parts of the bylaws or ordinances dealing with issues concerning the political system and/or order, e.g., in the statute of Toruń for urban villages (1605) in Articles 4-5. Sometimes the provisions concerning judicial procedure even formed such a compact whole that they could be regarded as a kind of small court ordinance.[8]

In principle, all the issues dealt with by these provisions were regulated in the villages by custom, which meant that written instructions were not needed at all for the proper conduct of court proceedings. In addition to deductive inference from general knowledge of early modern legal culture, we can be supported in this regard by evidence of practice in the form of village court books and a juxtaposition of the content of village statutes with lists of fees for the procedural acts (Pol. *taksy*). In the village court books, which contain the recognitions and judgments of village courts and the testimonies of the parties, one finds more formulas and rituals than in the statutes. In the

8 See e.g., Articles 8-11 in the "announcement" for Ptaszkowa of 1618, Articles 3-9 in the Chełmno statute for the village of Rozgarty of 1632, Articles 6-8 w in the ordinance for Lanckorona captainship of 1646, Articles 2-6 in the by-laws for Silno and Wielka Nieszawka and subsequent dependent texts from the 18th century, Articles 71-87 in the by-laws for Mały Lubień of 1756, and Art. 94–95/102–103 in the statutes for the Chełmno bishopric of 1756–1758.

latter, only the institution of *litkup* (ritual drinking to the transaction) is mentioned several times, and only as late as in the 18th century, as a condition for the validity of the transfer of the possession of real estate.[9] Twice, another custom known from the practice of land and rural law also appears in village statutes, consisting in publicly retracting a false claim, i.e., going under a table and pronouncing an appropriate formula, sometimes accompanied by the sound of a dog barking.[10] However, rural statutes lack some customs and practices well-known to the village books of records, such as the transfer of real estate "under a green twig". Court books, reflecting the practice of the administration of justice, also allow for the identification of a wider range of procedural law issues; for example, legal representation, referral back to a court of lower instance, judicial assistance, and reformative decrees.

The lists of fees for official acts also contain a much broader scope of these acts than the other parts of the village statutes. For example, in the statute for the village of Siedlce of 1637, Article 8 mainly discusses the division of judicial powers between the mayor and the manorial steward, but the fees for official actions give a very broad picture of the activities of the mayor, the jury and the scribe, including, inter alia, carrying out court settlements, recognition of private deeds, taking inventory and valuation of property by virtue of partition or inheritance, enforcement actions (summons for payment, seizure of property, taxation of property), *intromissio* (investure in possession), acceptance of oral petitions and drafting of written ones, complaints and rejoinders, procedural objections, filing lawsuits and interrogations, preliminary (*sententia interlocutoria*) and final judgements (*sententia diffinitiva*), long and short judgements, assignments of claims, etc. Of course, a list of fees may have covered actions which the mayor undertook very rarely or not at all, and their valuation was carried out "just in case". Nevertheless, the difference in detail between the provisions of the statute for Siedlce and the enumeration of possible actions in the list of fees indicates that, in the opinion of those responsible for the administration of the estate of St. Bridget's Monastery in Gdańsk, roughly the same procedural actions could potentially be performed before the village office there as before the municipal and land courts of the time. Moreover,

9 Article/point 9 of the statutes for Kotusz of 1729, Tuchorze of 1745 and Złotkowo of 1762.

10 I am referring here to the statutes of the 17th century for Czarże (Article 7) and the villages of the monastery in Czerna (Article 2). On the application of this procedure in practice, see Alfons Mańkowski, "Wilkierz miasteczka Czarza", *Zapiski Towarzystwa Naukowego w Toruniu* 11/2 (1938), 56 footnote 2; Ryszard Łaszewski, *Wiejskie prawo karne w Polsce XVII i XVIII wieku*, Toruń, 1988, 144–145, footnote 551; Grodziski, "*Kultura prawna wsi*", 87–88.

apparently the superiors believed that the village office of Siedlce did not need written instructions for this but only a price list for their services.

It is significant in this respect that among the provisions on the organisation of court proceedings, relatively few deal with such important matters as the composition of the court entitled to adjudicate and the time and place of conducting court sessions. It must be presumed that rural communities generally coped with holding courts at the right place and time and with the proper adjudication panel without the help of written laws, simply sticking to forms hallowed by tradition. If any provision concerning these matters appears in village statutes, it is rather in order to remove possible abuses (e.g., the arbitrariness of mayors, judging without a sufficient number of jurors), as sometimes explicitly stated in the texts in question.[11] An occasion to establish regulations concerning the time and place of the court proceedings could also be the ravaging of specific villages together with their records by an invasion, as was the case with Świlcza and Woliczka, destroyed by the Tatars in 1624. In the course of the reconstruction and reorganisation of both villages, in 1628, Mikołaj Spytek Ligęza granted both villages a statute together with a new court book.[12] Significantly, this statute even describes the elements of the judicial *theatrum*, providing in Article 22 for the opening during a court session of the court book on the page containing the contents of the oath of the advocate/voigt and jurors. However, this is an exception rather than a rule as in general, even in the statutes for newly founded villages, establishing them as new areas of self-governing jurisdiction, the performative elements of the judicial proceedings were very rarely reflected (even the court books are sometimes more detailed in this matter, e.g., denoting the gestures taken by parties or witnesses by making their oaths).

Village statutes also infrequently contain formulas for procedural actions. Of the 148 source texts reviewed for the purpose of this article, only five statutes pertaining to four demesnes contained detailed forms for the establishment of courts.[13] Most of these, however, did not involve ordinary village courts but rather criminal courts or other special proceedings which were held less frequently and with greater participation of demesnes. They are therefore rather

11 E.g., in the Greater Poland statute of 1514 or in the statute for the demesne of Tuchla of 1598.

12 *Ustawa dla wsi Świlczy i Woliczki z roku ok. 1628*, Adam Kamiński, Franciszek Kotula (eds.), Rzeszów, 1948, xii.

13 These were two statutes for Ptaszkowa of 1618, the statute for Siedlce of 1637, the ordinance for the urban villages of Kalisz of 1647 and the by-laws for the captainship of Gniew of 1676, and the ordinance for Drohobyczka/Дрогобичка issued in 1720.

examples of top-down legislative action undertaken by landlords, consisting largely of the reception of urban law rather than the codification of rural custom. On the other hand, there are only few formulas in the village statutes that were useful from the point of view of ordinary, everyday legal relations. Suffice it to say that only one statute (for Siedlce in 1637) contains a formula for the act most frequently noted in village books, i.e., the transfer of the possession of real estate. Thus, it appears that rural communities were perfectly capable of conducting court proceedings without written forms, and the demesnes very rarely saw the need to equip their villages with such aids.

The reason for this was probably prosaic: quite simply, both in the late Middle Ages and in the early modern period these were humans rather than written texts that were considered the primary carrier of law. This was probably true to a greater extent of procedural law, the expression of which was oral and public procedure, than of substantive law, potentially more susceptible to formation by the manor. The belief in a man as the main carrier of legal custom is clearly illustrated by Article 21 of the bylaws for Wielka Nieszawka, later copied into a number of other village statutes, according to which a field in a village could only be bought by "a German man aware of Dutch customs and laws, not a Polish man who would not know or understand Dutch customs."[14] With a limited supply of German settlers familiar with the Dutch customs, this provision was not very realistic, which can be seen even in its further evolution. In a variation of this provision in the 1729 bylaw for Grabowiec—but only in its Polish version!—the purchaser of a field in a village could either be a good and honest man or a German who knew Dutch customs.[15] The bylaw for Grabowiec, therefore, already acknowledged that it was also possible for a Polish person to learn Dutch legal customs but did not depart from the basic principle that it was the people who applied specific forms, rituals and rules, and not written normative texts, which determined the essence of the legal custom practised in a given place.

3 Hierarchy and Order as Guiding Ideas of the Rural Statutes

Only one type of formula is found in village statutes quite often. These are oath formulas of official persons which were mostly included in full but sometimes

14 Michał Targowski, "Wilkierz Wielkiej Nieszawki z 1771 roku", *Rocznik Toruński* 39 (2012), 156.

15 *Polskie ustawy wiejskie XV–XVIII w.*, Stanisław Kutrzeba, Alfons Mańkowski (eds.), Kraków, 1938, 248.

summarised. This does not seem to be a coincidence if one looks at the content of these oaths and the preambles of village statutes. The key words that recur in both are "order" and "fidelity". They lead to the source of village legislation, which was the concern of the lords for peace and order in villages, understood in many ways. From the point of view of the village owners, it was important that all fees and labour due should be on time and that neither the estate management apparatus nor the landlord should be involved in the day-to-day management of village affairs, questions of custom or the administration of justice, excluding of course the most difficult cases, appeals and criminal matters. A number of measures found in village statutes served to achieve these aims, including inter alia provisions concerning the judicial powers of the rural communal bodies and their proper composition, and provisions concerning the obligation to appear when summoned or sued by the mayor, to behave with dignity before the office and at court hearings, and to respect the office and not to challenge its rulings (see details in Table 5.1). Although the statutes very often guaranteed the possibility of appealing to the court against the judgments of village courts, the reservation that was sometimes added is very characteristic: the way to appeal was supposed to be closed for troublemakers who would insult the court of first instance (village court).[16] One might even get the impression that the dignity of the village office as the "arm of the lord" and the proper conduct of the parties before it was more important to the landowners than ensuring a fair trial for their subjects.

Here we touch upon a fundamental issue from the point of view of assessing village statutes as sources of understanding old law. Quite numerous provisions, and even entire statutes, place a powerful emphasis on organisational and disciplinary issues (see Table 5.1), thus representing the perspective of the landlords and village elites, who cared about the population's reverence for those representing authority and respect for their orders. As the judicial and administrative powers in a village office were inseparable, it is sometimes difficult to ascertain to what extent the provisions on, for example, appearing when summoned by the office applied to judicial assemblies, since a mayor could also "send a ball" (circulate a message summoning people to a meeting) in matters related to security or economic affairs. Sometimes, however, the statutes explicitly stated that failure to appear in court was punishable, indi-

16 See Article 10 of the statute for Żuławy Polskie of 1676; Article 3 of the statute for Gumienice and Straszniów of 1679; Article 42 of the statute for Kotusz; point 30 of the bylaws for Tuchorze of 1745; point 38 of the privilege for Złotkowo of 1762. Compare also Rafacz, *Ustrój wsi*, 368.

TABLE 5.1
Issues concerning the organisation and ritualisation of court proceedings in the rural statutes of the Crown of the Kingdom of Poland from the 15th to the 18th centuries (in chronological order)

Locality (demesne), year of issuing of statute	Composition and powers of the adjudicating bodies	Prescriptions concerning organisation of court sessions, their order and the dignity of village office	Formulas
Strzemięcino, a. 1443		Respect of the office	
Ustawa ławnikom... (Greater Poland), 1514	Composition of the court		
Rychemberk (Bogatka), 1551		Appearance in the community and respect for the office (Art. 3)	
Węgrzce, 1570	Competences of the steward when representing the landlord (Point 6)	Appearance in manor court (Point 7)	
Żuławy Gdańskie, 1598		Appearance in village court (Art. 5)	
Pruszcz Gdański, 1595 (1723)	Composition of the court (Art. 11)	Appearance in the community (Art. 7)	
Kartuzy, ca. 1600		Respect for the office (Art. 10); appearance in the community (Art. 11)	
Toruń, 1605	Judicial competences of authorities (Art. IV, Points 5, 6, 8, 12),	Appearance in court (Art. V, Points 5–6), and community (Art. V, Point 7); respect for the office (Art. 5, Point 3); behaviour before the court (Art. V, Points 2, 4, 8)	Oaths of officials (Art. 4, Points 4, 14; Art. 6, Point 6)
Ptaszkowa, 1618 (*Zapowiedzi*)		Appearance in court (Point 8); respect for the office (Point 9)	
Ptaszkowa, 1618 (*Sposób odprawowania...*)			Order of establishment of court; oaths of officials
Ptaszkowa, 1618 (*Sposob gaięnia...*)			Order of establishment of court

TABLE 5.1 Issues concerning the organisation and ritualisation of court proceedings (*cont.*)

Locality (demesne), year of issuing of statute	Composition and powers of the adjudicating bodies	Prescriptions concerning organisation of court sessions, their order and the dignity of village office	Formulas
Szotland, 1620	Judicial competences of authorities (Art. 36, 41)	Respect for the office (Art. 2, 37); appearance in court (Art. 4)	Oaths of officials (Art. 1)
Hoppenbruch, 1621		Respect for the office (Art. 16); appearance in court (Art. 16)	Oaths of officials (Art. 14)
Tuchla, 1621–23		Appearance in court (Art. 15); prohibition on encroaching on the boundaries of the disputed fields before court proceedings (Art. 20)	
Ellerwald, 1623 (1754)		Appearance in the community (cap. 3, Art. 3); behaviour in the community (cap. 3, Art. 4)	
Klimkówka, 1624		Appearance in the community	
Czarże, 1626 (1661)		Appearance before the village office (Art. 13)	
Sułoszowa, 1627		Respect for the office (Art. 2, Point 58)	
Świlcza/Woliczka, 1628		Appearance in the community (Art. 11); respect for the office (Art. 19); place of court proceedings (Art. 18); behaviour before the court (Art. 19)	Oaths of officials (Art. 1, 22)
Kasina, 1630		Respect for the office	
Rudna, 1630		Appearance in the community (Art. 1)	
Rozgarty, 1632	Judicial competences of authorities (Art. 8)	Appearance in the community and in court (Art. 3); behaviour before the court (Art. 3–4, 9); time of court proceedings (Art. 6)	
Kasina, 1636		Respect for the office	

TABLE 5.1 Issues concerning the organisation and ritualisation of court proceedings (*cont.*)

Locality (demesne), year of issuing of statute	Composition and powers of the adjudicating bodies	Prescriptions concerning organisation of court sessions, their order and the dignity of village office	Formulas
Siedlce, 1637	Judicial competences of authorities (tit. 8, Art. 1–2)		Order of establishment of court; formula for the transfer of real estate; oaths of officials
Gietrzwałd, bef. 1639; 1676	Judicial competences of authorities (Art. 69)	Respect for the office (Art. 2), appearance in the community (Art. 3–4) behaviour before the court (Art. 70)	
Tuchola, 1643 (1749)	Judicial competences of authorities (Art. 53)	Respect for the office (Art. 11)	Oaths of officials
Lanckorona 1646	Judicial competences of authorities (Art. 6)	Time of court proceedings (Art. 6); respect for the office; behaviour before the court (Art. 8)	
Kalisz, 1647			Order of establishment of court
Lubień Mały, 1650 (1756)	Judicial competences of authorities (Art. 10, 60), including prohibition of evocation to the manor court (Art. 76, 81, 85)	Appearance in the community (Art. 3); respect for the office (Art. 4, 73); behaviour before the court (Art. 71)	

TABLE 5.1 Issues concerning the organisation and ritualisation of court proceedings (*cont.*)

Locality (demesne), year of issuing of statute	Composition and powers of the adjudicating bodies	Prescriptions concerning organisation of court sessions, their order and the dignity of village office	Formulas
Silno, 1652 [?]; Wielka Nieszawka, 1665 (1771) [and derived texts: Kozibór, 1719; Grabowiec, 1729; Kopanino, 1730; Duliniewo, 1754]	Judicial competences of authorities (Art. 2–4, –/36); prohibition of evocation to the manor court (Art. 3)	Appearance in court on a lawsuit or mayor's claim (Art. 5–6); behaviour before the court (Art. 36/31) and nonchallenge of judgments (Art. 37/34)	
Klimkówka, 1660	Judicial competences of authorities (643a)	Respect for the office (643d); appearance in the community (643e)	
Wojanowo et al., ca. 1660	Judicial competences of authorities (Art. 11, 13)	Appearance in the community (Art. 8); respect for the office (Art. 9)	
Konarzyn, 1662		Appearance in the community (Art. 22, 36); respect for the office and behaviour before the court (Art. 28)	
Łącko, 1670, 1702		Respect for the office (Art. 2/2); appearance in the community (Art. 11/13)	
Czerna, 1672		Respect for the office (6); appearance in the community (12)	
Żuławy Malborskie, bef. 1676/1723		Appearance in the community (Art. 10, 12); behaviour before the court (Art. 11)	
Żuławy Polskie, 1676	Judicial competences of authorities (Art. 2, 3, 13, 15–17)	Respect for the office (Art. 10); time of court proceedings (Art. 14)	
Gniew, 1676			Order of establishment of court; oaths of officials

TABLE 5.1 Issues concerning the organisation and ritualisation of court proceedings (*cont.*)

Locality (demesne), year of issuing of statute	Composition and powers of the adjudicating bodies	Prescriptions concerning organisation of court sessions, their order and the dignity of village office	Formulas
Czarnowo, Pędzewo, Zła Wieś, 1678	Judicial competences of authorities (Art. 1)		
Gumienice and Strazsniów, 1679	Judicial competences of authorities (Art. 3–4)	Respect for the office, behaviour before the court (Art. 2–3)	
Strzeszyce and Żbikowice, 1679		Respect for the office (Point 2); appearance in the community (Point 9)	
Lichtenfeld/Jasna, 1682 (1728)	Judicial competences of authorities (Art. 20)	Appearance in the community (Art. 9)	
Klimkówka, 1685		Behaviour before the court	
Łąkorek, 1692 (1705)		Time of court proceedings (Part 2, Art. 7); appearance in the community (Part 2, Art. 10; Part 3, Art. 5); respect for the office (Part 2, Art. 11; cz. 3, Art. 5)	Oaths of officials (Part 2, Art. 2)
Kasina, 1695		Appearance in the community (Statute 3)	
Sucha, 1696	Composition of the court (Point 25)	Respect for the office (Points 1, 19); behaviour before the court (Points 1–2); time of court proceedings (Point 25)	Oaths of officials (Points 16–17)
Tuchla, 1698	Composition of the court (Art. 7); judicial competences of authorities (Art. 10)	Time and place of court proceedings (Art. 7)	
Strzeszyce and Żbikowice, 1702		Respect for the office (Point 2); appearance in the community and in court (Points 13, 21, 22)	

TABLE 5.1 Issues concerning the organisation and ritualisation of court proceedings (*cont.*)

Locality (demesne), year of issuing of statute	Composition and powers of the adjudicating bodies	Prescriptions concerning organisation of court sessions, their order and the dignity of village office	Formulas
Luboń, 1719	Judicial competences of authorities (Points 14, 20)		
Bystrzec, bef. 1728	Judicial competences of authorities (Art. 3–4)	Respect for the office (Art. 5, 46); appearing when summoned by the mayor (Art. 17); behaviour before the court (Art. 45); time of court proceedings (Art. 48)	
Kotusz, 1729	Judicial competences of authorities (Art. 41); prohibition of evocation to the manor court (Art. 42)	Appearance in the community (Art. 1); respect for the office (Art. 2–4); time of court proceedings (Art. 39)	
Ptaszkowa, 1729		Appearance in the community; respect for the office; behaviour before the court	
Zegrze, Rataje, 1733	Judicial competences of authorities (Art. 9, 80, 84, 85, 89, 91, 93, 94, 102)	Appearance in the community (Art. 38); Respect for the office (Art. 63); behaviour before the court (Art. 64, 66)	Oaths of officials (Art. 2, 5)
Ptaszkowa, 1736	Prohibition of evocation to the manor court	Appearance in the community	
Dębiec, 1737	Judicial competences of authorities (Point 8)		
Jazowsko, 1738	Judicial competences of authorities (Art. 6)	Appearance in the community (Art. 2–3) and in court (Art. 7); respect for the office (Art. 3)	
Sadłuki, 1739	Judicial competences of authorities (Point 40)	Appearing when summoned by the mayor (Point 30); behaviour before the court, respect for the office (Point 5)	

TABLE 5.1 Issues concerning the organisation and ritualisation of court proceedings (*cont.*)

Locality (demesne), year of issuing of statute	Composition and powers of the adjudicating bodies	Prescriptions concerning organisation of court sessions, their order and the dignity of village office	Formulas
Zegrze, 1745; Rataje, 1745	Judicial competences of authorities (Art. 28)		
Tuchorze, 1745	Judicial competences of authorities (Point 29)	Appearing when summoned by the mayor (Point 1); behaviour before the court (Point 2); respect for the office and its messengers (Points 2–4); time of court proceedings (Point 28)	
Jankowo, 1747	Composition of the court (Point 3)	Appearing when summoned by the mayor (Points 4, 31)	
Gołębiewo, 1754	Prohibition of evocation to the manor court without mayor's consent (Point 17)	Appearance in the community (Point 2); behaviour before the court (Points 13, 22)	
Skotniki, 1751		Appearance in the community	
Zagórzany, 1752	Judicial competences of authorities (Art. 1, 3)	Time and place of proceedings (Art. 3)	
Brankówka, 1753	Judicial competences of authorities (Art. 4)	Appearance in the community and in court (Art. 2); behaviour before the court (Art. 3)	
Chełmno bishopric (nobles' villages, table estates), 1756, 1758; Gruczno, 1763	Judicial competences of authorities (Art./ Points 13, 37, 87, 89/15, 46, 99, 100/ 15, 46, 99, 102)	Appearance in the community and in court (Art./Points 17, 28/18, 37/18, 37); respect for the office (Art./Points 18/19/19, 109); behaviour before the court (Art./Points 95/ 103/-)	Oaths of officials (Art./ Points 11/ 11, 14/ 11, 14)
Ptaszkowa, 1756	Judicial competences of authorities (Art. 7)	Appearance in the community (Art. 10); respect for the office (Art. 12)	

TABLE 5.1 Issues concerning the organisation and ritualisation of court proceedings (*cont.*)

Locality (demesne), year of issuing of statute	Composition and powers of the adjudicating bodies	Prescriptions concerning organisation of court sessions, their order and the dignity of village office	Formulas
Mogiła, 1756	Judicial competences of authorities (Art. 14)	Appearance in the community (Art. 16)	
Gwoździec/ Гвіздець, 1757	Judicial competences of authorities (Art. 4)		
Świątniki Górne, 1759, 1760	Composition of the court (Point 1)		Oaths of officials (*in initio*)
Sambor economy, 1759			Oaths of witnesses and parties (Art. 1–2)
Złotkowo, 1762	Judicial competences of authorities (Point 37)	Appearance in the community (Point 1); respect for the office (Point 3); behaviour before the court (Points 2, 4, 31); time of court proceedings (Point 34)	
Ilnik/Ільник, 1765		Respect for the office (Part 4, Art. 1)	Oaths of officials (Part 2, Art. 5)
Puck, 1767; Mirachowo, 1767	Judicial competences of authorities (Art. 41/ 41)	Appearance in the community (Art. 15/15); respect for the office (Art. 17/17); time of court proceedings (Art. 88/96)	
Ptaszkowa, 1767	Judicial competences of authorities		
Krowodrza, 1776	Judicial competences of authorities (Art. 6)	Appearance in court (Art. 5)	Oaths of officials (*in initio*)
Nieborów, 1777	Judicial competences of authorities (Art. 2)	Time of court proceedings (Art. 2)	

TABLE 5.1 Issues concerning the organisation and ritualisation of court proceedings (*cont.*)

Locality (demesne), year of issuing of statute	Composition and powers of the adjudicating bodies	Prescriptions concerning organisation of court sessions, their order and the dignity of village office	Formulas
Radzików, Kębłowice, 1778	Judicial competences of authorities (Art. 21, 23)		
Kicin, 1781		Time of court proceedings (Art. 1)	
Tyniec, 1785	Judicial competences of authorities		
Troszyn, 1788	Judicial competences of authorities (Art. 3)	Appearance in court (Art. 4) and village community (Art. 6); behaviour before the court (Art. 6)	Oaths of officials (*in fine*)
Ostróg/Острог, 1790; Rękoraj, 1791	Judicial competences of authorities (Art. 8/7)		
Znosicz/Зносич, 1791	Judicial competences of authorities (p. 79/80)		Oaths of officials (p. 79)

cating how important it was for the community to be present at procedural actions. The solemnity of village authorities was also addressed by the provisions in the village statutes, which were very numerous, concerning respect for the office, behaviour in the court and not challenging the decisions of village courts that had been made, as well as not mocking village judges whose judgements had been revoked by their superiors. Importantly, sources of judicial practice indicate that these provisions were by no means a dead letter.[17]

17 Compare Łaszewski, *Wiejskie prawo karne*, 98–99; Grodziski, "Kultura prawna wsi", 83–84 footnote 21.

Another issue very often addressed in village statutes was the scope of the judicial competence of the various bodies (the mayor or advocate/voigt, jury, the manorial officials and even the village community), which both the demesne and the village elite wished to define. On the one hand, certain cases—above all criminal and more difficult ones (e.g., inheritance cases which involved assessing the degrees of kinship and rights of relatives)—were reserved for the manorial instances. On the other hand, in some statutes there was an explicit prohibition of reference to the manor, i.e., the omission of the village court in cases not reserved for the demesne.[18] The provisions of some statutes also emphasised the role of the village community, which was to rule on matters too difficult to be decided by the village office alone.[19] Provisions of this kind were intended to limit the number of minor cases that would come before the lord or his officials for judgment, leaving only an appeal route for these matters. This built up the authority of the village office as an instance where appearance could not be avoided, and any appeals against its rulings involved additional expenses, the danger of conflict with the village community and the risk of defeat before the lord or his representative.

With the above in mind, it is hardly surprising that in the village statutes not only the provisions setting out the organisation of court proceedings but also those relating directly to the course of the trial (Table 5.2) covered a rather limited set of issues of potential interest from the point of view of dominial administration and village elites. This remark applied not only to statutes issued in the form of ad hoc legal rulings to remedy existing imperfections, but also to systematic ordinances and bylaws of a "micro-constitutional" nature, describing in detail issues from diverse spheres of life. In both, the most frequently mentioned procedural activity was the appeal, i.e., the procedure taking place at the intersection of rural and manorial jurisdiction. The term appeal in village statutes could sometimes include a motion (*mocja*), i.e., a complaint against the judge.[20] However, these concepts, which were not precisely separated even in landlaw,[21] could also have been applied imprecisely in rural law.[22] Therefore, when referring to appeal proceedings, I am writing

18 Compare e.g., Article 3 in the by-law for Silno and Wielka Nieszawka and derived texts; Article 42 in the statute for Kotusz of 1729; the statute for Ptaszkowa of 1736; Articles 81 and 85 in the by-law for Lubień Mały of 1756.

19 This was already the case in the Toruń by-law for urban villages of 1605, Article IV, point 8; compare also Article 4 in the statutes for Silno, Wielka Nieszawka and their derivatives.

20 Compare e.g., Article 86 and 90 for the ordinance for Zegrze and Rataje of 1733.

21 Wacław Uruszczak, *Historia państwa i prawa polskiego 966–1795*, Warszawa, 2021, 311.

22 Compare e.g., Łaszewski, *Wymiar sprawiedliwości*, 175, footnote 7.

TABLE 5.2 Issues concerning the course of the court trial in the rural statutes of the Crown of the Kingdom of Poland from the 15th to the 18th centuries (in chronological order)

Locality (demesne), year of issuing of statute	Procedural actions and other actions relevant to the procedure	Evidentiary proceeding and the means of evidence	Precautionary and enforcement proceedings	Varia
Krzemieniewo, a. 1413		Oath		
Pruszcz Gdański, 1485		Official damage assessment (Art. 19)	Seizure of cattle (Art. 12)	
Ustawa ławnikom... (Greater Poland), 1514		Official inspection of damage		
Kielce, 1576	Appeal, leniency by the dominion (p. 44)			
Żuławy Gdańskie, 1598			Seizure of cattle (Art. 30)	
Kartuzy, ca. 1600		Official damage assessment (Art. 45, 48)		
Pabianice, 1600				Conditions for the validity of legal transactions (§ 8)
Toruń, 1605	Appeal (Art. 4, Point 9)	Official damage assessment (Art. 12, Point 5), oath (Art. 14, Point 12)	Seizure of cattle (Art. 12, Points 3–4)	
Ptaszkowa, 1618 (*Zapowiedzi...*)	Appeal (Point 11)	Oath (Point 10)		
Szotland, 1620		Official search for stolen property (Art. 14)		Conditions for the validity of legal transactions (Art. 28–29, 35–36)

TABLE 5.2 Issues concerning the course of the court trial in the rural statutes (*cont.*)

Locality (demesne), year of issuing of statute	Procedural actions and other actions relevant to the procedure	Evidentiary proceeding and the means of evidence	Precautionary and enforcement proceedings	Varia
Hoppenbruch, 1621		Official search for stolen property (Art. 24)		
Tuchla, 1621–23		Prohibition on encroaching on the boundaries of disputed fields before court proceedings (Art. 20)		
Ellerwald, 1623 (1754)			Debt enforcement (Cap. 3, Art. 6)	
Czarże, 1626 (1661)	Appeal (Art. 15)	Oath (Art. 7); obduction (Art. 8); official inspection (Art. 11); survey of damage (Art. 11–12)		
Świlcza/Woliczka, 1628	Appeal (rt.. 1)			
Rozgarty, 1632	Lawsuit. Art. 6); aprt.l (Art. 8, 14)	Official inspection and damage assessment, including appeal procedure (Art. 7, 14)		Participation of women in proceedings (Art. 8)
Siedlce, 1637			Sequestration of movable property (tit. 8, Art. 5)	
Tuchola, 1643 (1749)			Assistance of the community in the enforcement of penalties (Art. 56)	Gravity of the *res iudicata* (Art. 12)

TABLE 5.2 Issues concerning the course of the court trial in the rural statutes (*cont.*)

Locality (demesne), year of issuing of statute	Procedural actions and other actions relevant to the procedure	Evidentiary proceeding and the means of evidence	Precautionary and enforcement proceedings	Varia
Lubień Mały, 1650 (1756)	Appeal (Art. 86)	Official inspection and damage assessment (Art. 38); oath (Art. 74)	Sequestration of movables for the sake of penalty (Art. 5); seizure of cattle (Art. 38–42)	Conditions for the validity of legal transactions (Art. 65); participation of women in proceedings (Art. 72)
Silno, 1652 [?]; Wielka Nieszawka, 1665 (1771) [and derived texts: Kozibór, 1719; Grabowiec, 1729; Kopanino, 1730; Duliniewo, 1754]	Appeal (Art. 3)	Official inspection and damage assessment (Art. 11, 17)	Seizure of cattle (Art. 14)	
Klimkówka, 1660				Conditions for the validity of legal transactions (643j)
Wojanowo et al., ca. 1660		Official inspection and damage assessment (Art. 55)		
Konarzyn, 1662	Lawsuit to the office and the community (Art. 18); lawsuit of a community (Art. 35)	Official inspection and damage assessment (Art. 4, 6, 15, 30)	Seizure of cattle (Art. 19)	
Żuławy Malborskie, bef. 1676/1723		Official inspection and damage assessment (Art. 26–27)		
Żuławy Polskie, 1676	Appeal (Art. 10, 12)		Enforcement of higher instance decisions (Art. 17–18, 23)	

TABLE 5.2 Issues concerning the course of the court trial in the rural statutes (*cont.*)

Locality (demesne), year of issuing of statute	Procedural actions and other actions relevant to the procedure	Evidentiary proceeding and the means of evidence	Precautionary and enforcement proceedings	Varia
Gumienice and Straszniów, 1679	Appeal (Art. 3)		Charging property for the sake of penalty (Art. 3)	
Lichtenfeld/Jasna, 1682 (1728)		Official inspection and damage assessment (Art. 24); witness statements (Art. 40)		
Tuchla, 1698	Appeal (Art. 10)			Participation of women in proceedings (Art. 11)
Luboń, 1719	Appeal (Point 20)			
Kasina, 1720		Extracts from court records for evidentiary purposes (ustawa 3)		
Bystrzec, bef. 1728	Appeal (Art. 3)	Proximity to evidence (Art. 36)	Seizure of cattle (Art. 23–27)	Conditions for the validity of legal transactions (Art. 37)
Kotusz, 1729	*Litkup* (Art. 9); lawsuit (Art. 39); Appeal (Art. 42)	Official inspection and damage assessment (Art. 32)	Seizure of cattle (Art. 26–29)	Participation of women in proceedings (Art. 5); conditions for the validity of legal transactions (Art. 9)

TABLE 5.2 Issues concerning the course of the court trial in the rural statutes (*cont.*)

Locality (demesne), year of issuing of statute	Procedural actions and other actions relevant to the procedure	Evidentiary proceeding and the means of evidence	Precautionary and enforcement proceedings	Varia
Zegrze, Rataje, 1733	Appeal (Art. 86, 90, 102)	Official inspection and assessment of damage (Art. 53, 88, 105) and of animals found (Art. 73); witness statements concerning loans (Art. 76)		
Ptaszkowa, 1736			Prohibition on delaying enforcement of decisions	
Dębiec, 1737	Appeal (Point 8)			
Sadłuki, 1739		Official inspection and damage assessment (Point 19)	Seizure of cattle (Point 22)	
Zegrze, 1745; Rataje, 1745	Appeal (Art. 28, 33)			Conditions for the validity of legal transactions (Art. 17)
Tuchorze, 1745	*Litkup* (Point 9); lawsuit (Point 28); Appeal (Point 30)	Official inspection and damage assessment (Point 22)	Seizure of cattle (Points 19–21)	Participation of women in proceedings (Point 5); conditions for the validity of legal transactions (Point 9)
Jankowo, 1747	Appeal (Point 3)			
Gołębiewo, 1754	Lawsuit (Point 13)	Official inspection and damage assessment (Point 13)	Seizure of cattle (Point 12)	
Skotniki, 1751	Appeal			

TABLE 5.2 Issues concerning the course of the court trial in the rural statutes (*cont.*)

Locality (demesne), year of issuing of statute	Procedural actions and other actions relevant to the procedure	Evidentiary proceeding and the means of evidence	Precautionary and enforcement proceedings	Varia
Brankówka, 1753	Appeal (Art. 4); ugoda (Art. 14)	Official inspection and damage assessment (Art. 12, 13, 15)	Seizure of cattle (Art. 10)	Participation of women in proceedings (Art. 3)
Chełmno bishopric (nobles' villages, table estates); Gruczno, 1756, 1758, 1763	Appeal (Art./Points 14, 94, 97/ 102/-); jury deliberation (Art./Points 94/ 102/-); *sententia diffinitiva* (Art./ Points 94/102/-)	Official damage assessment (Art./ Points 42/51/51); secret hearing of witnesses (Art./ Points 94/102/-)	Seizure of cattle (Art./Points 44/53/53)	Court sessions (Art./ Points 94/102-)
Ptaszkowa, 1756	Appeal (Art. 12)			
Świątniki Górne, 1759, 1760			Rules on enforcement of decisions by the advocate/voigt (Point 3)	
Sambor economy, 1759		Confidentiality of witness evidence (Art. 3)		
Złotkowo, 1762	*Litkup* (Point 9); lawsuit (Point 34); appeal (Point 38)	Official inspection and damage assessment (Point 29)	Seizure of cattle (Points 26–29)	Participation of women in proceedings (Point 5); conditions for the validity of legal transactions (Point 9)
Ilnik/Ільник, 1765;	Appeal (Art. 1)			
Jonne, Elżbiecin, 1765; Seroki, 1766; Olszewo, 1766);	Appeal (Art. 10/p. 199–200, p. 214)			
Puck, 1767; Mirachowo, 1767				Gravity of *res iudicata* (Art. 18)

TABLE 5.2 Issues concerning the course of the court trial in the rural statutes (*cont.*)

Locality (demesne), year of issuing of statute	Procedural actions and other actions relevant to the procedure	Evidentiary proceeding and the means of evidence	Precautionary and enforcement proceedings	Varia
Krowodrza, 1776		Official inspection and damage assessment (Art. 7)		
Kozłowice, 1786	Appeal (Art. 9)			
Troszyn, 1788	Appeal (Art. 3, 4); lawsuit (Art. 4)	Documentary and witness evidence (Art. 4); official inspection and damage assessment (Art. 4)	Charging property for the sake of penalty (Art. 7)	
Znosicz/Зносич, 1791	Appeal (p. 79)			

about appeals, although appeals *sensu strictiori* should be understood—as in the land law—only those filed immediately after the judgment of the court of first instance.[23]

The numerous mentions of the appellate procedure correspond to the no less numerous provisions, already indicated above and in Table 5.1, concerning the competences of the adjudicating bodies. Those two groups of provisions were aimed to remove possible ambiguities at the intersection of the two instances (the communal and the manorial), each of which, in its own well-understood interests, should have retained its authority and the scope of the subject matter of its jurisdiction. It may be inferred from the wording of the statutes that it was considered a danger for the dignity of the village courts to be burdened with cases that were too difficult, and for the lord's judiciary to be inundated with minor cases. Adequately regulating the issue of instances made the work of those in charge of the courts easier and, at the same time, guaranteed income for all of them: for the village bodies from allowing appeals and for the demesnes from trying cases in the second instance.

23 Compare Łaszewski, *Wymiar sprawiedliwości*, 83.

4 Provisions Concerning Evidentiary, Precautionary and Enforcement Procedures

The sections of village statutes concerning the evidentiary proceeding show a similar tendency to that seen with the other issues mentioned above: a focus on issues that the demesne, or village authorities, were willing to regulate or consolidate. This is probably why in numerous statutes one can read about the inspection and assessment of damage by specifically designated official persons from among the rural elite, as well as their searching of houses and farmyards for stolen property (see details in Table 5.2). Such activities were indeed carried out, as is known from sources of legal practice.[24] We will learn rather little from village statutes about the most common means of evidence used in practice, which were witness statements and evidence from court books and documents.[25] There is also only one mention in a village statute of official examination of injuries (obduction),[26] which was, in fact, very well known to the peasantry and also practiced outside the village forum.[27]

Provisions on evidence from witnesses and documents appear in village statutes as if, even without manorial legislation, the use of these basic means of evidence were sufficiently regulated by local custom or the common-sense practice of village courts. By the provisions of the laws, attempts were, of course, made to influence this practice, but the landlords were probably under no illusion that they were able to shape it in any arbitrary way. This can be illustrated by the example of the quite numerous provisions in village statutes establishing prerequisites for specific legal actions, especially property partitions and transfers of the possession of real estate. Quite often, provisions in statutes required certain acts to be performed with the knowledge of the lord, before the village office or the entry of transactions of a particular kind in the books. However, only a small number of these provisions were accompanied by any sanction, and only a few stated the constitutive nature

24 Compare Łaszewski, *Wymiar sprawiedliwości*, 75. See also e.g., footnote 96 in court book of Iwkowa, *Księga sądowa wsi Iwkowej 1581–1809*, Stanisław Płaza (ed.), Wrocław, 1969, 73–74.

25 On the most frequent use of these particular measures, compare Łaszewski, *Wymiar sprawiedliwości*, 69–74.

26 In the statute for Czarże of 1626/1661.

27 See Łaszewski, *Wymiar sprawiedliwości*, 75; Janusz Łosowski, *Dokumentacja w życiu chłopów w okresie staropolskim*, Lublin, 2013, 155–158.

of the entry in the book and the invalidity of transactions made without such an entry.[28] In most cases, therefore, the dominions, through the relevant provisions, indicated to the peasants their preferences regarding the documentation of particular types of transactions but going against them, even if it exposed the parties to some unspecified difficulties, did not entail the invalidity of the transaction. A glaring illustration of the phenomenon discussed here are the provisions of Articles 73 and 76 of the statute for Zegrze and Rataje of 1733. They established the sanctioned requirement to make loans before the village office, but in the event of failure to comply with this formality, in the situation of the debtor's serious illness, the possibility of proving the existence of the liability by means of witness testimony was provided anyway. Clearly, therefore, when issuing the statute in question, Poznań's authorities assumed in advance that the requirement to make loans before the office would be ignored.

It was not uncommon for village statutes to mention a means of evidence, which in a modern civil trial—and that was essentially the nature of the proceedings in a village court—was supplementary in nature,[29] namely an oath. The oath is even mentioned in the oldest known Polish village statute (*laudum*), dating back to the beginning of the 15th century. In its light, the inhabitants of the village of Krzemieniewo, with the approval of the noble owners of the village, passed a resolution that the defendant was to defend himself with an expurgative oath (an oath taken to exonerate oneself) of his neighbours from both sides.[30] Also concerning the same means of evidence are the provisions contained in two statutes from Chełmno Land issued in the 17th century for Czarże and Lubień Mały. However, the specific provisions of these laws were probably backed by quite different *rationes legis*: in the bylaw for Czarże, one can see the will to deter potential perpetrators (by adding sanctions for those making false accusations), while in the statute for Lubień Mały, the

---

28 See Article 18 of the by-law for Szotland of 1620; Article 17 of the statutes for Zegrze and Rataje of 1745.

29 See Uruszczak, *Historia państwa i prawa*, 306; this claim finds support in the theses of the legal scholarship of the time, compare Adam Moniuszko, "*Iuramentum corporale praestitit.* Przyczynek do badań nad przysięgą dowodową w koronnym procesie ziemskim u schyłku XVI stulecia", *Соціум. Альманах соціальної історії* 9 (2010), 363–364. In rural law, this thesis is well illustrated by Article XIV, point 12 of the Toruń statute for urban villages (*Polskie ustawy wiejskie XV–XVIII w.*, 56), which only allowed the oath to be taken in the absence of other evidence.

30 "Uchwała gromadzka z początku XV wieku", Kazimierz Tymieniecki (ed.), *Roczniki Historyczne* 6 (1930), 237–238.

desire to mobilise those slandered to take an oath to exonerate themselves (by indicating the time limits for taking these oaths and sanctions for failing to do so).

In addition to evidentiary actions, enforcement was also mentioned in the village statutes. The most mentions in this area relate to the procedure for the seizure of cattle which damaged crops. One can guess that the legislators had a similar goal here, as with many other provisions: to limit the extent of conflicts and preserve internal peace in rural communities. In this particular case, these objectives were to be achieved through the timely entry into action of the village office, which was to take over the care of seized cattle for an appropriate fee.

5 Conclusion

Summarising the above remarks, it should be stressed that the material collected does not make a quantitative analysis possible, if only because of the over-representation of village statutes from Royal Prussia and the existing phenomenon of copying specific provisions, or even entire statutes, between demesnes throughout the northwestern part of the Crown. Nevertheless, the available material does allow for some initial generalisations.

Undoubtedly, the phenomenon of juridification manifesting itself in the tendency to describe in detail the rights and obligations of various entities and the procedures for their implementation is evident. A clear primacy in this respect was led as early as the beginning of the 17th century by urban demesnes, followed closely by the estates of certain ecclesiastical institutions. This trend extended over time to all types of demesnes, although until the partitions of the Polish-Lithuanian Commonwealth (1772–1795), concise and ad hoc statutes did not completely give way, at least in the southern part of the Crown, to elaborate legal acts regulating diverse areas of rural life. As far as the formal and legal provisions contained in individual statutes are concerned, the increase in the number of statutes in general, and their elaborate types in particular, did not necessarily translate into the scope of the regulations concerning the formal law they contained. The fate of the 1665 bylaw for Nieszawka, the provisions of which in the area of procedural law were repeated in several further acts from 1719–1754, is telling in this respect. Thus, it seems that on the borderland between Royal Prussia and the Greater Poland lands of the Crown throughout this period there was no increase in the substantive scope of written regulations deemed necessary, only in the number of landed estates whose owners and/or local communities found it useful to have written laws.

Nor is it apparent that between the 17th and 18th centuries the comprehensiveness of procedural law regulations issued for villages surged, or that they covered a noticeably broader spectrum of issues, although the average size of the statutes themselves increased considerably during this period. Even the most detailed village statutes, including those containing compact parts devoted to court proceedings, were not actually local codifications of procedural law but covered only a certain scope of it.

It is clear from the remarks above that the provisions included in the statutes were those which the landlords, and possibly also the rural elite, were interested in writing down. These concerned issues relating to the preservation of the hierarchy and social peace (respectability of office, enforcement procedure) or the interface between the rights of the village community and the manorial jurisdiction (substantive competence of the adjudicating authorities, appeal/motion). As a general rule, however, many matters of overriding importance for the course of a trial (time limits, forms of petitions, procedural objections, postponement of a trial, etc.) were rarely or never regulated by village statutes. Particularly informative in this respect is a comparison of the provisions of statutes with lists of fees for official acts and sources of practice (court books), which shows that, at least potentially, village courts were able to carry out a wide range of actions with the necessary knowhow without having to support themselves either with their own written resolutions or with ordinances granted by the landlords.

Such a result provides a partial, if somewhat paradoxical, answer to a question that perplexed Adam Vetulani and his disciples, as to whether there was a separate peasant law in the Kingdom of Poland and then in the Polish-Lithuanian Commonwealth.[31] The sources discussed in this chapter do not allow us to fully answer this question but they surely show that there was much room for peasant legal culture underneath the superficial layer of juridification driven by the landlords. Moreover, the peasants were certainly able and ready to fill this space with their legal culture and practice. It was in no case a phenomenon unique to Poland-Lithuania, but also for other European countries. Several telling examples from various countries of ordinary people actively participating in legal relations and judicial proceedings still in the 17th and 18th centuries were brought about and commented on by Griet Vermeesch.[32] The only difference between Poland-Lithuania and some areas of the West could be the practical absence of state power as an active factor in

31 Compare Grodziski, "*Kultura prawna wsi*", *passim*, further reference there.

32 Griet Vermeesch, "Reflections on the relative accessibility of law courts in early modern Europe", *Crime, History* and *Societies* 19/2 (2015), 65–66.

the former. Until the very end of the Polish-Lithuanian polity, these were the landlords that had to be negotiated with in order to assure the space for legal action of peasants and villages.

The village statutes quite clearly show the limits of the demesnes' influence on the rural judiciary, obvious in the situation in which the primary instrument of this influence was the village office, which was also the organ of the rural community. The landlords were apparently neither willing nor able to influence the course of judicial proceedings in their villages in detail, as these were largely regulated by local tradition. Arguably, the demesnes were interested in involving themselves as little as possible in the tedious, day-to-day affairs of their subjects, which were to be resolved by the village offices (mayors/voigts and jurors/councillors). It was to the village offices that the lord's legislation gave succour, as far as the rules on behaviour in court and the solemnity of official persons were concerned. Nevertheless, the common interest between the village offices and the demesnes on judicial grounds ended there. Then there were the judicial proceedings themselves, essentially taking place among the representatives of common people, according to rules hallowed by tradition, though by no means in isolation from the other legal orders operating in the Crown, especially the land and municipal ones. The hosts of these proceedings were, to a greater or lesser extent, the rural communities themselves, able to carry out a wide range of legal actions in their courts.

TABLE 5.3 Detailed data concerning the rural statutes listed in Tables 5.1–5.2 (in alphabetical order). Abbreviations: AKP 11—*Polskie ustawy wiejskie XV–XVIII w.*, ed. S. Kutrzeba, ks. A. Mańkowski, Kraków 1938 [Archiwum Komisji Prawniczej, vol. 11]; SPPP 11–12—*Księgi Sądowe Wiejskie*, vol. 1–2, ed. B. Ulanowski, Kraków 1921 [Starodawne Prawa Polskiego Pomniki, vols. 11–12].

Locality (demesne), year of issuing of statute	Part of the Crown, voivodship	Domain	Edition/archival location of the statute
Bogatka (Rychemberk), 1551	Royal Prussia, Pomeranian voivodship	City of Gdańsk	AKP 11, no. 2
Brankówka, 1753	Royal Prussia, Chełmno voivodship	City of Chełmno	M. Targowski, *Wilkierz olęderskiej wsi Brankówka*, „Rocznik Grudziądzki" 21, 2013, pp. 233–245
Bystrzec, bef. 1728	Royal Prussia, Chełmno voivodship	noble estate	AKP 11, no. 45
Chełmno bishopric (nobles' villages), 1756	Royal Prussia, Chełmno voivodship	Chełmno Bishopric	AKP 11, no. 33
Chełmno bishopric (table estates), 1758	Royal Prussia, Chełmno voivodship	Chełmno Bishopric	AKP 11, no. 34
Czarnowo, Pędzewo, Zła Wieś, 1678	Royal Prussia, Chełmno voivodship	City of Toruń	AKP 11, no. 44
Czarże, 1626 (1661)	Royal Prussia, Chełmno voivodship	Noble estate	A. Mańkowski, *Wilkierz miasteczka Czarza*, „Zapiski Towarzystwa Naukowego w Toruniu" 11:1938, issue 2, pp. 54–58
Czerna, 1672	Lesser Poland, Cracow voivodship	Czerna Monastery	SPPP 12, nr 7403
Dębiec, 1737	Greater Poland, Poznań voivodship	City of Poznań	AKP 11, no. 28
Drohobyczka/Дрогобичка, 1720	Lesser Poland, Ruthenian voivodship	Noble estate	О. Вінниченко, *До історії сільського судочинства: "ругове право" в галицькому селі початку XVIII століття*, „Дрогобицький краєзнавчий збірник" 11–12, 2008, pp. 514–526
Duliniewo, 1754	Greater Poland, Inowrocław voivodship	Royal demesne	AKP 11, no. 32

TABLE 5.3 Detailed data concerning the rural statutes listed in Tables 5.1–5.2 (*cont.*)

Locality (demesne), year of issuing of statute	Part of the Crown, voivodship	Domain	Edition/archival location of the statute
Ellerwald, 1623 (1754)	Royal Prussia, Malbork voivodship	City of Elbląg	C. Leman, *Provinzialrecht der Provinz Westpreussen*, vol. 2, Leipzig 1832, no. XIII, pp. 42–57
Gietrzwałd, bef. 1639, 1676	Royal Prussia, Malbork voivodship (Warmian bishoply principality)	Frombork Chapter	AKP 11, no. 13, 16
Gniew, 1676	Royal Prussia, Pomeranian voivodship	Royal demesne	AKP 11, no. 15
Gołębiewo, 1754	Royal Prussia, Chełmno voivodship	Royal demesne	X. Fröhlich, *Geschichte des Graudenzer Kreises*, vol. 1, 2nd ed., Danzig 1884, p. 77–78
Grabowiec, 1729	Greater Poland, Land of Dobrzyń	Royal demesne	AKP 11, no. 25
Gruczno, 1763	Royal Prussia, Pomeranian voivodship	Gniezno Archbishopric	AKP 11, no. 35
Gumienice & Straszniów, 1679	Lesser Poland, Sandomierz voivodship	Noble estate	AKP 11, no. 17
Gwoździec/Гвіздець, 1757	Lesser Poland, Ruthenian voivodship	Royal demesne (Sambor economy)	J. Łosowski, *Dokumentacja w życiu chłopów w okresie staropolskim*, Lublin 2013, Annex 22
Hoppenbruch, 1621	Royal Prussia, Pomeranian voivodship	Peplin Monastery	AKP 11, no. 10
Ilnik/Ільник, 1765	Lesser Poland, Ruthenian voivodship	Royal demesne (Sambor economy)	J. Łosowski, *Dokumentacja w życiu chłopów w okresie staropolskim*, Lublin 2013, Annex 25

TABLE 5.3 Detailed data concerning the rural statutes listed in Tables 5.1–5.2 (*cont.*)

Locality (demesne), year of issuing of statute	Part of the Crown, voivodship	Domain	Edition/archival location of the statute
Jankowo, 1747	Greater Poland, Poznań voivodship	Poznań Bishopric Canon Chapter	AKP 11, no. 46
Jazowsko, 1738	Lesser Poland, Cracow voivodship	noble estate	*Księgi sądowe wiejskie klucza jazowskiego 1663–1808*, opr. S. Grodziski, Wrocław 1967, no. 110
Jonne, Elżbiecin, 1765	Greater Poland, Masovian voivodship	noble estate	AKP 11, no. 36
Kalisz, 1647	Greater Poland, Kalisz voivodship	Town of Kalisz	State Archives Poznań, Akta miasta Kalisza, sygn. 53/4328/0/-/I232, pp. 354–356
Kartuzy, ca 1600	Royal Prussia, Pomeranian voivodship	Monastery of Holy Virgin Mary in Kartuzy	AKP 11, no. 5
Kasina, 1630, 1636, 1695, 1720	Lesser Poland, Cracow voivodship	Dominican Convent in Cracow	SPPP 11, no. 3127, 3205, 3475–81, 3605–3608
Kicin, 1781	Greater Poland, Poznań voivodship	Poznań Bishopric	W. Rusiński, *Osady tzw. „Olędrów" w dawnym woj. poznańskim*, Poznań 1939 – Kraków 1947, pp. 145–150
Kielce, 1576	Lesser Poland, Sandomierz voivodship	Cracow Bishopric	*Ordynacje i ustawy wiejskie z Archiwów Metropolitalnego i Kapitulnego w Krakowie 1451–1689*, ed. S. Kuraś, Kraków 1960, no. 49
Klimkówka, 1624, 1660, 1685	Lesser Poland, Cracow voivodship	noble estate	*Księga sądowa kresu klimkowskiego 1600–1762*, opr. L. Łysiak, Wrocław 1965, nr 233, 643, 715

TABLE 5.3 Detailed data concerning the rural statutes listed in Tables 5.1–5.2 (*cont.*)

Locality (demesne), year of issuing of statute	Part of the Crown, voivodship	Domain	Edition/archival location of the statute
Konarzyn, 1662	Royal Prussia, Pomeranian voivodship	noble estate	M. Targowski, *Wilkierz wsi Konarzyn z 1662 r.: zapomniane źródło do badań nad historią Olędrów z Dolnej Grupy*, „Rocznik Grudziądzki" 13:2021, s. 207–219
Kopanino, 1730	Greater Poland, Land of Dobrzyń	Royal demesne	AKP 11, no. 26
Kotusz, 1729	Greater Poland, Poznań voivodship	Noble estate	W. Rusiński, *Osady tzw. „Olędrów" w dawnym woj. poznańskim*, Poznań 1939 – Kraków 1947, pp. 151–156
Kozibór, 1719	Greater Poland, Inowrocław voivodship	Royal demesne	AKP 11, no. 22
Kozłowice, 1786	Greater Poland, Masovian voivodship	Royal demesne	*Księgi Referendarii Koronnej z drugiej połowy XVIII w.*, eds. A. Keckowa, W. Pałucki, vol. 2, Warszawa 1957, s. 536–539
Krowodrza, 1776	Lesser Poland, Cracow voivodship	Cracow Canonry of St. Spirit de Saxia	SPPP 11, no. 4415
Krzemieniewo, a. 1413	Greater Poland, Poznań voivodship	Noble estate	*Uchwała gromadzka z początku XV wieku*, ed. K. Tymieniecki, „Roczniki Historyczne" 6:1930, pp. 237–238
Lanckorona Captainship, 1646	Lesser Poland, Cracow voivodship	Royal demesne	*Акты издаваэмыэ виленскою Коммисэю длиа Разбора Дриевнх Актов*, vol. 25, pp. 479–482
Lichtenfeld/Jasna, 1682 (1728)	Royal Prussia, Malbork voivodship	Noble estate	W. Nowosad, *Osadnictwo olęderskie w dobrach szlachty Prus Królewskich. Stan źródeł i możliwości badawcze*, in: *Archiwa – Kancelarie – Zbiory*, vol. 1, Toruń 2005, Annex VII

TABLE 5.3 Detailed data concerning the rural statutes listed in Tables 5.1–5.2 (*cont.*)

Locality (demesne), year of issuing of statute	Part of the Crown, voivodship	Domain	Edition/archival location of the statute
Lubień Mały, 1650 (1756)	Royal Prussia, Chełmno voivodship	Royal demesne	AKP 11, no. 14
Luboń, 1719	Greater Poland, Poznań voivodship	City of Poznań	AKP 11, no. 23
Łącko, 1670, 1702	Lesser Poland, Cracow voivodship	Clarissine Convent in Stary Sącz	*Księgi sądowe klucza łąckiego*, t. 1, wyd. A. Vetulani, Wrocław 1962, nr 544, 599
Łąkorek, 1692 (1705)	Royal Prussia, Chełmno voivodship	Royal demesne	AKP 11, no. 19
Mirachowo, 1767	Royal Prussia, Pomeranian voivodship	Royal demesne	AKP 11, no. 38
Mogiła, 1756	Lesser Poland, Cracow voivodship	Mogiła Cistercian Monastery	SPPP 11, nr 3833
Nieborów, 1777	Greater Poland, Rawa voivodship	noble estate	J. Wegner, *Instruktarz ekonomiczny dóbr nieborowskich z 1777 r.*, „Teki Archiwalne" 1:1953, pp. 9–43
Olszewo, 1766	Greater Poland, Masovian voivodship	noble estate	H. Stebelska, *Źródła do sprawy oczynszowania w dobrach mazowieckich Andrzeja Zamoyskiego*, „Teki Archiwalne" 5:1957, pp. 214–219
Ostróg/Острог, 1790	Lesser Poland, Wołyń voivodship	noble estate	AKP 11, no. 40
Pabianice, 1600	Greater Poland, Sieradz voivodship	Cracow Bishopric	*Ordynacje i ustawy wiejskie z Archiwów Metropolitalnego i Kapitulnego w Krakowie 1451–1689*, ed. S. Kuraś, Kraków 1960, no. 69
Pruszcz Gdański, 1485	Royal Prussia, Pomeranian voivodship	City of Gdańsk	W. Długokęcki, D. Kaczor, *Wilkierz gdańskiej wsi Pruszcz z 1485 roku*, „Zapiski Historyczne", 72, issue 2–3, 2007, pp. 177–184

TABLE 5.3 Detailed data concerning the rural statutes listed in Tables 5.1–5.2 (*cont.*)

Locality (demesne), year of issuing of statute	Part of the Crown, voivodship	Domain	Edition/archival location of the statute
Pruszcz Gdański, 1595 (1723)	Royal Prussia, Pomeranian voivodship	City of Gdańsk	D. Kaczor, *Wilkierz wiejski Pruszcza Gdańskiego z 1595 roku*, in: *Hortus Imaginum* ..., red. A. Paner et al., Gdańsk 2005, s. 104–109
Ptaszkowa, 1618 (*Sposób odprawowania* ...; *Sposob gaię̨nia* ...; *Zapowiedzi* ...); 1729; 1736; 1756; 1767	Lesser Poland, Cracow voivodship	Royal demesne	SPPP 11, no. 4100, 4103, 4114, 4161, 4162, 4177, 4186
Puck, 1767	Royal Prussia, Pomeranian voivodship	Royal demesne	AKP 11, no. 37
Radzików, Kębłowice, 1778	Greater Poland, Płock voivodship	Royal demesne	*Księgi Referendarii Koronnej z drugiej polowy XVIII w.*, eds. A. Keckowa, W. Pałucki, vol. 1, Warszawa 1955, pp. 437–441
Rękoraj, 1791	Greater Poland, Sieradz voivodship	noble estate	„Pamiętnik historyczno-polityczno-ekonomiczny", 10, 1791, pp. 790–803
Rozgarty (Kulmisch Rossgarten), 1632	Royal Prussia, Chełmno voivodship	City of Chełmno	P. Lettkemann, *Willküren der Dörfer in der Kulmer Stadtniederung*, [in:] *750 Jahre Kulm und Marienwerder*, Münster 1983, pp. 56–68
Rudna, 1631	Royal Prussia, Malbork voivodship	Royal demesne	AKP 11, no. 11
Sadłuki, 1739	Royal Prussia, Malbork voivodship	Noble estate	Z. Guldon, *Wilkierz wsi szlacheckiej Sadłuki (pow. sztumski) z r. 1739*, „Zapiski Historyczne", 28, 1963, issue 1, pp. 73–81
Sambor economy, 1759	Lesser Poland, Ruthenian voivodship	Royal demesne	J. Łosowski, *Dokumentacja* ..., Annex 21
Seroki, 1766	Greater Poland, Masovian voivodship	noble estate	H. Stebelska, *Źródła do sprawy oczynszowania w dobrach mazowieckich Andrzeja Zamoyskiego*, „Teki Archiwalne" 5:1957, pp. 197–202

TABLE 5.3 Detailed data concerning the rural statutes listed in Tables 5.1–5.2 (*cont.*)

Locality (demesne), year of issuing of statute	Part of the Crown, voivodship	Domain	Edition/archival location of the statute
Silno, 1652 [?]	Greater Poland, Land of Dobrzyń	Royal demesne	AKP 11, no. 3
Skotniki, 1751	Lesser Poland, Cracow voivodship	Royal demesne	SPPP 12, nr 7482
Strzemięcino, a. 1443	Royal Prussia, Chełmno voivodship	Town of Grudziądz	Mentioned in: X. Fröhlich, *Geschichte des Graudenzer Kreises*, vol. 1, 2nd ed., Danzig 1884, p. 335
Strzeszyce & Żbikowice, 1679, 1702	Lesser Poland, Cracow voivodship	Clarissine Monastery in Stary Sącz	SPPP 11, nos. 3914–15; 3921
Sucha, 1596	Lesser Poland, Cracow voivodship	Royal demesne	AKP 11, no. 20
Sułoszowa, 1627	Lesser Poland, Cracow voivodship	Noble estate	PAU/PAN Library Cracow, Ms 1875, p. 57–59
Szotland/Szkoty, 1620	Royal Prussia, Pomeranian voivodship	Cuyavian Bishopric	AKP 11, no. 8
Siedlce (Schiedlitz), 1637	Royal Prussia, Pomeranian voivodship	Monastery of St. Bridget in Gdańsk	AKP 11, no. 12
Świątniki Górne, 1759, 1760	Lesser Poland, Cracow voivodship	Cracow Bishopric	SPPP 12, nos. 7216, 7223
Świlcza/Woliczka, 1628	Lesser Poland, Ruthenian voivodship	Noble estate	*Ustawa dla wsi Świlczy i Woliczki z ok. 1628 r.*, ed. A. Kamiński, F. Kotula, Rzeszów 1948
Toruń, 1605	Royal Prussia, Chełmno voivodship	City of Toruń	AKP 11, no. 6
Troszyn, 1788	Greater Poland, Masovian voivodship	Royal demesne	*Księgi Referendarii Koronnej z drugiej połowy XVIII w.*, eds. A. Keckowa, W. Pałucki, vol. 2, Warszawwa 1957, s. 662–670

TABLE 5.3 Detailed data concerning the rural statutes listed in Tables 5.1–5.2 (*cont.*)

Locality (demesne), year of issuing of statute	Part of the Crown, voivodship	Domain	Edition/archival location of the statute
Tuchla, 1621–1623, 1698	Lesser Poland, Ruthenian voivodship	Noble estate	AKP 11, no. 9, 21
Tuchola, 1643 (1749)	Royal Prussia, Pomeranian voivodship	Royal demesne	AKP 11, no. 31
Tuchorze, 1745	Greater Poland, Poznań voivodship	Noble estate	F. Guntram Schultheiss, *Die Nachbarschaften in den Posener Hauländereien nach ihrem historischen Zusammenhang*, „Archiv für Kulturgeschichte“, Berlin 1908, pp. 28–34
Tyniec, 1785	Lesser Poland, Cracow voivodship	Tyniec Benedictine Monastery	SPPP 12, no. 7279
Ustawa ławnikom … (Greater Poland), 1514	Greater Poland	not specified	E. Raczyński, *Wspomnienia Wielkopolski, to jest województw poznańskiego, kaliskiego i gnieźnieńskiego*, Poznań 1842, vol. 1, Additions, pp. X–XI
Węgrzce, 1570	Lesser Poland, Cracow voivodship	Cathedral Chapter in Cracow	SPPP 12, no. 7333
Wielka Nieszawka, 1665 (1771)	Greater Poland, Inowrocław voivodship	Royal demesne	M. Targowski, *Wilkierz Wielkiej Nieszawki z 1771 roku*, „Rocznik Toruński“ 39, 2012, pp. 147–160
Wojanowo et al., ca 1660	Royal Prussia, Pomeranian voivodship	Private estate of a Gdańsk burgher	S. Hoszowski, *Ustawa dla wsi dziedzicznych Edwarda Rüdigera, rajcy gdańskiego, z drugiej połowy XVII wieku*, „Zapiski Historyczne“, 24, 1958/1959, pp. 85–98
Zagórzany	Lesser Poland, Cracow voivodship	Benedictine Monastery in Tyniec	SPPP 11, no. 4282
Zegrze, Rataje 1733	Greater Poland, Poznań voivodship	City of Poznań	AKP 11, no. 27

TABLE 5.3 Detailed data concerning the rural statutes listed in Tables 5.1–5.2 (*cont.*)

Locality (demesne), year of issuing of statute	Part of the Crown, voivodship	Domain	Edition/archival location of the statute
Zegrze, 1745; Rataje, 1745	Greater Poland, Poznań voivodship	City of Poznań	AKP 11, nos. 29, 30
Złotkowo, 1762	Greater Poland, Poznań voivodship	noble estate	C. Brandenburger, *Das Hauländer-Dorf Goldau bei Posen*, „Zeitschrift der Historischen Gesellschaft für Provinz Posen", vol. 18, 1903, Annex 3, pp. 44–49
Znosicz/Зносич, 1791	Lesser Poland, Wołyń voivodship	noble estate	W. Smoleński, *Sprawa włościańska w Polsce wieku XVIII*, [in:] *Pisma historyczne*, vol. 3, Kraków 1901, pp. 75–81
Żuławy Gdańskie, 1598	Royal Prussia, Pomeranian voivodship	City of Gdańsk	P. Szafran, *Ustawa wiejska dla Żuław Gdańskich z 6 II 1598 r.*„ Rocznik Gdański" 32:1972, pp. 193–203
Żuławy Malborskie, bef. 1676/1723	Royal Prussia, Malbork voivodship	Royal demesne	AKP 11, no. 24
Żuławy Polskie, 1676	Royal Prussia, Pomeranian voivodship	Royal demesne	AKP 11, no. 43

CHAPTER 6

The French *Code de procédure civile* in Polish Territories in the 19th Century

Dorota Malec

The annihilation of the Polish state as a result of the three partitions (1772, 1793, 1795) executed by neighboring powers (Russia, Austria, and Prussia) led to the imposition of foreign legal systems across Polish territories. The establishment of the Duchy of Warsaw in 1807 on a portion of Polish lands rekindled aspirations for the revival of native legal traditions. The necessity for legal reforms, as mandated by the constitution promulgated by Napoleon Bonaparte, culminated in a substantial reform and modernization of the legal system. The reforms implemented during this period were particularly significant in the domain of civil law, as Article 69 of the Constitution of the Duchy of Warsaw explicitly stipulated that the Napoleonic Code would serve as the governing civil law.

The adoption of the *Code civil* of 1804 necessitated further legislative adjustments. These encompassed civil procedure, modern principles for the organization of common judiciary systems, the legal profession, and notarial services. It was during this time that the institution of prosecutors, whose functions closely mirrored those of the French model, was introduced into Polish territories.[1] The regulations enacted in this era assumed considerable importance, extending far beyond the territorial boundaries of the Duchy of Warsaw and its brief existence (1807–1814), persisting throughout much of the 19th century and, to some extent, into the first half of the 20th century within certain regions of Poland.

The evolution of civil procedure in Polish territories during the 19th century, particularly the history of French civil procedure in the Duchy of Warsaw and the Kingdom of Poland, has been the subject of extensive scholarly inquiry. However, such analyses have often remained overshadowed by studies

---

1 Dorota Malec, "Wpływy *Code civil* oraz innych kodyfikacji napoleońskich na ziemiach polskich (część II)", *Czasopismo Historyczno-Prawne*, 57 (2005), 2, 69–87; Wojciech Witkowski, "Uwagi o modernizacji sądów i prawa na ziemiach polskich w czasach zaborów", in *Państwo —Prawo—Myśl Prawnicza. Prace dedykowane profesorowi Grzegorzowi Leopoldowi Seidlerowi w dziewięćdziesiątą rocznicę urodzin*, Artur Korobowicz (ed.), Lublin, 2003, 304.

 | DOI:10.1163/9789004736672_008

focusing on substantive law.[2] The *Code de procédure civile* of 1806 exerted a profound influence not only on the development of Polish law during the 19th century but also served as a foundational model for modern European codes of civil procedure. Its direct application extended to other states within the sphere of French influence during the era of the French Revolution and Napoleonic Wars, including Belgium (1795), the Netherlands (1810), Geneva (1798), and territories on the left bank of the Rhine (1790).[3]

The principles for the implementation of Article 69 of the Constitution of the Duchy of Warsaw were set forth in a decree issued by the King of Saxony and the Duke of Warsaw on January 27, 1808. According to its provisions, "the Napoleonic Code, as a constitutional law, under Title IX, Article 69, designated for 'Our Duchy of Warsaw', was to be implemented starting from May 1, 1808, for all civil judicial authorities. Civil judges of any rank, in newly received cases from May 1 onwards, were to issue their judgments in accordance with the provisions and laws of the Napoleonic Code."[4]

French legislation played a significant role, and its prolonged validity caused the Napoleonic codes to become deeply integrated for many years into the legal system of the central lands: the Duchy, later the Kingdom of Poland, and eventually—to a significant extent—the central provinces of the Second Polish Republic during the interwar period. Napoleonic law remained in force until 1852 in the territories of the Free City of Kraków as a

2 See among other Hipolit Chwalibóg, *Wykład Kodeksu Postępowania Cywilnego*, Warszawa, 1874; August Heylmann, *Wykład historyczno-praktyczny porządku i postępowania cywilnego w sądzie apelacyjnym i trybunałach Królestwa Polskiego*, Warszawa, 1835; Jan Szymanowski, *Wykład kodeksu postepowania cywilnego*, Warszawa, 1866; Eugeniusz Waśkowski, *Zasady procesu cywilnego*, Wilno, 1932; Katarzyna Sójka-Zielińska, "Postępowanie cywilne", in *Historia państwa i prawa Polski*, vol. 3: *Od rozbiorów do uwłaszczenia*, Juliusz Bardach, Monika Senkowska-Gluck (eds.), Warszawa, 1981, 158 and 517; Konstanty Grzybowski, "Postępowanie cywilne", in *Historia państwa i prawa Polski*, vol. 4: *Od uwłaszczenia do odrodzenia państwa*, Warszawa, 1982, 255–259; Władysław Sobociński, *Historia ustroju i prawa Księstwa Warszawskiego*, Toruń, 1964, 258–272; Artur Korobowicz, "Pozostałości francuskiej procedury cywilnej w sądownictwie Królestwa Polskiego po reformie z 1876 r.", in *'Vetera novis augere'. Studia i prace dedykowane Profesorowi Wacławowi Uruszczakowi*, eds. Stanisław Grodziski, et al. (eds.), Kraków, 2010, 437–445; Tadeusz Ereciński, "Znaczenie francuskiego *Code de procédure* z 1806 r. dla rozwoju procesu cywilnego w Polsce", *Czasopismo Prawno-Historyczne* 57 (2005), 2, 133–144; articles of Michał Gałędek and Anna Klimaszewska and Piotr Zbigniew Pomianowski in *Krakowskie Studia z Historii Państwa i Prawa* 1 and 2 (2019) and 1 and 4 (2021); see also Anna Stawarska-Rippel, *Elementy prywatne i publiczne w procesie cywilnym w świetle prac kodyfikacyjnych w Polsce (1918–1964). Studium historycznoprawne*, Katowice, 2015, 19–28.

3 Stawarska-Rippel, *Elementy prywatne*, 22.

4 *Journal of Laws of the Duchy of Warsaw*, vol. 1 (1807), 5.

kind of legacy from the period when these lands belonged to the Duchy of Warsaw. The broad application of the French regulations introduced at the beginning of the 19th century was thus fully possible in areas that gained some autonomy within quasi-state entities formed on the ruins of the Duchy of Warsaw: the Kingdom of Poland and the Republic of Kraków. Their liquidation, carried out by the partitioning powers, was simultaneously associated with the replacement of the existing legal order with the norms of the partitioning states.

The provisions of the *Code de procédure civile* were introduced in the Duchy of Warsaw in an informal manner, bypassing the constitutional order. This was effected pursuant to an instruction issued on May 23, 1808, by the Minister of Justice, Feliks Łubieński. The instruction was intended to apply temporarily, only until the issuance of proper regulations. Although such regulations were never enacted, the code retained its binding force. In 1810, following the expansion of the territory of the Duchy of Warsaw, the code was also introduced in the newly established Galician departments, including Kraków. After the fall of the Duchy, it was applied in the Kingdom of Poland and was ultimately replaced only by a tsarist decree dated March 6/18, 1875, which introduced the Russian Civil Procedure Law of 1864—a law that, incidentally, was also based on French models.[5]

The introduction of French legislation initially met with distrust from the ruling classes and legal professionals of the Duchy of Warsaw. This distrust stemmed from prejudice against foreign and rigid forms, which, during the initial period, were regarded as too difficult to understand and master.[6] French civil procedure gradually gained supporters despite the initial criticism of the law's excessive formalism (according to its opponents) and the relatively high costs of proceedings. This shift was associated with the growing recognition among legal professionals of its similarities to the former Polish legal process and procedural principles known from the pre-partition period.[7] This sentiment was expressed, among others, by the distinguished lawyer and notary Jan Wincenty Bandtkie. In 1815, he observed that experienced Polish lawyers considered the civil procedure to be good and necessary, attributing its perceived flaws to limited knowledge of the provisions and their incomplete implementation.[8] The advantages of the French code were noted in the simplified forms of proceedings in justices of the peace

5 Sójka-Zielińska, "Postępowanie cywilne", 153–154; Grzybowski, "Postępowanie cywilne", 255.

6 Sobociński, *Historia ustroju*, 269.

7 Sobociński, *Historia ustroju*, 263, 272.

8 Sobociński, *Historia ustroju*, 269.

courts, the mandatory conciliation proceedings required before filing a lawsuit, the straightforward method of appointing legal representatives, and the direct exchange of legal documents between them.[9]

As was the case with the *Code civil*, the authentic text of the Code of Civil Procedure in the Duchy remained the French original. The translation commissioned by the Minister of Justice and prepared by Antoni Łabędzki, published twice (in 1807 and 1810), did not acquire the status of an official version. Efforts to publish the code in a revised edition adapted to the Duchy's needs also proved unsuccessful.[10]

It is important to emphasize the considerable diversity in judicial practice, which arose from differences in the application of procedural provisions when compared to France. The courts of the Duchy of Warsaw were authorized to draft internal regulations independently, which undoubtedly impeded the uniform application of the *Code de procédure civile*. According to the aforementioned instruction of the Minister of Justice dated May 23, 1808, the courts established such internal regulations independently, providing a basis for the development of their own procedural practices, particularly regarding case preparation, adjudication, and the types and maintenance of court records. This diversity was not mitigated by the Minister of Justice's efforts to standardize judicial practice through numerous circulars and detailed regulations. Among legal professionals, there was a prevailing belief in the fundamental compatibility of the former Polish procedural system with the new French one. On the other hand, this facilitated the retention of certain former Polish legal institutions in judicial practice, which were not always consistent with the French procedural code.[11]

It is worth highlighting that, along with the French civil procedure, new remedies for appealing civil judgments were introduced in the Duchy of Warsaw. In addition to appeals, which were already known in Polish law, *cassation* was introduced as the most important remedy against final judgments.[12] Cassation was adapted to Polish conditions by the provisions of the decree dated April 3, 1810.[13] However, during the era of the Kingdom of Poland, it

9 Korobowicz, "Pozostałości francuskiej", 432.

10 Sobociński, *Historia ustroju*, 259–260, 262.

11 Sobociński, *Historia ustroju*, 262.

12 Władysław Sobociński, "Sądownictwo Księstwa Warszawskiego a problem kasacji. Pierwsze pomysły i zaczątki organizacji kasacyjnej", *Czasopismo Prawno-Historyczne* 34 (1982), 2, 141 ff; Artur Korobowicz, "Rys dziejów kasacji w polskim systemie sądowo-odwoławczym", in *Polska lat 90-tych. Przemiany państwa i prawa*, vol. 2, Lublin, 1998, 307 ff; Ereciński, „Znaczenie", 139.

13 *Journal of Laws of the Duchy of Warsaw*, vol. 2 (1809/1810), 151–185.

was largely replaced by the revision system, only to reappear in these territories again in 1876.

Cassation complaints were reviewed by the Council of State (modeled after the French *Conseil d'État*), an organ whose existence and competencies were derived from the Constitution of the Duchy and further specified in the decree of April 3, 1810, regarding the organization of the Court of Cassation, as well as in the decree of September 19, 1810, concerning the Council's other functions.[14] The interpretation of a cassation judgment by the Council was not binding, and a judgment challenged for a second time was to be reviewed by an expanded nine-member panel. Only after a judgment had been challenged three times for the same reasons would the Council refer the case to the King, who would issue a binding explanation in the matter.

The extensive responsibilities assigned to the Council of State resulted in delays in its functioning as a court of cassation. These delays were further exacerbated by a conflict between the Minister of Justice and the majority of the members of the Council of State.[15] The 1810 decree introduced a degree of selection for cassation complaints, which was to be conducted by the Commission for Petitions and Instructions. An even more intriguing modification was introduced in cassation proceedings before the third-instance court in the Free City of Kraków. Until 1833, in cases where the judgments of the first and second instances were consistent, the admissibility of a cassation complaint was determined by professors and doctors of the Faculty of Law at the then Jagiellonian University.[16]

The Napoleonic era introduced a new and creative reliance on the role of judicial case law in Polish territories, despite the fact that in former Poland, the influence of legal doctrine and judicial decisions on court law was not known. This marked another element aimed at unifying judicial practice, a focus that was later emphasized during the era of the Kingdom of Poland.[17]

The *Code de procédure civil* was supplemented in subsequent years with judicial instructions and regulations, as well as rescripts issued by the Ministry

14 *Journal of Laws of the Duchy of Warsaw*, vol. 2 (1809/1810), 151–185, 379–426.

15 Sobociński, *Historia ustroju*, 248.

16 Andrzej Dziadzio and Mateusz Mataniak, *Protokoły posiedzeń Wydziału Profesorów i Doktorów Prawa Uniwersytetu Jagiellońskiego (1817–1833). Opinie o stosowaniu Kodeksu Napoleona przez sądy Wolnego Miasta Krakowa*, Kraków, 2022, 7 ff; Andrzej Dziadzio, "Stosowanie francuskiej procedury cywilnej przez sądy Wolnego Miasta Krakowa (1815–1846)", *Prawo i Więź* 4 (2023), 155–176.

17 Wojciech Witkowski, "Dyskusja o jurysprudencji wśród prawników Królestwa Polskiego", in *Prawo wczoraj i dziś. Studia dedykowane prof. K. Sójce-Zielińskiej*, Grażyna Bałtruszajtys (ed.), Warszawa, 2000, 383 ff; Ereciński, "Znaczenie", 135–136.

of Justice. In this modified form, the code became deeply entrenched in the judicial practice of these lands. Even the draft of a new civil procedure code prepared by the Legislative Commission in 1820 during the Kingdom of Poland, which sought to standardize the previously inconsistent judicial practice, was based not only on the principles but also on the structure and content of the French law. It departed from the French model only in the domain of enforcement proceedings.[18]

After the establishment of the Kingdom of Poland in 1815, formed from parts of the Duchy of Warsaw, the French *Code de procédure civil* of 1806 remained in force. Although the Constitution of the Kingdom of Poland of 1815 announced the introduction of a new system of common courts, which would have influenced procedural rules, in practice, the network of courts from the previous period was retained. Ultimately, significant changes affecting civil procedure occurred only at the level of the highest instance. The organization of courts, the system of substantive civil law (supplemented in 1818 and 1825 by mortgage laws and the Civil Code of the Kingdom of Poland), and the French civil procedure, all originating from the Duchy, became for many years a key factor distinguishing the Kingdom of Poland from Russia. Moreover, these elements were regarded by legal practice and doctrine as native and intrinsic law, playing a vital role in the creation of a national legal culture and in defending Polish identity against russification.[19]

However, the continued applicability of the *Code de procédure civile* did not mean the complete unification of procedural rules in the Kingdom of Poland. This was influenced by the persistence of traditions from pre-partition judicial practice and the impact of procedural norms from other partitioning states. Courts also continued to issue their own instructions and internal regulations.[20] Although the Government Commission for Justice, acting as the Ministry of Justice, attempted to influence the uniformity of judicial practice (for instance, by resending rescripts issued by the minister in the previous period to the courts), it also permitted deviations from the French model due to local customs and requirements.

As previously mentioned, in 1820, alongside efforts to reform the civil code, work was undertaken to amend civil procedure. Despite initial intentions to create an entirely original code of procedure, the creators of the draft were instructed, in line with the directives of the Government Commission for Jus-

18 The project did not enter into force—despite the acceptance of the Council of State, it was not passed by the Sejm, see Sójka-Zielińska, "Postępowanie cywilne", 518.

19 Korobowicz, "Rys dziejów", 432.

20 Sójka-Zielińska, "Postępowanie cywilne", 517.

tice, to adhere to the structure and content of French provisions. The draft, ultimately introducing changes only in the area of enforcement proceedings, was presented to the Council of State of the Kingdom of Poland in 1820. Despite its approval, it was never enacted.[21]

Significant changes to the *Code de procédure civile* of 1806 arose from the adoption by the Sejm of the Kingdom of Poland of the Mortgage Law of 1818, which was crucial for the development of Polish law and later supplemented in 1825. The distinctiveness of mortgage proceedings also stemmed from the decree of the Viceroy of the Kingdom of Poland dated January 22, 1822, which regulated appellate proceedings in such cases, along with other detailed provisions.

The most significant change during the era of the Kingdom of Poland was the abolition of cassation, resulting from the establishment of the Supreme Court in civil matters in 1815. Proceedings before this court adopted a revisionary character.[22] At the same time, the principles of written, indirect, and inquisitorial procedure were strengthened, and the involvement of a prosecutor was abolished, with their functions transferred to the reporting judge.[23]

The changes in the highest judicial instance, despite partial attempts at reform, exacerbated its flaws. Not only did the number of instances increase, but their character also changed. The principle that every case would pass through two substantive instances, with the cassation court ensuring uniformity in the application of law, was undermined. The highest courts were granted not only the right to annul judgments rendered in violation of the law but also the authority to issue substantive decisions in cases. In the 1840s, following the establishment of the Departments of the Governing Senate in Warsaw, these bodies became the third judicial instance with a revisionary role. The increase in the number of instances led to higher litigation costs and prolonged proceedings.[24]

In 1876, the Russian authorities in the occupied territories implemented the unification of the legal system in the Polish lands that had once formed part of the former Kingdom of Poland. However, changes in civil procedure had already begun earlier, with the introduction of municipal courts in 1864. Pro-

21 Sójka-Zielińska, "Postępowanie cywilne", 518.

22 Sójka-Zielińska, "Postępowanie cywilne", 518.

23 See Stanisław Zawadzki, *Prawo cywilne obowiązujące w Królestwie Polskim*, vol. 3, Warszawa, 1863, 400 ff.

24 Artur Korobowicz, "Organizacja sądownictwa", in *Historia państwa i prawa Polski*, vol. 3: *Od rozbiorów do uwłaszczenia*, Juliusz Bardach, Monika Senkowska-Gluck (eds.), Warszawa, 1981, 470.

ceedings before these courts were characterized by orality, transparency, and the absence of costs.[25] The most significant reform was enacted by virtue of a tsarist decree dated March 6/18, 1875, which took effect in 1876. This reform introduced a new Russian judicial system and the Russian procedural laws of 1864: the criminal and civil codes of procedure.

The unification of civil procedural law was not absolute, as certain distinctions were either preserved or newly introduced. The most significant of these arose from the continued distinctiveness of substantive civil law. Even after 1876, the legislation referred to as French-Polish—namely the Napoleonic Code, the Civil Code of the Kingdom of Poland, and Polish mortgage laws—remained in force in the territories of the former Kingdom of Poland.

The Russian civil procedure also retained its binding force in these territories after Poland regained independence in 1918, until the adoption of a unified civil procedure code. This code, prepared by the Codification Commission of the Republic of Poland, was issued in the form of a presidential decree on November 29, 1930, and became known as the Code of Civil Procedure (came in force in 1933).[26] Russian civil procedure had already been introduced in the eastern Polish territories under Russian rule, which had not previously been part of the Kingdom of Poland.

When assessing the impact of the introduction of the Russian civil procedure of 1864, it is important to note that it was significantly modeled on the French *Code de procédure civile* of 1806. The differences, which included the reduction of procedural formalism and the abandonment of the requirement for mandatory legal representation, aimed to simplify the proceedings.

An important reform was the reinstatement of cassation as an extraordinary remedy for challenging judicial decisions.[27] Under the new judicial organization introduced at the same time, cassation complaints from the territories of the former Kingdom of Poland were to be reviewed by the Governing Senate in St. Petersburg. Russian regulations required that when a judgment was annulled by the cassation court, the case was to be referred to another assembly of justices of the peace or another judicial chamber. However, their application in the Kingdom of Poland was not feasible because only one court operated at the judicial chamber level—the Warsaw Judicial Chamber. In

25 Grzybowski, "Postępowanie cywilne", 254.

26 *Journal of Laws* 1930, No. 83, item 651. The Code came into force in 1933 and was in force until the introduction of the next codification of civil procedure in 1964. This last code, after numerous amendments, is still in force today.

27 Korobowicz, "Rys dziejów", 404–406.

practice, therefore, the case was referred to a different panel of judges within the same chamber.[28]

It is worth noting that, under transitional provisions, in subsequent years (even into the 1890s), courts in the former Kingdom of Poland continued to apply the French *Code de procédure civile* to cases initiated before July 13, 1876, that is, before the unification of the legal system with the Russian Empire came into effect.[29]

Even after the introduction of Russian civil procedure, many customs and procedural principles developed under the French norms applied in the Duchy of Warsaw and the Kingdom of Poland until 1876 retained their vitality. This persistence was influenced by the attachment of judges to both the old regulations and the procedural practices they had followed. In the new, heavily Russified judicial structure, nearly half of the judges ruling in civil cases still came—out of necessity—from the ranks of local Polish lawyers. These lawyers had gained their education and professional experience while practicing under the French civil procedure for many years.

The continuation of established customs was further supported by the professional experiences of Polish attorneys practicing before the courts, whose role in the judicial process had been strengthened by the previously applied regulations.[30] The persistence of old procedural customs and the prominent role of attorneys were revealed during a review of the state of the judiciary and the application of the new procedural laws conducted in 1886, ten years after the changes took effect.[31] This review highlighted, among other things, the continued significant role of attorneys in civil proceedings, most of whom were Polish, the role was similar to the practices under the former French procedural regulations.

The continuation of old procedural customs was possible as long as many legal professionals, who had gained their professional experience before 1876, remained on the bench. However, their numbers began to decline from the 1890s onward due to natural causes (death, retirement) and the intensive Russification of the judiciary, which increasingly entrusted judicial positions to Russians.[32]

It is worth noting that the similarity between the French civil procedure and former Polish law was recognized even in 1875, when the Russian civil

28 Grzybowski, "Postępowanie cywilne", 257.

29 Korobowicz, "Pozostałości francuskiej", 433–434.

30 Korobowicz, "Pozostałości francuskiej", 435.

31 Korobowicz, "Pozostałości francuskiej", 435–436.

32 Korobowicz, "Pozostałości francuskiej", 436.

procedure was introduced in the territories of the Kingdom of Poland. A well-known Warsaw lawyer, Adolf Suligowski, reflected on the implications of this change and observed that, "by a strange coincidence, the procedure currently in force in our country, dating back to 1808, was entirely consistent in terms of civil procedure principles with the old Polish regulations."[33]

This perspective, deeply rooted in the consciousness of legal professionals from the territories of the former Kingdom of Poland, persisted even after Poland regained independence in 1918. When the Code of Civil Procedure, issued in the form of a presidential decree on November 29, 1930, was analyzed, it was noted—albeit with some idealization—that the French civil procedure from the era of the Duchy of Warsaw was akin to the old Polish law and had become ingrained in the national psyche.[34]

Shortly after Poland regained independence in 1918, some legal professionals from the central provinces, accustomed to these principles, advocated for the restoration of at least some institutions that had been developed in the practice of civil procedure in the territories of the Duchy of Warsaw and the Kingdom of Poland until 1876.[35] However, this view did not gain acceptance. During the work of the Codification Commission, there was even a proposal to expedite the codification process and quickly unify the regulations by extending the Austrian civil procedure law of 1895, which was in force in the former Austrian partition, to the entire country.[36] This proposal was successfully opposed by Professor Franciszek Ksawery Fierich, the President of the Codification Commission.[37]

When analyzing the provisions of civil procedure applicable in the Polish territories under the partitions, it is also necessary to mention the regulations in force in the Austrian and Prussian partitions. At the beginning of the 19th century, in the Polish territories under Habsburg rule (the so-called Kingdom of Galicia and Lodomeria), the General Judicial Ordinance (*Allgemeine Gerichtsordnung* of Emperor Joseph I, dated May 1, 1781) was introduced as part of judicial reforms on January 1, 1784. Following the annexation of new

---

33 Adolf Suligowski, "O reformie sądowej w Królestwie Polskim", *Niwa* (1875), 56, cited after Władysław Sobociński, *Historia ustroju*, 272; on work on the Code of Civil Procedure see Stawarska-Rippel, *Elementy prywatne*, 35 ff.

34 Alfons Parczewski, "Wspomnienia patrona trybunału", *Wileński Przegląd Prawniczy* (1932), 1–10.

35 Stanisław Taylor, "Ustrój sądowy w Księstwie Warszawskim i Królestwie Polskim do 1876 r.", *Gazeta Sądowa Warszawska* (1918), 381–384, 403–405.

36 Stawarska-Rippel, *Elementy prywatne*, 43.

37 Leonard Górnicki, *Prawo cywilne w pracach Komisji Kodyfikacyjnej Rzeczpospolitej Polskiej (1919–1939)*, Wrocław, 2000, 74.

Polish territories (the so-called Western Galicia) to Austria after the Third Partition in 1795, a new civil procedure code, titled the General Judicial Law for Western Galicia (*Allgemeine Gerichtsordnung für Westgalizien*), was implemented there under regulations issued on May 1, 1796. In 1807, it was also introduced in Eastern Galicia.[38]

The foundations of Austrian codifications were criticized in the Polish territories, particularly for procedural shortcomings that caused, among other issues, excessive delays, excessive formalism, and reduced legal certainty. In 1852, the provisions of the Western Galician code were extended to the Free City of Kraków, where, as previously mentioned, the French *Code de procédure civile* of 1806 had been in force as a legacy from the Duchy of Warsaw period. Partial reforms of civil procedure in Austria, carried out until 1875, did not diminish the criticism of the regulations that remained in force.[39]

It was not until 1893 that a comprehensive reform was undertaken. As a result, the laws of 1875 were implemented, covering civil procedure and enforcement ordinances. The Austrian law, popularly referred to as the "Klein Code" (after its author, Franz Klein), remained in force in this part of the Polish territories even after independence was regained, until the Polish Code of Civil Procedure of 1930 came into effect. Furthermore, it influenced the content of the Polish Code.[40]

In the Polish territories under Prussian rule, the General Judicial Ordinance (*Allgemeine Gerichts-Ordnung*) of 1795 was in force, which established the principle of written proceedings.[41] Between 1833 and 1846, this principle underwent changes, but a fundamental reform of the regulations in this part of the Polish lands occurred only as a result of the legislative changes of the German Empire between 1877 and 1897.[42] The German Civil Procedure Code of 1877 also remained in force in this part of Polish territories until the Code of Civil Procedure of 1930 was enacted.

The role of French civil procedure in Polish territories in the 19th century extended beyond the period of its direct applicability in the Duchy of Warsaw and the Kingdom of Poland until 1876. The principles of the *Code de procédure civile* set the direction for the evolution of civil procedure, reflected in the

38 Stanisław Grodziski, "Postępowanie cywilne 1772–1784", in *Historia państwa i prawa Polski*, vol. 3: *Od rozbiorów do uwłaszczenia*, Juliusz Bardach, Monika Senkowska-Gluck (eds.), Warszawa, 1981, 768.

39 Grzybowski, "Postępowanie cywilne", 455.

40 Andrzej Dziadzio, *Powszechna historia prawa*, Warszawa, 2008, 236.

41 Sójka-Zielińska, "Postępowanie cywilne", 645.

42 Grzybowski, "Postępowanie cywilne", 624.

foundations of modern codifications of civil procedure, such as the Russian law of 1864, the German law of 1877, and the Austrian law of 1895. There were notable differences between the Austrian and German laws, with the Austrian law breaking away from the traditional French model and setting a new direction for the evolution of civil procedure in many European countries.

Considerations on the history of the *Code de procédure civile* in Polish territories form part of broader reflections on the reception of law. It is a historical paradox in the history of law in Poland that French provisions in the fields of substantive and procedural civil law, although effectively imposed and implemented during the Duchy of Warsaw era to the initial dissatisfaction of the elites and legal professionals, over time came to be regarded as native law, serving to protect the distinctiveness of Polish legal culture. The questionable formal basis for the introduction of the French procedure was no longer contested, and its applicability was accepted for decades as a provisional measure. At the same time, the recognized similarities to former Polish law fostered diversity in judicial rulings and occasionally led to interpretations of the provisions that significantly diverged from the French model.

CHAPTER 7

An Appeal to the Faculty of Law at the Jagiellonian University against Violation of the French *Code Civil* by the Courts of the Free City of Cracow (1815–1833)

Andrzej Dziadzio

Jagiellonian University, as an important research and national institution, held a high position in the political and judicial structures of the Free City of Cracow (1815–1846).[1] According to the Constitution of the Free City of Kraków of 1815 professors and doctors of the university had the active right of election to the Assembly of Representatives as a legislative body, independently of their financial status; the university could delegate three doctors to the chamber. The university had the right to elect two members of the Governing Senate, acting as the executive authority. By virtue of Article XV of the Constitution, the Faculty of Law of Jagiellonian University also became an institution with an important function in the organisation of the judiciary of the Free City of Cracow.[2] The Constitution provided for an extraordinary appeal procedure in the form of an appeal (recourse) to the Faculty of Professors and Doctors of Law. It consisted of the right of the parties to a civil trial to appeal against the judgments of the Court of First Instance and the Court of Appeal, which were in conformity with their content, to the Faculty of Law of Jagiellonian University.

1 The Free City of Cracow was established at the Congress of Vienna in 1815 under the protectorate of Austria, Russia and Prussia. Its internal relations were defined by the original constitution of 3 May 1815 (renewed on 11 September 1818), imposed by these states, which, inter alia, placed legislative (Assembly of Representatives), governmental (Senate) and judicial (Court of First Instance and Court of Appeal) powers in the hands of the Poles. However, the policies of the Free City authorities were under the permanent control of three residents. It encompassed the area of Cracow and its surroundings (including Chrzanów, Trzebinia, Nowa Góra), with an area of 1150 km². The population in 1815 was approximately 90,000 (by 1843 the population rose to 145,787, 10 percent of which were Jews). The Free City of Cracow was abolished and incorporated into Austria in 1846.

2 "Constitution de la Ville libre de Cracovie et de Son Territoire", in *Constitutions of the World from the Late 18th Century to the Middle of the 19th Century. Sources on the Rise of Modern Constitutionalism*, Horst Dippel (ed.), Europe: vol. 5, Berlin, Boston 2008, 147–148.

 | DOI:10.1163/9789004736672_009

An appeal against unanimous judgments issued in a civil case could be based on an allegation that the courts violated substantive law or essential forms of court procedure. The Faculty of Law, after reviewing the case, i.e., the judgments and pleadings of the parties, would draw up a legal opinion stating that there had been a violation of substantive or procedural law, or that there had been no violation of law. However, no such power was granted by the Constitution to parties to criminal proceedings. They could indeed appeal directly to the Court of Last (Third) Instance, but only if the courts of both instances unanimously ruled on the death penalty or infamy.[3] The exclusion of criminal cases from the constitutional appeal procedure to the Faculty of Law may have been due to the fact that the application of substantive and procedural criminal law was based on Austrian legislation, which was well known in Cracow through the long-standing adjudicatory practice of the courts (from 1798 onwards).

In contrast, Napoleonic legislation (the *Code civil* and *Code de procédure civile*), which was to apply temporarily in the Free City, formed the basis of private-law relations in Cracow from 1810. This was because the Guardian States considered it an expression of Napoleon's "usurpation" and aimed for its prompt repeal. French law was therefore less familiar in judicial practice, which may have justified the need for a new remedy. This may also have been supported by the fact that the court system of the Free City of Cracow abandoned the Court of Cassation, which had been established in 1810 according to the French model in the Duchy of Warsaw. A similar fate was to be shared by French law. By order of the Organising Commission established by the Guardian States, the Legislative Committee was set up as early as January 1816, which began work on new codes. However, the draft codes prepared by the committee were not implemented. French civil law, both substantive (*Code civil*) and procedural (*Code de procédure civile*), with only partial modifications, re-

3 The interpretation of the constitutional provision therefore led to the conclusion that if there were unanimous judgments in a criminal case, there was no right to request the Faculty of Law of the Jagiellonian University to issue an opinion on the question of violation of substantive or procedural law by the criminal courts. Nevertheless, the professors and doctors of law—contrary to the literal wording of the Constitution—adopted the principle that also in criminal cases a convicted person could appeal to the Court of Last (Third) Instance on the basis of an *opinio facultatis* in the event of cassation-like grounds with respect to concurring judgments of the Court of First Instance and the Court of Appeal. This is because they assumed that the accused should not be in a worse legal position than a party to civil proceedings. The minutes of the legal faculty meetings therefore contain opinions also issued in criminal cases, but the percentage of these was small in the total number of decisions, which mainly concerned private law disputes.

mained in force in Cracow until 1855, when the Austrian Empire introduced its own civil legislation (inter alia the ABGB).[4]

The Faculty of Law of Jagiellonian University, when examining appeals against judgments of the Court of First Instance and the Court of Appeal, which contained a unanimous verdict, therefore primarily assessed the correctness of the application of the provisions of French civil law, mainly the *Code civil*. The faculty's opinion that there had been an infringement of substantive or procedural law in a case under consideration opened the way for a party to refer an appeal to the Court of Last (Third) Instance. The finding by the Law Faculty that there were no grounds for appeal ended the case. The judgments appealed against became final and binding. Between 1815 and 1833, the Faculty of Law thus acted as a court *par excellence*. The remedy adopted by the Constitution of the Free City of Cracow was an original and unique institution. Although it combined elements of the French cassation and the German procedure of the so-called *Aktenversendung*, neither of them found full expression in this hybrid construction. On the one hand, the law faculty's acknowledgement of the grounds for cassation to the Court of Last (Third) Instance did not mean that the contested judgments were set aside and the case sent back to the Court of Appeal, since the Court of Last Third) Instance had the power to make a substantive, adjudicatory ruling. On the other hand, the Court of Last (Third) Instance was not bound by the opinion of the Faculty of Law. It could have assumed that there were no grounds for appeal and upheld the judgments.

The procedure related to an appeal submitted by the parties to the Faculty of Law against the unanimous judgments of two court instances was never

4 Lesław Pauli, "Prawa obce w Rzeczypospolitej Krakowskiej", *Zeszyty Naukowe Uniwersytetu Jagiellońskiego* 97 (1982), 143–417. In 1822, the Mortgage Act was passed in the Free City of Cracow, which repealed Title XVIII of Book III of the *Code civil* (Articles 2092–2203). In 1825, the Guardianship Law repealed the provisions of Titles X (Articles 388–487) and XI (Articles 488–515) of Book I. However, the provisions on secular matrimonial law, including the right to divorce, were retained. The provisions of the French Code were supplemented by a number of specific acts of *lex specialis* nature, such as the law on Jewish marriages, which was intended to counteract marriages concluded by Jews exclusively in a religious form. This was because Jews rejected secular marriage law. One of the measures to force Jews to marry in a civil form, in addition to a fine, was the sanction of recognising the illegitimacy of children from marriages in which the religious marriage was concluded before and not after the marriage in a secular form. This was a reference to the old Polish institution of *proles illegitima* and a land law that rejected the principle canon law *legitimatio per subseqens matrimonium*. Civil litigation was also based on French procedure until 1855, which was amended in 1823 by the ordinance "Law of Judicial Enforcement" and in 1825 as regards provisions under the law on "Proceedings before the Courts of Peace."

regulated by law. The procedure followed by the professors of the Faculty of Law in this regard was based solely on practice and custom. Although the Ruling Senate submitted a bill to the Assembly of Representatives defining "the form of proceedings in appeals to the Faculty of Professors and Doctors of Law against two concurring judgments", it was not enacted either in 1826 or 1827.[5] The bill provided, inter alia, that faculty resolutions would retain the form of court judgments, except for the addition of an enforcement clause. A resolution of the Faculty of Law was to consist of an invocation, operative part and justification. It was stipulated that resolutions passed by the faculty on a complex appeal were to include the full content of the appellant's request, the arguments of the opposing party and the report of a clerk. However, the practice in this regard was different. The minutes of a meeting of professors and doctors of the law faculty on a single day sometimes included several cases that had been examined. An examined case was signed by the chairman of the meeting and the secretary. For each case, the day and place of the meeting were stated in the minutes. The participants were then listed, followed by a brief description of the case, stating the personal details of the parties, the subject matter of the dispute and the judgments of the Court of First Instance (or the judgment of the Court of Peace) and the Court of Appeal, which were contested by a party. The presence of at least five persons was required for a resolution to be adopted. This was the composition of the faculty, as a rule, in session, as well as when the case was dealt with by circulation. In such a case, the clerk prepared a written proposal of the content of the resolution, on which the other members of the faculty wrote "agreement with the clerk."[6]

If the law faculty, after reviewing the case and the judgments, found no violation of the law, then it formulated a conclusion at the end of the opinion that an appeal to the Court of Last (Third) Instance did not take place. The decision of the Faculty of Law that there were no legal grounds for an appeal to the Court of Last (Third) Instance did not contain a statement of reasons. In contrast, the faculty justified its resolution when it found that the courts had violated substantive or procedural rules, writing in the conclusion of the opinion that an appeal to the Court of Third Instance was legitimate. However, when it found that the appealed judgments were not compatible with each other it issued an opinion that a party without a resolution of the Law Faculty

---

5 Andrzej Dziadzio, "Udział Wydziału Prawa Uniwersytetu Jagiellońskiego w stosowaniu *Code Civil* w Wolnym Mieście Krakowie (1815–1833)", in *Miasto i państwo na przestrzeni dziejów. Studium historyczno-prawne. Księga Jubileuszowa z okazji czterdziestopięciolecia pracy naukowej oraz 70. urodzin profesora Tadeusza Maciejewskiego*, Warszawa, 2020, 189–202.

6 Dziadzio, "Udział Wydziału Prawa", 190.

could appeal to the Court of Last (Third) Instance. The court acted similarly when it found that a party had appealed judgments that did not differ in their content. It would then refer it to the proceedings before the Faculty of Law, making the determination of the appeal conditional on the faculty accepting that the rulings of the courts violated the law.

The *modus procedendi* developed on the basis of Article XV of the Constitution was quickly adopted and established in practice. A party challenging the content of concurring judgments of two court instances on the grounds of an infringement of the law addressed a request for an opinion from the Faculty of Law to the rector of Jagiellonian University. In the appeal sent, the appellant presented the essence of the case and pointed out *in concreto* the violation of the law by the courts. However, he had to comply with the limitation period for lodging an appeal on pain of rejection, which was eight days from the delivery of the Court of Appeal's judgment to the party. This time limit was set out in the Enforcement Ordinance of 1823. At the same time, the party was obliged to submit the judgments under appeal. The Faculty of Law could call upon a party to supplement the documents. As a rule, the reply to the appeal was filed by the litigation opponent of the appealing party.

When an appeal was received, the rector of the university would appoint a clerk in each case and summon the professors and doctors of law to a meeting, designating the day, time and place. The rector required the clerk to prepare a statement of position in writing, including a presentation of the factual and legal background to the case submitted. At the meeting of the Faculty of Law, the clerk would familiarise the other members with the file of the case and propose the content of the opinion. According to the resolution of the Assembly of Representatives, the law faculty meeting had to be held within 12 or 14 days of the receipt of the appeal. The obligation of the professors and doctors to give an opinion on the grounds of appeal to the Court of Last (Third) Instance within the two-week deadline required them to be constantly ready to perform this task. The increasing number of appeals filed with the rector over time meant that the professors and doctors of the Faculty of Law either dealt with them by circulation or issued resolutions on more than a dozen cases in a single day. This must in part have had a negative impact on the degree of fair examination of each case of judicial appeal. Thus, it sometimes happened that the Faculty of Law adopted resolutions in which the legal assessment of the case differed from the correct ruling of all court instances.

The exercise of the adjudicatory function given to the Faculty of Professors and Doctors of Law under Article XV of the Constitution was not an easy task. The Faculty of Law issued a legal opinion essentially having at its disposal the content of the judgments under appeal, the arguments of the appellant and, as a rule, the reply of the adverse party. Although it was in the interest of the party to demonstrate the violation of specific provisions of law in the appealed judgments, sometimes the type of violation of law had to be determined by the law faculty on its own, as there were no formal-legal criteria as to the content of the appeal filed. As a rule, however, the pleadings filed with the division contained a description of the status of the case, an indication of the violation of the law and the relevant demand. Judicial rulings in civil law disputes in the Free City of Cracow in light of the resolutions of the professors of the Faculty of Law were generally correct. In the case of the two unanimous court judgments, only about a quarter of the university opinions contained a view of a violation of substantive or procedural law. Moreover, from a review of the surviving judgments of the third instance court, it can be concluded that the number of cases in which it did not share the law faculty's view of a violation of the civil code remained at about one-fifth. An analysis of several cases in which judgments of lower instances were approved, despite the finding by the Faculty of Law of the existence of grounds for cassation certifies that the legal rationale was not always on the side of the professors of the faculty.

The most common examples of misapplication of the *Code civil* by the Krakow courts concerned the form of the contract for evidentiary purposes, the provisions on forced heirship under the law of succession or the determination by trial of the separation of property.[7] The misinterpretation of the provisions in this regard was due to the fact that they concerned legal institutions that did not exist in Austrian law applied by the courts until the introduction of the *Code civil*. The provisions of the *Code civil*, which were a legacy of French legal culture, were therefore the most difficult to interpret by Cracow's judges and professors in the Faculty of Law. Such legal constructions included, in particular, the inheritance provisions, which were a compromise in the French Code between the inheritance rules of written law (*droit écrit*) and customary law (*droit coutimière*) of pre-revolutionary France.

---

7 In one of the opinions issued, professors and doctors of law stated that the courts should grant a judgment in favour of a wife to establish a marital separation of property, as long as she demonstrated a "disorder" in her husband's business, causing her to fear that her dowry brought into the marriage would be at risk (Article 1443 of the *Code civil*). In contrast, the courts of all instances held that the wife's claim for property separation could be granted provided that she proved the amount of the dowry brought into the marriage. As the plaintiff did not provide proof of the amount of the dowry, the courts dismissed the claim. For more, see Andrzej Dziadzio, "Opinie profesorów i doktorów prawa Uniwersytetu Jagiellońskiego jako źródło badań nad stosowaniem Kodeksu Napoleon w Wolnym Mieście Krakowie", in *Krakowskie Studia z Historii Państwa i Prawa* 13/3 (2020), 308–309.

Thus, succession law cases resulted in decisions that did not fully correspond to the correct interpretation of the provisions of the *Code civil*.[8]

Difficulties in correctly interpreting the provisions of the *Code civil* were experienced by Cracow's courts in the case of legal constructions that restricted freedom of contract by imposing requirements on the forms of contracts entered into by parties to a contractual relationship. In the early days of the application of French law by Cracow's judges, there were cases of rulings that were based on a misunderstanding of the content of the provisions of the *Code civil*. French law was more formalised in terms of the forms of contracts concluded than Austrian law. Therefore, Cracow's judges did not immediately succeed in correctly assessing the institutions of French law. It was only the correct interpretation of the provisions by professors and doctors of law in appeal proceedings that shaped judicial practice in accordance with the actual content of French legislation. For example, Cracow's judges interpreted the content of Article 1341 of the *Code civil* as a statutory prohibition on refuting the content of a document by witness testimony. They overlooked that this provision regulated the construction of a form of contract for evidentiary purposes (*ad probationem*), which was typical of French law. In one case, two court instances recognised the validity of an oral land exchange agreement worth more than 150 francs on the basis of witness evidence. The courts admitted the witness evidence on the assumption that, since the rule prohibited this evidence against the document, it therefore *a contrario* allowed the witness evidence in the absence of a written agreement. It was only the Court of Last (Third) Instance that found that the lower courts had violated the evidentiary prohibition of article 1341 of the Napoleonic Code, following the opinion of the Faculty of Law.[9]

The second case in which French law formalised the form of contracts was that the *Code civil* for bilateral contracts required that a contract should be concluded in two identical copies with this fact clearly noted in the contract. Conclusion of a bilateral contract in one copy, or without mention in the contract of its two originals, entailed its nullity (Article of 1325 of the *Code civil*). Due to formal deficiencies, a party to the contract could bring an action in court to have it annulled, unless it had executed the contract itself. Cracow's

8 See Piotr Michalik, "Stosowanie przepisów prawa spadkowego *Code civil* przez sądy Wolnego Miasta Krakowa", in *Krakowskie Studia z Historii Państwa i Prawa* 14/3 (2021), 307. However, the opinions of the Faculty of Law have contributed to a better understanding of the nature of French inheritance law, although the professors of the Faculty of Law can be criticised for not fully understanding the special features of French inheritance law.

9 For more, see Dziadzio, "Opinie profesorów", 314.

courts, accustomed to the freedom of contract under Austrian law, which allowed the parties to choose any form of contract, recognised the validity of bilateral oral contracts or those concluded in writing in a single copy. For Cracow's courts, the validity of a contract drawn up in two copies was not subject to any doubt, but in a different form: written and notarial deed.[10]

Such a case was encountered by the Krakow courts in their adjudication practice and they fully recognised the claim of one of the parties to the contract to comply with its provisions. It was only the literal and grammatical interpretation of Article 1325 of the *Code civil*, carried out by the Faculty of Law in appeal proceedings, that led the Court of Last (Third) instance, guided by the opinion of professors and doctors of law, to rule that a contract concluded by the parties in a form not permitted by the *Code civil* was invalid. At this point it should be noted that the case law of the French or Baden Courts, unlike that of Cracow's courts, reached for a systemic and functional interpretation of Article 1325 of the *Code civil*, bearing in mind the need to safeguard freedom of contract and the principle of *pacta sunt servanda*. Indeed, they adopted the ruling line according to which a deed with private signatures containing a bilateral contract, although invalid due to violation of the disposition of Article 1325 *Code civil* (not having been drawn up in as many originals as there are parties with different interests), it could nevertheless be treated as the beginning of written evidence according to Article 1347 of the *Code civil*, permitting the taking of evidence by witnesses regarding the conclusion of a contract.[11] Noteworthy, however, are the examples of the opinions of the Faculty of Law of Jagiellonian University in which it referred to key principles of the *Code civil*, such as precisely the freedom of contract and the obligation to observe contracts, which were even more strongly expressed in Austrian law than in the French Code.[12]

One of the issues before the Faculty of Law was the interpretation of a notarial agreement whereby a contractual lien was created on real estate as security for possible claims under a concluded contract for the lease of landed property. The parties entered into a temporary lease contract for landed property, in which the tenant encumbered his house with a certain sum, represent-

10 Dziadzio, "Opinie profesorów", 309.

11 Andrzej Dziadzio, Dziadzio, "Vertragstypenzwang im Code civil? Gültigkeit gegenseitiger Verträge in der Judikatur der Freien Stadt Krakau (1815–1846)", in *Zeitschrift der Savigny-Stiftung für Rechtsgeschichte, Germanische Abteilung* 139 (2022), 281.

12 See Zeiller's commentary on Article 919 of the ABGB in *Materialien für Gesetztkunde und Rechtspflege in den österreichischen Erbstaaten*, Carl Joseph von Pratobevera (ed.), Wien, 1814, 182–183.

ing the amount of the deposit made in favour of the lessor, secured by a mortgage entry in his favour. However, the tenant stipulated in the contract that the lessor would only be able to enforce his claims under the lease from the mortgaged house for a period of six months after the termination of the lease. A few years after the termination of the lease, the tenant's successor, who had inherited the tenement, brought an action to have the mortgage cancelled. The Court of First Instance and the Court of Appeal unanimously dismissed the action for the deletion of the mortgage entry. The Faculty of Law, however, held that in their judgments the courts had violated Articles 1134, 1162 and 1163 of the *Code civil*. The professors and doctors of law made the assumption that a judgment in favour of the plaintiff should be determined by the fundamental *Code Civil* principle of freedom of contract and autonomy of the will of the parties.[13]

In the case law of the Faculty of Law of Jagiellonian University, we come across numerous examples of the interpretation of procedural rules of French legislation which affected proceedings before Cracow's courts. One of the more frequent violations of the general rules of civil procedure, found in the opinions of the Faculty of Law, was that the courts ignored the principle that the burden of proof rests on the one who asserts and not on the one who denies.[14] In particular, this was the case for claims by testamentary legatees for payment of the legacy by statutory heirs. The courts awarded the claim under the legatee's will, even though the amount claimed by the plaintiff, according to sued forced heirs, breached the mandatory portion guaranteed to them by the *Code civil*. The courts did not respect the principle that it was incumbent on the legatee to provide evidence of the amount of the estate in order to show that the amount of the legacy did not exceed the mandatory portion due to the forced heirs. Indeed, they provided a valuation of the estate, according to which an order for payment of the requested legacy would prejudice their rights to the mandatory portion. The plaintiff, claiming payment of the legacy in breach of the compulsory portion, should have proven that there was a greater estate left than the calculation provided by the defendants.[15] In

13 Dziadzio, "Udział Wydziału", 194–195.

14 The principle that the burden of proof rests with the plaintiff and not the defendant was stipulated in Art.1315 of the *Code civil*: "Whoever demands the performance of an obligation should prove it."

15 Jagiellonian University Archives (henceforth cited as JU Archives), ref. WP I 57, Faculty of Professors and Doctors of Law of Jagiellonian University (henceforth cited as JU Faculty of Law), meeting of 28 October 1822. In the above case, there were five sons of the heir who, according to Article 913 *C.c.*, were entitled to three-fourths of the estate. The testamentary bequest in this case should not exceed one-fourth of the value of the estate.

another case, the Faculty of Law, in an issued opinion, held that the plaintiff claiming a fee for an easement established on an owner's land must prove the existence of a limited the defendant owner should provide proof of removal from the mortgage books of the legal obligation incumbent on him, according to the principle of: *asserenti, non neganti, incumbit probatio*.[16]

An interesting issue from the point of view of the correctness of the courts' application of procedural provisions was the qualification of civil law disputes in the context of a claim of the inadmissibility of the judicial route. The opinions of the Faculty of Law, among several others, included a case in which the parties challenged the judicial route, arguing that the dispute concerned a matter of administrative (public) law and not civil law. This case is interesting in that the courts were faced with interpreting Article 6 of the Civil Code, which set the limits of freedom of contract by stating that "the laws pertaining to public order and good morals may not be infringed by private contracts."[17] The dispute was conducted by the Department of Public Revenue and Treasury in the Governing Senate, as the administrator of the national (state) property, with the lessee of an inn located on a public estate. The lessee brought an action before the court of first instance to terminate the lease. The Department of Revenue, as the defendant, raised a plea of inadmissibility of court proceedings on the grounds that in the lease contract the plaintiff had waived court proceedings, agreeing to the parties to the contract pursuing their claims in administrative proceedings. The Court of First Instance and the Court of Appeal dismissed the plea that the court lacked jurisdiction to hear the dispute, finding the contractual provision in which the parties had waived the court route to be a breach of the limit of freedom of contract, which was set by public order acts.[18]

In justifying their position, the courts cited Article XV of the Constitution of the Free City of Cracow, according to which "these two courts shall adjudicate in all cases regardless of their nature or the status of the persons." In the opinion of the courts, the contractual waiver of the judicial route in the adjudication of a civil dispute was not within the limits of freedom of contract, as it

---

As mentioned above, the Cracow' judges had, at the beginning of the application of the *Code civil* provisions on testamentary succession, some difficulties in correctly reading the institution of the reserve as a means of securing the succession rights of forced heirs, e.g., they granted the inheritance under the will to the testator's wife without showing the contents of the will, which prevented the forced heirs from claiming a breach of the compulsory part: see the session on 4 July 1822.

16 JU Archives, ref. WP I 57, JU Faculty of Law, meeting of 16 February 1830.

17 *Kodex Napoleona z przypisami*, 2 vols., Warszawa, 1808, 4.

18 JU Archives, ref. WP I 57, JU Faculty of Law, the meeting on 6 July 1829.

contravened the legal order. The law faculty, on the other hand, in its opinion, referred to Article 1712 of the *Code civil*, which allowed for the application of special provisions in relation to the lease of national property. Such provisions, in the opinion of the law faculty, were the provisions of the decree of 14 January 1812, in force from the time of the Duchy of Warsaw, according to which all receivables arising from contracts were subject to the jurisdiction of the administrative authorities.[19] On the basis of the cited provisions, the Faculty of Law argued that the parties, by excluding the judicial route in the lease agreement, did not so much violate public policy by doing so, but acted in accordance with its legal dimension! It must be assumed that the courts adjudicating the case found that the administrative route concerned the administrative enforcement of the rent, but regarded the claim for termination of the contract itself as a civil dispute, subject to judicial jurisdiction under Article XV of the Constitution. The position of the Krakow courts regarding the interpretation of the constitutional provision should be considered correct, contrary to the legal view of the law faculty.

The largest percentage of court rulings that were appealed to the Faculty of Law on the grounds of violation of procedural rules were payment disputes (approximately 65%).[20] As a rule, the source of these claims were contracts, often concluded orally. In these types of cases the appeals to the Faculty of Law most often involved allegations of defective conduct of the evidentiary proceedings, mainly through violation of the statutory conditions for the admissibility of oath evidence. For this reason, the law faculty's opinions were more concerned with assessing the courts' application of the procedural rules contained in the *Code civil* than the Code of Civil Procedure itself. It was a feature of French legislation that in the *Code civil* the norms of substantive law occurred in conjunction with procedural rules. The best example of this was precisely the law of obligations of the *Code civil*, where in Title III "on Contracts, or contractual obligations in general", entire Section VI, was devoted to the provisions for "proof of obligations and payment." The *Code civil* included, inter alia, provisions on the types of oaths and the legal conditions for taking this evidence, but the very definition of an oath was given in the Code of Civil Procedure.[21]

19 JU Archives, ref. WP I 57, JU Faculty of Law, the meeting on 6 July 1829.

20 Dziadzio, "Udział Wydziału", 189.

21 *Kodex postępowania cywilnego wyłuszczony przez swoie powody i przez przykłady, z rozwiązaniem pod każdym artykułem trudności, a oraz głównych zagadnień, nastręczających się w texcie, jako też z opisaniem znaczenia wszelkich wyrazów prawnych: dzieło przeznaczone dla uczących się prawa, dla osób trudniących się przystosowaniem przepisów*

The provisions of French law on oaths as a means of evidence in civil proceedings confirm that not only did the very essence of the contract in the *Code civil* have a foundation in Roman law, but also the Roman model had provisions on evidence in obligation relations. The *Code civil* followed Roman law in adopting, in articles 1357–1369, two types of oaths: a decisory oath, which one party tendered to another—and an oath administered to one party or the other by the court. A decisory oath was admissible only to establish the personal acts of the party to whom it was tendered. It could be ordered in any state of the case, even before any other evidence was adduced. It could only be tendered to the opposing party if it concerned acts common to both parties. The firmness of a decisory oath consisted on the fact that its evasion entailed the admission of a proven fact contrary to that covered by its content. The taking of an oath precluded the possibility of proving its falsity in civil proceedings; for when one party called for an oath, the other party was obliged either to tender it or take it, or to submit to the consequences of not taking it. It was not possible for the opposing party to refuse a proposed oath without the negative consequences of such a refusal. An oath could be ordered to be taken by one of the parties *ex officio* by the court in order to settle the dispute, but only if neither the action nor the allegations against it had been completely proven (justified) or completely devoid of evidence.[22]

Despite the clear tendency of the Civil Code to eliminate religious aspects from the law, it may be somewhat puzzling that an oath as a means of evidence of a firm nature in a civil trial was retained. Although the drafters of the code asked themselves whether the numerous examples of societal corruption undermined the rationality of maintaining the ancient institution of an oath, this doubt did not result in the elimination of this means of evidence from procedure. This was because French law, as mentioned above, prohibited the taking of witness evidence when a legal act with a value exceeding 150 francs was not concluded in written form or by notarial deed (Article 1341 of the *Code civil*). The form of a legal transaction for the purposes of evidence (*ad proba-*

---

procedury i dla wszystkich innych, którzy życzą poznać takowe a nie mogli oddawać się szczególney ich nauce, podług drugiéy edycyi przez J. A. Rogrona; przeł. na polski język z zastosowaniem prawodawstwa polskiego i własnem staraniem i nakładem wyd. przez Damazego Dzierożyńskiego, Warszawa, 1829, 29. Article 55 of the Code defined an oath as "a solemn declaration at which a party calls Deities to witness that the truth is asserted." The Code of Civil Procedure defined the conditions for the conduct of an oath by a judge of peace differently from the *Code Civil*, as a judge of peace could not order an oath *ex officio* because he was acting as a conciliator.

22 Bolesław Rotwand, "Przysięga jako dowód w procesie cywilnym", in *Kwartalnik Prawa Cywilnego i Karnego* 1/1–4 (1918), 448.

tionem) found in the *Code civil*, which in court excluded proceedings the evidence of witnesses, imposed, as it were, the necessity of maintaining an oath. Otherwise a party would be deprived of any opportunity to assert its claim if the written document was not prepared, or was lost or destroyed.

For the above reasons, it is understandable that in proceedings before Cracow's courts, an oath was a fairly frequently used means of evidence in payment disputes, as most claims of this type arose from contracts—as already mentioned—mostly concluded orally. The taking of evidence by oath was also the subject of numerous complaints to the Faculty of Law, alleging either a misclassification of the type of oath (firm or *ex officio*) that was admissible in the factual and legal state of a particular case, or an incompatible order to take the oath in court. The content of a decisory oath was determined by a party to the proceedings, but, as the law faculty instructed the courts, it was the court's duty to amend it if it included circumstances that had been admitted by the opposing party. The faculty in this case invoked the general rule of civil procedure that the facts admitted by a party were to be regarded by the court as proven.[23]

A common mistake repeated in court rulings was the administration of an oath *ex officio* according to its content established by the court in a situation where there was no—as the law faculty opinions put it—any "initial evidence" in the case. Cracow's courts thus had some difficulty in applying the provisions of the *Code civil*, which distinguished between a firm oath and an oath *ex officio*. The Law Faculty's opinions from the final period of its judicial function reflected a case in which the plaintiff, claiming payment of a certain amount, tendered an oath to the defendant, who, however, neither accepted it nor referred to it. The court, however, in such a state of affairs, instead of awarding the amount to the plaintiff, imposed an oath *ex officio* on her, although the court had no evidence in the case.[24]

In addition to instances of misapplication of oaths *ex officio* by the courts, where the action was completely devoid of evidence in the light of the facts established by the law faculty, a source of serious controversy between it and the courts was the issue of the very interpretation of the concept of "initial evidence", conditioning, according to the law faculty, the statutory admissibility of oaths *ex officio*. Namely, in one case, the courts ordered the plaintiff to

23 JU Archives, ref. WP I 57, JU Faculty of Law, meeting of 4 June 1817. This principle was reminded to the courts by the Faculty of Law in the first opinion issued under Article XV of the Constitution: see also the meeting of 19 November 1821 and 23 October 1822.

24 JU Archives, ref. WP I 57, JU Faculty of Law, the meetings on 6 February 1828, 17 July 1829, 15 June 1832, 12 September 1833 r.

reimburse the successors of a deceased person for whom he had performed certain services under a power of attorney. This is because the courts held that the evidence of the power of attorney was precisely a prerequisite for the admissibility of an oath *ex officio* ("the claim was not entirely devoid of evidence"), and, following its execution by the plaintiff, accepted the action. In contrast, the faculty of law, in its opinion in this case, assumed that such "initial evidence", justifying the admissibility of the plaintiff's oath *ex officio*, could only be the plaintiff's submission of receipts documenting the costs of actions arising from the power of attorney.[25] The Faculty of Law therefore concluded that there were grounds to allow the appeal. However, the Court of Last (Third) Instance confirmed the lawfulness of the appealed judgments.[26] Which legal position should therefore be considered correct?

The opinion of the professors and doctors of law does not appear to be correct in that the prerequisites for the admissibility of witness evidence and evidence of oaths ordered *ex officio* were treated equally. According to the *Code civil*, witness evidence could be admissible in respect of oral contracts exceeding 150 francs when the party provided "the beginning of evidence in writing" (Article 1347 of the *Code civil*); similarly, evidence of oaths ordered *ex officio* could be taken if the demand "was not completely devoid of evidence" (Article 1367 of the *Code civil*). The Faculty of Law equated the legal meaning of the two terms, assuming that the court could admit an oath *ex officio* if a party presented "the beginning of the evidence" (within the meaning of Article 1347 of the *Code civil*), rather than any evidence, even circumstantial, to justify the demand. The courts, on the other hand, rightly assumed that the two premises of the evidentiary prohibition did not coincide, since the prohibition of evidence of an oath *ex officio* came into play when the claim or allegation was not supported by any evidence (!). In the case analysed above, the courts considered the contents of the power of attorney on which the plaintiff based his claim as evidence within the meaning of the *Code civil* provision on an oath *ex officio*.

It should also be noted in favour of the Cracow courts that, in adjudicating civil cases, they tried to follow the principle of the free assessment of evidence, which was expressed in Article 1353 of the *Code civil*. The remnants of the formal theory of evidence in French procedure could be seen, inter alia, in

25 JU Archives, ref. WP I 57, JU Faculty of Law, meeting of 27 December 1824.

26 National Archives in Cracow (henceforth cited as ANKr,), WM 251, Judgment of the Court of First Instance of 6 April 1824, Judgments of the Court of Appeal of 15 September 1824 and 23 November 1824. The Court of Last (Third) Instance upheld the judgments of the lower courts in a judgment of 14 April 1825 (WM 187).

the provisions on oaths cited above and the prohibition of refuting the content of a document by witness testimony. However, the legal theory of evidence was nevertheless transferred to civil proceedings from the Austrian criminal procedure of 1803, which, as mentioned above, had the acceptance of the Cracow' legal community. The professors and doctors of law of Jagiellonian University were not free from this attachment to the legal theory of evidence. This is evidenced by one case, which concerned a claim for payment of a certain sum of money by the heirs of a professor and the rector of the university, Walenty Litwiński, brought by a woman caring for his mentally ill wife. As the basis of her claim, she presented a letter written in Litwiński's own handwriting, in which he promised to pay a certain amount for a service rendered by the plaintiff. The courts of both instances awarded the amount of 600 zlotys to the plaintiff, finding the evidence presented sufficient to rule in favour of the plaintiff.[27] However, following an appeal by the defendants, the Faculty of Law, in its opinion, found a procedural error on the basis that the letter submitted, in its view, constituted only "half of the evidence", with the result that the courts should order either an *ex officio* oath or the examination of witnesses.[28] As in the above-mentioned case, the Faculty of Law treated the letter submitted by the plaintiff only as "the beginning of written evidence" that required supplementary proof.

The undoubtedly positive side of the law faculty's supervision of the case law of Cracow's courts with regard to the use of a decisory (firm) oath in court proceedings was that it consistently instructed them that an oath was an extraordinary means of evidence with subsidiary application. In other words, the courts could not rely on a firm oath as a means of evidence if they had other evidence in the case, such as a letter presented by the defendant in which the plaintiff waived the benefit now claimed in the petition. The court in such a case was to rule on the basis of the document presented, not the decisory

27 ANKr, WM 190, Judgment of the Court of Appeal of 2 June 1824. Unfortunately, it was not possible to find the judgment of the Court of Last (Third) Instance in this case.

28 JU Archives, ref. WP I 57, JU Faculty of Law, meeting of 17 July 1824. The Faculty of Law stated in a brief opinion in its conclusion: "Bearing in mind that the letters by M. Padlewska's letters are not full evidence, but semi-evidence, yet the courts, in the face of such incomplete evidence from these letters, in the face of denials from Litwiński's successors, regardless of the fact that Marianna Padlewska herself referred to witnesses and oaths to prove her claim which was not fully proven, firmly decided to award the sum of 600 zlotys to Padlewska. Thus, having apparently violated Articles 1347 and 1367 of the *Code civil*, the Faculty of Law Professors and Doctors stipulates that an appeal in this case to the Court of Last (Third) Instance shall take place."

oath.[29] The Faculty of Law also limited the ability of the courts to use evidence of a firm oath in certain categories of civil cases, although the *Code civil* contained a general declaration that "the oath decisory may be tendered in any description of dispute whatsoever" (Article 1358 of the *C.c.*).

In this category of cases the Faculty of Law included an action to establish a right in rem, referring to the old Polish legal tradition and the evidentiary procedure provided for by the provisions of *Processus variarum recognitionum et inscriptionum in iudicio terrestri. Formulae inscription perpetuarum* of 1523.[30] In one case, the Faculty of Law considered the lawfulness of the refusal to register mortgages in favour of, inter alia, hospitals, collegiate churches and Jagiellonian University, encumbering the defendant's real estate. According to the faculty, the appellant representative of the national government had failed to prove the lawfulness of the transfer of the mortgage encumbrances to the respondent's hereditary estates by way of proof of entry of the disputed sums in the court books. The government's representative, relying on the provision of the Napoleonic Code that evidence of a decisory oath may be admissible in any case, demanded that it be filed by the defendant to prove the possession of the document of the taking of the hereditary estates together with the mortgage encumbrances. The faculty, in dismissing the claim, admonished the government's representative that he had attempted to prove a right in rem by oath, although such evidence was inadmissible because, as the opinion stated: "For a right in rem not by a firm oath, but by a tabular instrument by the constitutions referred to above (i.e., of 1523 and 1543 AD) should be indicated and proved."[31]

The participation of the professors and doctors of law in the administration of justice of the Free City of Cracow should be assessed positively, irrespective of the objections that may be raised against both the manner in which they performed the duty entrusted to them by the Constitution of 1815 and the accuracy of their legal opinions. The role of the Faculty of Law in shaping judicial practice in the Republic of Cracow must be fully appreciated. Its

---

29 JU Archives, ref. WP I 57, JU Faculty of Law, meeting of 3 June 1826. The faculty stated in its opinion: "Considering further that evidence by oath is extraordinary, and therefore only takes place where there are no ordinary ones, the courts of both instances, by giving place to the oath to be performed by Drobner, irrespective of the receipt given by him, insofar as the plaintiff has not demanded payment of the claimed sum for 8 years, have infringed Article 1322 of the *Code civil.*" Compare also the sessions of 4 September 1826 and 8 March 1828.

30 See *Volumina Constitutionum*, Part 1: 1493–1549, vol. 1: 1493–1526, Stanisław Grodziski, Irena Dwornicka, Wacław Uruszczak (eds.), Warszawa, 1996, 401.

31 JU Archives, ref. WP I 57, JU Faculty of Law, meeting of 22 March 1828.

legal opinions often influenced the proper interpretation of the *Code civil* by the courts. This was of particular importance in the situation of the polycentric legal system of the Free City of Cracow, in which, in addition to French law, Cracow's judges had to refer to Austrian law or old Polish law in their rulings.

The analysis of the opinions allows for a general observation that a large group of appeals filed by the parties on the violation of procedural rules concerned the *Code civil's* regulation of evidence. In particular, the most frequent basis was the courts' admission of evidence in the form of a firm and *ex officio* oath, contrary to the regulations. An oath was widely used in civil disputes adjudicated by Cracow's courts for the reason that the majority of court cases concerned claims for payment, in which—due to statutory limitations on the possibility of taking evidence from witnesses—an oath was the only means for a party to pursue a claim. The law faculty's opinions attest that the general rule of civil procedure, which the courts violated most often in the adjudicated cases, was to disregard the statutory injunction that the burden of proof is on the plaintiff, not the defendant. On the other hand, the courts correctly determined their subject matter jurisdiction in adjudicated cases, despite the sometimes different position of professors and doctors of law.

CHAPTER 8

The Development of German Civil Procedure from the 16th to the 20th Century

Martin Löhnig

1 Starting Point: The Cameral Procedure

The rules of cameral procedure were rooted in the common law procedural law of the ecclesiastical courts. They gradually formed according to practical needs. The respective Reichskammergerichtsordnungen of 1500, of 1521 and finally of 1548/1555 represent the focal points of this development. In this respect, too, the Reichskammergericht played an essential role in the implementation of written common procedural law in Germany. However, essential aspects of procedural law remained unregulated by law and left to judicial practice or the "common decisions" of the court. The procedure was exclusively written and therefore dominated by the appointment system (*Terminsystem*): because the procedure was based on written recesses, there were as many appointments as there were procedural acts of the parties, compliance with which was incumbent on the parties.[1] In addition, there was the contingency maxim (*Eventualmaxime*), according to which, in order to accelerate the proceedings, similar competing procedural acts were also to be filed simultaneously.[2] Cameral procedure was governed by the disposition maxim (*Dispositionsmaxime*) and the principle of submission (*Beibringungsgrundsatz*). The evidence procedure (*Beweisverfahren*) was also written. The basis for the collection of evidence was the written records of witnesses, which were attached to the files. The cameral procedure had a considerable influence on the German territorial court systems, which adopted its procedural principles in part verbatim. In the territories of the Holy Roman Empire of the German Nation, civil proceedings were conducted until the late 18th century according to the common law procedure, whose roots lie in the Roman canon law of

1 Bettina Dick, *Die Entwicklung des Kameralprozesses nach den Ordnungen von 1495–1555*, Köln, Wien, 1981, 104 ff.

2 Dick, *Die Entwicklung des Kameralprozesses*, 112 ff.

 | DOI:10.1163/9789004736672_010

procedure[3] and the statuary laws of the upper Italian cities. The procedure, with all the different manifestations it found, was always "written, indirect and secret, [it] adheres to legal rules of evidence, the contingent maxim and a division of proceedings."[4]

2 The Break with Common Law

With the Corpus Iuris Fridericianum of 26 April 1781, Prussia gave itself a code of procedure whose instruction procedure (*Instruktionsverfahren*) broke thoroughly with the common law procedure. This new procedure, with a judicial determination of facts strictly divorced from disputes over questions of law, served first and foremost to determine the material truth independently of the actions of the parties;[5] as a result, lawyers became state-salaried assistant counsels.[6] In addition, litigants were to be protected against arbitrary treatment. In an absolutist state model, civil proceedings do not serve solely to enforce private claims, but have above all the function of enforcing certain state concepts of order and justice.[7] Even if in the end the Prussian Instruktionsverfahren could not prevail due to factual deficiencies and the history of its almost one hundred years of validity must be told as the history of numerous reforms and reform attempts:[8] the prelude to procedural reform had

3 See Peter Landau, "Die Anfänge der Prozeßrechtswissenschaft in der Kanonistik des 12. Jahrhunderts", in *Der Einfluß der Kanonistik auf die europäische Rechtskultur*, Orazio Condorelli, Franck Roumy, Mathias Schmoeckel (eds), Cologne, 2010, 7 ff.

4 Gerhard J. Dahlmanns, *Der Strukturwandel des deutschen Zivilprozesses im 19. Jahrhundert*, Aalen, 1971, 17.

5 The quotations are from a letter by Svarez from 1785, printed in Adolf Stölzel and Carl Gottlieb Svarez, *Ein Zeitbild aus der zweiten Hälfte des achtzehnten Jahrhunderts*, Berlin, 1885, 19.

6 Compare Martin Löhnig, "Are lawyers still needed or can they go? Zur Geschichte der Anwaltschaft im 19. Jahrhundert", in *Justiz und Baukultur im 19. Jahrhundert. Beiträge zur Tagung: 150 Jahre Gerichts- und Gefängnisbau am Görlitzer Postplatz vom 24. bis 26. September 2015*, Andreas Bednarek et al. (eds), Görlitz, 2018, 86 ff.

7 Cf. Martin Löhnig, "Der Zivilprozess zwischen Staat und Gesellschaft bei Grolman", in *Naturrecht und Staat in der Neuzeit*, Jens Eisfeld, Martin Otto, Louis Pahlow, Michael Zwanzger (eds), Tübingen, 2013, 420.

8 Knut Wolfgang Nörr, *Reinhardt und die Revision der allgemeinen Gerichts-Ordnung für die Preußischen Staaten*, Tübingen, 1975. See Martin Ahrens, *Prozeßreform und einheitlicher Zivilprozess: Einhundert Jahre legislative Reform des deutschen Zivilverfahrens vom Ausgang des 18. Jahrhunderts bis zur Verabschiedung der Reichszivilprozeßordnung*, Tübingen, 2007, 83 ff.

been made[9] just as the unity of German civil procedural law had been shattered.

After the dissolution of the Holy Roman Empire of the German Nation, the French civil procedure soon joined the common law and Prussian civil procedure as a third model. In France—and thus also in the former Prussian, Bavarian and Hessian territories on the left bank of the Rhine—the Code de procédure civile came into force in 1807. In 1809, a new code of procedure closely based on the Code was enacted in the Kingdom of Westphalia.[10] In 1811, the Code came into force in the Grand Duchy of Berg.[11] After the Congress of Vienna, French law continued to apply as "Rhenish law" in these territories, which fell back to Prussia, Bavaria and Hesse.[12] What remained was a judicial constitution characterised by revolutionary principles with an independent administration of justice,[13] in which a large part of the principles that are still decisive today had already been fully developed.[14] The executive and judiciary were clearly separated, all citizens were equal before judge and law, publicity and orality were basic principles of every court proceeding, and the requirements for the professional competence of judges were strict. French civil procedural law as such, on the other hand, was largely unaffected by the philosophy of the Revolution;[15] it went back to the regulations of an Or-

---

9 See also Knut Wolfgang Nörr, *Naturrecht und Zivilprozess. Studien zur Geschichte des deutschen Zivilprozeßrechts während der Naturrechtsperiode bis zum beginnenden 19. Jahrhundert*,Tübingen, 1976, 24 ff.

10 On this Heinz Mohnhaupt, "Richter und Gerichtspraxis im Verfassungsgefüge des Königreichs Westphalen", in *Napoleon und das Königreich Westphalen. Herrschaftssystem und Modellstaatspolitik*, Andreas Hedwig, Klaus Malettke, Karl Murk (eds), Marburg, 2008, 167–190; idem, "Die Gerichtspraxis zum Code civil im Königreich Westphalen zwischen Transplantation und Restauration (1807–1813)", in *Richterliche Anwendung des Code civil in seinen europäischen Geltungsbereichen außerhalb Frankreichs*, Barbara Dölemeyer, Heinz Mohnhaupt, Alessandro Somma (eds.), Frankfurt/Main, 2006, 37–60. A first commentary was also published immediately: Johann W. Rosenthal, *Die neue bürgerliche Prozeß-Ordnung des Königreichs Westphalen*, Quedlinburg, 1809.

11 See also Martin Löhnig, "La réforme de la justice dans le Grand-Duché de Berg: de la réception de l'organisation judiciare française en Allemagne", *Revue historique de droit français et étranger* (2012), 255 ff

12 Werner Schubert, *Französisches Recht in Deutschland zu Beginn des 19. Jahrhunderts. Zivilrecht, Gerichtsverfassungsrecht und Zivilprozeßrecht*, Cologne, Vienna, 1977.

13 Adolf Klein, "Die rheinische Justiz und der rechtsstaatliche Gedanke in Deutschland", in *Recht und Rechtspflege in den Rheinlanden 1819–1969. Festschrift zum 150jährigen Bestehen des Oberlandesgerichts Köln*, Adolf Klein, Josef Wolffram (eds.), Cologne, 1969, 113 ff.

14 Antonio Grilli, "Konzeptionen für die Justiz der Rheinlande in der französischen Zeit", in *Napoleonische Herrschaft in Deutschland und Italien-Verwaltung und Justiz*, Christoph Dipper, Wolfgang Schieder, Reiner Schulze (eds.), Berlin, 1995, 243 ff.

15 Schubert, *Französisches Recht*, 570.

donnance of Louis XIV,[16] which had created a uniform procedural law for France for the first time. Nevertheless, revolutionary demands could be fulfilled on this basis, for example, in that oral and public proceedings were to be conducted (Art. 87 ff. CdPC), and the principles of party rule (*Parteiherrschaft*) and negotiation maxims (*Verhandlungsmaxime*) came into play. The Rhine Province was thus an enclave of liberal judicial constitution in the respective states. This aspect is not dealt with, or only marginally, in many works on the reception of French law in the Rhineland,[17] although French procedural law and French court constitutions probably had a much more lasting effect in 19th-century Germany than the *Code Napoléon*. The gaps and shortcomings of French civil procedural law—of which the contemporaries were well aware[18]—initially took a back seat to the function of safeguarding freedom that was attributed to the procedure.[19]

The development of German civil procedural law in the 19th century can be described as a gradual adaptation of civil procedure in the individual German states that emerged after 1806 to the maxims of French procedural law. Finally, a French-inspired draft reform emerged in Prussia in 1864.[20] In Bavaria, an even more French-influenced code of civil procedure came into force in 1869 with the Code of Civil Procedure for the Kingdom of Bavaria (*Prozeßordnung in bürgerlichen Rechtsstreitigkeiten für das Königreich Bayern*).[21] The unity of German civil procedural law, broken by Prussia in 1781, was finally restored a good hundred years later under Prussian leadership with the Civil Procedure Code of 1877/79 (*Reichszivilprozeßordnung*). In this context, the

16 *Ordonnance civile touchantla réformation de justice du mois d'Avril 1667*=First part of the Code Louis elaborated by Jean-Baptiste Colbert and published in 1667/1670; see on this Alfred Aymé, *Colbert promoteur des grandes ordonnances de Louis XIV*, Remquet, 1860.

17 See e.g., Elisabeth Fehrenbach, *Der Kampf um die Einführung des Code Napoléon in den Rheinbundstaaten,* Wiesbaden, 1973; Helmut Berding, *Napoleonische Herrschafts- und Gesellschaftspolitik im Königreich Westfalen 1807–1813*, Göttingen, 1973; but Schubert, *Französisches Recht*, footnote 13.

18 On this Elisabeth Koch, "Zum Einfluß des Code de procédure civil auf die deutsche Zivilprozeßrechtsreform", in *Französisches Zivilrecht in Europa während des 19. Jahrhunderts*, Reiner Schulze (ed), Berlin, 1994, 162 ff.

19 Ahrens, *Prozeßreform*, 50 ff.

20 The text can be found in *Entwurf und Motive einer Prozeß-Ordnung in bürgerlichen Rechtsstreitigkeiten für den Preußischen Staat*, Werner Schubert (ed.), Goldbach, 1994.

21 Annotated by Marquard Adolph Barth, *Kommentar zur neuen Zivilprozessordnung für das Königreich Bayern*, Nördlingen, 1871; Albert Vierling, *Die Prozeßordnung in bürgerlichen Rechtsstreitigkeiten für das Königreich Bayern mit Erläuterungen*, Nördlingen, 1870; Johann Wernz, *Commentar zur Prozeßordnung in bürgerlichen Rechtsstreitigkeiten*, München, 1871; Johann Nepomuk von Lengriesser, *Leitfaden zur Civilprozeßordnung für das Königreich Bayern*, München, 1871.

Prussian draft from 1864 had "significance as important preliminary work."[22] A conclusive but quite incomplete narrative, because the roots of the *Reichszivilprozeßordnung* are to be found neither in France nor in Prussia, but in Hanover.

3 The Birth of Modern German Civil Procedure in Hanover

In the Kingdom of Hanover,[23] a temporary liberalisation occurred following the bourgeois revolution of 1848, at the end of the reign of Ernst August (1837–1851) and in the early years of George V (1851–1866). This phase also saw a fundamental reform of the organisation of justice, which was flanked by two new codes of procedure, the Civil Procedure Code of 8 November 1850 (BPO)[24] and the Criminal Procedure Code of the same date. These reforms were driven forward by Otto von Düring, who was appointed Minister of Justice in 1848,[25] who appointed the Hanoverian lawyer Adolf Leonhardt as an academic assistant in his ministry and entrusted him significantly with the drafting of the reform laws. We must remember this name because Leonhardt himself later became Minister of Justice in Hanover (1865) and—after the annexation of Hanover by Prussia in 1866—also in Prussia (1867–1879).[26] He is the father of modern German civil procedure, the foundations of which still exist today. Leonhardt designed a completely new type of procedure in 1850. In Germany, a new fourth type of procedure existed alongside the common law, the Prussian and the French. On the one hand—following the revolutionary demands raised in the Vormärz period[27]—it placed the oral and public[28] proceedings

22 *Entwurf und Motive einer Prozeß-Ordnung in bürgerlichen Rechtsstreitigkeiten für den Preußischen Staat*, Werner Schubert (ed.), Goldbach, 1994, xxxi.

23 On the historical background, see Bertram Mijndert, *Das Königreich Hannover—Kleine Geschichte eines vergangenen deutschen Staates*, Hannover, 2003.

24 Sammlung der Gesetze, Verordnungen und Ausschreiben für das Königreich Hannover 1850, Abtheilung I, 341 ff.

25 On the person of Düring, see Katrin Rieke, "Otto Albrecht von Düring", in *300 Jahre Oberlandesgericht Celle*, Norbert Steinau (ed.), Celle, 2012, 52 f.; Bernhard Mühlhan, "Düring Otto Albrecht von", in *Neue Deutsche Biographie* 4 (1959), 170 f.

26 On the person of Leonhardt, see Werner Schubert, "Leonhardt, Adolf", in *Neue Deutsche Biographie* 14 (1985), 253 f.

27 See also Martin Löhnig, "Introducing the participation of laymen into the judicial system in 19th century Germany—The Exampla of Bavaria", in *Popular Justice in Europa 1750–1870*, Emanuel Berger, Emilié Delivré (eds.), Bologna, 2014, 115.

28 The parties could not dispose of the publicity, which could only be restricted under narrow conditions; according to Leonhardt, they served a higher purpose, see Adolph

with genuine alternating speech at the centre of civil proceedings. On the other hand, he framed this procedure with common law elements, thus standing, as it were, between common and French civil procedure. The "common law mass of proceedings" previously prepared in various drafts was thus "broken on the ideas of the bourgeois revolution."[29]

The principle of orality (*Mündlichkeitsgrundsatz*) is "more correctly expressed" by Leonhardt as the "principle of immediacy" (*Unmittelbarkeitsgrundsatz*).[30] The two principles, which are indeed closely related, are thus not yet clearly distinguished; Leonhardt may have been primarily concerned with the elimination of the "probably most profound feature"[31] of the common process, the immediacy (*Mittelbarkeit*), one only has to think of the sending of files, and the secrecy inevitably associated with it.[32] According to common law, only the content of the files had been decisive (*quod non in actis non in mundo*). Now, the subject matter of the proceedings was solely the oral submissions of the parties within the framework of the hearing, which—even if several dates took place—now formed a unit. The *Eventualmaxime* that characterised the written procedure no longer applied. The maxim of negotiation (*Verhandlungsgrundsatz*) applied, but without full party control; in this way, a streamlined conduct of the proceedings was to be ensured.[33] The form of oral proceedings, which would be codified in the Imperial Code of Civil Procedure in 1877/79, already appears here.

This oral hearing, which could be divided into different factual sections if necessary, ended with a judgement on the evidence (which, in deviation from the common-law interlocutory evidence (*Beweisinterlokut*), was, however, binding only on the recognising court). This was followed by the evidentiary procedure (*Beweisverfahren*), which had a strong common law character; here, the principle of orality and immediacy applied only to a limited extent, be-

Leonhardt, *Die Justizgesetzgebung des Königreichs Hannover unter besonderer Berücksichtigung der Regierungs- und ständischen Motive zum practischen Gebrauche*, vol. 2: *Die bürgerliche Proceßordnung und deren Nebengesetze*, Hanover, 1851, 55.

29 Ahrens, *Prozeßreform*, 481.

30 Adolph Leonhardt, *Die Justizgesetzgebung*, 13

31 Compare Dahlmanns, *Der Strukturwandel*, 18.

32 However, the Badische Prozeßordnung in bürgerlichen Rechtsstreitigkeiten of 1831 in §§ 1112 ff. BadPO 1831 at least softened the written nature of the proceedings to such an extent that it allowed the written proceedings to end with an oral final hearing—although this was dispensable in numerous exceptional cases; other individual states followed this model, cf. Johann Christoph Schwartz, *Vierhundert Jahre deutsche Zivilprozeßgesetzgebung*, Berlin, 1898, 601.

33 Ahrens, *Prozeßreform*, 645 ff.

cause Leonhardt allowed evidence to be taken by a judge commissioned to do so. The common law rules of evidence also continued to apply to a large extent. The Civil Procedure Code thus did not arrive at the principle of free judicial assessment of evidence. If the case was ready for decision, the court had to close the hearing and pass a judgement in closed session, which had to be pronounced within a week. The sole ordinary legal remedy was the appeal (Berufung), which opened up a full second instance of the facts. Enforcement, if necessary, was carried out according to the French model by a court bailiff to be appointed by the plaintiff. All in all, a "groundbreaking new model of litigation",[34] which came into being on perhaps a historically unique occasion. The Civil Code of Procedure of the Kingdom of Hanover was soon dubbed the "model book of procedural reform."[35]

On 17 July 1862, the Commission for the Drafting of a Common Civil Procedure Law of the German Confederation (*Deutscher Bund*) was appointed.[36] It was not by chance that it met in Hanover—the choice of the conference venue testifies to the high esteem in which the Code of Civil Procedure was held and also signified a certain setting of the course in terms of content, especially since Adolf Leonhardt had been appointed as a member of the Commission for the Kingdom of Hanover, who thus had a home game, so to speak. His Hanoverian Code of Procedure was chosen as the working basis. Between autumn 1862 and July 1864, the Commission then drew up a draft law, which was discussed in a second reading between February 1865 and February 1866 and—despite a few deviations—was largely based on the model of the Civil Procedure Code of the Kingdom of Hanover. Even though the taking of evidence was still separated from the first stage of the trial according to the common law model, the threshold was nevertheless lowered considerably. The evidentiary judgement was replaced by a non-binding evidentiary order, which marked the transition to the evidentiary procedure. In addition, the draft abandoned the statutory rules of evidence (*Beweisregeln*) and arrived at the principle of free assessment of evidence (*Grundsatz der freien Beweiswürdigung*).[37] As a result, the central principle of immediacy, unlike in the Civil Procedure Code, now also applied in principle to the pro-

34 Ahrens, *Prozeßreform*, 481.

35 Wilhelm Endemann, "Betrachtungen über einige Hauptgrundsätze des preußischen Entwurfs einer Civilprozeßordnung", *AcP* 49 (1866), 1–42.

36 ProtDBV 1862, § 243 (412 ff.).

37 Initially, this was a discussion of criminal procedure, which was then also received in the field of civil procedure, cf. the fundamental monograph by Wilhelm Endemann, *Die Beweislehre des Zivilprozesses*, Heidelberg, 1860.

cedural stage of the taking of evidence. On 30 April 1866, the Commission submitted the draft with minutes to the Federal Assembly,[38] which referred it to the Committee for the Establishment of a Federal Court on 19 May 1866. On 21 June 1866, the Committee requested that the draft be sent to the governments of the individual states, which were to declare their support for it. By this time, the war between the German Confederation and Prussia had already broken out; the motion was accepted by the Federal Assembly, which had been decimated by Prussia and its allies.[39]

After the foundation of the North German Confederation through the entry into force of the Federal Constitution on 1 July 1867, the project of a uniform code of civil procedure was immediately taken up again, this time of course on Prussian initiative. The constitutional environment had changed completely, for now a federal state existed with corresponding legislative competence and Prussia, now unchallenged in dominance, went from being a stumbling block to being the driving force. At the Federal Council meeting of 4 September 1867, Prussia requested the appointment of a commission to prepare a draft code of procedure in civil disputes.[40] The president of the commission was Adolf Leonhardt, by then Prussian Minister of Justice. The commission deliberated from January 1868 to 20 July 1870. These deliberations[41] can be read, as it were, as the third reading of the draft created in Hanover.[42] Prussia thus worked with looted property from the Kingdom of Hanover, which had been annexed in 1866, in terms of both content and personnel.

When the draft of a code of civil procedure for the North German Confederation was completed in September 1870, which did not bring any substantial innovations (Schubert characterises the negotiations as "not very decisive and not very creative"[43]), it was destined for a fate just as unfavourable as that of its predecessor. The North German Confederation dissolved and, in the course of

38 *Protocolle der Commission zur Berathung einer allgemeinen Civilprozeßordnung für die deutschen Bundesstaaten*, Werner Schubert (ed.), 18 vols., Frankfurt/Main, 1985.

39 ProtDBV 1866, § 188 (243).

40 *Protokolle der Kommission zur Ausarbeitung des Entwurfs einer Civilprozeßordnung für die Staaten des Norddeutschen Bundes*, Werner Schubert (ed.), vol. 1, Frankfurt/Main, 1985, xvii.

41 *Protokolle der Kommission zur Ausarbeitung des Entwurfs einer Civilprozeßordnung für die Staaten des Norddeutschen Bundes*, Werner Schubert (ed.), 5 vols., Frankfurt/Main, 1985.

42 Martin Ahrens, "Von Hannover nach Berlin—Wegmarken der Prozessrechtsentwicklung", in *Wendepunkte der Rechtswissenschaft*, Werner Heun, Frank Schorkopf (eds.), Göttingen, 2014, 136.

43 *Protokolle der Kommission zur Ausarbeitung des Entwurfs einer Civilprozeßordnung für die Staaten des Norddeutschen Bundes*, xx.

the accession of the South German states, a new German Confederation, the German Empire, was created with the constitution of 1 January 1871. Some of these southern German states, namely Baden,[44] Württemberg[45] and Bavaria[46] had just passed procedural codes after long reform deliberations and did not agree at all to the North German draft coming into force in their territories.

4 The Imperial Code of Civil Procedure of 1879

The "Draft of a German Code of Civil Procedure and its Reasons. Edited by the Royal Prussian Ministry of Justice"[47] brought new momentum. Adolf Leonhardt himself is said to have corrected a copy of the North German draft in autumn 1870, thereby creating the framework for a new code of procedure. The concept of immediacy and orality continued to dominate in the draft that Leonhardt drew up with his colleagues on this basis. On the other hand, the two-part procedure originally favoured by Leonhardt[48] had been completely eliminated; instead, the model of oral proceedings had also been extended to the taking of evidence. The hearing of facts and the taking of evidence were now no longer separated from each other, and the court orders on evidence only had a procedural function. Leonhardt had thus abandoned a final defining element of the common law procedure, but also of his own Code of Procedure of 1850.[49] Leonhardt seems to have distinguished himself by a pronounced capacity for self-criticism and probably wanted to deliver a clear, politically enforceable procedural model again after the North German negotiations, which were not very fruitful in terms of content. This draft was finally passed as law without any significant changes.

On 1 January 1879, the new Code of Procedure was finally able to come into force as the Reichszivilprozeßordnung. It is the result of a productive competition and synthesis of procedural models, especially in the long Hanover deliberations in the late phase of the German Confederation. In these, the principle of orality, as regulated in the Civil Procedure Code of the Kingdom of

44 *Prozeß-Ordnung in bürgerlichen Rechtsstreitigkeiten für das Großherzogthum Baden* (1864).

45 *Civilprozeß-Ordnung* (1868).

46 *Prozeßhandlung in bürgerlichen Rechtsstreitigkeiten für das Königreich Bayern* (1869).

47 N.N., *Entwurf einer deutschen Zivilprozeßordnung nebst Begründung. Edited by the Royal Prussian Ministry of Justice*, Berlin, 1871.

48 Compare Dahlmanns *Der Strukturwandel*, 54 ff.

49 Ahrens, *Prozeßreform*, 615.

Hanover, prevailed in an expanded form as a procedural model.[50] Thus a far-reaching consensus had been reached on the basic lines of procedural reform in Germany. After the foundation of the German Empire, the Hanoverian procedure, which was divided into two parts according to the model of the common law procedure, was transferred into an independent, undivided procedure by its author Adolf Leonhardt. The *Reichszivilprozeßordnung* thus not only realised legal unity, but also, as the result of decades of work, brought to fruition a completely new, systematic and principled dogmatic edifice. A building whose shell was erected during the time of the German Confederation and which still exists today despite ongoing renovation work.

The inspiration for the first renovations came from Austria. There, a new Code of Civil Procedure[51] came into force in 1898. Franz Klein,[52] who drafted this code of procedure, oriented himself to the principles developed during the time of the German Confederation in the form that these had found in the Reichszivilprozeßordnung. However, based on a different understanding of the process than Adolph Leonhardt, he went a step further: away from the liberal and towards the "social civil process". He did not understand the process as a continuation of the struggle on the market by other means, but as a social conflict,[53] so that the administration of justice had to appear to him as a state welfare task.[54] Moreover, in shaping the structure of the procedural process by strengthening the power of the judge at the expense of the negotiation maxim,[55] he was able to take into account the criticism that had meanwhile been levelled at the German Code of Civil Procedure. The German Code of Civil Procedure and the Austrian Code of Civil Procedure are therefore two fruits of the same tree that grew in Hanover, but the Austrian fruit did not ripen until 20 years later.

---

50 Ahrens, *Prozeßreform*, 639.

51 Law of 1 August 1895 on judicial proceedings in civil disputes (Code of Civil Procedure), RGBL. no. 113/1895.

52 On Klein as a person, see Hans Schima, "Klein, Franz", in *Neue Deutsche Biographie* 11 (1977), 738 f.

53 Mario Marinelli, "Die Konzeption des Rechts und des Prozesses von Franz klein im Wein des Fin de Siècle", in *Die Aktualität der Prozeß- und Sozialreform Franz Klein*, Mario Marinelli, Ena-Marlis Bajons, Peter Böhm (eds.), Vienna, 2015, 31 ff.

54 Peter Böhm, "Der Streit um die Verhandlungsmaxime. Zum Einfluß der Verfahrenstheorie des 19. Jahrhunderts auf das gegenwärtige Prozeßverständnis", *Ius Commune* 7 (1978), 136 ff., emphasises the character of the Austrian Code of Civil Procedure as a "political code" that formulates a rejection of the belief in the self-regulating powers of purely individualistic endeavours.

55 Walther J. Habscheid, "Richtermacht oder Parteifreiheit. Über Entwicklungstendenzen des modernen Zivilprozeßrechts", *Zeitschrift für den Zivilprozeß* 81 (1968), 175.

Friedrich Stein, who we still encounter today in the title of the most important commentary on the German Code of Civil Procedure, the "Stein/Jonas", wrote in 1921 in the preface to his *Grundriß des Zivilprozeßrechts*: "For me, the trial is technical law in its very sharpest form, dominated by changing expediencies, devoid of eternal values."[56] This statement by the scholar, who died in 1923, is the statement of a classical liberal proceduralist, a determined opponent of reforms modelled on Austrian civil procedural law. Thus, the competition between two models of civil procedure already dates back to the Empire[57] and extended into the Weimar period, which then gained in importance due to the catalyst of the crises of the war and post-war period.[58] Adolf Baumbach, who founded Baumbach's Commentary on the Code of Civil Procedure in 1924, which is still published today, would have strongly disagreed with Friedrich Stein. In the introduction to the second edition of his commentary, published in 1925, he writes: 'Every code of procedure stands in indissoluble relations to the state, social and economic structure of its time, which a cultural historian could develop from it like the zoologist develops the body of a vertebrate from its skeleton.'[59] According to this, civil procedure is not a matter that obeys only technical necessities, and certainly not one that would suffice and legitimise itself out of itself.

After the end of the Great War, the question arose as to whether civil procedural law serves exclusively to enforce the subjective rights of the parties.[60] Whether it creates, as it were, a state-free space in which the state provides a neutral arbitrator in the form of the judge, but leaves the parties complete control over all elements of the proceedings. Whether civil procedural law is simply a "rule of combat for the parties' dispute, which takes place in the free play of forces before a court that remains passive."[61] Or whether civil proce-

56 Friedrich Stein, *Grundriß des Zivilprozeßrechts*, Tübingen, 1921, iii.

57 See also the debates at the German Jurists' Days of the imperial era on strengthening the power of the judge to conduct proceedings (1902), on court proceedings and the right of appeal (1908) and on orality and immediacy (1912).

58 However, the amendment to the district court on 1 June 1909 had already strengthened the judicial powers to conduct proceedings in the district court and introduced the office operation for service of process and summonses.

59 Adolf Baumbach, *Taschenausgabe der neuen Zivilprozeßordnung mit Entlastungsverordnung, Gerichtsverfassungsgesetz und Einführungsgesetzen mit erläuternden Einführungen und Anmerkungen*, Berlin, 1925, 2.

60 For a detailed discussion, see Martin Löhnig, "Weimarer Zivilprozeßrecht", in *Weimarer Zivilrechtswissenschaft*, Martin Löhnig, Mareike Preisner (eds.), Tübingen 2014, 135–150.

61 Friedrich Stein and Martin Jonas, *Die Zivilprozeßordnung für das Deutsche Reich*, Tübingen, 1925, Introduction § 6, xxxi.

dure also serves state purposes[62] such as the enforcement of certain postulates of justice or the fulfilment of community tasks. Or whether—as Martin Jonas put it in 1925—on the basis of a modern conception of the state, "in addition to the idea of security recognised by the liberal concept of the state alone, the idea of welfare"[63] is being promoted, the realisation of which requires state intervention in the struggle of the parties. Or whether, in addition, civil procedural law is even placed predominantly or exclusively in the service of a state for which the enforcement of the rights of individuals becomes a by-product in the proving of the legal order. Whether, in other words, "the powers of the parties must take a back seat to consideration for the national community",[64] and the adversarial opposite of the liberal basic rule applies: "The judge is the master of the proceedings."[65]

In 1924, the first drastic change in liberal German civil procedure took place, which was based on the cornerstones of orality, uniformity of the trial, party operation and immediacy of the taking of evidence and regulated the classical contentious trial. In the words of Adolf Baumbach, the novella "laid an axe to the foundations of the present civil procedure."[66] For Martin Jonas, it appeared "more as an anticipated part of a future code of procedure than a supplement to the old law."[67] The introduction of certain powers of the judge

---

62 The term "welfare institution of the state", by the way, is open to many things here: Is it a welfare institution for the objective probation of the legal order or exclusively for the protection of subjective private rights? In any case, the state seems to be able to unilaterally determine the purposes of this welfare.

63 Stein and Jonas, *Zivilprozeßordnung*, Introduction § 6, xxix.

64 Erich Volkmar DJ (1934), 1623.

65 Stein and Jonas, *Zivilprozeßordnung*, Einleitung § 6, xxii. The 16th edition 1938/39 was published under the authorship of Martin Jonas. Max Friedländer writes: "[Friedrich Stein] was indisputably the greatest civil proceduralist of his time. He 'bequeathed' his main work, the great commentary on the Code of Civil Procedure, which Gaupp had founded in the 1970s, but which in its present form came only from Stein, to the Ministerial Councillor Dr Jonas, who continued it after his death and did so in a creditably conscientious manner. But when a new edition appeared after 1933, the National Socialists considered it impossible for the commentary to continue to be called Stein-Jonas; for even if Jonas was an Aryan, his name was still Jewish; and even if Stein was a neutral name, Stein was still a Jew. So the old Gaupp was brought up from obscurity again and the book was suddenly called Gaupp-Stein-Jonas. In the following edition, however, Mr Jonas drew alone and the intellectual property of the great Stein was ignored; it was indeed 'Jewish thought', but seems to have been 'Aryanised' by the suppression of his name" (Max Friedländer, *Life Memoirs*, http://www.brak.de/w/files/01_ueber_die_brak/friedlaender.pdf).

66 Adolf Baumbach, *Zivilprozeßordnung*, 2.

67 Stein and Jonas, *Zivilprozeßordnung*, Introduction § 6, xxxi.

to conduct the proceedings at the expense of the parties' exclusive control over the proceedings, the strengthening of the concentration maxim through the creation of preclusion norms, making it more difficult to amend the complaint or the possibility of a decision on the basis of the case file as a break with the principle of orality do not necessarily eliminate the liberal basic orientation of a procedural law as such. It falls short of characterising acceleration, concentration and rationalisation of proceedings solely in the way that the rights of the parties had to take a back seat to the public interest in achieving these goals.[68] After all, effective civil jurisdiction also serves the effective enforcement of subjective rights.

In contrast, the preface of the Civil Procedure Code, which was then revised on 1 January 1934, testifies to clearly changed ideas: "The parties and their representatives must be aware that the administration of justice serves not only them, but at the same time and primarily the legal security of the people as a whole"[69] and the preservation of peace (Rechtsfrieden).[70] This does not mean, however, that the new Civil Procedure Code is a "Nazi law" in terms of its content. Based primarily on a draft by the Reich Ministry of Justice, which was influenced by the 14th edition of Stein/Jonas (1928/29) and published in 1931,[71] this reform simply continued along the path taken in 1924. Thus, like many reforms of 1933, it took up developments of the Weimar years, but with the addition of some specific, ideologically influenced additions. Both in the explanatory memorandum of the 1931 draft and in the preface of the 1933 law, a "swift" and "popular"[72] procedure was set against the traditional liberal procedure. Erich Volkmar, who was responsible for the 1931 draft and had always invoked the "social spirit",[73] and Martin Jonas must have initially seen National Socialism primarily as a means of implementing the concepts they

68 But so Knut Wolfgang Nörr, *Zwischen den Mühlsteinen: Eine Privatrechtsgeschichte der Weimarer Republik*, Tübingen, 1988, 229.

69 Preamble 2 to the Act Amending the Procedure in Civil Law Disputes of 27 October 1933, RGBL. I 781 ff. Karl Blomeyer, "Erneuerungsbewegung und Zivilprozeßreform", *Deutsches Recht* 4 (1934), 473.

70 Thus Höhn (1934) DR 473.

71 Incidentally, the attempted reform of 1931 was prepared in the literature by the Stein/Jonas commentary, the 14th edition of which was published in 1928/29.

72 Draft 1931, Explanatory Memorandum p. 242 as well as Preamble 1 to the Act Amending the Procedure in Civil Law Disputes of 27 October 1933, RGBL. I 781 ff.

73 For example: Erich Volkmar, "Das Goldene Jubiläum der ZPO", *Deutsche Juristenzeitung* (1927), 187 f.

had developed before 1933.[74] Not only the Weimar discourse, but also the "further civil procedural reform discussion in the committees of the Academy for German Law (1934–1943) and in the two civil procedure commissions of the Federal Republic (1955–1959; 1964–1974) stands", according to an accurate statement by Werner Schubert, "in large parts in the tradition of the late imperial period."[75]

The development of civil procedural law consists of a "constantly repeated struggle between orality and written form, acceleration and thoroughness, freedom and boundedness of procedure, party rule and the power of judges",[76] according to Leo Rosenberg in the introduction to his major textbook on the ZPO. This struggle has been going on for decades and is still one-sided today: away from liberal civil procedure and towards social civil procedure. The term "social", of course, could (and can) hide very different contents, but that is another story.

74 Thus, with a view to the reform of compulsory enforcement law on 1 January 1934, also Werner Schubert, "Reform der Zwangsvollstreckung nach 1933", ZRG (Germ) 121 (2004), 350.

75 Werner Schubert, "Die Entstehung der Amtsgerichtsnovelle von 1909", ZRG 126 (2009), 174.

76 Leo Rosenberg, *Lehrbuch des deutschen Zivilprozessrechts*, Berlin, 1927, 5.

CHAPTER 9

The Evolution of Austrian Civil Procedure from the 18th to the 20th Century

Kamila Staudigl-Ciechowicz

Until the codifications of the 18th century, the law in the Austrian *Länder* was characterised by a high degree of fragmentation and legal pluralism. This state of affairs is also clearly evident in the area of civil procedure. In the individual crown lands, there were different courts with varying designations; Martin Schennach called this phenomenon "designation pluralism (*Bezeichnungspluralismus*)."[1] A typical feature was the coexistence of different judicial bodies, some of which simultaneously fulfilled administrative tasks according to modern understanding. Some of these organs were anchored in the order of the estates, others were created by the sovereign or sprang from autonomous areas, such as the universities. Ecclesiastical jurisdiction also played an important role, to which for example matrimonial disputes were subject until the Josephinian reforms of the late 18th century. The pluralism of the courts within the individual crown lands was accompanied by complex jurisdictions, some of which were derived from court regulations and others from customary law. A customary law character is also typical for the procedural law of the lower courts in this period.[2] In the higher instances and in the courts of the Holy Roman Empire, the procedure was shaped by the principles of the Roman canonical process.[3] There were isolated attempts on the part of the sovereigns to create upper courts that were not only to serve as the apex of the sovereign court system, but also to control the jurisdiction of the estates and thus to strengthen the position of the sovereign vis-à-vis the estates. This development was seen as linked to the "overall state idea (*Gesamtstaatsidee*)", the beginning of which was dated 1526.[4] It is noteworthy that the professionalisation of judges took place particularly in the sovereign courts; these ten-

1 Martin P. Schennach, "Habsburgermonarchie", in *Konfliktlösung in der Frühen Neuzeit*, Wim Decock (ed.), Berlin, 2021, 425.

2 Schennach, "Habsburgermonarchie", 428.

3 Raban v. Canstein, *Lehrbuch der Geschichte und Theorie des Oesterreichischen Civilprozessrechtes*, vol. 1, Berlin, 1880, 93.

4 Canstein, *Lehrbuch*, 87f.

 | DOI:10.1163/9789004736672_011

dencies were enshrined in law under Joseph II with the introduction of compulsory legal training.[5]

1 The General Court Code 1781 (Allgemeine Gerichtsordnung—AGO)

The Austrian hereditary lands under Maria Theresa and Joseph II underwent significant changes in the structure of the authorities, but also in the legal system. The aim was to strengthen central power in order to transform the union of states into a unitary state. The establishment of uniform authorities for all crown lands and the creation of uniform law in as many areas of the legal system as possible played a decisive role in this. The establishment in 1749 of a new authority, the Supreme Judicial Office (*Oberste Justizstelle*), which functioned as a joint supreme court and additionally exercised some of the tasks of the administration of justice, was a major step towards separating the judiciary from the administration.[6] Until then, these matters, together with other administrative tasks, had been the responsibility of authorities, the Court Chancelleries (*Hofkanzleien*), which were organised according to territorial rather than factual aspects. Under Joseph II there were changes in the constitution of the courts. For the purpose of centralising and consolidating the judiciary as a state competence, special courts (*Sondergerichte*) were dissolved with a few exceptions,[7] these reforms made it necessary to change the organisation of the courts. Several courts of appeal were set up as courts of second instance, which were further expanded until 1817.[8]

A central project in the area of legal unification was the creation of a uniform court and procedural code. The "fluctuating jurisdictional relations (*schwankenden Jurisdictionsverhältnisse*)" within the individual crown lands alone led to frequent conflicts of jurisdiction.[9] Spatially limited, uniform legal codification projects had already existed for Bohemia and Moravia at the beginning of the 18th century.[10] In 1781, the General Court Code (*Allge-*

5 See § 430 AGO, Patent v. 1. 5. 1781, Joseph des Zweyten Römischen Kaisers Gesetze und Verfassungen im Justiz-Fache Nr 13.

6 Canstein, *Lehrbuch*, 152.

7 Canstein, *Lehrbuch*, 159.

8 Canstein, *Lehrbuch*, 154f.

9 Alphons v. Domin-Petrushevecz, *Neuere österreichische Rechtsgeschichte*, Wien, 1869, 26.

10 Michael Loschelder, *Die österreichische Allgemeine Gerichtsordnung von 1781. Grundlagen- und Kodifikationsgeschichte*, Berlin, 1978, 26; Gerhard Dahlmanns, "Österreich", in *Handbuch der Quellen und Literatur der neueren europäischen Privatrechtsgeschichte*, Helmut Coing (ed.), vol. 3/2, München, 1982, 2699–2753, 2701.

meine Gerichtsordnung—AGO) was published.[11] It had been preceded by many years of preparatory work. Almost 40 years passed between the appointment of the commission and the final result. The aim was to enact a uniform law, but the idea of modernising procedural law was in the background.[12] In 1753, Maria Theresia appointed a commission as Compilation Commission to compile the fragmented existing procedural laws and to draft a new law on this basis.[13] The original plan was for the Commission to draft a uniform code that would encompass both civil law and civil procedure.[14] The Commission departed from this in the 1770s, and a fully developed draft for the court code as a separate law emerged in 1775.

The drafting was the responsibility of Joseph Hyazynth Froidevo. It is noteworthy that French, Sardinian, Dutch, Prussian and Danish law, as well as the Holy Scriptures, the New and Old Testaments, were consulted in the preparation of the draft and in the deliberations.[15] Although the content of the AGO was ready in 1776 and also received imperial approval, it nevertheless failed.[16] Canstein blamed conflicts with the Supreme Judicial Office, which he described as an "opponent of uniform and codified legislation",[17] for this. In recent legal history, this argumentation is evaluated in a more differentiated manner. Loschelder locates the failure in the context of conflicting interests of the crown lands and the difficulties of adapting the court organisation to the new court order.[18] Further expert opinions and revisions followed in the codification work, internal differences of opinion between the Compilation Commission and representatives of the Supreme Judicial Office (called the Deputation), who were appointed to consult on the draft, hampered the progress of the work.[19] The work was only accelerated after the death of Maria Theresia, when Joseph II resolved any outstanding differences of opinion and promulgated the AGO at the beginning of May 1781.[20]

---

11 See Loschelder, *Die österreichische Allgemeine Gerichtsordnung*; Canstein, *Lehrbuch*, 163–184.

12 Loschelder, *Die österreichische Allgemeine Gerichtsordnung*, 21; Norbert A. Schoibl, *Die Entwicklung des österreichischen Zivilverfahrensrechts*, Frankfurt/Main, 1987, 37.

13 Loschelder, *Die österreichische Allgemeine Gerichtsordnung*, 25.

14 Loschelder, *Die österreichische Allgemeine Gerichtsordnung*, 25.

15 Canstein, *Lehrbuch*, 168.

16 Loschelder, *Die österreichische Allgemeine Gerichtsordnung*, 67–71.

17 Canstein, *Lehrbuch*, 172; Phillipp Harras v. Harrasowsky, *Geschichte der Codification des österreichischen Civilrechtes*, Wien, 1868, 140–142.

18 Loschelder, *Die österreichische Allgemeine Gerichtsordnung*, 67–71.

19 Canstein, *Lehrbuch*, 173–184.

20 Patent v. 1. 5. 1781, Joseph des Zweyten Römischen Kaisers Gesetze und Verfassungen im Justiz-Fache (JGS) Nr 13. Loschelder, *Die österreichische Allgemeine Gerichtsordnung*, 79f.

Although the AGO was strongly oriented towards "Bohemian and Austrian procedural law of the seventeenth and eighteenth centuries" and was based on "common procedure on Roman and canon law basis",[21] it also reflects the influence of foreign legislation and natural law considerations.[22] According to the AGO, the civil process was dominated by the parties, the judge had a weaker position. In this context, one speaks of *Parteienbetrieb* and the principle of negotiation (*Verhandlungsprinzip*). The idea behind this corresponded to the civil process as the interest of the parties rather than the general good, which was in the interest of the state. Dahlmanns characterised this manifestation as a "conception of the court's function as an arbitrator only" based on natural law and reason.[23] Characteristic of the new civil procedural law was the extensive written form, indirectness, non-publicity and legally standardised rules of evidence.[24] It is noteworthy that during the deliberations on the codification, there were opposing positions precisely on the question of written form and the structure of the evidentiary procedure. The Deputation advocated oral proceedings as the rule, emphasising the speed and fairness of oral proceedings.[25] At the same time, the judge should be able to decide in individual cases whether oral or written proceedings should be used, which strengthened his position vis-à-vis the parties. The oral nature of the proceedings, which repeatedly came up as a demand in the late 19th century, was nothing revolutionary or new; some court rules of the 17th century provided for oral proceedings, and the Deputation took its cue from these.[26] As a counter-argument, the Compilation Commission put forward the "thoroughness and reliability" of a written procedure as the "basis of the decision."[27] In the end, the AGO provided for a written procedure with three exceptions: According to § 15 AGO, oral proceedings could take place "in the countryside, [...] in small claims matters" and in cases of insults of honour.[28] The decisive factors here were, on the one hand, the lack of legally competent persons outside the cities and, on the other hand, in the case of small claims, the

21 Dahlmanns, "Österreich", 2702. See also Werner Ogris, *Die Rechtsentwicklung in Österreich 1848–1918*, Wien, 1975, 41.

22 Canstein, Lehrbuch 183.

23 Dahlmanns, "Österreich", 2703.

24 Emil v. Schrutka, "Civilprocessreform", in *Oesterrichisches Staatswörterbuch. Handbuch des gesammten österreichischen öffentlichen Rechtes*, Ernst Mischler, Josef Ulbrich (eds.), vol. 1, Wien, 1895, 267.

25 Loschelder, *Die österreichische Allgemeine Gerichtsordnung*, 89.

26 Loschelder, *Die österreichische Allgemeine Gerichtsordnung*, 87–89.

27 Canstein, *Lehrbuch*, 177.

28 § 15 AGO.

circumstance that the costs for a pleading could exceed the value of the dispute. In the case of libel/slander, *Franz Georg v. Keess* explained in his commentary on the AGO that the exception was based on the fact that "through writings, the injustices are only renewed, extended and perpetuated, also brought to more publicity, and the bitterness of the minds is nurtured."[29]

In retrospect, the AGO—especially in comparison to the ZPO 1895—was often viewed negatively, as backward and outdated. Franz Klein described it —admittedly from the perspective of the ending 19th century—as "the stagecoach in the age of the railways."[30] In the first decades after it came into force, however, the reception of the AGO was quite positive. In 1809, Franz von Zeiller noted that the AGO "lacks none of the essential, inner qualities of a purposeful legal procedure."[31] Zeiller named the "natural order, definiteness, clarity and precision" of the code as its "[external] advantages."[32] A favourable assessment of the AGO can also be found in Canstein's textbook of 1880: according to this, the AGO was "a masterpiece for its time", which even a hundred years after its enactment "deserve[d] full respect and recognition."[33] Canstein even went a step further and declared that the AGO "achieved almost the highest that could be achieved in the field of written procedure."[34]

The application of the AGO in practice highlighted its weaknesses. Especially the disposition maxim (*Dispositionsmaxime*) and the *Parteibetrieb* led to protracted proceedings.[35] § 437 AGO, which imposed restrictions on the judge in the area of interpretation and analogy, also caused difficulties. In case of doubt "about the meaning of the law", the judge had to turn to the emperor and await his decision. Numerous supplementary decrees appeared, dealing with unclear provisions and having the character of authentic interpretations. Canstein cited the teachings of Montesquieu on the one hand and Russian law under Empress Catherine II as a model on the other as the back-

29 Franz Georg v. Kees, *Kommentar über Josephs des Zweyten allgemeine Gerichtsordnung*, Wien, 1789, 22.

30 Franz Klein, "Die neuen österreichischen Civilprozess-Gesetzentwürfe", in *Zeitschrift für deutschen Zivilprozeß* 19 (1894), 2.

31 Franz v. Zeiller, "Grundzüge einer Geschichte der Oesterreichischen bürgerlichen Gerichtsordnung", in Franz v. Zeiller, *Jährlicher Beytrag zur Gesetzkunde und Rechtswissenschaft in den Oesterreichischen Erbstaaten*, vol. 4, Wien, 1809, 9.

32 Zeiller, *Grundzüge*, 9.

33 Canstein, *Lehrbuch*, 170.

34 Canstein, *Lehrbuch*, 183.

35 Schoibl, *Entwicklung*, 38.

ground for this provision,[36] which was definitely in line with the trend of the time.[37] Other Austrian laws or law projects of this period also provided for comparable provisions, in particular the *Codex Theresianus* as a draft[38] and the *Josephinisches Gesetzbuch* from 1786 in § 26.[39] The *Allgemeines Preußisches Landrecht* (ALR) also contained similar norms (§§ 47f. ALR).[40]

2 The West Galician Court Order 1796 (Westgalizische Gerichtsordnung—WGO)

It was precisely the numerous supplementary ordinances and the resulting confusion that prompted Emperor Leopold II to initiate a revision of the AGO in 1790.[41] Already within the first ten years since the AGO came into force, so many supplementary ordinances had been issued that they exceeded "the text of the AGO" with its 437 paragraphs.[42] The commission set up for this purpose was chaired by the important jurist and representative of natural law, Karl Anton v. Martini.[43] While the revision work was still in progress, an amendment to the rules of interpretation in civil law was enacted,[44] so that the problem of authentic interpretations in this area was defused.[45] Within a few years, the Commission, in cooperation with other bodies, prepared a project based on the AGO, taking into account the numerous supplementary ordinances. The final product, the West Galician Court Order (WGO), was sanctioned in 1796 and—spatially limited—initially applied only in West Ga-

36 Canstein, *Lehrbuch*, 184. This restriction also corresponded to the Landesordnung from 1627.

37 Loschelder, *Die österreichische Allgemeine Gerichtsordnung*, 200 footnote 40; Anton Menger, *System des oesterreichischen Civilprocessrechts in rechtsvergleichender Darstellung*, vol. 1, Wien, 1876, 61f.

38 See Franz-Stefan Meissel, "*Aequitas austriaca*—Zur Billigkeit als Rechtsquelle in der Kodifikationsgeschichte des ABGB", in *Festschrift für Thomas Simon zum 65. Geburtstag*, Gerald Kohl, et al. (eds.), Wien, 2020, 172f.

39 General Civil Code (*Josephinisches-Gesetzbuch*), Patent v. 1. 11. 1786, Joseph des Zweyten Römischen Kaisers Gesetze und Verfassungen im Justiz-Fache (JGS) Nr. 591.

40 Dahlmanns, "Österreich", 2704.

41 Ogris, *Rechtsentwicklung*, 41.

42 Dahlmanns, "Österreich", 2704.

43 Canstein, *Lehrbuch*, 185.

44 § 2 Patent v. 22. 2. 1791, Leopold des Zweyten Römischen Kaisers Gesetze und Verfassungen im Justiz-Fache (JGS) No. 115.

45 Canstein, *Lehrbuch*, 185.

licia,[46] an area that only fell to the Habsburg Monarchy in 1795 in the course of the third partition of Poland and was to be incorporated into the Austrian legal system as quickly as possible.[47]

The literature states that "factual differences" between the AGO and the WGO were "minor",[48] even describes the WGO as a "new edition" of the AGO.[49] However, it must be emphasised that the enactment of the WGO was preceded by extensive debates with different proposals for solutions. Immediately after the promulgation of the WGO, it was far from being a copy of the AGO, but rather a further development of it, so that there were definitely differences—despite great similarities.[50] In the following years, these differences in content were largely overcome by adapting the AGO to the WGO.[51] The lasting differences were the different numbering of the paragraphs, as well as the different scope of the two court codes, due to the inclusion of the procedural law before commercial courts, mining and military courts in the WGO.[52]

In the following years, the territorial scope of the WGO was extended more and more—among others to the whole of Galicia, but also Salzburg and Tyrol[53] at the same time, the AGO still applied in parts of the Habsburg Monarchy, so that, at least from a formal point of view, a legal fragmentation existed in the area of civil procedure law until the introduction of the ZPO in 1895.

3 Reform Attempts

Reform discussions dragged on for almost a hundred years. The initial consideration of essentially extending the West Galician Court Order to the other Austrian provinces[54] was soon abandoned and the question "whether the

46 Patent v. 19. 12. 1796, Seiner Majestät des Kaisers Franz Gesetze und Verfassungen im Justiz-Fache (JGS) Nr. 329.

47 The same applied to private law; see Kamila Staudigl-Ciechowicz, "Civil Law in Forced Unions. The Austrian Civil Code and its Significance for the Development of Civil Law in Central Europe", in *Krakowskie Studia z Historii Państwa i Prawa* 13/3 (2020), 291.

48 Ogris, *Rechtsentwicklung*, 40.

49 Dahlmanns, "Österreich", 2704.

50 For a list, see Canstein, *Lehrbuch*, 187–203. For details, see Franz Xaver Nippel, *Erläuterung der allgemeinen Gerichts-Ordnung vom 1. Mai 1781*, vol. 2, Wien 1847, 583–772.

51 Canstein, *Lehrbuch*, 204.

52 Menger, *System*, 64.

53 An overview of the scope and entry into force is given in Menger, *System*, 65.

54 Dahlmanns, "Österreich", 2705f.

West Galician Court Order should be revised" was discussed.[55] At first, the commission pursued the plan of drafting a law that would include both contentious and non-contentious proceedings. Delays in the work led to the completion of only the contentious part, but this draft, submitted in 1816, did not receive imperial sanction.[56] The same fate befell the draft from 1820.[57]

With the Revolution of 1848, the constitutional situation in the Austrian lands changed; already with Pillersdorf's Constitution of April 1848,[58] state guarantees of the independent administration of justice were introduced,[59] § 29 Pillersdorf's Constitution prescribed public oral proceedings for the courts. The provisions in the March Constitution of 1849 were in the same tone. A separate section was now dedicated to judicial power. In terms of content, § 103 of the March Constitution corresponded to § 29 of the Pillersdorf Constitution. However, § 103 of the March Constitution contained a legal reservation, according to which exceptions to the public and oral nature of the proceedings were possible by law in favour of order and morality. In constitutional practice, both provisions were mainly only of limited relevance; Pillersdorf's constitution was only in force for a little less than a year and the March Constitution was not implemented in large parts, thus resembling a Potemkin village. With the first Sylvester Patent in 1851, the March Constitution was abolished anyway; the few principles of the neo-absolutist phase provided for a return to written and non-verbal proceedings, with a few exceptions.[60] A lasting achievement of the Revolutions 1848/49, on the other hand, was the complete nationalisation of the judiciary through peasant liberation and the abolition of patrimonial jurisdiction. The new court organisation provided for district courts (*Bezirksgericht*), provincial courts (as courts of first instance but also courts of appeal, *Landesgericht*), higher regional courts (*Oberlandesgericht*) and the Supreme Court (*Oberster Gerichtshof*) as the highest court. The constitutional development envisaged the complete separation of judiciary and administration, but this separation was temporarily not realised during the neo-absolutism in the first instance through the

55 Schrutka, "Civilprocessreform", 267.

56 Schrutka, "Civilprocessreform", 267.

57 Schrutka"Civilprocessreform", 267; Dahlmanns, "Österreich", 2706.

58 Verfassungs-Urkunde des österreichischen Kaiserstaates v. 25. 4. 1848, Politische Gesetze und Verordnungen (PGS) LXXVI (1848), Nr. 49.

59 However, the term "independence of judges" does not appear in Pillersdorf's constitution. § 28 only speaks of irremovability and non-assignability.

60 Grundsätze für organische Einrichtungen in den Kronländern des österreichischen Kaiserstaates, Allgemeines Reichs- Gesetz- und Regierungsblatt für das Kaiserthum Oesterreich (RGBL) 4/1852, Beilage.

creation of mixed district offices as judicial and administrative bodies. In the meantime, work on reforming civil procedure continued. A draft from 1858, which was still based on the old process principles, was not approved.[61]

With the gradual return to constitutionalism, principles such as orality and publicity gained more weight again. These were taken into account in further drafts, and from 1861 drafts and memoranda of the Ministry of Justice were also produced in printed form and were consequently accessible to a wider public.[62] From 1862 to 1866, legislative work was conducted on a supranational level. Immediately after the completion of the General German Commercial Code, negotiations began in the German Confederation on a common code of civil procedure. The responsible commission was chaired by Austria, represented by the section head Theobald von Rizy. In April 1866, the draft of the *Allg.* C.P.O. *für die deutschen Bundesstaaten* was completed; the dissolution of the German Confederation prevented its further treatment at the international level. Instead, the Ministry of Justice revised this draft, and in December 1867 it was presented in the House of Representatives as the "Draft of a C.P.O. for the Länder of the Austrian Crown not belonging to the Hungarian Crown" but in the end it was not dealt with.[63] A similar fate befell the later drafts. In 1876, Justice Minister Julius Glaser presented a draft that was oriented towards the Code of Criminal Procedure in the area of legal remedies.[64] This draft, like the one based on it from 1881, was not successful.

4 Corrections and Reforms through Individual Laws

Although overall reforms of civil procedure failed for decades, some necessary changes—limited to individual types of proceedings—were carried out by way of individual legislation and at the same time paved the way for the later overall reform.[65] The new, special types of proceedings were intended to ensure faster proceedings, mostly orality was provided for and the judge

61 Schrutka, "Civilprocessreform", 267.

62 *Denkschrift über einige Hauptfragen betreffend die neue bürgerliche Proceß-Ordnung*, Wien, 1862.

63 66th Meeting of the 4th Session of the House of Representatives on 18.12.1867, StenProtAH II. GP 4th Sess 1899.

64 Otto Leonhard, "Zur Geschichte der österreichischen Justizreform vom Jahre 1898", in *Festschrift zur Fünfzigjahrfeier der österreichischen Zivilprozessordnung 1898–1948*, Wien, 1949, 131.

65 Dahlmanns, "Österreich", 2709.

had more competences. Thus, in procedural law, there was an indirect weakening of the dominance of the parties by narrowing the scope of application of the AGO or WGO and consequently a "decline in the practical significance" of the AGO or WGO.[66] It is noteworthy that several of the special laws were originally part of an (unsuccessful) overall reform—in particular the marriage procedure law of 1819.[67]

Special features were standardised in 1819 for matrimonial proceedings,[68] thus separation and divorce matters. Compared to the AGO, orality was more pronounced, and the judge had an active role in determining the substantive truth.[69] In practice, "written protocolary forms" were resorted to despite the envisaged orality.[70] A highly simplified procedure was provided for in the summary patent (*Summarpatent*) of 1845.[71] The summary procedure was used for disputes of low value—primarily monetary claims. The new procedure served to "accelerate the legal process", did not require a lawyer and weakened the principle of negotiation towards the principle of investigation.[72] The judge had to instruct the parties and first work towards a settlement. The judge's duty of manduction existed regardless of whether the parties were represented by lawyers.[73] In practice, the summary patent did not prove its worth. The adherence to the indirectness of the proceedings with an investigating and a discerning judge made elaborate recordings necessary, but corresponding clerks were not available. This circumstance and the judges' lack of preparation for the new oral procedure system led to numerous problems in practice. The proceedings dragged on, the costs were—due to the involvement of lawyers—no longer proportional to the amount in dispute and the legal reality did not correspond to the legal text.[74] Further types of proceedings, some of which were based on summary proceedings, were intro-

66 Paul Oberhammer, Tanja Domej, "Germany, Switzerland, Austria (c. 1800–2005)", in *European Traditions in Civil Procedure*, Cornelis Hendrik van Rhee (ed.), Oxford, 2005, 118.

67 Schrutka, "Civilprocessreform", 267.

68 Hofdekret v. 23. 8. 1819, Seiner Majestät des Kaisers Franz Gesetze und Verfassungen im Justiz-Fache (JGS) No. 1595.

69 Gabriele Schneider, *Das Bagatellverfahren im österreichischen Recht*, Wien, 2001, 16.

70 Dahlmanns, "Österreich", 2709.

71 Regulation on summary proceedings in civil disputes (Summarpatent), Justiz-Hofdekret v. 24. 10. 1845, JGS No. 906. Schneider, *Bagatellverfahren*, 17–24.

72 Dahlmanns, "Österreich", 2710; Schneider, *Bagatellverfahren*, 19.

73 § 25 Summarpatent.

74 Schneider, *Bagatellverfahren*, 20–24.

duced: property disturbance proceedings in 1849,[75] enforcement proceedings in 1839,[76] bill of exchange proceedings in 1850,[77] *Mandatsprozess* in 1855,[78] proceedings from tenancy agreements in 1858[79] and—following the Prussian and Hanoverian example[80]—dunning proceedings in 1873.[81]

Of particular importance for further developments in civil procedural law was the Small Claims Procedure Act of 1873, drafted by Julius Glaser.[82] Glaser was guided by contemporary Prussian legislation, but also took particular account of English and French law[83] and created a procedural law based on orality, immediacy, publicity and free assessment of evidence. In contrast to the ordinary court rules, there was no *Eventualmaxime* in the small claims procedure, and the position of the judge also differed from the AGO or WGO due to the "expansion of the judicial management powers."[84] In the literature, this very law, which introduced the modern procedural principles in Austria, is understood as the precursor of the ZPO 1895: On the one hand, it "gradually accustomed judges [...] to those modern procedural principles", on the other hand, the first instance procedure of the ZPO 1895 was based on the small claims procedure.[85]

5 The Code of Civil Procedure (ZPO) 1895

Only the draft of a Code of Civil Procedure, which was introduced in the Imperial Council in 1893, was ultimately successful. A look at the political, social and legal developments of the late 19th century as a background for the legis-

75 Imperial Decree of 27. 10. 1849, RGBL 12/1849, with a provisional regulation on the procedure in property disturbance disputes.

76 Hofdekret v. 7.5. 1839, Gesetze und Verordnungen im Justiz-Fache vom Jahre 1839, für die deutschen Staaten der österreichischen Monarchie (JGS) No. 358.

77 Decree of the Ministry of Justice of 25 January 1850, RBGL 52/1850, promulgating the [...] provisional regulation on the procedure in matters of bills of exchange.

78 Imperial Decree of 21 May 1855, RBGL 95/1855, on the procedure for bringing those claims which are proven by notarial deed.

79 Imperial Decree of 16 November 1858, RGBL 213/1858, on the judicial procedure in disputes arising from the tenancy agreement.

80 Dahlmanns, "Österreich", 2713.

81 Law of 27. April 1873, RBGL 67/1873 on the dunning procedure.

82 Law of 27 April 1873, RGBL 66/1873, on the procedure in small claims cases (*Bagatellverfahren*). Schneider, *Bagatellverfahren*, 39.

83 See Schneider, *Bagatellverfahren*, 44–52.

84 Schneider, *Bagatellverfahren*, 16.

85 Schneider, *Bagatellverfahren*, 138.

lative work on the ZPO 1895 shows that industrialisation and the slow democratisation now also made social issues more prominent in politics and law.[86] We encounter the growing awareness of the need for social legislation in the discussions on the drafts of the German Civil Code, but also in papal letters such as, in particular, Pope Leo XIII's encyclical *Rerum Novarum*. In Austria—after an economically liberal phase—there was increased social legislation from the beginning of the 1880s. The fruits of this era were workers' protection laws,[87] laws on compulsory accident insurance and health insurance. To a certain extent, the ZPO 1895 also ranks among these socio-political projects: moving away from the idea of liberal procedural law that dominated the German Code of Civil Procedure in 1877 and towards litigation as an outgrowth of state legal protection. Here, too, the social idea is evident, which presupposes a judiciary that works efficiently, quickly and cheaply. In Klein's conviction, the trial is a "social evil" that must be resolved quickly.[88]

Although the work on the ZPO 1895 thus followed the trends of the time, it is nevertheless a particularly remarkable reform in several respects. With the ZPO 1895, a needs-oriented code of procedure that reflected the time was created in Austria. Franz Klein, a hitherto little-known jurist, was responsible for this. With the ZPO 1895, he created a novelty throughout Europe that received much attention and imitation. At the same time, the ZPO 1895 is the product of decades of development, as the draft codes from the middle of the 19th century were its "preliminary stages",[89] but also the small claims procedure as an experimental model facilitated the rapid creation of the ZPO 1895.

Klein had already developed an interest in civil procedure during his student days; he was one of the early listeners of the civil procedural expert and social theorist Anton Menger,[90] a fighter of the propertyless classes and critic of the first draft of the German Civil Code. Klein was a man of many talents. After his studies, he not only passed the bar exam, but also the judge's exam and habilitated at the University of Vienna for civil procedure law.[91] It is significant that Klein's first lecture at the University of Vienna in the winter semester of 1885/86 dealt with "Small Claims Procedure and [the] Civil Proce-

86 Dahlmanns, "Österreich", 2730 f.

87 E.g., Act of 21 June 1884, RGBL 115/1884, on the employment of young workers and women, on daily working hours and Sunday rest in mining.

88 Oberhammer, Domej, Germany, Switzerland, Austria 121 with further references.

89 Dahlmanns, "Österreich", 2716.

90 Peter G. Mayr, "Die Studien- und Praxiszeit Franz Klein", in *Historiarum ignaris semper sunt pueri. Festschrift Rainer Sprung*, Bernhard König (ed.), Wien, 2001, 259–282, 270f.

91 On his life, see Rainer Sprung, "Der Lebensweg Franz Klein", in *Forschungsband Franz Klein (1854–1926). Leben und Wirken*, Herbert Hofmeister (ed.), Wien, 1988, 13–78.

dure Reform (based on the draft of a Civil Procedure Code of 1881)."[92] Only a few years later, he wrote the decisive essays for the civil procedure reform in the *Juristische Blätter*. In 19 issues of the *Juristische Blätter*, beginning at the end of October 1890, Klein discussed the problems of civil procedure reform in his essay series "Pro futuro."[93]

In his essays, Klein criticised the jurists' lack of concern with the question of the concrete design of a new Code of Civil Procedure. Apart from the buzzwords "orality, publicity, free assessment of evidence",[94] there was hardly any consideration of how an efficient course of proceedings could be ensured. He problematised six topics, including judicial participation in the process and means of accelerating the process. In his essays he attempted to derive the existing principles historically and pointed out alternatives—including legal comparisons with Germany and France.

It was precisely this series of essays that attracted the interest of the Minister of Justice, Count Schönborn, in Klein. Even before it was finished being printed in the *Juristische Blätter*,[95] Klein was appointed Ministerial Secretary in the Ministry of Justice on 17 February 1891.[96] Within two years Klein drafted an entire package of judicial laws: the Jurisdiction Code, the Civil Procedure Code and the Enforcement Act. Klein's drafts, in which he tried to implement his ideas already published in Pro futuro, met with interest, approval but also rejection in Austria and abroad. As a contrast to the German Code of Civil Procedure of 1877, Klein's draft also earned criticism from the representatives of party-led procedural law. The departure from the negotiation maxim and especially the judge's search for the material truth was understood by some jurists as crossing the line between the pursuit of public-law interests and private interests. Rudolf Leonhard, professor in Marburg, formulated this view pictorially in his criticism of the proposed "authority of the judge to take evidence *ex officio*."[97] Thus, it would be the "peculiarity of the private law system" that forbids "peering over to the forbidden fruits of material truth, which only thrive in the garden of criminal proceedings."[98]

---

92 Sprung, "Lebensweg", 63.

93 The essays were collected in a special monographic edition: Franz Klein, *Pro futuro. Betrachtungen über Probleme der Civilproceßreform in Oesterreich*, Leipzig, Wien, 1891.

94 Klein, *Pro futuro*, 5.

95 The last part appeared on 1 March 1891, *Juristische Blätter* 20 (1891), 101–103.

96 Bernhard Schöniger-Hekele, *Die österreichische Zivilprozeßreform 1895*, Frankfurt/Main, 2000, 20.

97 Rudolf Leonhard, "Zur Reform des Civilprocesses", in *Juristische Blätter* 20 (1891), 249.

98 Leonhard, "Reform", 249.

As early as March 1893, all three of Klein's drafts were introduced as government bills in the Imperial Council. A separate law, the so-called Consultation Law (*Beratungsgesetz*), was to guarantee their rapid completion.[99] In view of the numerous failed reforms of civil procedure law that had repeatedly been introduced in the *Reichsrat* but had never been fully examined, this law was aimed at speedy treatment. Another motivation for this special treatment was the concern that the deliberations would not be completed in time for the end of the legislative period (i.e., by 1897).[100] At the same time, the possibility of amending the bill in the *Reichsrat* was restricted. The Consultation Law was proposed by the MP Josef M. von Baernreither.[101] It provided for the formation of two special commissions, one for the House of Representatives (Permanence Committee) and one for the House of Lords (Permanence Commission), each of which would be responsible for the substantive treatment of the bills. A Joint Conference consisting of representatives of both commissions served as a consultative body between the two houses and signed off on the joint report. In the plenum of the two legislative chambers, on the other hand, there was no special debate; the two houses of the Imperial Council could either accept the entire project as a whole or reject it after the rapporteurs had presented their report, but amendments to the content could not be made. The Consultation Law referred to very specific legislative projects already introduced in the *Reichsrat*: on the one hand, Klein's three drafts on the reform of civil procedure already mentioned, and on the other hand, the project to introduce labour courts. In the summer of 1895, both chambers passed the ZPO 1895, and the imperial approval came two weeks later.[102]

The new ZPO 1895 consisted of 602 paragraphs. It was based on the Hanoverian Code of Procedure of 1850 and took into account the earlier Austrian drafts, in particular that of Julius Glaser of 1876.[103] The aim was to establish an expedient and practicable procedure. The essential cornerstones of the reform were the judge's power to lead proceedings, he had to ascertain the material truth as far as possible (weakened principle of investigation), immediacy in

99 Law of 5 December 1894, RGBL 227/1894, concerning the consultation and adoption of resolutions on the draft laws relating to the introduction of a new code of civil procedure.

100 Franz Matscher, "Die Entwicklung des zivilprozessualen Rechts", in *Parlamentarismus und öffentliches Recht in Österreich*, Herbert Schambeck (ed.), vol. 1, Berlin, 1993, 475–518, 479.

101 Matscher, "Entwicklung", 479.

102 Law of 1 August 1895, RGBL 113/1895, on judicial proceedings in civil disputes (Civilprocessordnung).

103 Dahlmanns, "Österreich", 2734.

connection with orality supplemented by elements of written form, which also guaranteed reviewability in the appellate courts. Further procedural principles—more or less pronounced in the ZPO 1895—are the free assessment of evidence, publicity, departure from the *Eventualmaxime* to freedom of submission and procedural concentration. An essential aspect of the reform was the restriction of procedural delay. In order to ensure efficient and fair proceedings that were as short as possible,[104] on the one hand, the judge was in charge of the proceedings and ensured that they continued without the need for further motions.[105] On the other hand, adjournments were only possible within strict limits, even reinstatement to the earlier state was only allowed within narrow limits to prevent "procedural negligence."[106] At the same time, an application for a judgement on the part of the plaintiff was required in order to open proceedings at all. This step could not be taken *ex officio*. Thus, the Austrian Code of Civil Procedure 1895 was characterised by a mixture of a disposition maxim and an official maxim. In the literature, the latter is referred to as the principle of judicial operation (*Richterbetrieb*) as well as the principle of court operation (*Gerichtsbetrieb*).

The ZPO 1895 provided for three legal remedies: the appeal, the revision and the recourse. These were limited, not full remedies.[107] The prohibition of novelty applied in these proceedings. According to the ZPO 1895, all judgments of the courts of appeal could be challenged by means of revision, except in minor cases; already with the first amendments to the law, restrictions on revision were introduced. Revisions were decided solely by the Supreme Court (OGH).

The importance of judges and lawyers for the actual application of the procedural laws in the sense of the legislator was already emphasised by Klein in *Pro futuro*, when he wrote: "The law gives a lot of rules and regulations, which in themselves and in their composition, judged purely scientifically, represent the best process. But what becomes of them in reality is decided by those who apply the law: Judges and lawyers. It depends on them whether the good seeds will sprout."[108] Even before the ZPO came into force, Klein drafted a new court organisation law that was to ensure the success of the ZPO in practice.[109] This was associated with an increase in the number of judges, as well as a precisely designed preparatory service that future judges had to successfully complete.

104 Leonhard, "Geschichte", 134.
105 Hans Sperl, *Lehrbuch der Bürgerlichen Rechtspflege*, vol. 1, Wien, Leipzig, 1930, 361.
106 Dahlmanns, "Österreich", 2735.
107 Karl Wolff, *Grundriß des österreichischen Zivilprozeßrechts*, Wien, 1936, 333.
108 Klein, *Pro futuro*, 6.
109 Leonhard, "Geschichte", 140–143.

At the same time, Klein took care of setting up courses for existing judges and lawyers in order to ensure the law-abiding application of the new procedural rules.[110]

6 Developments in the 20th Century

The ZPO 1895 as a modern social code of procedure served as a model for foreign law projects.[111] After the collapse of the Habsburg Monarchy, it served as the basis or even model for the civil procedure codes of the successor states.[112] But other states that did not have at least a partial legal tradition in common with Austria also oriented themselves to the Austrian Code of Civil Procedure 1895, in some cases even shortly after it came into force, or adopted it almost verbatim. In the literature, the Liechtenstein Code of Civil Procedure of 1912 is described as "almost a copy" of the Austrian ZPO.[113] The ZPO 1895 provided impulses for the development of civil procedure in the Scandinavian countries, Germany, but also in Italy and Greece.[114]

Only a brief look shall illuminate the development of the ZPO 1895 in Austria in the 20th century.[115] The first amendment of the ZPO took place in 1914, about twenty years after its enactment. This amendment, as well as others made in the interwar period, was primarily aimed at simplifying proceedings and reducing the burden on the courts.[116] The main changes to civil court proceedings up to 1938 included: "the gradual introduction of single judges

110 Leonhard, "Geschichte", 143–146.

111 Schöniger-Hekele, *Zivilprozeßreform*, 123–155.

112 Helmut Slapnicka, *Österreichs Recht ausserhalb Österreichs*, Wien, 1973, 49f.; Hans Schima, "Die österreichische Zivilprozeßordnung im Lichte neuerer Prozeßtheorie", in *Festschrift zur Fünfzigjahrfeier der österreichischen Zivilprozessordnung 1898–1948*, Wien, 1949, 250–280, 256; *Die Entwicklung des Zivilprozessrechts in Mittel- und Südosteuropa seit 1918*, Walter Rechberger (ed.), Wien, 2011.

113 Schöniger-Hekele, *Zivilprozeßreform*, 145.

114 Slapnicka, *Österreichs Recht*, 50; Walter H. Rechberger, "Die Ideen Franz Klein und ihre Bedeutung für die Entwicklung des Zivilprozessrechts in Europa", *Ritsumeikan Law Review* 25 (2008), 104–110.

115 See in more detail, Andreas Konecny, "Österreich", in *Die Entwicklung des Zivilprozessrechts in Mittel- und Südosteuropa seit 1918*, Walter Rechberger (ed.), Wien, 2011, 1–38; Schoibl, *Entwicklung*, 61–113; Rainer Sprung, "90 Jahre Zivilprozeßgesetze", in *Neuerungen im zivilgerichtlichen Verfahrensrecht*, Bundesministerium für Justiz (ed.), Wien, 1984, 1–35; Matscher, "Entwicklung", 494–518.

116 See Kamila Staudigl-Ciechowicz, "Civil Procedure Law in Austria in the Interwar Period", in *Varieties of Social Civil Procedure*, Martin Löhnig (ed.), Berlin, 2025, 33–64, 41–47.

(*Einzelgerichtsbarkeit*) at the court",[117] simplifications in the dunning procedure,[118] as well as restrictions on revision of court sentences. Particular difficulties arose in the implementation of the institute of Rechtspfleger,[119] which were introduced in various areas with the 6th Court Relief Amendment and were supposed to settle certain "simple legal cases."[120] As a long-fought innovation, women were generally admitted as party representatives in civil proceedings in 1920,[121] until then they had been excluded from this. The ZPO 1895 underwent numerous amendments during the Second Austrian Republic. Larger ones to be mentioned are, for example, the expansion of legal aid in 1973[122] and especially the Civil Procedure Amendment in 1983[123] as a particularly extensive amendment.[124]

7 Concluding Remarks

Finally, we will take a brief look at the question of which factors were decisive for the successful creation and actual effectiveness of the ZPO 1895. The recipe for success consisted of several ingredients that together made this great success possible. Decisive for the actual modernisation and adaptation to the needs of the people seeking justice was the interplay of various basic principles, which were anchored in the ZPO 1895 in different forms—depending on their practicability.[125] For example, experience with the matrimonial procedure 1819 and the summary patent 1845 showed that the principles within

117 Hans Schima, "40 Jahre österreichische Jurisdiktionsnorm und Zivilprozeßordnung", in *Juristische Blätter* 64 (1935), 421–425, 423.

118 Rudolf Hermann, "Zehn Jahre Novellengesetzgebung im Zivilprozesse", in *Österreichische Richterzeitung* 22 (1929), 33–41, 35.

119 Individual areas of enforcement upon movable goods were allowed to be carried out by judicial officers as early as 1926.

120 *Reichspost* No. 345 v. 15. 12. 1930, 2. See also Gustav Ratzenhofer and Ernst Bettelheim, "Die privatrechtliche Gesetzgebung Österreichs in der Zeit vom 1. Juli 1929 bis zum 31. Dezember 1930", in *Zeitschrift für ausländisches und internationales Privatrecht* 5 (1931), 86–114, 97–99.

121 Law of 22. 3. 1920, StGBl 136/1920, on party representation by women.

122 Federal Act of 8 November 1973, BGBl 569/1973, amending the Introductory Act to the Code of Civil Procedure, the Code of Civil Procedure, [...] amending it to regulate procedural assistance (Procedural Assistance Act).

123 Federal Act of 2 February 1983, BGBl 135/1983, amending the provisions on civil proceedings (Civil Proceedings Amendment Act 1983).

124 See on both, Schoibl, *Entwicklung*, 67–69, 75–87.

125 Schöniger-Hekele, *Zivilprozeßreform*, 27.

each procedure were so strongly interconnected that the amendment of a single principle—such as written form—hardly had any effect in practice. Only with the introduction of the principle of immediacy could the principle of orality truly take effect. Essential for facilitating access to legal protection in the area of private law for the less privileged population was the judge's power to conduct proceedings and duty of manduction.

The rapid and successful parliamentary treatment secured the Consultation Law. Thus, unlike many other important contemporary projects, the ZPO was able to pass both chambers smoothly in 1895. At first glance, this restriction of the legislative body's members' right to have a say is admittedly problematic from a modern democratic perspective. At the same time, however, it must be emphasised that it was precisely the participation of the Imperial Council in lawmaking at the turn of the century that repeatedly experienced restrictions that were more pronounced than these provided by the Consultation Law. The December Constitution provided for the emperor's right to issue emergency decrees (so-called § 14 decrees).[126] This right was used rampantly in the years immediately following the enactment of the ZPO 1895. In comparison, the Consultation Law with the treatment of draft laws in commissions of the Imperial Council and the overall vote in the respective plenum represented a lesser evil.

An important contribution to the actual application of the new ZPO 1895 was made by the training of judges. Particularly in the case of earlier reforms, such as the summary patent, the legal text provided for modern basic principles, but legal practice remained entrenched in the old schemes. The controls by the newly created court inspectors offered additional security. Added to this was the personality of Klein as a determined social politician and jurist with an excellent command of his craft.

The Code of Civil Procedure 1895 has been in force in Austria for almost 130 years, despite some far-reaching amendments. The ZPO 1895 created—as Andreas Konecny stated in 2011—"by no means a flawless civil procedure", even after the numerous amendments,[127] yet it provided and still provides the basis and principles for a modern, long-lasting procedural law.

126 Helmut Gebhardt, "Die Praxis des § 14-Notverordnungsrechts von 1868 bis 1914", in *Normsetzung im Notstand*, Christian Neschwara, et al. (eds.), Wien, 2018, 247–258, 252 f.

127 Konecny, "Österreich", 38.

CHAPTER 10

Russian Law of Civil Procedure of 1864

Grzegorz Smyk

The second half of the 19th century in Russia was a period of deep political and legal reforms undertaken in this country on the initiative of Tsar Alexander II after the lost Crimean War. Their goal was to eliminate the most striking relics of the feudal era and modernise the inefficient state apparatus. These reforms led to the abolition of peasants' personal serfdom, the reconstruction of the school system, the introduction of self-government institutions, and the reform of the justice system and judicial law.[1] In 1864, independent institutions of common justice and modern judicial procedures—criminal and civil—were introduced in Russia, based on the principles of equality of parties, openness, adversarial and dispositive proceedings, with the right to free assessment of evidence by a judge and instance control of appealed decisions.[2] As a result of these reforms, for which the model and reference point was the Western European tradition and the legal idea, the legal and judicial system in the Russian Empire became part of the Western legal culture. For the first time in the history of Russia, an individual could seek fair and impartial protection of his or her rights in the courts through a trial before an independent and assumedly objective judge, expecting that he would enforce compliance with the law with his professionalism and authority. Therefore, whether the reformed Russian justice system in civil matters would achieve its goals depended on the appropriate selection of educated judges and on the rationality and coherence of procedural regulations.[3]

Court proceedings, forming since the early Middle Ages in the Russian lands, where the Russian state emerged in the 15th and 16th centuries, initially

1 More on the political situation and reforms of the political system and law in the Russian Empire during the reign of Tsar Alexander II: Richard Pipes *Rosja carów*, Warszawa, 1990, 47–51; Michał Sczaniecki, *Powszechna historia państwa i prawa*, Warszawa, 1985, 545–552; Karol Koranyi, *Powszechna historia państwa i prawa*, part 4, Warszawa, 1967, 296–304; Marian Klementowski, *Powszechna historia ustroju*, Warszawa, 2012, 561–564.

2 These reforms only covered the so-called central "Great Russian", governorates of the Russian Empire and after 1876, governorates of the Kingdom of Poland, Baltic and Transcaucasian governorates, Artur Korobowicz, *Sądownictwo Królestwa Polskiego 1876–1915*, Lublin, 1995, *passim*.

3 Tadeusz Maciejewski, *Historia powszechna ustroju i prawa*, Warszawa, 2000, 643–666.

 | DOI:10.1163/9789004736672_012

took the form of a complaint process. It was a uniform process, which did not distinguish proceedings in criminal cases from proceedings in civil cases, initiated at the request of the plaintiff, open oral and adversarial, in which the evidentiary proceedings depended on the legal, social and economic status of the party. The principles of this process were included in a scattered manner in the oldest list of Ruthenian law in Pravda Ruska from the 11th to the 12th centuries, and then in the *Sudebnik* (*Судеьник*) of Ivan III from 1497, the Tsar's *Sudebnik* of Ivan IV the Terrible from 1550, and finally in the) all-Russian collection of law *Sobornoye Ulozheniye* (*Соборное Уложение*) published during the reign of the Tsar Alexius in 1649.[4]

The departure from the native tradition in the field of judicial proceedings occurred in Russia in the 18th century, i.e., during the reign of Peter I and his successors. The influence of Western models—primarily German—was visible in all modernization projects of the Russian state of that era. They also covered the institutions of civil proceedings. In this area—following the example of Western countries—Russia has separated proceedings in civil cases from proceedings in criminal cases and, consequently, separated the civil proceedings from the criminal proceedings. The separate civil process in Russia that has been developing since the 18th century was based on the principles of the German common civil process (*deutsches gemeines ziviloprozess*), which was a combination of native elements and the principles of the Roman-canonical process. This form of civil trial took over from the Roman-canonical trial the principles of complaint, writing, dispositivity and the legal theory of evidence, supplementing them with the principle of contingency and the so-called *judgment as evidence*. The principle of contingency (forethought) forced the parties to immediately present all the plaintiff's demands as well as the defendant's denials along with the presentation of evidence. The institution of the *judgment as evidence* determined only which of the parties and by what means was to prove their case, which often determined the outcome process. These rules excluded the institution of an articulated complaint, known in the Roman canonical process, in which the plaintiff separately formulated short allegations to which the defendant had to respond. The court issued a judgment based on the files of the evidentiary proceedings, and the judge was bound by the principle of formal truth, i.e., he passed the judgment on the basis of the so-called Formal truth, i.e., the evidence presented to him by the indicated party, regardless of his own belief in the value of this evidence and his own information about the case. The means

4 Andrzej Dziadzio, *Powszechna historia prawa*, Warszawa, 2008, 107–112; Katarzyna Sójka-Zielińska, *Historia prawa*, Warszawa, 1993, 78–79.

of appeal against judgments was an appeal, and against final judgments—the review.[5]

The above rules and institutions of the civil process were comprehensively codified in Russia for the first time in volume X, part 2 of the *Свод Законов Российской Империи* (*Svod Zakonov Rossijskoj Imperii—Code of the Laws of the Russian Empire*) of 1832.[6] The proceedings were—as in the German general civil trial—secret and written. The court judged without any contact with the parties to the proceedings solely on the basis of a summary of the pleadings prepared by the court office, usually edited by secret advisors and according to the rules of formal legal theory of evidence, and the court could—unlike in a common German civil trial—on its own initiative, collect information regarding the case, e.g., using documents not included in the files but held by other offices. In everyday court practice, this collection was a way of delaying trials in the interests of influential defendants not interested in quickly resolving the dispute and collecting monstrous amounts of court files.[7]

The awareness of the backwardness of the Russian model of civil proceedings in relation to the developed countries of Western Europe, the chaos of regulation of procedural institutions and the permanent inefficiency of the state judicial system in Russia caused that in the years 1850–1852, on the initiative of the Minister of Justice Viktor Panin, two special commissions were established to develop projects for the reform of Russian civil and criminal procedure. However, their work was slow and did not bring the expected results. Only the defeat of Russia in the Crimean War, the death of Tsar Nicholas I and the accession to the Russian throne of his son Alexander II—who was aware of the need for deep and quick reforms of the Russian state—led to a change in the situation and acceleration of work on judicial reform and a new civil procedure. By order of the emperor, Sergei Ivanovich Zarudny, a lawyer, specialist in civil law and an outstanding expert in the civil procedure, became the secretary of the commission for the development of the civil procedure. The basic principles of the future Russian civil procedure developed under his supervision were established in this commission on April 14, 1860 and submitted for approval to the State Council—the main legislative body of the then

5 Stanisław Płaza, *Historia prawa w Polsce na tle porównawczym*, part 2: *Polska pod zaborami*, Kraków, 2002, 148–149; Dziadzio, *Powszechna historia*, 447–452; Sójka-Zielińska, *Historia prawa*, 202–204; Koranyi, *Powszechna historia*, 357–358.

6 *Гражданское Судопроизводство, Свод Законов Российской Империи*, vol. 10 part 2, Санкт Петерсьург, 1832, *passim*.

7 Płaza, *Historia prawa*, 148–149; Dziadzio, *Powszechna historia*, 447–452; Sójka-Zielińska, *Historia prawa*, 202–204; Koranyi, *Powszechna historia*, 357–358.

Russian Empire. As a result, on October 24 1860, the State Council appointed a special commission to prepare and carry out judicial reform in the Russian Empire and develop the principles of new court procedures. The outstanding Russian lawyer Vladimir Petrovich Butkov was personally appointed by Tsar Alexander II as the chairman of this commission with the rank of secretary of state. Its members were experienced and comprehensively educated Russian lawyers—both practitioners, scholars and state officials: Nikolai Ivanovich Stoyanovsky, Dimitry Aleksandrovich Rowinsky, Nikolai Adreevich Buckowski, Konstantin Petrovich Pobedonostsev and the previously mentioned Sergei Ivanovich Zarudny.[8]

After two years of work, the Commission presented to the State Council of the Russian Empire a catalogue of basic principles that were to become the foundation of the reform of the Russian justice system, the organization of the judiciary and judicial procedures. These principles were to be: the independence and separation of the common courts from the administration, the liquidation of state courts, the irremovability of judges from the judicial offices entrusted to them and guaranteeing their independence in adjudicating. In the field of civil proceedings, the principles that were to be followed by the designers of the new Russian civil procedure were: the principle of complaint, adversarial nature, directness and dispositivity, oral openness and, above all, the principle of free assessment of evidence by the judge and the introduction of means of appeal and control of judgments, i.e., appeal and cassation. Another novelty in the Russian justice system was the principle of representation, which allows the parties to act in proceedings through professional representatives—lawyers, appointed by individual courts. These rules were adopted from the French model of civil procedure, implemented in the French Code of Civil Procedure of 1806. On September 29, 1862, they gained the approval of the State Council and the Emperor's acceptance.[9]

The principles of the proposed judicial reform have been subject to consultations with Russian legal circles. Butkov asked professors of law faculties of almost all Russian universities at that time and selected judges and prosecutors to present their opinions on the proposed solutions. In response, as many as 488 representatives of the Russian legal world submitted their remarks and comments. In December 1863, the chairman of the Commission, Butkov, offi-

8 The above findings were made in the work of Anna Stawarska-Rippel, "Rosyjska procedura cywilna w pracach sekcji postępowania cywilnego Komisji Kodyfikacyjnej II RP na przykładzie projektu „Tytułu o dowodach" J.J. Litauera", in *Z Dziejów Prawa*, vol. 3, Katowice, 2010, 79–91.

9 Don Chenoweth, *Soviet Civil Procedure. History and Analysis*, Philadelphia, 1977, 5 ff.

cially transferred the draft legal acts of judicial reform to the Second Department of His Imperial Majesty's Chancellery and to the then Minister of Justice—Dimitry Nikolayevich Zamijatin. After taking into account his amendments, on October 2, 1864, the project was sent to the State Council of the Russian Empire, and on November 20 of that year, Emperor Alexander II sanctioned three legal acts: *Учреждение Судебных Установлений* (*Uchrezhdeniye Sudebnych Ustanovniy—the Law on the Organization of Judicial Authorities*), *Устав Уголовного Судопроизводства* (*Ustaw Ugołownogo Sudoproizvodstva—the Law on Criminal Procedure*) and *Устав Гражданского Судопроизводства* (*Ustaw grazhdanskogo sudoproizvodvostva—the Law on Civil Procedure*) that interests us.[10]

The Russian *Law of Civil Procedure* of November 20, 1864, in its original version, consisted of 1,460 articles, divided into four Books, of which the *First Book* (Articles 29-201) regulated the proceedings before justices of the peace and assemblies of justices of the peace, and the *Second Book* (Article 202-1281)—proceedings before general courts, i.e., district courts and court chambers. Each of these books is divided into titles containing provisions on: jurisdiction of the court, representatives, complaints and rules for filing a lawsuit, service, deadlines, mode of proceedings before the court (ordinary proceedings and abbreviated proceedings), evidence, summons, secondary intervention, precautionary measures, judgments, their execution (execution) and provisions on the means and procedure for appealing against judgments. The *Third Book* (Articles 1282-1400) contained exceptions to the general procedure of court proceedings regulated in the *First* and *Second Books*, i.e. the so-called *separate proceedings.* In Russian civil procedure, these included: proceedings in cases in which state bodies managing public property (*statio fisci*) were parties (Art. 1282-1315), cases for compensation for damage caused by state officials (judges, prosecutors, officials) with faulty decisions (Art. 1316-1336) as well as: proceedings in matrimonial and family matters (determining marriage, alimony, parental authority, determining the parentage of a child—Art. 1337-1356). *Book Three* ended with the provisions on conciliation and arbitration (Articles 1357-1400). The *Fourth Book* (Articles 1401-1460) contained the whole of provisions of security proceedings in matters of: inheritance (secur-

10 *Учреждение Судебных Установлений, Свод Законов Российской Империи*, vol. 16 part 2, Санкт Петерсьург, 1892, *passim*; *Устав Уголовного Судопроизводства, Свод Законов Российской Империи*, vol. 16 part 2, Санкт Петерсьург, 1892, *passim*; *Устав Гражданского Судопроизводства* (further *у.г.с. из 1864 г.*), *Свод Законов Российской Империи*, vol. 16 part 2, Санкт Петерсьург, 1892, *passim*; Юрий Орлов, *Неизвестная Темида. Документы, событя, лудя*, Москва, 2003, 149 ff.

ing the inheritance assets, division of the inheritance), property (protection of possessions), personal matters (declaration of death) and obligations (placing the subject of the obligation in a court deposit and auction sale). These books were preceded by *General Provisions* (Articles 1-28), containing the basic rules of civil procedure. Moreover, in 1876, *Book Five* was provided for the Kingdom of Poland and the Baltic and Caucasian governorates, which contained separate provisions, applicable only in these territories and taking into account the differences in the local civil law (e.g., the *Napoleonic Code* in the Kingdom of Poland) and local customs (Article 1461-1798).[11]

Russian civil procedure was based on the principle of complaint, adversarial and dispositive nature, with the right to a court being available in every civil case.[12] Judicial and procedural capacity in civil matters was granted to every person by law, and its exercise could be carried out by him personally or by proxies—professional legal deputies of lawyers (*присяжные поверенные*).[13] The proceedings were to be open and public, and the actions taken by the court, the parties and participants of the proceedings were to be oral.[14] In adjudicating, the court was to be guided by the principle of legalism, requiring action on the basis and within the limits of applicable law, and in the event of their absence or ambiguity—in accordance with its *general principles*.[15] Fol-

---

11 *Устав Гражданского Судопроизводства, Свод Законов Российской Империи*, vol. 16 part 2, Санкт Петерсьург, 1912, *passim*.

12 "Всякий спор о праве гражданском подлежит разрешению судеьных установлений."—art. 1 *у.г.с. из 1864 г.*; "Судеьныя установления могут приступатъ к производству гражданскихъ делъ не иначе, какъ вследсвие просъбы о томъ лицъ, до коихъ теъ дела касаются, и разрешитъ ихъ не иначе, квк по выслушаний обснения противной стороны, или по истечений назначенного дла предлавления онаго срока."—art. 4 *у.г.с. из 1864 г.*

13 "Каждый признается способнымъ отискиватъ и защищатъ на судъ свои права, исключения изъ сего правила означены въ нижеследующнхъ статъяхъ."—art. 17 *у.г.с. из 1864 г.*; "Все деиствия по производству дела, о коих упоминается въ настоящем уставе, могутъ ьытъ совершаемы не толко тяжущимися, но и их поверенными, за исключением лишъ случаевъ, положителъно законом отъ сего изъятых."—art. 16 *у.г.с. из 1864 г.*; "Тяжущиеся имеютъ право присылатъ вместо сеья въ судъ поверенных по всям делам, производящимсяя въ судеьных установлениях."—art. 14 *у.г.с. из 1864 г.*

14 "При всех дейсвиях судеьных установлений по производству гражданских делъ, за исключенем случаевъ, положителъно въ законе указанных, допускаетя присутсвие тяжущихся и остронных лицъ и представление тяжущимися словесных обяснений."—art. 13 *у.г.с. из 1864 г.*

15 "Въсе судебныя установления объязаны решатъ дела по точному разуму существующихъ законов, а въ случае их неполноты, неясности, недостатка или противоречия, основыватъ решение на общем смысъле законов."—art. 9 *у.г.с. из 1864 г.*; "Воспрещается останавливатъ решегие дела под предлогом неполноты,

lowing the example of French solutions, Russian civil procedure adopted the principle of instance, according to which each civil case could go through two substantive instances and one formal instance—cassation.[16] Due to the fact that the Russian judicial organization of 1864 provided for a two-vertical structure of common courts, i.e., a division of peace justice and a division of general justice, for the former the first instance was the justices of the peace (*мировыя судя*) and the second instance was the substantive congress of justices of the peace (*мировые сесды*), and for general courts, the first instance was district courts (*окружные суды*) and the second instance was court chambers (*судебные палаты*). Cassation control was entrusted to the cassation departments of the Ruling Senate (*Правителствующий Сенат*) in St. Petersburg.[17]

A lawsuit in courts of the peace could be oral or written, but in district courts it could only be written.[18] Pursuant to Art. 257 of the *Law of Civil Procedure* Civil from 1864, the complaint should include: the name of the plaintiff and the defendant, their place of residence, clearly formulated demands of the plaintiff, outlining the limits of the court ruling, factual circumstances and legal grounds for the claim, and evidence justifying the request for the complaint.[19] Failure to comply with one of these requirements resulted in the ineffectiveness of the complaint and its return to the plaintiff. The lawsuit was submitted to the court in person, by proxy or by post, and the court served it on the defendant. The defendant was not obliged to respond in writing to the lawsuit, but was obliged to present all allegations against the lawsuit (exceptions) and provide evidence at the first hearing. If he presented them later, it was up to the court whether to consider them as filed for the sake of delaying

---

неясности, недостатка или противоречия законов. За нарушенпе сего правила виновные подвергаются ответственности, как за отказ въ правосудий."—art. 10 *у.г.с. из 1864 г.*

16 "Гражданския дела подлежатъ разрешению по существу въ двух судебных инстанциях."—art. 11 *у.г.с. из 1864 г.*; "Судебное дъело не подлежитъ расмотрению по существу въ двух толъко инстанциях."—art. 12 *у.г.с. из 1864 г.*

17 Walenty Miklaszewski, *Rys organizacji władz sądowych*, Warszawa, 1876, 1–147.

18 "Суд приступаетъ къ производству дела не иначе, какъ по исковому прошению, которое пишется на гербовои бумаге, по форме, при сем прилагаемои."—art. 256 *у.г.с. из 1864 г.*

19 "Исковое прошение должно содержатъ, 1. Означение суда, въ который прошение подается, 2. Имя, отчество, фамилю или прозвище, звание и миесто жителъствакакъ истца, так и ответчика, 3. Означение цены иска, 4. Изложение обстоятелъства дела,, из коих иск проистекает, 5. Указание доказателъств и законов, на коих иск основан, 6. Проситнлъный пункт, заключающий въ себе требования истца, то естъ, о чем он просит суд постановитърешение."—art. 257 *у.г.с. из 1864 г.*

the case and refuse to admit them, or to accept them for the substantive resolution of the dispute.[20]

The court hearing began with a presentation by the judge-rapporteur of the so-called *case status reports* (*доклад*). It was a short summary of the parties' positions, prepared on the basis of the plaintiff's complaint and the defendant's response to it. Its purpose was to define the scope of the dispute and at the same time outline the limits of the court's adjudication. After it was read, the parties were heard, and the failure of one of them to appear did not impede the process. The hearing before the court was oral and public, with the possibility of being excluded from the public at the request of both parties granted by the court. The provisions of Russian civil procedure tried to prevent excessive length of proceedings and obliged the court and the parties to strive to determine the essence of the dispute (*litis contestatio*) and its factual and legal basis as quickly as possible. Therefore, already at the first hearing, the parties were obliged to present all the factual circumstances, legal basis and evidence of their claims as well as the objections directed against the opponent's claims. A party's conscious delay in the process exposed it to financial penalties. Nevertheless, in accordance with the principle of dispositivity, the parties could bring counterclaims and even modify the scope of the claim submitted in the lawsuit. The chairman of the adjudicating panel was responsible for managing the hearing and the entire course of the trial. He allowed the parties to carry out procedural activities, disciplined them and strived to complete the process as quickly and cheaply as possible. For this purpose, he had the right to persuade the parties to end the dispute amicably. If this was impossible, after determining the partie' positions and resolving all formal objections (exceptions), the chairman ordered the conduct of evidentiary proceedings.[21]

20 "Словесное состояние тяжущихся въ изложени сперва истцом, а за тем ответчиком какъ требовний их, так и обстоятелъностъ и доводов, на коих сий требования основаны."—art. 330 *У.Г.С. из 1864 г.*

21 "Доклад дела производится членом суда, оснований представленных тяжущимся къ делу бумаг и документов."—art. *У.Г.С. из 1864 г.*; "Ответчик имеет право заявитъ встречный иск не позже какъ въ первой ответной бумаге, а если таковая неибыла подана, то въ первом заседани по делы."—art. 340 *У.Г.С. из 1864 г.*; "Истец может уменшит свои требования, заявленныя въ исковом прошении, но не въ праве увеличиватъ их, изменятъ по существу или предявлятъ новыя требования, разве бы они истекали непосредственно из заявленных въ исковом прошениих."—art. 332 *У.Г.С. из 1864 г.*; "При словесном состоянии председателъ суда склоняет тяжущихся къ примирению, если признает ето возможным. Въ случае примирения, составляется, за подписъю тяжущихся, протокол, который имеет силу окончателъного решения и не подлежитъ обжалованию."—art. 337 *У.Г.С. из 1864 г.*; "Словесным

The basic principles of evidentiary proceedings in the Russian Civil Procedure Act of 1864 included the principle of equality of the parties, free assessment of evidence and the obligation of the party to prove the facts and circumstances on which it bases its claim. The principle of equality of the parties required the court to enable both parties to use the same procedural means, including evidentiary means. In order to comply with this principle in evidentiary proceedings, the court was obliged to examine all the circumstances of the case and all evidence applications and claims submitted by the parties. The burden of taking evidence rested with the party who, by submitting its demands or allegations, derived legal consequences from them. Therefore, reporting and taking evidence was solely the responsibility of the parties. In no case did the court seek or conduct any evidence *ex officio*. Nevertheless, the chairman of the adjudicating panel could point out to the party any evidence gaps that were important for clarifying the dispute.[22]

In the catalogue of means of evidence, to which the Russian *Law of Civil Procedure* devoted almost 200 detailed articles, it listed first the testimony of witnesses (Articles 370-411) and then the evidence: from the hearing of representatives of the local community (Articles 412-437), from documents (Article 438-478), admission (Articles 479-484), oath (Articles 485-498), inspection (Articles 507-533) and expert opinions (Articles 515-533).

Each side had an equal right to call its witnesses to confirm its claims and facts. The law only required them to indicate the circumstances that were to be proven by such testimony. Persons called by the parties as witnesses—apart from strictly mentioned exceptions—could not refuse to testify. The hearing of witnesses took place in an open court session, in the presence of the parties and their representatives. The hearing was led by the chairman, who took the oath from the witness and then asked him questions. Only after that the parties asked questions to the witness. In the event of contradiction in the testimony of two or more witnesses, the court ordered their confrontation,

---

состоянием руководит председателъ суда. Когда он найдет, что дело достаточно разъяснено, то прекращает словесное состояние, по не прежде, какъ по выслушании обеих сторон въ равном числе изустных обяснений."—art. 338 *у.г.с. из 1864 г.*

22 "Решение суда должно бытъ основано на документах и других писменных актах, представленных сторонами, равно и на доводах, изясненных при изустном состоянии."—art. 339 *у.г.с. из 1864 г.*; "Истец должен доказатъ свой иск. Ответчик, возражающий против требований истца, обязан, съ своей стороны, доказатъ свои возражения." — art. 366 *у.г.с. из 1864 г.*; "Суд ни въ каком случае не собирает сам доказателъсв или справок, а основывает решения исключителъно на доказателъствах, представленных тяжущимися."—art. 367 *у.г.с. из 1864 г.*

i.e., a *face-to-face* hearing. The court was not bound by the witnesses' testimonies but freely assessed their credibility and power at its own discretion. A special form of witness evidence was the interrogation of representatives of the local community, often combined with an inspection of the place (*on-site visit*). They were ordered by the chairman of the adjudicating panel at the request of one or both parties, in cases of delimitation or determination of ownership of real estate or in cases where the parties invoked local customs. Such a hearing, combined with an "on-site visit", often with the participation of experts, was conducted "in the field" by a delegated judge. Witnesses gave evidence under oath and their credibility was subject to the free assessment of the court.[23]

Documents occupied an important place among the means of evidence provided for in Russian civil procedure. This concept included not only official documents, such as notarial deeds or acts of public authorities, but all letters and documents—both private and public—on the basis of which the legal status of the subject of the dispute could be determined. The purpose of conducting this measure of evidence was to unquestionably demonstrate the truthfulness of the party's statements contained therein and to establish its authenticity. The party could only question this measure of evidence if it accused the document of lacking authenticity.[24]

---

23 "Никто не имеет права отказыватся отъ свидетелъства. Изъ етого правила исключаются толъко, 1. Родственники тяжущихся, 2. Имеющие выгоду отъ решения дела въ полъзу тои или дркгой стороны."—art. 370 *у.г.с. из 1864 г.*; "Допрос свидетелей прозводится въ открытом заседани суда"—art. 385 *у.г.с. из 1864 г.*; "Тяжущиеся и их поверенные имеют право присутсвоватъ при допросе свилетелей, хотя бы он производился и въ частном доме, и привестп съ собою постронных лиц, но не более двух съ каждой стороны."—art. 390 *у.г.с. из 1864 г.*; "Сила свиделъственных показаний, смотря по достоверности свидетели, ясности, полноте и вероятности его показания, определяется судом, который обязан привести въ решении основания, по коим свидетелъския показания приняты им за доказателъство, или почему дано предпочтение показанию одного свидетеля прнд показапем другаго."—art. 411 *у.г.с. из 1864 г.*; "При споре о пространстве, местности или продолжителъности поземелъного владения, суд, по ссылке той или другой стороны на свидетелъство местных жителей, хотя бы ета ссылка была и непоименная, может назначитъ особое дознание чрез околъных людей."—art. 412 *у.г.с. из 1864 г.*; "Суд может, по просбе тяжущагося или по своему усмотрению, назначит осмотр па месте, съ участем или безъ участя сведущих людей."—art. 507 *у.г.с. из 1864 г.*; „Определение достоверности и силы показаний околъных людей предоставляется усмотрению суда."—art. 437 *у.г.с. из 1864 г.*

24 "Каждая сторона обязана, по требованию своего противника, представлят находящиеся у неи документы, служащие къ подтверждению спорных обстоятелъств дела."—art. 442 *у.г.с. из 1864 г.*; "Къ писменным доказателъствам относятся не то-

Another measure of evidence was an admission. It could concern each party's recognition of the factual circumstances of the dispute as undisputed or the defendant's recognition of the plaintiff's procedural claim submitted in the lawsuit. A party's declaration containing an admission could be made in writing or orally during the hearing at any stage of the process. The admitted facts or admission of the claim did not require further evidentiary proceedings and were irrevocable. The party could avoid its consequences only in the event of acting under the influence of error—which had to be proven by other means of evidence.[25]

A special means of evidence provided for in Russian civil procedure was an oath. The law allowed the parties—upon their unanimous request—to ask the court to resolve disputes by admitting evidence by oath. The oath could concern individual controversial issues, as well as the entire claim of the plaintiff—and therefore could lead to the end of the trial. It had a sacred character. It was ceremonially taken in the church of the religion of the party taking the oath, according to the text of the oath approved by the priest of the appropriate religion. It had an evidentiary value equal to other means of evidence and it was impossible to avoid its effects by other means of evidence.[26]

лъко акты крепостнуе, явочные и домашние, о коих упоминается въ законах гражданских, но и другия бумаги."—art. 438 *у.г.с. из 1864 г.*; "Акты крепостные, а равно и явочные, если существо содержащейся въ них сделки не противно законам, имеют силу доказательства какъ между сторонами, участвовавшыми въ договоре, так и между их наследниками и преемниками, разве бы они опровергнули подлинност актов, или доказали, что акты потеряли свою силу."—art. 457 *у.г.с. из 1864 г.*; "Поверка акта может бытъ назначена судом, если тяжущийся, против коего представляется акты, заявит сомнение въ его подлинности,или объявит спор о подлог."—art. 541 *у.г.с. из 1864 г.*

25 "Признание может бытъ сделано перед судом писменно, въ одной из бумаг, на суд подаваемых, или словесно, во время словеснаго состояния. Въ последнем случае, если противная сторона желает восполъзоватся признанием, то по ея просъбе оно должно бытъ записано въ протокол."—art. *479 у.г.с. из 1864 г.*; "Когда одна из сторон самс признает действителъностъ такого обстоятелъства, которое служит къ утверждению прав ея противника, то оно считается не требующим далънейших доказателъств."—art. 480 *у.г.с. из 1864 г.*; "Сторона, учинившая признание, может опровергатъ его въ таком толъко случае, когда признание относилосъ не къ личным ея действиям и когда она может доказатъ, что была введена въ заблуждение неведенем такого обстоятелъства, которое открылос лишъ впослествий."—art. 481 *у.г.с. из 1864 г.*

26 "Тяжущимся не запрещается, по взаимному их соглашению, просит суд о решений дела на основании принимаемой одним из них присяги, но суд может ни принудит тяжущихся къ принятию присяги, ни предлагатъ её от себя истцу или ответчику."—art. 485 *у.г.с. из 1864 г.*; "Присяга должпа бутъ изустная,на основании изготовленного тяжущимися присяжнаго листа, который подписывается прийве-

The last means of evidence mentioned by the *Law of Civil Procedure* of 1864 was the opinion of experts. It was ordered by the court at the request of the parties or on its own initiative when specialist knowledge was necessary to resolve the disputed issues. One to three experts could be appointed and they presented their expertise to the court in writing. However, the court was not bound by the findings and conclusions of the expert opinion and could omit it if it had other means of evidence that it considered more convincing.[27]

After conducting the evidentiary proceedings, the court closed the hearing and proceeded to issue a judgment. The party's failure to appear did not suspend the issuance of the judgment, which in such a case was a default judgment, from which the party had the right to file an opposition against it within two weeks of its delivery. The judgment was issued at a closed session, during which the chairman reported the findings made by the court and asked the other members of the jury about their opinions on the main issues of the dispute. The decision to accept the operative part of the judgment was made by a simple majority of the judging panel, but each judge could submit his or her dissenting opinion to the minutes. Then, the presiding judge began to draft the operative part of the judgment and announced it to the parties and participants in the proceedings at an open session. The one-month period necessary for the judgement to become final ran from that date.[28]

денным къ присяге тяжущимся и священником, или духовным лицом его исповедания."—art. 495 *у.г.с. из 1864 г.*; "Присяга принимается за доказателъство того, въ чем она учинена, и не можетъ бытъ опровергаема никакими другими доказателъствами."—art. 498 *у.г.с. из 1864 г.*

27 "Суд может, по просъбе тяжущихся или по свему усмотрению, потребоватъ заключение сведущих людей о таком предмете, коего разсмотрение или оценка требует особых ученых, технических или хозяйственных сведений."—art. 515 *у.г.с. из 1864 г.*; "Сведущие люди назначаютсия, въ определенный судом, срок, не последует, то исбираютсясамим судом."—art. 518 *у.г.с. из 1864 г.*; "Суд не обязан подчинятся мнению сведущих людей, несогласному съ достоверными обстоятелъствами дела."—art. 533 *у.г.с. из 1864 г.*

28 "По окончани словесного состязания, судия удаляются въ особую комнату, где, обсудивъ выслушанное дело, постановлают по оному решение."—art. 693 *у.г.с. из 1864 г.*; "... Если не явится ответчик, то истец может просит о допущение его къ представлению словесных обяснений и постановлени заочного решения."—art. 718 *у.г.с. из 1864 г.*; "Неявившийся ответчик имеет право, по делам, производящимся обыкновенным порядком, въ месячный срок, а по делам, производящимся порядком сокращенным, въ течение двух неделъ, податъ против заочнаго решения отзыв въ суд, постановивший решение."—art. 727 *у.г.с. из 1864 г.*; "Суждению о деле предшествует постановление председателем суда вопрос, выводимых из требований и возражений тяжущихся."—art. 694 *у.г.с. из 1864 г.*; "Решения постановлаются по болъшинсву голосов. Въ случае раенства голосов

The parties had the right to appeal against non-final court judgments to a higher court (an assembly of justices of the peace or a judicial chamber). The appeal was submitted through the court that issued the contested decision. An appeal complaint should specify the scope of the appeal, the factual and legal basis for the appeal allegations and the complainant's demands. After accepting the appeal, the court of appeal notified the opposing party and requested it to submit a written response to the applicant's allegations. The appeal proceedings were conducted according to general rules. It was public, oral and adversarial. The parties could use the same procedural means, and the court assessed the evidence freely. After examining the appeal, the court of appeal could uphold the contested judgment and dismiss the appeal, or accept it and rule, changing the contested judgment in whole or in part. The appellate court did not have the right to overturn the appealed judgments and refer the case back to the first-instance court, but it had to rule on the merits of the case.[29]

The annulment of final court judgments could occur as a result of cassation, restitution or the opposition of a third party. The basis for cassation could be a clear violation of law, failure to comply with the basic principles of the judicial process, or the court's violation of the provisions on jurisdiction; restitution—new circumstances revealed after the final judgment was issued, and the third opposition—violation of the rights of third parties who did not participate in the trial. These complaints were sent to the Cassation Departments of the Ruling Senate in St. Petersburg. Taking them into account resulted in the judgment being annulled and the case being re-adjudicated by the congress of justices of the peace—in cases belonging to the peace court or the court chamber—in the general court division. The ruling of the Ruling Senate issued

---

мнение председателя дает перевес."—art. 698 *у.г.с. из 1864 г.*; "Решения и определения суда считаются обявленными в денъ, назначенный тяжущимся для прочтения или частнаго определения."—art. 714 *у.г.с. из 1864 г.*

29 "На всякое решение суда по существу дела тяжущиеся имеют право принестъ апелляционную жалобу."—art. 743 *у.г.с. из 1864 г.*; "Апелляционная жалоба подается въ суд, постановивший решение."—art. 744 *у.г.с. из 1864 г.*; "Въ апелляционной жалобе должно бытъ обяснено 1. На все ли решение приносится жалоба или толко на некоторыя его части, 2. Какими обстоятелъствами дела или законами опровергается правилъност решения, 3. Въ чем заключается ходотайство приносящаго жалобу."—art. 745 *у.г.с. из 1864 г.*; "Палата обязана решитъ всякое

under the cassation procedure was binding on the court that was to rule on the case again and in practice had precedent significance.[30]

Alexander II's reforms in Russia in the second half of the 19th century aimed to eliminate feudal elements and reform the state system. These reforms led to the abolition of peasants' personal serfdom, the reconstruction of the school system, the introduction of self-government institutions, and the reform of the justice system and judicial law. In 1864, independent institutions of common justice and modern judicial procedures—criminal and civil—were introduced in Russia, based on the principles of equality of parties, openness, adversarial and dispositive proceedings, with the right to free assessment of evidence by a judge and instance control of appealed decisions. As a result of these reforms, for which the model and reference point was the Western European tradition and the legal idea, the legal and judicial system in the Russian Empire became part of the Western legal culture. For the first time in the history of Russia, an individual could seek fair and impartial protection of his or her rights in the courts through a trial before an independent and assumedly objective judge, expecting that he would enforce compliance with the law with his professionalism and authority. Therefore, whether the reformed Russian justice system in civil matters would achieve its goals depended on the appropriate selection of educated judges and on the rationality and coherence of procedural regulations.

30 "Просбы объ отмене решений могут бытъ трех родов: 1. Просбы о кассаци решений, 2. Просбы о пересмотр решений, 3. Просбы не участвовавших въ деле лица."—art. 792 *у.г.с. из 1864 г.*; "Просбы объ отмене решений подаются въ кассационный департамент Правителствующаго Сената."—art. 801 *у.г.с. из 1864 г.*; "въ случае отмены обжалованнаго решения, Сенат обращает дело къ новому производству и решению, назначая для сего другую палаты,ближайшую кътой, где дело производилосъ."—art. 809 *у.г.с. из 1864 г.*; "Все определения Сената по просбам объ отменение решений публикуются во всеобщее сведение, дла руководства къ единообразному истолкованию и применению законов."—art. 815 *у.г.с. из 1864 г.*

CHAPTER 11

The Influence of Foreign Laws on the Polish Code of Civil Procedure (1930/33)

Andrzej Dziadzio

After Poland regained its independence in 1918, three codes of civil procedure were in force on its territory: Russian, German and Austrian, which were to remain binding until Poland introduced its own codification of procedural law. In addition, the Hungarian Code of Civil Procedure was applied on the small territory of Spiš and Orava, in the southern part of the state. The abolition of legal particularism in the reborn Polish State thus became one of the first tasks of the legislative Sejm. Within less than four months of convening, the Sejm, on 3 June 1919, passed the Act on the Establishment of a Codification Commission, whose function was to prepare "drafts of uniform legislation in the field of civil and criminal law."[1] The draft acts were to be submitted to the Sejm by the minister of justice. The Codification Commission began legislative work on the unification of the various branches of law in the autumn of 1919. The preparation of codes and acts was carried out in parallel by the divisions and sections established for this purpose. Within the Civil Division, in addition to the Civil and Commercial Law Section, the Civil Procedure Section began its activities, which was to draft the provisions of the Code of Civil Procedure.

However, preliminary work on the assumptions of the future Polish Code of Civil Procedure began as early as two years before the establishment of the Codification Commission. The proclamation of the Polish kingdom by the central states in 1916—after part of the Polish lands with Warsaw had been taken away from Russia—initiated the creation of Polish public administrative bodies. The Provisional Council of State was then established, followed by the Regency Council, within which the Civil Law Commission functioned from the beginning of 1917. Its primary task was to prepare a Polish code of civil procedure to replace Russian procedure. This is because it had been imposed on Polish soil in 1876 in place of the French Code of Civil Procedure. French civil law, both substantive (the Napoleonic Code) and formal law, in-

1 "Act of 3 June 1919 on the Codification Commission", *Journal of Laws of 1919*, no. 44, item 315.

 | DOI:10.1163/9789004736672_013

troduced in the Duchy of Warsaw in 1808, was for a long time an expression of the legal separation of the Polish lands from the Russian Empire. The French-Polish system of civil law, dating from the enactment in 1825 of the Civil Code of the Kingdom of Poland (only some provisions of the *Code civil* were changed in within it) continued to be in force (until 1945), despite the repeal of the French Civil Procedure Code. The end of Russian rule in central Poland therefore created a chance for the Kingdom of Poland to introduce its own civil procedure. For this reason, the established the Civil Law Commission was to be charged with developing the principles of a Polish code of civil procedure. Thus, in the years preceding the establishment of the Codification Commission, the Polish legal community of Warsaw and Krakow conducted a broad discussion on the assumptions of a future code of civil procedure. Therefore, the principles of Polish civil procedure had been defined long before the Codification Commission started its work, and it recognized them as the guiding idea for the provisions of the Code of Civil Procedure. This was also the case because the preparatory work carried out at that time involved practically the same representatives of Polish scholarship, jurisprudence and the bar, who were part of the Codification Commission and played a key role in it.

A characteristic feature of the debates of Polish legal bodies on the model of the future code was the extensive use of the law-comparative method in selecting the most pertinent procedural institutions. In the papers presented, the authors justified their position, generally based on a critical or approving analysis of the contents of a number of codes: the French (1806), Russian (1864), German (1877), Austrian (1895), and Hungarian (1911), as well as the code of the Swiss cantons of Zurich (1913) and Bern (1918). The methodology adopted for the analysis of the rules was intended to lead to the creation of a code of civil procedure, which was not so much to be characterized by novelty and innovation, but which, through a rational selection of the best solutions—supported by positive judicial practice—was to guarantee the efficient and fair resolution of civil disputes. A code of civil procedure was therefore intended by the Polish codifiers to be a synthesis of the achievements of European civil-procedural legislation. The aim of this study is to show, on the one hand, to what extent the Polish Code of Civil Procedure 1930 (enacted in 1933 after a *vacatio legis* of more than two years)[2] was an original synthesis of the

2 "Regulation of the President of the Republic of Poland of 29 November 1930—Code of Civil Procedure", *Journal of Laws of 1930*, no. 83, item 651. The entry into force of the code was planned for 1 January 1933. During the *vacatio legis* period, however, some provisions were amended by virtue of the regulation of the president of the Republic of Poland of 27 Octo-

provisions of the codes taken as a model for the implemented legal provisions. On the other hand, it will be important to answer the question of which model of civil procedure had a decisive influence on the content of this code: the French (Russian) or the Austrian (German)?

1 The Principles of the Code of Civil Procedure in the Opinion of the Polish Legal Community (1917–1918)

The French type of civil proceedings was in force on Polish soil for the longest time of all modern procedures applied before 1918. In central Poland, both in the Duchy of Warsaw (1807) and later in the Kingdom of Poland (1815), the French Code of Civil Procedure was in force for almost 70 years. The Russian procedure of 1864, which was introduced on Polish soil in 1876, although imposed by the Russian partitioning power, was for the most part modelled on the French code. The Napoleonic Code of Civil Procedure was also applied in Krakow and the surrounding area for almost 45 years (1810–1855). French civil procedure, as well as the *Code civil,* blended with Polish legal culture to such an extent that legislative work in the reborn Second Republic (1918–1939) saw French law as a national legacy at the times of the partitions.

This was expressed by Jagiellonian University professor Franciszek Ksawery Fierich—the father of Polish scholarship on legal procedure and the first president of the Codification Commission-when he asked, at a meeting of the Krakow Law and Economics Society in 1918, whether the French procedure, which had been in force in Poland for so long, should not become one of

ber 1932, *Journal of Laws of 1932*, no. 93, item 802. U 1932, no. 93, item 802. Through the regulation, the law on judicial enforcement proceedings, based on a draft prepared by the Codification Commission, *Journal of Laws 1932*, no. 93, item 803 was promulgated with effect from 1 January 1933. On 1 December 1932, a proclamation of the minister of justice on the announcement of the uniform text of the Code of Civil Procedure was published in the Journal of Laws, *Journal of Laws 1932*, no. 112, item 934. The uniform text of the Code of Civil Procedure included the law on judicial enforcement proceedings and amendments to the original text of the code contained in the regulation of 27 October 1932. The Code of Civil Procedure in its new unified version entered into force on 1 January 1933. It consisted of two parts: the first, covering contentious proceedings (Articles 1-507), and the second, containing provisions on enforcement proceedings and proceedings to secure claims (Articles 508-862). The draft on non-contentious proceedings was not promulgated before the outbreak of the Second World War in 1939. The code came into force through a regulation of the president of the republic of Poland. who, by virtue of the amendment of the Constitution in 1926, was empowered to issue statutory instruments.

the most important bases for Polish civil procedure.[3] This was to be supported by the fact that the French model of civil procedure corresponded to the Polish procedural tradition set by the codification of 1523. This is because the old Polish procedure, despite the reforms of civil procedure in neighboring countries towards secrecy and written proceedings, remained faithful to the principle of openness and orality. Historical considerations and the continuity of legal culture were therefore to determine the wider application of French solutions in the Polish Code of Civil Procedure. Fierich regarded the French procedure as the mother procedure also in relation to the German and Austrian codifications of civil procedural law, which had taken over its fundamental principles: openness, orality, and directness of court proceedings, as well as the free assessment of evidence by the judge. However, both the discussion within the Warsaw Civil Law Commission (1917–1918) and the debate conducted by the Krakow Legal and Economic Society focused more attention of their participants on the analysis of Austrian and German civil procedure, as well as the related Hungarian law. French and Russian procedure occupied a secondary position in the consideration of the future code.

The Polish legal community was therefore aware that French civil procedure was the starting point for defining the fundamental principles of civil procedure for the Germanic legal orders as well. However, they were subjected to a certain revision and reconstruction due to the differently defined purpose and essence of court proceedings. Polish lawyers were fully aware of the evolution which civil procedure underwent in the 19th century. Indeed, the French model of the organization of civil trial served to secure the autonomy of the will of the parties in the establishment of private law relations and their protection in the form of the chief principles of accusatorial and adversarial procedure, as well as the principle of disposition. The role of a court was reduced to that of an arbitrator in resolving a dispute between the parties, who themselves provided evidence to support their claims. The parties were the host of the trial. The court determined the facts of the case solely on the basis of evidence provided by the parties. The court was deprived of evidentiary initiative and therefore based its decision on a determination of formal truth; in French procedure, the burden of proof was on the plaintiff. The French procedural model corresponded to the requirements of legal transactions associated with a system of a free competition economy, laissez-faire

3 *Czasopismo Prawnicze i Ekonomiczne: organ Wydziału Prawa i Administracji Uniwersytetu Jagiellońskiego oraz Towarzystwa Prawniczego i Ekonomicznego w Krakowie. Year 17*, 4 vols., (1917–1918), 108 ff.

economics, and a liberal approach to individual activity—*volenti non fit iniuria*.

The development of procedural law in the second half of the 19th century was an outcome of a change in the state's function from one of protection to one of organization. Liberalism in the shaping of economic mechanisms was overshadowed by the active intervention of the state in the sphere of economic and social relations in order to protect weaker and poorer groups.[4] The new model of civil procedure was adopted by the acts of the Germanic area: the German Act of 1877 and the Austrian Act of 1895. The aim of civil procedure in the German-Austrian model was to take into account, first of all, the interest of the state, expressed in the guarantee of substantive equality of litigants, and secondly, as it were, to satisfy the legitimate interest of a party. A civil trial was thus to establish the actual state of affairs, i.e., the material truth as the basis for a judicial decision, and this was to be served by the active role of a judge in a civil trial. Therefore, the new procedures ignored the issue of regulating the burden of proof, as the court could take evidence on its own initiative, which it assessed freely, forcing the parties to respond to the evidence thus gathered.

These requirements were met by all civil procedural acts from the German Act of 1877 through the Austrian Act of 1895, and the Hungarian of 1911 to the Berne Act of 1918. It was therefore a direction of change of civil procedure that the Polish legal community considered modern, progressive, and innovative in comparison to the already "archaic" French procedure. Therefore, the discussion of the new Polish civil code focused on such issues as the combination of oral court proceedings with written elements, or the preservation of the principle of adversarial and dispositive procedure while increasing the role of the judge in a trial.[5] The different experiences with the application of procedures that were different in content, i.e., mainly Russian (modelled on French) procedure in the lands of central Poland and Austrian procedure in the south of the Polish state (Lesser Poland) also marked the axis of the dispute on the most desirable solutions in the Polish code, namely the definition of the scope of the judge's activity, the catalogue of evidence and means of challenge.

4 *Czasopismo Prawnicze*, 119 ff.

5 "Dodatek. Protokół z posiedzeń Sekcji prawa cywilnego formalnego Komisji Kodyfikacyjnej w sprawie zasad postępowania procesowego. Posiedzenie w Warszawie w dniu 15 maja 1920 roku", in *Polska procedura cywilna. Projekty referentów z uzasadnieniem. Przedruk wyczerpanych druków z 1921 i 1923 r.*, vol. 2, Warszawa, 1928, 262 ff.

2 The Warsaw Commission for Civil Law

The first statements by representatives of the Polish legal elite on the principles of Polish civil procedure, as already mentioned, came from members of the Warsaw Commission for Civil Law, which was able to assess the functioning of Russian civil procedure from the practical side. However, for the most part, they presented views in which the postulate of equipping the judge with evidentiary initiative shone through. The passive role of the judge in a civil trial, which was a distinguishing feature of the French model, was clearly contested. According to the chairman of the commission, Jan Jacob Litauer—a judge of the Supreme Court and later a member of the Codification Commission in the role of deputy and then chairman of the Civil Procedure Section—the active role of a judge was to be expressed in cooperation with the parties in order to establish the substantive truth.[6] The commission summarized its findings by passing the conclusion that the future Civil Procedure Code "is to be based on the principles of openness and orality with due regard to the written nature and directness. The adversarial principle is to be combined with the official-investigative principle, while, however, the rights of the parties to dispose of the trial are to be preserved."[7]

In addition to its general conclusion on the direction of future work on the Polish Code of Civil Procedure, the Warsaw Commission devoted considerable attention to specific institutions of civil procedure. One of these was the issue of the means of evidence in a civil trial in the form of an oath of the parties. The issue of admitting this means of evidence in a civil trial was, by the way, later vigorously discussed within the civil procedure section of the Codification Commission. An oath as a means of evidence was present in French and German procedure, while it was not provided for in the Russian code. The drafters of the Russian procedure rejected an oath on the grounds that "taking a party's oath as the basis for deciding a case in its favor transforms the party into the judge of its own case." They were of the opinion that a party's oath could only serve to discover the truth if it was ordered by a party having goodwill. On the other hand—as the Russian legislator justified the position—"he who has bad will always turn it to his advantage; the result is

6 Anna Stawarska-Rippel, *Elementy prywatne i publiczne w procesie cywilnym w świetle prac kodyfikacyjnych w Polsce (1918–1964). Studium historyczno-prawne*, Katowice, 2018, 44–45.

7 Stanisław Gołąb, *Projekty polskiej procedury cywilnej. Powstanie—Uzasadnienie—Zdanie odrębne*, Kraków, 1930, 41 ff.

that an oath in most cases gives service to an unconscientious party and often becomes a provocation of perjury."[8]

The attitude of the members of the Civil Law Commission towards an oath as a means of evidence varied, although the majority agreed that this evidence should be retained in the Code of Civil Procedure. The necessity of the use of an oath in a civil trial was pointed out by Bolesław Pohorecki, a judge in the Court of Appeal, later the President of the Civil Chamber of the Supreme Court, and from 1932 the president of the Codification Commission. In his view, oath evidence should be admitted in all cases where the substantive law required written evidence and therefore excluded the possibility of witness evidence. Pohorecki believed that a rational trial required the existence of a means of evidence in the form of an oath, since in the absence of a written document or if it was lost, there would be no possibility of asserting rights in a court.[9] In contrast, the objection to the oath evidence was on the grounds that it was not subject to the court's assessment due to its decisive nature, which contravened the principle of free assessment of evidence.

In the end, the members of the commission agreed to take the position that evidence under oath would only be admissible after all other evidence had been exhausted and in connection with the hearing of the parties according to the model given by the Austrian procedure, including the oath both at the request of the parties and *ex officio*. However, an oath was not intended to constitute decisive evidence, as the consequences of evasion were to be freely assessed by the court. The Warsaw lawyers therefore opted for the evidentiary measure of hearing the parties under oath according to the rules of Austrian procedure, thus recognizing the inadequacy of the Russian procedure. They also chose not to reinstate the French version of an oath on the grounds that the court's free assessment of this evidence was excluded.

An important issue raised during the deliberations of the Warsaw Civil Law Commission was the determination of the bindingness of a civil court on a criminal court judgment. French and Russian procedure took the position that the contents of a final criminal court judgment had binding force in a civil trial. This regulation was not accepted by the members of the commission. Instead, they approved the provisions of Austrian law, according to which only a final conviction in a criminal case was binding on a civil court. Finally, the commission decided to adopt a somewhat more relaxed position, according to which the preliminary binding effect of a criminal conviction was limi-

8 Bronisław Rotwand, "Przysięga jako dowód w procesie cywilnym", in *Kwartalnik Prawa Cywilnego i Karnego* 1/1–4 (1918), 448 ff.

9 Stawarska-Rippel, *Elementy prywatne*, 69.

ted to situations in which the defendant was the accused or his/her heirs. In this way, it sought to broaden the scope of the civil judge's discretionary assessment of the evidence in a case that had also been the subject of a criminal judgment.[10]

With regard to appeal measures in the future code, the Warsaw legal community was clearly in favor of the need to retain the French cassation. Only Judge B. Pohorecki proposed that a future cassation tribunal could exceptionally pass a judgment on the merits. He referred this to a case in which the contested judgment could be revoked on the grounds of an infringement of substantive law and the case was, in factual terms, ready for adjudication.[11] The introduction of an appeal in the form of a cassation, or revision into the Polish Code was one of the most controversial issues which had to be resolved by the Codification Commission. This was because Krakow's lawyers were accustomed to the institution of a revision in Austrian procedure. A large group therefore opted for the adoption of this type of means of challenge, which was a feature of Germanic legal culture.

3 Krakow Law and Economics Society

A draft of the main principles of Polish civil procedure was sent in early 1918 by the Warsaw Civil Law Commission—as noted earlier—to Fierich for evaluation of the draft at a meeting of the Krakow Legal and Economic Society. The analysis of the draft was carried out by a committee of the society consisting of professors from Jagiellonian University: F.K. Fierich, Tadeusz Dziurzyński and Stanisław Gołąb.[12] All of them were later active members of the Codification Commission and its civil procedure section. Professor Stanislaw Gołąb's dissertation, published in print in 1930, entitled "Drafts of Polish Civil Procedure. Creation—Justification—Dissenting Opinion," contained the argument that found its way into the contents of the official justification of the draft of the Code of Civil Procedure drawn up by the Codification Commission.[13] Co-reports of the society's meeting were also drawn up by Cracow's advocates, including Józef Skąpski and Jerzy Trammer, who later played an active role in the work of the Codification Commission. The Commission of the Krakow Society was the first team to undertake the preparation of the preliminary

10 Stawarska-Rippel, *Elementy prywatne*, 73.

11 *Czasopismo Prawnicze*, 176 ff.

12 *Czasopismo Prawnicze*, 106 ff.

13 See footnote 7.

assumptions of the Polish Code of Civil Procedure.[14] This is because the evaluation of the work of the Warsaw Civil Law Commission became an inspiration for discussing key issues in the field of procedural law from the point of view of legislative work on the Civil Procedure Code. The speeches of the representatives of Krakow academia and the bar took the form of reasoned theses which were to serve as preparatory material for the future code. Therefore, the question should be asked whether there was a difference in designing the contents of the Polish code between Warsaw's and Krakow's lawyers.

The main ideas of civil procedure, which found expression in a resolution of the Warsaw Commission, in principle met with the appreciation of the Krakow' community. This was the position of Fierich, who argued that the structure of civil procedure, which had existed for 110 years (French and later Russian procedure) on the territory of the Kingdom of Poland, and which was based on the principle of oral procedure with only some manifestations of a written form, openness, free theory of evidence and directness in the taking of evidence, should be preserved in the Polish code, as it corresponded, on the one hand to the rational requirements of court proceedings, and on the other hand, to legal tradition.[15] At the same time, he recognized the importance of properly situating the position of the judge in the gathering of trial material, but in terms of reconciling the principle of free trial of the parties with the principle of official investigation. Like Warsaw's lawyers, Fierich believed that the rules of Russian procedure, assigning the judge an entirely passive position in the search for evidence, should be abandoned. While the collection of trial material (facts, evidence) was still the responsibility of the parties, the court was to cooperate actively and on its own in the collection of evidence. He pointed to the Austrian, German and Hungarian procedural acts as models to follow.

The majority of the discussants of the Krakow Society were in favor of the adoption of the investigative principle in the version of the Austrian procedural act. Those in favor of adopting the Austrian model with regard to the formal and material leadership of the judge in civil litigation were especially advocates, who argued that in this respect the Austrian procedure had proven itself in practice. They therefore supported its solutions that enabled the court to arrive at material truth and imposed an obligation on the parties to act in good faith. They regarded the extension of the judge's procedural powers as an obvious consequence of the principle of free assessment of evidence. They

14 Stanisław Grodziski, "Komisja Kodyfikacyjna Rzeczypospolitej Polskiej", in *Czasopismo Prawno-Historyczne* 33/ 1 (1981), 48.

15 *Czasopismo Prawnicze*, 130 ff.

cited observations from judicial practice, where one did not encounter cases of appeals on the grounds that the court had gone too far in its pursuit of the truth, but appeals based solely on the fact that the adjudicating court had not exhausted all means of discovering the truth were very frequent. Professor Gołąb's view that an investigative principle going too far would often be of little use for the final outcome of the dispute and would only prolong proceedings was in the minority. What is worse, he argued, it could also bring about negative ethical consequences, since, for example, evidence from the hearing of a party against his/her will would, in many cases, have the character of coercion. He would thus be in a coercive position from which "the way out for an individual with fewer scruples of a religious or ethical nature might be to give evidence that does not correspond to the truth."[16]

The thesis of the Warsaw commission on the need to maintain the principle of oral proceedings with the possibility of the parties to file pleadings also did not raise serious objections. The scope of the use of a pleading in a trial and its function in the course of an oral hearing constituted an important part of the legal issues discussed throughout the codification works. As one of the participants in Krakow's debate aptly put it, the essence of the problem was to ensure that the extension of the principle of written proceedings in an adversarial oral trial did not lead to orality in the form of the freely spoken word at the trial, turning it into an "oral reading."[17] Finding the optimum relationship of the principle of written proceedings to the principle of orality was also one of the most important legislative challenges faced by the Codification Commission. However the coherent conception of the organization of a trial developed by it in this respect was modified by the government in the final version of the Code of Civil Procedure promulgated in 1930, as will be discussed below.

The participants in Krakow's debate on the new civil procedure code also supported the position of the Warsaw Commission that the parties' oath, albeit of subsidiary use, should remain an evidence measure, but in the modified form provided for in the Austrian code. As it was argued, without evidence of the parties' oaths, no rational trial could exist, since, in the absence of other means of proof, it would often be impossible to establish the facts relevant to the outcome of the dispute. The view therefore prevailed that the Polish legislator should be guided in this respect by the Austrian rules on the evidence of the hearing of parties, including a possible hearing under oath. An oath taken by a party was to be subject to the judge's assessment. The decisive oath, which existed in French or German procedure, was rejected because it was

16 *Czasopismo Prawnicze*, 122 ff.

17 *Czasopismo Prawnicze*, 120.

incompatible with the principle of the judge's free assessment of evidence. Difficulties in the use of this means of proof by the court were also pointed out, often consisting in the incorrect or erroneous formulation of the thesis of evidence in the wording of the oath.[18] These objections were not devoid of reason, as indicated by the judicial practice on Polish soil based on French regulations. The unanimous position of the Polish legal community as to the procedural advantages of the evidence of hearing the parties, as evidence characterized by simplicity and unconstrained by any form, compared to an oath, was not questioned during the work of the Codification Commission. Only objections were raised to the hearing of the parties under oath, as it was pointed out that all legal constructions of a religious nature should be removed from the civil procedure. Krakow's lawyers also commented on the question of the prejudiciality of a criminal judgment in a civil case, criticizing the idea of adopting in the Polish code the principle of the absolute binding force of a criminal judgment in a civil case. F.K. Fierich was of the opinion that a criminal judgment should be treated like any other public document and should be subject to the free assessment of a civil judge, otherwise, it would be an acceptance of the legal theory of evidence, which should no longer have a place in the modern code. In any case, a common position could not be reached on this issue, which was discussed at a later stage of the codification work.[19] The concept of the relative binding force of a criminal conviction in a civil trial was upheld by the Codification Commission because the thrust of the Code of Civil Procedure was the principle of the judge's free assessment.[20] It was not until the ministerial stage of work on the code, already during the *vacatio legis*, that the scope of the civil judge's binding of the criminal court's judgment was further expanded.[21] The codification commission's original treatment of the 1930 provision of the Code of Civil Procedure defining the extent to which a civil court is bound by a criminal court judgment was re-

18 *Czasopismo Prawnicze*, 160 ff.

19 Stawarska-Rippel, *Elementy prywatne*, 73–74.

20 Stawarska-Rippel, *Elementy prywatne*, 146. Article 7 of the Code of Civil Procedure in the Codification Commission's version reads: "The findings of a final criminal conviction as to the commission or non-completion of an offence shall be binding on a civil court unless they have been overturned in proceedings before that court."

21 Article 7 of the Code of Civil Procedure was given the following wording: "§ 1. The findings of a final judgment of conviction in criminal proceedings as to the commission of an offence shall be binding on a civil court. § 2. These findings, however, may be overturned before the civil court when the case concerns the civil liability of a person against whom the accusation has not been brought, or of a person who has not defended him or herself in criminal proceedings."

placed in 1933 by a regulation similar to the proposal of the Civil Law Commission, which, as mentioned above, modelled itself on the Austrian act.

The most serious difference of opinion between the members of the Warsaw Civil Law Commission and the Krakow Legal and Economic Society was over the type of means of challenge in the new code. In the case of an appeal as a means of challenging a judgment of a court of first instance to a court of second instance, the dispute centered around the adoption of a full appeal *cum beneficio novorum* or one in which a party was not allowed to raise new circumstances in the case. The first type of appeal was found in Russian law, the second in Austrian law. The line of demarcation in views regarding the approach to this issue did not run along geographical lines, but rather on the level of purely dogmatic considerations. The choice of a means of challenge to the Supreme Court, on the other hand, as the third judicial instance, was dictated by a different legal tradition. For in the lands of the Kingdom of Poland there was a cassation appeal, while in the lands of the former Austrian and Prussian partition there was a revision. Despite the fact that the Warsaw commission was in favor of cassation in principle, and the Krakow law society was in favor of revision, there was no lack of voices among the Krakow theoreticians emphasizing the advantages of the French cassation.

In his paper, Professor Dziurzyński pointed out that from a theoretical point of view, the cassation could not be faulted with anything, as it was characterized by a clear concept (protection of public order) and a simple form (revocation of a judgment), while the revision combining two separate points of view (interest of the party and interest of the state) was a complicated and artificial legal creation. Nevertheless, he found interesting the proposal of B. Pohorecki to entrust the cassation court with the possibility of issuing a substantive judgment to a limited extent. Fierich's position was also isolated. He supported the resolution of the Warsaw body postulating the preservation of a pure cassation type, as it was connected with a simple system of judicial organization, which consisted of two court instances ruling *in merito*, an appeal *cum beneficio novorum*, and a cassation.[22] However, as part of the work of the Codification Commission, Fierich proposed the concept of cassation with elements of revision proceedings.

A synthetic review of the first stage of the activity of Polish lawyers directed at reflecting on the main assumptions of the new civil procedure code proves that a clear vision of future changes was set at that time. The guiding principles of civil procedure developed by Polish legal scholarship and judicial prac-

22 *Czasopismo Prawnicze*, 177 ff.

tice were creatively developed in the Codification Commission's draft code of civil procedure. The results of the legal-comparative studies undertaken on civil procedural law showed that the Polish legal elite was capable of carrying out codification and unification of the law in a relatively short period of time. The Codification Commission could already boast the first drafts of the Code of Civil Procedure in 1922. In view of the intensive work of the Codification Commission, the idea of extending one of the existing codes to the whole area of the Polish state was abandoned. In the field of civil procedural law, this code was to be the Austrian Act of 1895.

4 The course of work on the Polish Code of Civil Procedure by the Codification Commission

In its work on the draft code of civil procedure, the Codification Commission's task was made easier by the fact that the procedural rules it had to revisit had previously been widely discussed. The adopted mode of operation of the Civil Procedure Section referred in part to its course of action. This is because Fierich, as chairman of the section, proposed to settle the fundamental questions of civil procedure before the drafting of the rules of the various sections of civil procedure. These included categories of issues already discussed among specialists, namely: (1) the relationship of a pleading to the word and, in particular, the importance of preparatory pleadings in the structure of a trial, (2) the openness and secrecy of proceedings, (3) the investigative principle or the principle of the disposition of the parties, (4) the freedom of assessment of evidence, (5) the question of an oath of the parties or evidence of hearing the parties, (6) the structure of an appeal and (7) the question of whether a review or a cassation is to be introduced. The exchange of views between the members of the Civil Procedure Section of the Codification Commission replicated the arguments that had been voiced earlier, although there were sometimes changes of position.[23]

The principle of an oral trial was emphasized by virtually all discussants, but differences marked the definition of the meaning of preparatory pleadings. The orality of the trial was defined, on the one hand, as requiring the court's decision to be based exclusively on that material which the parties had verbally cited at the trial (Józef Skąpski). Preparatory pleadings were to be admissible, within the necessary limits, as a pre-trial announcement of the

23 "Dodatek", 262 ff.

trial material (Fierich). However, they should not, according to some, have an obligatory character (Maurycy Allerhand—a professor at the University of Lwów). On the other hand, the view was expressed that a court should take into account not only what the parties cited orally at the hearing, but also what they included in the pleadings filed before the hearing (Litauer). The approach to the principle of orality and its relation to the parties' pleadings varied among the members of the sub commission. However, there was fairly widespread acceptance of the existence of the oral rule in the code with limited admission of preparatory pleadings.

Combining the principle of orality with the right of the parties to file preparatory pleadings was not an easy legislative task, as it was feared that incorrectly constructed provisions of the code would not transform a trial from being "oral" merely in name to being written. German judicial practice was cited as an example of such a phenomenon. Although it adopted the oral principle almost in its pure form, after its amendment (1909), pleadings took on a key role in a trial. Indeed, the parties were allowed to invoke pleadings at a trial if they did so in agreement and the court considered them appropriate.[24] This led to preparatory writings being read out in full at an oral trial, after which only the presentation of evidence took place and there was a judgment. For this reason, the Polish codifiers wanted to avoid this danger at all costs.

Therefore, in the Codification Commission's draft code, it adopted the principle that parties were not allowed to refer to the contents of submitted preparatory pleadings at the hearing, unless it was necessary to cite the literal wording of a document. The response to the action and other pleadings were for the court's information only. A court based its judgment on the oral statements of the parties. In the proceedings before regional courts, the code provided neither the obligation nor the possibility to cite the legal principles of the claim in the action. The citation of the legal grounds of the claim was to be made orally during the hearing.[25] Determining how to properly prepare an oral hearing in regional courts was an issue to which the Civil Procedure Section devoted considerable attention. This is because it was a question of giving preparatory pleadings such procedural significance

24 *Komisja Kodyfikacyjna Rzeczypospolitej Polskiej. Sekcja Postępowania Cywilnego. Polska procedura cywilna. Projekty referentów z uzasadnieniem*, vol. 1, Warszawa, 1928, 163 ff.

25 See Articles 206 and 225 § 1 of the 1930 Code of Civil Procedure (henceforth cited as CCP). On 1 December 1932, a proclamation by the Minister of Justice announcing the consolidated text of the Code of Civil Procedure was published in the *Journal of Laws 1932*, no. 112, item 934. The Code of Civil Procedure entered into force on 1 January 1933.

in order to create the concept of proceedings that are as simple, fast and inexpensive as possible.

Fierich, as the reporter of this part of the code, was against the concept of an optional exchange of preparatory pleadings at the trial stage between the delivery of a complaint and an oral, adversarial hearing. By contrast, he advocated the introduction of a mandatory response by the defendant to the complaint, which he linked at the same time to the preservation of the compulsory representation by an advocate before regional courts. The compulsory response to a complaint was present in Austrian procedure. According to the Austrian legislator, the purpose of the compulsory response to an action was to inform the court and the plaintiff in which direction the defense would be conducted and what evidence would be used.[26] The intention of the order to respond to an action was to show the full picture of the case before trial, but to exclude the possibility of the court basing its judgment on a mandatory pleading. Similarly, Fierich justified his proposal for a mandatory response to the action by arguing that only an oral trial offered the opportunity to present the material announced in the preparatory pleadings, since "the field of the parties' litigation is not the preparatory pleadings, but only the oral trial." The defendant's failure to comply with his obligation to file a response to the action had the effect that the court was entitled to issue a default judgment. On this point, Fierich's concept was in line with the provisions of the 1918 Berne Code. He regarded the obligatory response to the action as the "backbone of a trial" in the structure of the provisions of the code.[27] In the view of the defenders of the solution adopted in the code, the mandatory response to an action, by putting the trial material in order before the trial, improved the course of the trial, eliminating an element of gaming and randomness.[28] However, the Codification Commission's coherent idea of combining the principle of an oral trial with elements of a written trial was derailed at the stage of ministerial amendments to the draft code of civil procedure. The filing a response an action became optional in the code. The code provided, following the model of Austrian law, that in intricate and settlement cases the presiding judge

---

26 *Das zivilgerichtliche Verfahren in und äußern Streitsachen gemeinverständlich erläutert von Dr. Alfred Bloch, Dr. Max Leopold Ehrenreich. Dr. Michael Heller und Oswald Kastner*, Wien, 1912, 327–328. § 243 of the Austrian act provided for a mandatory response to an action, but this obligation was subject to the discretion of the judge.

27 *Komisja Kodyfikacyjna*, 208 ff.

28 Albert Thon, "Główne problemy w dyskusji nad K.P.C.", *Głos Sądownictwa* 8/1 (1936), 16 ff.

could order the filing of a response to the action before the hearing, as well as the exchange of further preparatory pleadings.[29]

However, the Codification Commission's civil procedure section devoted the most attention to considering the introduction of investigative elements into civil procedure. The investigative principle was raised in the context of the fundamental question of whether a civil judge should be granted the right to take evidence which had not been requested by the parties. The question of the scope of the judge's discretionary power to freely assess evidence and the ability to take evidence from an oath or examination of the parties *ex officio* was directly linked to the court's evidentiary initiative. Despite some voices stating that the investigative principle violates the main principle of private law, i.e., the principle of party autonomy and sometimes interferes with their private interests (Stanisław Gołąb and Alfons Parczewski—professor at the University of Warsaw), the section was in favor of adopting the investigative principle within the limits of the Austrian procedure.[30] It thus upheld the direction of changes to civil procedure in the Polish lands adopted at the very beginning of the construction of the rules of the Code of Civil Procedure. Accordingly, the members of the Codification Commission section decided that the results of evidentiary proceedings would be subject to the free assessment of the court, including the right to examine the admission of facts by the parties. In this respect, the position adopted was similar to Austrian law. In the French legal system the admissions of the parties were binding on them, and this solution was supported by a minority of the section members (Alfons Parczewski and Kamil Stefko—professor at the University of Lwów).

The opinions were somewhat differently distributed when discussing the admissibility in a civil trial of the parties' oath or the parties' examination (unsworn or under oath). The vast majority of the discussants were of the opinion that the Austrian solutions should be chosen, providing for the examination of the parties as subsidiary evidence in the form of an unsworn hearing, but also with the obligation for the parties to take an oath. The oath provided for in French and German law did not find too many supporters (Alfons Parczewski). The choice of this means of evidence following the Austrian model was determined by the fact that it had already been explicitly supported. The procedural superiority of the examination of the parties over an oath was also determined by the fact that the examination of the parties was subject to free judicial assessment, while an oath was an evidentiary rule,

29 See Article 222 of the CCP.

30 "Dodatek", 262 ff.

as a remnant of the legal theory of evidence.[31] The authors of the Polish Code consistently rejected this theory of evidence, so that the prohibition of refuting the contents of a document with witness testimony was only introduced at the stage of ministerial work on the code. This is because the authors of the draft code were convinced of the need to treat all evidence equally in view of the adoption of the principle of free evaluation of evidence by a court as the best way to establish material truth in a trial. In the opinion of the drafters, this objective was to be served first and foremost by the formal and material direction of the judge equipped with discretionary authority. In this respect, they saw the Austrian Code as an unsurpassed model, in addition supported by positive courtroom experience.

A difference of opinion among the members of the Codification Commission's civil procedure section was also revealed by the issue of the choice of a means of challenge to a court of second instance. The essence of the problem to be resolved was that it had to be decided what purpose a means of challenge was supposed to serve, whether, in the appeal proceedings, the court should examine the claim further or examine the case on the basis of the procedural material of the court of first instance. The former system was to be supported in the first place by the fact that it was more likely to lead to the discovery of the material truth in the trial (reporter Dziurzyński). According to the reporter, a party should be given the opportunity to present new evidence in the appeal proceedings, as it was not uncommon for a party to gain a full understanding of the entire case only after the first instance judgment. A law excluding new circumstances in appeal would have to be based on the assumption that the court of first instance was always able to consider the dispute extremely carefully and comprehensively in terms of facts and evidence. As long as there are doubts about this—the reporter argued—the legislator cannot limit the accumulation of procedural material to a single instance if the purpose of the trial was to be achieved.[32]

Dziurzyński was thus in favor of introducing a full appeal into the Polish code. Allerhand, on the other hand, did not share the reporter's position and declared himself in favor of adopting the Austrian system, which did not allow novelty in appellate proceedings. In his view, the Austrian appellate procedure was fully sufficient, as in the event of an error by the judge there was either a revocation of the judgment with an order for a supplementary hearing or the possibility of renewed evidence on appeal.[33] The opinion against a full

31 "Dodatek", 262 ff. The session in Warsaw on 16 May 1920.
32 *Polska procedura cywilna. Projekty*, 7 ff.
33 "Dodatek".

appeal was sparse among the section members. The majority supported the reporter's position. However, there was also an emphasis on the need for a provision allowing an appellate court to disregard new circumstances where a party could and should have cited this new procedural material in the court of first instance (Trammer, Stefko, and Litauer). Although the draft section adopted the appeal *cum benefcium novorum* and allowed for an objective re-examination of the dispute on a changed factual basis, the subsequent work of the Codification Commission echoed the call for an exception to the general rule of recognition of new circumstances by the appellate court. The code of civil procedure stated that an appellate court may disregard new facts and evidence if a party could have cited them in the proceedings before the district court, unless the opportunity or need to cite them arose later.

A debate on the choice of cassation or revision as a means of challenge to a court of third instance was initiated by Dziurzyński, who spoke in favor of cassation, but with the modification that the Supreme Court, as a cassation court in those cases in which it accepted the cassation, and the case was suitable for a substantive ruling, could issue a substantive ruling. The remaining members of the Section were in favor of cassation, although there was also no shortage of supporters of a revision according to Austrian law (Stefko).[34] Although there was a prevailing conviction among the section members that, for both rational and historical reasons, a cassation should be introduced in the Polish code, it was not definitively decided whether it should take the form of a pure cassation in the French version or with elements of a revision in nature. For this reason, in the further work of the Codification Commission's civil procedure section, the issue of a means of challenge to the third instance probably aroused the greatest emotion. The draft prepared in this respect by Fierich met with the assessment of two co-reporters, i.e., Skąpski and Litauer, the former having previously declared himself in favor of a revision according to the Austrian act, the latter being an ardent defender of the French cassation. Also Trammer, who opted for a revision by virtue of the fact that it was applied in the lands of the former Prussian and Austrian partition, presented an extended argument.[35]

In his report, Fierich gave a historical and doctrinal assessment of cassation, showing its advantages over the revision system, in which he was somewhat consistent, as he advocated the adoption of cassation at a meeting of the Krakow Society, contrary to the position of the majority. He saw the advantage of cassation in the fact that a judge of a cassation court does not judge the case in

34 "Dodatek".

35 *Polska procedura cywilna. Projekty*, 10 ff.

dispute, but judges the "judging." He therefore assumed that the activity of the Supreme Court consisted of this kind of control. Indeed, he ruled out the possibility that a case could be tried *in merito* once again in its entirety by a court of third instance. He argued that the concept of revision, from the point of view of the needs of rational judicial proceedings, had a significant flaw. Fierich's assumption was that a case could and should be decided on its merits only by the court that had the opportunity to conduct the entire case on the basis of the material it had collected. Any *revisio in iure*, involving not only control but also a ruling on the merits, had the disadvantage that the judge was ruling on the basis of the state of affairs established by another judge. Indeed, the foundation of civil procedure was to remain the principle of directness. Given a choice between cassation and revision, he strongly preferred the former, as it better served the administration of justice.[36] A cassation court did not decide the case, did not examine the facts, but only considered whether a provision of substantive or procedural law had been correctly applied. If it found an error of law it revoked the contested judgment and referred it back to the court of lower instance for reconsideration.

The draft submitted by Fierich, however, contained a provision that the Supreme Court could exceptionally issue a judgment on the merits, ending the case. He justified such a solution on opportunistic grounds. For the sake of speeding up proceedings and reducing litigation costs, Fierich opted for a provision according to which the Supreme Court could rule on the merits of a case when, after the judgment had been revoked on the grounds of an infringement of substantive law, the case was suitable for resolution and if this was requested by both parties. In his proposal, he did not see a move away from cassation to revision, as the Supreme Court's decision on the merits depended on the request of both parties.[37] In this proposal there was also a tribute to the views that the French cassation should be modified if the Supreme Court were to be part of the ordinary judiciary and not a tribunal outside the ordinary judiciary system.

What was striking about the position of the co-reporter Skąpski was that he essentially supported the concept of Fierich, although he had previously been in favor of the introduction of a revision for he considered the most important function of the court of cassation to be that of guardian of the uniformity and consistency of the case law of the lower courts. In France, it was the guardian of the "unity of French law." Consideration of precisely this aspect of the cassation procedure seems to have prevailed in favor of the change in the co-

36 *Polska procedura cywilna. Projekty*, 10 ff.

37 *Polska procedura cywilna. Projekty*, 10 ff.

reporter's views, since, he believed, the Supreme Court in its role as a cassation court could break down legal particularism and be an integrating factor for the state. Skąpski, like the draft's reporter, juxtaposed German and Austrian review with cassation to conclude "the superiority of the construction of cassation." The *revisio in iure* of the German procedure was, in his view, distinguished from the French cassation only by the fact that the German Supreme Court not only revoked the judgements under appeal, but also ruled *in merito* if the defect in the judgement consisted in an erroneous application of the law with respect to the material established, and the case was capable of being decided from the point of view of factual basis. On the other hand, he stressed that a revision according to the Austrian procedure was, as far as its scope was concerned, more extensive than the German revision, as it also dealt with defects in factual findings. It was therefore a revision not only *in iure*, but also *in facto*. The Austrian revision court was a third instance court and therefore could not ensure uniformity in the application and interpretation of the law. Skąpski argued that the revision case law against the background of the Austrian procedure was not only unsatisfactory but required thorough reform. For this reason, he advised against copying this institution, although he had previously "for practical and economic reasons" supported its introduction into the Polish code.[38]

Skąpski's extensive and excellently constructed theoretical analysis also sought to cast doubt on the proposal to transfer revision powers to the Supreme Court, even to such a limited extent as Fierich's draft did. He thus posed the question to the author of the draft as to whether it was worthwhile by an exceptional norm "to break down the straight lines of the cassation construction tested by a century of experience." Preempting the answer, as it were, he was of the opinion that although "the problem of pure doctrine must give way to the principle of purposefulness, but where that purposefulness is precisely problematic, one must turn to the general elements of the principle."[39] In this sentence, a certain disappointment could be seen on the part of the co-reporter, who had, as it were, succumbed to the "charm" of cassation under the influence of the clear arguments of the section chairman expressed at earlier stages of the discussion of appeals in the Polish code. In addition to his reservations of a legal-dogmatic nature to the presented draft, Skąpski drew attention to the practical consequences of the reporter's proposal that the Supreme Court should rule on the merits at the unanimous request of both parties. I– ·leed, he pointed out the illusory nature of the proposed solution, as

…ocedura cywilna. Projekty*, 10 ff.

…cedura cywilna. Projekty*, 10 ff.

there was little likelihood that a substantive ruling would be sought by a party who had not filed a cassation on account of the settlement of the dispute in his or her favor. In other words, such a provision would, in practice, be dead, since the consent of three entities, the court and both parties, was required for the examination of a case on the merits. As there was far-reaching disagreement among the members of the section as to the choice of a means of challenge to the third instance, Fierich proposed three alternative solutions as to whether the Supreme Court could rule on the merits.[40] First, the Supreme Court, without referring back the case, could have ruled on the application of both parties on the grounds of violation of substantive law and only if the factual situation was ripe for adjudication. Second, the Supreme Court could have proceeded in the above manner but at the request of one of the parties. Third, the Supreme Court could rule on the merits under the same conditions but at its own discretion. Eventually, the draft code of procedure adopted by the Codification Commission included a provision that made the examination of the cassation on the merits by the Supreme Court subject to the application of one of the parties. This provision, however, was amended in 1932, according to which the examination on the substance of a cassation case was taken by the Supreme Court at its sole discretion.[41] The adoption of the third solution from those proposed by the section chairman by the Polish legislature consequently meant that a means of challenge to the Supreme Court adopted in the Code of Civil Procedure in 1930/33 increased the possibility of judgments on the merits. Thus, it acted in a dual role, as a cassation and revision instance. The construction of the Polish means of challenging an appeal was original, being a creative combination of two extreme legal institutions, also using the model of the Berne Code (1918). However, the Polish cassation in its final form adopted in the code was for many, including members of the Codification Commission, a covert revision (Gołąb and Skąpski).

---

40 Stawarska-Rippel, *Elementy prywatne*, 317–19.

41 Article 439 of the CCP stipulated: "If the Supreme Court finds that there is no violation of essential procedural rules, but there is a violation of substantive law, it may rule on the merits of the case instead of sending the case back for reconsideration. When issuing a judgment, the Supreme Court is bound by the facts established in the challenged judgment." The cassation appeal could be based on the following grounds: (1) on violation of substantive law by misinterpretation or misapplication; (2) on violation of essential procedural rules, if the defects could have decisively affected the outcome of the case (Article 426 of the CCP).

5 A Legal Comparative Assessment of the Procedural Institutions of the Polish Code (1930/33)

The draft code of civil procedure prepared by the Codification Commission was implemented with only some changes and additions, made at the level of the Ministry of Justice. Although the scope of the changes was quite limited, some of them violated the essential assumptions of the code, which guided the members of the Civil Procedure Section. Undoubtedly, an undeniable advantage of the code's provisions was their clear, simple, and transparent drafting, without unnecessary casuistry or lengthiness in the description of legal constructions. The creators of the code followed the model of the Swiss codes in this respect. The general structure of the code according to the criteria: court, parties, proceedings, enforcement, adopted by the Civil Procedure Section at the beginning of its work, did not change, whereas the systematics of the code with its division into titles, sections and chapters, on the other hand, was mostly based on the Austrian and German procedural acts. An important novelty of the code was the introduction of a general part to the procedural provisions which referred to each category of courts, which had the beneficial effect of shortening the layout and contents of the code. This was a technique modeled on the structure of the Swiss codes. Although there was a title of "general provisions" at the beginning of the code it was short, comprising eight articles, which were in part a duplication of the provisions of the introductory part of the Russian code. This part included a provision on the prejudiciality of a criminal judgment in a civil case. The Codification Commission's draft did not contain such an introduction; it was added during the ministerial work. The Codification Commission did not consider it advisable to introduce the guiding principles of civil proceedings in the introductory part.

Most of the provisions in the general part on court proceedings were modelled on the provisions of codes of Germanic provenance, mainly the Austrian code. This was particularly true of the provisions defining the powers of the presiding judge, since in the model of civil procedure adopted by the authors of the code, the host of a trial was the court and not the parties, as in the romance system (French and Russian). Therefore, the duty to deliver pleadings rested with the court, following the model of the Austrian act, and not with the parties, as was the case of the French Code. The court was not obliged to conduct a conciliation between the parties, as was the case under French (Russian) law. The Codification Commission's draft introduced a mandatory response to an action in proceedings before regional courts, regardless of the value of the subject matter of the dispute, on pain of a default judgment. This type of solution was based on the provisions of the Bern procedure (1918), which shifted a civil trial more to a trial with a greater role of the principle of written proceedings at the expense of orality. The authors of the draft code were right to link the mandatory response to an action with compulsory representation by advocates in proceedings before regional courts. This is because the assumption was to prepare a trial well and to conduct it efficiently and quickly. However, the Polish legislator did not support this concept, but reached for the Austrian model, according to which a written response was dependent on the discretion of the judge hearing the case.[42]

6 Evidence from Witness Testimony and the Examination of the Parties

The Polish Code of Civil Procedure of 1930/33 took over the types of means of evidence and defined their procedural significance in the way provided for by the Austrian Code (1895). Like Austrian law, the code did not contain a provision on the burden of proof (*onus probandi*) in a civil trial, which was defined in the French and Russian codes. Although the Civil Procedure Section of the Codification Commission discussed the issue in some detail, taking a provision of the Hungarian code as a reference, this was eventually abandoned. The Polish legislator probably assumed that the rule on the burden of proof was of a substantive legal nature. Therefore, it should be included in the provisions of the future civil code. Moreover, the code definition of the burden of proof may have conflicted with the rules on the distribution of evidence under the applicable substantive law, which was of a particular nature. The Polish Code of Civil Procedure, following the project of the Codification Commission, deleted from the catalogue of means of evidence the decisory oath and the *ex officio* oath (Napoleonic Code), which had existed in the lands of the Kingdom of Poland until 1876 (in Krakow until 1855), and which at the time of the drafting of the Polish code was still retained in French and German law. In its place, the code took over the evidence from the examination of the parties, under which, however, the court could conduct the examination after taking an oath from a party. The decision of the Codification Commission to implement this means of evidence into the Polish legal order determined that it has remained in Polish law until the present day, except that the oath was replaced by taking

42 The final shape of the code was influenced by Warsaw lawyers, whose views were taken into account by the ministerial team in the final stage of the code revisions; see Stanisław Goldsztein, "Uwagi do projektu Kodeksu Postępowania Cywilnego", *Palestra* 7/8–9 (1930), 345 ff.

an affirmation from the parties under pain of criminal liability for giving false testimony (see Articles 299 and 303 of the Code of Civil Procedure of 1964).

The procedural consequences of the introduction of evidence from the examination of the parties into the Polish procedure did not quite correspond, comparing the provisions of the draft by the Codification Commission and the contents of the promulgated Code of Civil Procedure. As mentioned earlier, the code, following the investigative principle, provided that the court could admit evidence even not invoked by the parties provided that the code did not contain a provision to the contrary (Article 244 of the CCP). Thus, the code did not allow the taking of evidence either from a document or the testimony of witnesses if both parties opposed it (cf. Articles 266 and 282 of the CCP). On the other hand, court could admit visual or expert evidence without the consent of the parties. In accordance with the principle of the free assessment of evidence by the judge, the drafters did not introduce a provision that would prohibit the refutation of the contents of a document with the testimony of witnesses, as was the case in the Russian procedure. The draft code also did not provide for a provision along the lines of Russian law, which stated that "witness testimony could not be evidence of such events for the establishment of which the law required proof in writing."[43]

According to civil law in force in the Kingdom of Poland, the written form of a contract was required for evidentiary purposes, e.g., when concluding a partnership agreement. Failure to observe the written form for this type of legal action had the effect that, in the event of a dispute between the parties, witness evidence was not admissible. The institution of the form of legal act for evidentiary purposes was a product of French legal culture, which has survived in the Polish lands to the present day.[44] The absence of a prohibition on refuting the contents of a document by witness testimony in the Code of Civil Procedure, according to the Codification Commission's draft, had the consequence that even such facts, for the establishment of which substantive civil law required written evidence, could be established by examining the parties.

The taking of evidence from witnesses on the circumstances of a contract entered into by the parties which had not been drawn up in writing for evidentiary purposes was possible, but on condition that both parties did not

43 Feliks Zadrowski, "Dowód z przesłuchania stron w projekcie kodeksu postępowania cywilnego", *Palestra* 6/3–4 (1929), 61 ff.

44 On this subject, see Andrzej Dziadzio, "Forma dla celów dowodowych (ad probationem) w europejskiej perspektywie historycznej", in Verba volant, scripta manent. *Księga jubileuszowa dedykowana Profesor Bogusławie Gneli*, Warszawa, 2023, 227–244.

object to it. The provisions in this respect were amended at the ministerial stage in such a way that the prohibition of evidence from witnesses against or beyond the wording of a document was introduced (Article 265 of the CCP). Thus, a provision adopted from Russian procedural law appeared in the final stage of work on the code. This had its legal consequences with regard to the possibility of taking evidence from the examination of the parties, since, according to a provision of the code, evidence from the examination of the parties could be ordered by the court, except in cases where evidence from witnesses was not admissible (Article 323 § 1). Thus, a court could order the parties to be heard on the contents of a contract, but only if both parties did not object to it. When the parties objected the court could not take evidence from the examination of the circumstances related to the contents of a document.

In both cases, the judicial practice that would arise on the basis of the above-mentioned provisions of the Code of Civil Procedure would be detrimental to the contents of civil law in force in the lands of the former Kingdom of Poland, which had introduced an absolute prohibition on the evidence from witnesses as to the contents of a concluded contract, if it was to be concluded in written form for evidentiary purposes. Therefore, the Polish legislator had to prevent this by establishing, in the regulation introducing the Code of Civil Procedure, a relevant provision applicable only in the lands of the former Kingdom of Poland. This provision stated that "as regards facts for which, according to civil law, evidence from witness testimony was inadmissible, this evidence, as well as evidence from the examination of the parties, could only be admitted if there was a beginning of written evidence" (Article XIX, § 3[1] and [2]).[45] It followed from this provision that facts which hitherto could not be proven by witness testimony due to the requirements of substantive law (e.g., the conclusion of a partnership) could also not be established by the examination of the parties unless there were a beginning of written evidence.

The French construction of the form of legal acts for evidentiary purposes, was taken over by the Polish Code of Obligations of 1933, which stated that "the requirements of the Act or the contract, without danger of invalidity, that the written form be observed, has only the meaning that in case of a dispute the evidence of witnesses is inadmissible without the consent of both parties" (Article 110 of the Code of Obligations).[46] This was a provision that the Civil

45 Regulation of the President of the Republic of Poland of 29 November 1930. Provisions introducing the Code of Civil Procedure, *Journal of Laws 1930*, No. 83, item 652.

46 Regulation of the President of the Republic of Poland of 27 October 1930, the Code of Obligations, *Journal of Laws 1933*, no. 82, item 598.

Procedure Section wanted to introduce into civil procedure at the very beginning of the Codification Commission's work. However, this provision did not find its way into the Civil Procedure Code, as the view prevailed that the substantive civil law provisions should be found in the future Civil Code. The provision on the form of a contract for evidentiary purposes was introduced throughout the Polish state by the Code of Obligations. For this reason, Article XI §3 of the provisions, introducing the Code of Obligations, provided that "the force of Article XIX of the provisions introducing the Code of Civil Procedure extends to the territory of the entire State."[47]

The change in the legal situation carried out by the Code of Obligations and the introductory provisions meant that, in the case of a dispute between parties which had entered into a contract without keeping it in writing for evidentiary purposes, the court could not take either from witness evidence or the examination of the parties unless there were a "beginning of written evidence" in the disputed case or both parties agreed to it. The decision of the Polish legislator in the inter-war period determined that these provisions are now in force in the legal order in the form in which they were established one hundred years ago.[48] Although the foundation of Polish civil procedure was formed by Germanic legal culture, it must also be noted that the influence of the Romanic tradition was strong in the lands of central Poland, which is best demonstrated by the above-described genesis of the provisions of the Code of Civil Procedure regarding means of evidence.

7 Appeal and Cassation

In the jurisdictional part of the provisions of the Code of Civil Procedure, the influence of the Austrian code was clearly noticeable. Complementary in nature, as a source of inspiration in the drafting of the provisions by the members of the Codification Commission, were later procedural acts such as Hungarian and Berne procedural acts. However, at the stage of ministerial revision of the draft, changes were introduced that were ideologically linked to the Russian model of civil procedure. On the other hand, the dominant part of the provisions in the field of means of challenge was the reference to French and Russian solutions rather than Austrian ones. The appeal appearing in the Polish Civil Procedure Code was aimed at correcting the mistakes of both a

47 Regulation of the president of the Republic of Poland of 27 October 1930, provisions introducing the Code of Obligations, *Journal of Laws 1933*, no. 82, item 599.

48 Compare Article 74 of the Civil Code of 1964.

court and the parties. The rule was that new facts and evidence could be cited in an appeal, with the exception that they could be disregarded by the appellate court when a party could have cited them before a regional court, unless the opportunity and need to cite them arose later. The code allowed novelties not cited in the appeal pleadings to be taken into account if they were discovered by a party after the pleading had already been filed. The admission of new facts and evidence was intended to serve the purpose of conducting the appeal proceedings in full (*cum benefcium novorum appeal*). In contrast, the possibility provided for in the code for the court to disregard novelty was intended to discipline the parties. An appellate court conducted a re-examination of the case in whole or in part, depending on the party's request. The model of appeal set by the work of the Codification Commission, whereby parties could present new facts and evidence is also applicable in the current Polish Code of Procedure (Article 368 of the 1964 Code of Civil Procedure).

It was not only the construction of the appeal in the Polish code that diverged from the Austrian model, but also the appeal to the court of third instance called cassation, although the French model of this means of challenge was creatively reworked by incorporating elements of a revision. The creators of the Polish code decided on this name, referring to the strong tradition of French law on Polish soil, on the one hand, while they persisted in the conviction that French legal thought prevailed in the construction of this means of challenge. The cassation took its final form in the code after a thorough rethinking on the part of the members of the Codification Commission, who were looking for the most appropriate means of challenge of the Polish judicial system to the Supreme Court. However, there is no doubt that the cassation concept, formulated by the chairman of the Codification Commission at the initial stage of its work, contributed to the contents of the provision of the Code of Civil Procedure. The originality of the solution finally adopted was that the cassation in the Polish version was a successful compromise between the French cassation and the German revision, without reproducing the defects of each. The strength of the influence of the Codification Commission's work on Polish legal scholarship is undoubtedly evidenced by the fact, as already mentioned, that cassation in the same form functions in the contemporary legal order. Just as the Codification Commission's draft made the possibility of the Supreme Court issuing a judgment on the merits conditional on the request of one of the parties, so now the Code of Civil Procedure makes the issuance of a judgment on the merits conditional on the request of the appellant.

8 The Influence of Foreign Laws on the Model of Enforcement Proceedings in the Polish Code of Civil Procedure

Prepared by the Codification Commission (subcommission for enforcement law and proceedings), the draft provisions on enforcement and proceedings to secure claims constituted the second part of the Code of Civil Procedure. As in the case of the provisions on contentious civil proceedings, the authors of the draft aimed to create optimal enforcement proceedings on the basis of the tried and tested solutions which had been in force in the Polish lands at the time of the establishment of an independent state. Therefore, their field of interest included the provisions of enforcement proceedings contained in three legal systems: the German (1877), Austrian (1896) and Russian (1864). Although Polish enforcement proceedings were modelled on the legislation of the partitioning states, they were not without novelty.

The Polish legislator opted for a model of enforcement proceedings in which enforcement actions were divided between a court and a bailiff. Thus, it did not take over the Austrian system, in which enforcement actions were carried out exclusively by a court.[49] The bailiff as an enforcement authority existed in Russian and German law. According to the Polish code, all enforcement activities were performed by bailiffs, with the exception of those activities which were delegated to the competence of a court. They worked at municipal courts (in Polish, *sądy grodzkie*). In cases transferred to the exclusive jurisdiction of a court, a bailiff was the executive body in the event that enforcement actions were delegated to him or her by the court. In such a case, the bailiff fulfilled the instructions of the court (Article 508 § 3 of the CCP). On the other hand, the bailiff was the executive and adjudicating authority in matters within his competence. However, a court could, *ex officio*, give orders to the bailiff to ensure the proper performance of the enforcement and to remedy any deficiencies observed (Article 508 § 4 of the CCP). The *ratio legis* of this provision consisted in the fact that, due to the complicated nature of enforcement proceedings, which could result in numerous breaches, there was an *ex officio* review of the bailiff's actions by the court—regardless of complaints and allegations.[50] The legislator's aim was to reduce the possibility

---

49 Rafał Łyszczek, "Wpływ regulacji prawnych państw zaborczych dotyczących organów egzekucji sądowej na zunifikowane ustawodawstwo polskie w okresie II Rzeczypospolitej: wybrane zagadnienia", *Krakowskie Studia z Historii Państwa i Prawa* 2 (2008), 233–251.

50 Wacław Zylber, "Nadzór sądu nad czynnościami komornika według kodeksu postępowania cywilnego", in *Polski Proces Cywilny: dwutygodnik poświęcony zagadnieniom wykładni i praktyce prawa procesowego* 3/10 (1935), 296 ff.

of the infringement of regulations in order to guarantee the interests of the parties to the fullest extent possible. The solution adopted was an original one, not found in other acts, which was introduced at the ministerial stage of the drafting of enforcement law.

The division of enforcement actions between a court and a bailiff was also, as mentioned, a feature of Russian and German enforcement. The difference, however, was that the German procedure delegated essentially all enforcement actions to a court, with the exception of those strictly listed in the act, which were delegated to a bailiff. In contrast, the Russian act delegated all enforcement actions, with the exceptions reserved to a court, to the bailiff's jurisdiction. The Polish Code of Civil Procedure referred to the Russian provisions on this point. A bailiff in Russia was a non-judicial body, loosely linked to the court, whose control over enforcement actions was minimal. In this respect, the Polish legislator chose a different model for the legal relationship between a court and a bailiff, introducing *ex officio* control of the court over the enforcement execution by a bailiff. Following the model of Russian law, the Polish legislator also introduced one means of challenge available to the parties to the enforcement proceedings, in the form of a so-called complaint against the actions of a bailiff (Article 512 of the CCP).

One of the fundamental guarantees for the proper conduct of enforcement actions was the introduction of a provision in the Polish Code of Civil Procedure obliging a bailiff to compensate for damages caused by his negligence or bad will. The civil liability of a bailiff came into play if the aggrieved party could not have prevented the damage in the course of the proceedings by means provided for in the code (Article 521 § 1 of the Code of Civil Procedure). The bailiff was jointly and severally liable to the state treasury for the damage caused (Article 521 § 2 of the Code of Civil Procedure). This structuring of the provision indicated that, in terms of the bailiff's liability for damages, the Polish legislator relied on Austrian provisions.[51] However, the conditions for the bailiff's liability in Austrian law were more limited compared to the provision in the Polish code. In contrast to the adopted model of civil proceedings in disputes modelled primarily on Austrian procedure, the influence of Russian law was much more pronounced in the enforcement provisions. The Polish enforcement procedure of 1930 (33) adopted systemic assumptions that have

51 The civil liability of judicial officials was regulated in Austria by the act of 12 July 1872. On this subject, see Andrzej Dziadzio, "Odpowiedzialność odszkodowawcza sędziów w dobie tworzenia się podstaw państwa prawa", in *Prawo i Państwo. Księga jubileuszowa 200-lecia Prokuratorii Generalnej Rzeczypospolitej Polskiej*, Warszawa, 2017, 87–101.

stood the test of time, as they still form the core of the provisions of the 1964 Code of Civil Procedure.

9 Conclusion

Civil procedural law was the branch of law which was the first to become of interest to scholarship and practice when confronted with the need to unify the law in the reborn Polish state. Throughout the period of work on the adoption of its own code of civil procedure, the Polish legal community presented a consensual position on many fundamental issues. First of all, it should be noted that there were no fundamental differences as to the definition of the guiding principles of the future code. The principles of an open, oral and adversarial trial, based on a free assessment of evidence directly taken at trial, were not questioned by any participant in the Polish debate. The need to increase the role of a judge in a civil trial was also widely accepted, albeit with varying emphasis on the investigative principle and the judge's evidentiary initiative. For this reason, the provisions of the Polish code concerning the jurisdictional part of the conduct of civil proceedings at the trial stage before a court of first instance were clearly modelled on Austrian law.

The structure of means of challenge was based on the use of the legacy of Romanian legal culture. The institution of appeals and cassation was in opposition to the legal solutions of Austrian law, which was also a point of reference in the discussion on the catalogue of means of challenge in the Polish Code of Civil Procedure. The Polish legislator also departed from the Austrian model of enforcement proceedings towards the introduction of provisions modelled on Russian legislation. It should be emphasized, however, that there were solutions adopted in the Polish Code of Enforcement Proceedings which allowed for the control of bailiff enforcement by a court to a much broader extent than was the case under Russian legislation.

CHAPTER 12

Judges' Independence and Accountability: 500 Years of Adjudication in Civil Law

Grzegorz J. Blicharz

A judge's independence and accountability, along with the shape of judicial power, have always been discussed in the Polish legal tradition. Importantly, judiciary reforms played a crucial role in the gradual change of the constitutional design of the state over the past 500 years. This chapter aims to present three key features of the judiciary in the Polish legal tradition, and why the *Formula Processus* enacted in 1523 played a key role in shaping them. First, the introduction of the appellate procedure to the Sejm court in *Formula Processus* was set to guarantee an impartial and independent court for the nobility. It embodied the principle of judges' independence, which Oswald Balzer described as "a characteristic of the old Polish judiciary."[1] Second, the innovative appellate procedure eventually overloaded the Sejm court and caused enormous delays in resolving disputes. The way out of this situation—a long-term consequence of *Formula Processus*—was the establishment of the Crown Tribunal in 1578, an unprecedented example of the separation of the judiciary from state power long before the modern era. As Stanisław Kutrzeba expressed it, during "Stefan Batory's reign, Poland saw a major reform in the field of justice, a reform that remained unchanged until the dismemberment of the old Polish Republic" at the end of the 18th century.[2] Third, the personal accountability of judges realized by the parties through *nagana sędziego* (motion or removal of a judge—*motio iudicis*) was limited and eventually abandoned due to the appellate procedure introduced by *Formula Processus*, which was targeted to review the judgment, not the judge.

1 Oswald Balzer, *Geneza Trybunału Koronnego. Studyum z dziejów sądownictwa polskiego XVI wieku*, Warszawa, 1886, 44.

2 Stanisław Kutrzeba, "La Réforme Judiciaire en Pologne a l'époque d'Etienne Báthory", in *Etienne Báthory, roi de Pologne, prince de Transylvanie*, Imre Lukinich, Jan Dąbrowski (eds.), Cracovie, 1935, 292.

 | DOI:10.1163/9789004736672_014

1 Judges' Independence as Universal Legal Phenomenon

In the modern legal doctrine, independence of judges and independence of courts are understood as a fruit of the separation of powers: that is, the judiciary from the legislative and executive powers.[3] The question, thus, is whether or not and to what extent Polish judges can be described as independent prior to the emergence of the modern concept of a state and independent judiciary.

In Polish legal vernacular, two different terms are used to describe independence, whereas judges or courts are *niezawiśli* and *niezależni* (art. 45 and art. 178 of the Polish Constitution of 1997). Although there is no clear distinction between these two terms, since they are both expressed by one English term, *independent*, the doctrine draws a slight difference in the usage. Historically, the term *niezawiśli* is older than *niezależni*, since it was used in the Polish Constitutions of 1921 and 1935. The current Constitution retains both terms when referring to judges and courts. The principle of independence understood as *niezależność* guarantees the separation and autonomy of judges from other state powers, as well as from any other individuals or entities. Differently, the principle of independence understood as *niezawisłość*, being a more overarching notion, expresses that judges are subordinated exclusively to the Constitution of the Republic of Poland and the laws of Poland. In certain contexts, *niezależność* is considered to be a set of guarantees that allows a judge not to be subjected to any external influences (*niezawisłość*).[4] Sometimes, *niezawisłość* is expressed in a positive way and points to the inner sphere of a judge, who should make impartial decisions solely according to the law and his own opinion and conscience. Conversely, in a negative way, it refers to the external aspect, meaning that no one can exert influence onto a judge's decision.[5] Overall, however, *niezawisłość* is sometimes referred to judges, whereas *niezależność* to courts.[6]

Similarly, in ancient Roman republican procedures, the archaic process called the *legis actiones*, with the later variation called a formulary system, allowed for any Roman citizen, whom the parties unanimously approved or whom the *praetor* randomly chose in the absence of such approval, to be nominated as a judge; regardless, it was expected that a judge be independent

3 Joanna Derlatka, *Wyłączenie sędziego w postępowaniu cywilnym*, Warszawa, 2016, 30.

4 Czesław Jaworski, "Niezależność i niezawisłość", in *Etyka zawodów prawniczych, Etyka prawnicza*, Hubert Izdebski, Paweł Skuczyński (eds.), Warszawa, 2006, 112.

5 Derlatka, *Wyłączenie sędziego*, 29.

6 Aneta Łazarska, *Niezawisłość sędziowska i jej gwarancje w procesie cywilnym*, Warszawa, 2018, 30.

and held accountable. Among the ancient Roman legal maxims, a universal rule of *nemo est iudex in propria causa*[7] retained a prominent place. It allowed for challenging a judge who was partial or who imposed a disservice through unprofessional, unethical conduct; in so doing, a judge was held accountable for his actions (*iudex qui litem suam fecit*). At the same time, this rule highlighted that a judge must be independent both from the parties, and from the *praetor*—a public official who appointed (*nominatio*) him to adjudicate a specific case. In fact, the Roman republican formulary system evolved not with regard to subordination towards *praetor* as jurisdictional authority, but rather with respect to the degree to which judges were subordinate to a legal opinion of Roman jurists, as a source of law, and to the extent to which they were free to choose between various legal interpretations.

In the times of Hadrian (2nd century AD), it held that when faced with the submission of two contradictory opinions of jurists, it is likely that the judge had to choose his final position according to the strength and authority of the jurist in question and the circumstances of the case. As Roman jurist Gaius informs us, "the judge is allowed to follow the opinion he wishes" (*iudici licet quam velit sententiam sequi*—G. 1,7).[8] The power of the interpretation of Roman jurists was already strengthened by Augustus (27 BC–14 AD) by way of distributing among jurists the privilege of *ius publice respondendi*—giving opinions with the authority of the *princeps*.[9] In the case of concurring opinions of jurists, since the time of Hadrian, they had the force of statute (*legis vicem optinet*- G. 1,7), so they bound judges in all cases. One can look at Hadrian's move as an interference with the independence of the Roman jurisprudence and indirectly of judges, motivating jurists to coordinate their opinions and determine uniform future sentences.[10] This could also be viewed as a move towards final confirmation of power of the jurists to create law,[11] who became "legislators, *homines politici* at the highest level."[12]

7 See C. 3,5,1 Valens, Gratian, and Valentinian (376) and D. 5,1,17 Ulpian, *Edict*, Book 22.

8 Antonio Palma, "Lo ius controversum quale espressione dell'artificialità del diritto romano", *Studia et Documenta Historiae et Iuris* 81 (2015), 93.

9 Johannes Michael Rainer, "Homo Politicus—Homo Privatus", in *Die Idee der Person als römisches Erbe?*, Hans-Dieter Spengler, Benedikt Forschner, Michael Mirschberger (eds.), Erlangen, 2016, 17.

10 Palma, "Lo ius controversum", 94.

11 Paulina Święcicka, Il *consensualismo* della legge nel pensiero dei giuristi romani del III secolo d.C. e nella riflessione dei giuristi contemporanei: paradosso o necessità razionale?, *Legal Roots: The International Journal of Roman Law, Legal History and Comparative Law* 5 (2016), 138–139.

12 Rainer, "Homo Politicus—Homo Privatus", 17.

Roman legal thought teaches us yet another aspect of judges' independence, which refers us to their subordination only to law (*ius*), especially as expressed by the Roman jurisprudence. This relates us to the idea of "interior independence" of Roman jurists and, later, professional judges. It is impossible to look at a judge's role only as a mechanical application of the body of law. This body is alive, because it refers to basic goods and values. Thus, in the "inner court" of every judge, there is ongoing process of choosing basic goods and values in order to properly resolve the conflict of principles.[13] A broader perspective on law is expressed by many Roman principles, which show that interpreting and applying law require the consideration of outside factors, such as: social context when executing law (*summum ius summa iniuria*), morality (*non omne quod licet honestum est*), and human flourishing (*hominum causa omne ius constitutium sit*). Anthropological assumptions are implicit in the law. The idea that the human person is at the core of the law, as expressed by Roman jurists, "is not rhetorical flimflam, nor the illusions or dreams of a lawyer."[14] Not following this broad context of the law would make a judge arbitrary, but not independent.

As it is argued in the modern Polish legal doctrine, the principle of impartiality, so vividly expressed in Roman law (*nemo est iudex in propria causa*), is correlative to the principle of independence.[15] Impartiality refers us to the conduct of each judge in a specific case, with the independence of judges towards relations with legislative and executive powers.[16] Similar views are presented in the Polish jurisprudence: "impartiality is the externalization of independence."[17] "*A contrario*, a pendent judge, i.e., one who is or may be subject to pressure from other persons, organizations, or authorities by virtue of the fact that they have the legal and economic advantage over him to exert this pressure, cannot be impartial."[18] Having said that, a judges' independence and accountability should be considered universal requirements that were commonly desired by the conflicted parties long before the modern separation of powers took precedence in democratic societies.

13 Franciszek Longchamps de Bérier, "Problemy podporządkowania prawu", in *Etyka zawodów prawniczych, Etyka prawnicza*, Hubert Izdebski, Paweł Skuczyński (eds.), Warszawa, 2006, 159–160.

14 Franciszek Longchamps de Bérier, "*Persona:* Bearer of Rights and Anthropology for Law", in *Human dignity and law. Studies on the dignity of human life*, José María Puyol Montero (ed.), Valencia, 2021, 48.

15 Derlatka, *Wyłączenie sędziego*, 31.

16 Łazarska, *Niezawisłość sędziowska*, 153.

17 Supreme Administrative Court of Poland, I GSK 931/08 (2010).

18 The Constitutional Tribunal of Poland, K 1/98 (1999).

2 The Original Independence of Polish Judges

Even before the *Formula Processus*, the independence of judges permeated Polish legal thought. The oldest Polish legal monuments refer to this principle. A Polish judge *judges according to his own opinion, which he deems most right —zo richtet her noch synem zynne zo her rechteste kan* (*Księga elbląska*—the Book of Elbląg, KE 3.2), and the juridical authority of Polish judges *does not flow from the Emperor, as (the authority of) the German princes and judges—Unde wen irgericht von dem keyser in gywerlt nicht enkumt, alzdutscher-vurstenunderichter tut* (KE 2.1). It presents Polish judges as more independent than German judges, since they do not depend on the emperor. These references are already present in the oldest known collection of Polish laws—the Book of Elbląg—which dates back to the 13th century and was written down in old German dialect for the purposes of Teutonic Order and its jurisdiction over Poles living under its reign. Oswald Balzer, when commenting on it, stated that judges' independence is "a characteristic of the old Polish judiciary."[19] Wacław Uruszczak stated that it confirmed "autonomy of Polish judges and their independence from rulers."[20] He highlighted that the 14th century *Statuty Kazimierza Wielkiego* (Statutes of Casimir the Great) also showed "concern for the independence of judges in the handling of court cases"[21] by ordering judges to maintain impartiality, fairness, and justice in passing judgments.[22] Even earlier literary sources, like *Chronica Polonorum* (Chronicle of the Poles) of Wincenty Kadłubek (12th/13th century), showed both judicial abuses and the ideals of providing just and merciful judgement. According to *Magister Vincentius*, the first judgment of innate (intuitive) justice may, if wrong, be corrected by legal justice in a just trial in which *Racio iuris imperat*, i.e., where the legal reasonableness rules (*Chronica Polonorum* IV, 2).[23] This elevates the independent judiciary to be the core principle of our legal tradition and is certainly not a mere coincidence. References to the role

19 Balzer, *Geneza Trybunału Koronnego*, 44.

20 Wacław Uruszczak, "Statuty Kazimierza Wielkiego jako źródło prawa polskiego", *Studia z Dziejów Państwa i Prawa Polskiego* 3 (1999), 101.

21 Wacław Uruszczak, *Historia państwa i prawa polskiego 966–1795*, Warszawa, 2021, 98.

22 Wacław Uruszczak, "Niezależność sądów, niezawisłość i samorządność sędziowska w dawnej i niedawnej Polsce", in *Krajowa Rada Sądownictwa. XX-lecie działalności*, Piotr Tuleja (ed.), Warszawa, 2010, 14–15.

23 Grzegorz J. Blicharz, "Wincenty Kadłubek, Magister Vincentius (ca. 1150–1223)", in *Law and Christianity in Poland. The Legacy of the Great Jurists*, Franciszek Longchamps de Bérier, Rafael Domingo (eds.), London, New York, 2023, 27–28; 31.

of judges, their independence, and their accountability occupy a prominent place in the oldest monument of Polish law, dating back long before the *Formula Processus* (1523).

The Book of Elbląg is a foundational text for our knowledge about Polish law. It starts by presenting the geopolitical situation of Poland and the German Empire, and most particularly by comparing Polish judges with German judges. Even more, it is preceded by a very broad and concise, almost lyrical, historical outline of what happened before Polish customary law was established, which focuses exactly on the general role of the judiciary. The characteristic preface to the Book of Elbląg testifies more to the erudition of the author himself than it is a serious source of knowledge about Polish law. Antoni Helcel even recognizes that the author of the text "preaches various oddities."[24] But from our point of view, it is an important source of knowledge about the way of thinking at the time and for imagining the foundations of the legal order. This aspect is usually overlooked in the literature. The analysis will follow Antoni Helcel's reconstruction and his translation of the Book of Elbląg into Polish.

The very first sentence of the introduction to the Book of Elbląg instructs us that the courts were created so that everyone could be lawfully obliged to observe customs, to avoid feuds, and to avoid lawlessness: *Once upon a time in the old days, when people feuded and allowed lawlessness, a council of wise men invented courts by which everyone was forced to have customs, and by this they attracted many people, that for some they had indulgence, for others the recognition of great guilt—Hy byvor by alden zyten / Do dy lute beganden stryten, / Un uben ungerichte, Der wysen rat tichte / Dy ding, do man twunge mete / Iclichen, daz her hette / Zetin, und czugin volkys vil do mete, / Daz ze hatten gedolt, Und obir vilen ingrose scholt.*

The author of the Book of Elbląg sets the history of law and judicial power in three contexts: Jewish, Roman, and Greek law. While he attributes the first attempts to establish judicial power to the Israelites, considering the time of Solomon as its peak, there is no doubt that the author gives the greatest merit in this field to the Romans: *In later times these laws were abandoned, so that they passed away and no one obeyed them. Only the Romans picked them up—Daz is waz zeu gan, / Und sich nymant karte dor an. / Romere hub en is wedir an* and next that *The Romans were outraged by this* [lawlessness] *and took it* [*law*] *under their protection—Dy romere daz mute. / Und schufen dorundir hute.* The pivotal role of Roman law, which is far superior to that of the Greeks, resounds

24 *Starodawne Prawa Polskiego Pomniki*, vol. 2, Antoni Helcel (ed.), Kraków, 1870, 6.

extremely clearly: *This came to the Greeks because the Romans gained great honor from here, that they bound the old and the young with their courts, and even the higher families were subject to them—Dis ding qwam den krychen vur, / Daz dy romere / Hattin michel ere, / Do von sy twungen / Dy alden und dy jungen / Myt irs gerichtes rechte.* According to the author, the judicial and juridical system of Rome was so much appreciated that the Greeks decided to "borrow" law from the Romans:—*This having been considered by the Greeks, they resolved to reach out to the Roman Senate, so that it would be willing to send them a law that would be useful to them, and which would curb the people's swagger, as is now happening in some cities—Daz ze ho geslechte / In udertenik machten. / Hir uf dy krychen dochten / Und worden daz czu rate, / Daz ze zcu dem senate / Zcu rome butyn ire hende, / Daz her in welde zenden / Recht, daz in tochte, / Und do man mete mochte / Twingen des volkes obir mut; / Alz man manchen stetin nu tut.* This mysterious "loan" took place, and *The Romans gladly accepted this request, and sent to the Greeks in writing their law, which they devised by their sages—Dys empfingyn dy Romer vor gut. / Den krichen santen ze mit schrift / Waz ze hattin geticht, / Und ouch mit eren wysen getracht, / Hatten stete gemacht.*

Poland and the Poles are already portrayed in the introduction as an independent people who also rejected Roman law as the law of the German empire: *The Romans also took possession in time of the country called Germany, and at once gave it their law. To the Germans the neighboring people were very heavy; but this people, though often reviled, yet persevered in resistance, so that with their families, in their laws, they are not subject to any country—Romer betwungen ouch zedir mannich lant; / Dy dutschin genant. / Ir recht saczten ze yn zcu hant. / Dy dutschen zeu nokbuer / Eyn volc, daz waz sere suer; / Alleine sy is nu vornarret, / Zo hat doch beharret, / Daz iz mit synem geslechte / An synem rechte / Dy keinem lande ist undirtan.* However, Poland formulated its own legal tradition. Poland's independence as a state with its own history and legal order shines throughout the text: *Its wise men have also long ago devised and arranged for it the laws to which it has recourse. This people is called Poles, and its laws I proclaim to you here—Syne wysesten ouch han / In zin recht getichtit / Von aldir, und berichtet, / Daz is dor an zich hat gewant. / Polen ist daz volk genant: / Syn recht tun ich euwch hy bekant.* It is repeated in the first paragraph which presents the legal order of Poland, that *the Poles have been subject to the Roman capital of the Pope since the moment of (their adoption) of Christianity, and not to the Emperor, because the Roman capital took them under its protection making them all the more willing to become Christians—dazdy Polen, von ircristenheitangende, habin den rinyschebstule des bobistesun-*

dirtenikgewesinundenict dem styl in synem schirm impfing, dorchdazzedestegernircristenwordin (KE 1.1)

The Book of Elbląg presents the Polish judge as different from German judge: *While their judgments do not emanate from the Emperor into the world, like the judgments of German princes and judges, therefore they do not call sessions of their bench courts from a higher authority, like the German Judges; whatever they judge, and whatever is testified or denied before them, has as firm a force as the judgments of the Margraves and German princes; for their judgments have the force of a bench court everywhere—Unde wen irgericht von dem keyser in gywerlt nicht enkumt, alzdutschervurstenunderichter tut, zoenhabinzedez keine gewoneit, das zeirgerichthegyn von obirgewalt, alzdutscherichter pflegen zcu tun. Wazabirzegerichtin, adirwaz vor in bekantwirt, adirgeloukint, daz hat zo getane macht, alzemarkgreven unde etlicher dutschenvursten, dyir ding nicht enhegin* (KE 2.1–2.2).

Moreover, Polish judge is independent from the advice of those present who were asked by him to join the proceedings: *But if he sees near him, when he judges, more fit men, then he invites them towards him, and asks their advice; and if he likes whose advice, then he judges according to that; but if not, then he judges according to his own opinion, which he deems most right—zyt her abir nucze lute by im, wen her riehtet, dy leet her zcu im, und leget in dy rede vor; und dunkit in ir keynis rede recht, dornoch richtet her; behaget im abir ir keynis rede, zo richtet her noch synem zynne zo her rechteste kan* (KE 3). According to the oldest Polish collection of laws, Polish judge are independent, and judge what they deem most right.

The same idea that a judge must follow his conscience and justice was expressed later in the art. 113 of the Statutes of Casimir the Great: *ne velud ... contra eorum conscientiam et iustitiam ... faciant partis in gravamen.*[25] The judges at that time were representative of the king, wherein their judgements were final, which held to be true especially in the most dominant form of courts, so called *sądy wiecowe* (*in colloquio*—higher court colloquia), that were held outside of the court of king (*in curia*). This was a way of providing justice much sooner on the local level. Although the system of courts and variety of judicial functions developed over time, the main feature of a judge as a representative of a king remained. Irrespective of this, at the core of Polish legal tradition remained a request and desire that a judge be impartial and independent, although subjected to the higher power of the king.

---

25 *Starodawne Prawa Polskiego Pomniki*, 129.

3 The Crown Tribunal of 1578: Toward the Modern Separation of Powers

State judiciary in private cases grew out of amicable justice. Stanisław Wróblewski[26]—one of Poland's most prominent jurists—made this observation in 1928 and enunciated that the judiciary has not always been a function of state power, expressing the need to establish a new arbitration form of courts. Ten years later, Seweryn Rosmarin referred to Wróblewski's statement, indicating that the "public service" of the judiciary may in time pass from the state into the hands of corporations, becoming a decentralized and internal function of each corporation.[27] Rosmarin pointed out the risk of courts' arbitrariness and detachment from public expectations and public opinion as a possible reason for opting for arbitration or corporate courts. Stanisław Gołąb explained, however, that: "Well-organized professional arbitration and conciliation courts can provide help and relief here, as long as their creation is not just an expression of resentment and distrust of the state judiciary."[28]

In ancient Roman *legis actio* and formulary proceedings, private and non-professional judges exercised judicial functions delegated by *praetors* (state officials who had *iurisdictio*, but who were not judges) in deciding civil law cases. Even then, such judges differed from arbitrators, who were chosen by the parties themselves based on an agreement (*compromissum*). Roman private judges, however, are a reminder of the private origins of conflict resolution mechanisms and an example of judicial power exercised by the general citizenry. In the Roman Empire, judges eventually became public officials incorporated into imperial bureaucratic structures, when *cognitio extra ordinem* became the only civil law procedure. Henceforward, Roman emperors and later medieval kings and absolute monarchs began to be considered holders of judicial power. This was an expression of their *imperium*, along with their legislative and executive powers. Even then, judicial power was delegated to judges, who, this time, became representatives of the ruler. It was evident for the author of the Book of Elbląg, who, however, peculiarly stressed independence of Polish judges. The change started with the emergence of another idea of the sovereign and the idea of separation of powers, when the judicial power began to be considered independent of the legislature.

26 Stanisław Wróblewski, "Sądy polubowne w historji prawa", in *Rocznik Polskiej Akademii Umiejętności. Rok 1927/1928*, Kraków, 1929, 84.

27 Seweryn Rosmarin, "Blaski i cienie sądownictwa polubownego", *Głos Prawa* 6–8 (1938), 395.

28 Stanisław Gołąb, *Proces cywilny we współczesnej sytuacji gospodarczej*, Kraków, 1932, 17.

The history of judicial power in Poland exemplifies attempts to appropriately balance the influence of state (i.e., royal power) and to ensure citizen participation in the administration of justice. As Oswald Balzer described it, the nobility gradually brought all cases under the submission of the king as supreme judge in order to mitigate the influence of the magnates on the Polish judges, who served as representatives of the king and ensured impartiality of the court at all levels of judicial system.[29] The culmination of this process was the introduction of an appeal procedure to the Sejm court (*in Conventione Generali Regni*) under the *Formula Processus* (1523). At the Sejm court, the king ruled himself in the presence of the entire Sejm, which also allowed the nobility to ensure the king's independence and impartiality in administrating justice. The normal appeal procedure was to *sądy wiecowe* (higher courts colloquia), but when they do not come to pass—*et in defectu terminorum generalium*, there was created an open way to appeal directly to the Sejm court.[30] Anyway, it was possible to appeal from the higher courts colloquia decisions to the Sejm court: *quilibet appellare de terminis praedictis generalibus ad Regiam Majestatem, tamquam jurium omnium Regni Dominum superiorem, pro Justitia consequenda*. As *Formula Processus* highlighted, anyone could appeal from the aforesaid higher courts colloquia to the King, as the supreme "Lord of all the rights of the Kingdom," for obtaining justice.[31]

The introduction of an appeal procedure to the Sejm court under the *Formula Processus* was related to the rise of the Polish *szlachta* (noblemen) as an important element of power structure in the Polish *Rzeczpospolita* (Commonwealth).[32] It sealed that noblemen were judged by the king himself, ensuring more impartial judgement independent from influences of the great lords and magnates (*możnowładcy—magnateria*). The innovative appellate procedure, however, eventually overloaded the Sejm court and caused enormous delays in resolving disputes. The way out of this situation—a long-term consequence of *Formula Processus*—was the establishment of the Crown Tribunal in 1578. The noblemen gained their own court independent of royal authority,[33] with judges elected by the nobility which extended its cognition also to the civil cases of the clergy. This Tribunal was designed to be

29 Balzer, *Geneza Trybunału Koronnego*, 17.

30 *Formula Processus*, in *Volumina Legum*, vol. 1, Petersburg, 1859, 205 (f. 409).

31 *Volumina Legum*, vol. 1, 205 (f. 409).

32 Anna Grześkowiak-Krwawicz, *Queen Liberty: The Concept of Freedom in the Polish-Lithuanian Commonwealth*, Leiden, Boston, 2012, 13–14.

33 Andrzej Dziadzio, "Konstytucja 3 maja 1791 roku na tle koncepcji ustrojowych oświecenia", *Państwo i Społeczeństwo* 4 (2006), 167.

the supreme and ultimate court of the whole of Poland, and in several drafts sought to become the court of all social strata.[34] This supreme court, adjudicating mainly civil cases, appears to be an example, unprecedented in Europe at that time, of the modern separation of legislative and judicial powers; this was long before Montesquieu and the true return of the judiciary to the general citizenry. Oswald Balzer highlighted that the Tribunal was instituted only one year after Jean Bodin "for the first time boldly made a theoretical claim about the need for a firm separation of legislation and the judiciary."[35] What we know about Jean Bodin, however, is that he highlighted that "these sovereign powers of legislation and judicature were merely two sides of the same coin of sovereignty"[36] and warned against too direct an involvement of the sovereign by "*intermeddling* with the legislative and judicial powers of state."[37] Thus, his favorite topic was the idea of delegation of *imperium* and *iurisdictio* to magistrates who cherished their own autonomy in power, which was given from above. Bodin traced it back to the Papinian rule of D. 1,21,1 (Papinian, *Questions*, Book 1): ... *verius est enim more maiorum iurisdictionem quidem transferri, sed merum imperium quod lege datur non posse transire* ... According to *the custom of our ancestors* iurisdictio *is transferable, but not the very power of* imperium *which is conferred by a statute*. This idea influenced political theories of medieval and early modern age. These ideas were certainly influential for Polish noblemen, even more given the influence of Bodin on Jan Zamoyski;[38] in fact, the latter was crucial for the 1578 reform, when he effectively negotiated with the clergy to support the establishment of the Crown Tribunal. From a broader perspective, the Crown Tribunal, however, was a symbolic takeover of the jurisdiction of the king, so Poland went beyond what Bodin expressed in his writings, especially in *Six Livres de la Republique* published in 1577. The Constitution of May 3, 1791 retained the tribunal of the nobility, although it allowed several governmental commis-

34 Felicia Roșu, "Monarch, Citizens, and the Law under Stefan Batory: The Legal Reform of 1578", in *Citizenship and Identity in a Multinational Commonwealth: Poland—Lithuania in Context 1550–1772*, Karin Friedrich, Barbara M. Pendzich (eds.), Leiden, Boston, 2009, 27–28.

35 Balzer, *Geneza Trybunału Koronnego*, 335.

36 Daniel Lee, *The Right of Sovereignty. Jean Bodin on the Sovereign State and the Law of Nations*, Oxford, 2021, 169.

37 Daniel Lee, *Popular Sovereignty in Early Modern Constitutional Thought*, Oxford, 2016, 219.

38 Summerfield Baldwin, "Jean Bodin and the League", *The Catholic Historical Review* 23/2 (1937), 174–175.

sions to have judicial powers, which was an exception to the separation of powers principle.[39]

The Crown Tribunal furthermore embodied yet another principle: the election of judges by the noblemen themselves: for example, by the provincial *sejmiki* (dietines), as opposed to the nomination or delegation of *iurisdictio* by the king. To this day, this issue is the crucial element in the conversation surrounding judges' independence. Nevertheless, although the Constitution of May 3, 1791, highlighted that the legitimacy of judges came not from the nomination or election, but from the pledge that a judge swears when entering the office,[40] the judges' pledge was the constant element of Polish legal tradition and was particularly underscored in the case of the *Formula Processus* and the Crown Tribunal. *Formula Processus* wanted that judges to be very careful in providing judgements, and especially diligently consider the capacity of parties: *Judices diligenter considerare debent*.[41] Moreover, not only were the judges' pledges not sufficient to guarantee *de facto* judges' independence, but neither were the requirements that the Tribunal's judges should be elected from those who are "worthy, God-fearing, virtuous, lawful and in the judicial customs of the country skillful, and settled";[42] this highlights the importance of judges' accountability.

4 Judges' Accountability: Departure from Personal Liability

Formula Processus additionally influenced the accountability of judges. The old way of "reviewing" the judicial decision was to claim the personal accountability of a judge, which in fact focused on judging the judge, not the judgement itself. The party who lost the case could initiate the procedure of *nagana sędziego* (motion of a judge or removal of a judge, later called in Latin—*motio iudicis*). It, however, did not affect the other party, since it started a new trial between one of the parties and the judge, which led to obtaining damages from him or to removing the judge from the judicial position. This personal liability, as it was already defined, also had ancient Roman roots. However, Stanisław Wróblewski warned, that history does not repeat itself, *although it is worth asking whether there are indeed similarities between the phenomena*

39 Dziadzio, "Konstytucja 3 maja 1791", 170.

40 Uruszczak, "Niezależność sądów", 18–21.

41 *Volumina Legum*, vol. 1, 208 (f. 416).

42 "Konstytucja Sejmu Walnego Warszawskiego Roku Pańskiego 1578", in *Volumina Legum*, vol. 2, Petersburg, 1859, 182 (f. 963).

and where they go.[43] In the Polish legal history, *Formula Processus* brought what already was well known in the late Roman law and in Canon law of the time: that is, the appellate procedure. It was designed to replace the motion against the judge (*nagana sędziego*). Appellate proceedings were already known in Mazowsze province since 1453, and in Podlasie since 1516.[44] Art. 39 of the *Formula Processus* stated that everyone should be allowed to appeal against the decision of *sąd ziemski* (land court) or *sąd grodzki* (castle court) *non per viam motionis Iudiciis, sed simpliciter verbo appellare ad terminus generalis*. The appeal to *roki generalne* (*ad terminus generalis*), so to *sąd wiecowy* (higher court colloquia) evolved into the direct appeal to the Sejm court, so to the king himself. According to the law enacted in 1523, the direct appeal to the Sejm court was possible only if there was *defectus terminorum generalium*, so only if cadency of *sąd wiecowy* "does not come to pass for certain reasons, and unlawful reasons, the party no longer needs to expect a further *sąd wiecowy* cadency, but can refer directly to the Sejm court."[45] The law theoretically allowed the gradual erosion of *sądy wiecowe* in practice as higher courts of the Polish Land Law. Since *sądy wiecowe* started not to be invoked, unlike the Sejm gatherings, the nobility started to send appeals directly to the Sejm court, establishing *appellatio per saltum* in practice. The king started to adjudicate decisions made by *sądy ziemskie* (land courts), *sądy grodzkie* (castle courts), chamberlain courts (*sądy podkomorskie*), commissar courts (*sądy komisarskie*), and provincial courts (*sądy wojewódzkie*, especially with regard to the jurisdiction over Jews).[46]

The old institution of personal liability of judge, however, returned quite soon. In 1538, the constitution *De motione iudiciis* was passed.[47] It reinstated the institution of *motio iudicis* due to abuses among judges: *Quia iudicum incuria et negligentia frequenter evenire solet, quod sententiae contra iuris et consuetudinis dispositionem ab eis feruntur—carelessness and negligence of judges are increasingly happening, so that judgments contrary to the dispositions of law and custom are issued by them*. This time, however, the motion against a judge was limited to the case of negligent and careless conduct of the court proceedings, and only if a judge's decision influenced the main issue of the

43 Wróblewski, "Sądy polubowne", 85.

44 Stanisław Kutrzeba, *Dawne polskie prawo sądowe w zarysie*, Lwów, Warszawa, Kraków, 1927, 112.

45 Balzer, *Geneza Trybunału Koronnego*, 83.

46 Balzer, *Geneza Trybunału Koronnego*, 26.

47 *Volumina Legum*, vol. 1, 262 (f. 533).

case, not just ancillary matters.[48] In fact, because of a rising number of appeals in front of the Sejm court, constitutions in 1543 and 1557 forbid appellate proceedings in accessory matters, just like it was enacted in the case of motion against a judge. The practice gradually assimilated *motio iudicis* and appellate proceedings.[49]

Even the cherished example of the Crown Tribunal was not free from *de facto* dependence of judges from the parties, and especially from the magnates. The predecessor of modern separation of judiciary from the legislative and executive power developed legal and juridical awareness among the nobility. It generated the phenomenon of considering court proceedings as impartial and independent, as a crucial element of "mixed republic." Alas, it fell short due to gradual erosion of social fabric, good morals, and good faith among those who served as judges, those who elected them, and those who appealed to them. Lack of the university degree in law as a requirement of being a judge diminished the quality of court decisions. Term was limited to one year, which did not allow for ample time to gain adequate experience and create the tradition of jurisprudence. Lack of proper remuneration invited judges to take bribes. The Tribunal influenced our current legal system with the maxim—*iustitias vestras iudicabo* ("I will judge your justice"), written down in the Crown Tribunal's room in Lublin, which Lech Gardocki, First President of the Polish Supreme Court, considered the most important one.[50] It was placed next to a crucifix, as the symbol of the Christ-judge. The ongoing reforms did not manage to fix the growing crisis of declining opinions of judges. The Tribunal started to be considered a symbol of the injustice that occurred due to the incompetence and slavish behavior of judges who forgot their conscience and justice. This was depicted in the legend of the devil's trial, which happened in the Crown Tribunal in Lublin. In 1637, a poor widow lost her trial against a wealthy magnate due to bribed judges. The widow exclaimed "that if the devil were judging her, not people, then a fairer sentence would be passed."[51] In fact, during the night, unknown judges with devilish eyes and raven hair masking horns arrived, opened the courtroom, and once again decided the widow's case, giving her justice. Christ on the crucifix

48 Kutrzeba, *Dawne polskie prawo*, 111.

49 Kutrzeba, *Dawne polskie prawo*, 112–113.

50 Franciszek Longchamps de Bérier, "*Audiatur et altera pars*. Szkic o brakującej kolumnie Pałacu Sprawiedliwości", in *Leges sapere. Studia i prace dedykowane profesorowi Januszowi Sondlowi w pięćdziesiątą rocznicę pracy naukowej*, Wacław Uruszczak, Paulina Święcicka, Andrzej Kremer (eds.), Kraków, 2008, 271.

51 Marek Kuryłowicz, "*Aequitas* i *iustitia* w rzymskiej praktyce prawnej", *Annales Universitatis Mariae Curie-Skłodowska*, sectio G (Ius) 66/1 (2019), 176–177 footnote 21.

turned His face away and wept bloody tears over this display of human anger far worse than the devil's. The chairman of the devil's court put his hand onto the table and burned upon it its mark. This story remains in our history as a *memento* for those who would like to see a judge's independence as freedom from accountability.

5 Conclusions

According to the preamble of the current Constitution of the Polish Third Republic, Poland's legal order consists of the best traditions of the Polish First and Second Republic. Undoubtedly, these include what today is called the independence of the courts and the independence of judges. The purpose of this chapter was to capture the best traditions of judicial independence in the historical development of the Polish civil judiciary. Firstly, it was resolved that Polish judges can be described as independent before the emergence of the modern concept of a state and independent judiciary, and even before *Formula Processus*. Secondly, the main judicial reform of the Crown Tribunal (1578) had a long-term effect on *Formula Processus* and shines as an example of the most modern practical separation of judiciary and its return to the general citizenry. Thirdly, the *de facto* dependence of judges and their lack of impartiality are recurring problems of the judiciary in Polish history, which highlights the need for accountability as a counterpart to independence, further demonstrating the role of the underlying social fabric.

CHAPTER 13

Civil Procedure on the Road Ahead: Toward a Fully Digital, Amicable Civil Procedure?

Abdoul Yatera

The disappearance of the private justice of primitive societies has given way to the State justice of modern societies, where the resolution of disputes is governed by a specific process: civil procedure. This allows individuals to turn to the courts to obtain the realization of their rights and freedoms. In this respect, civil procedure is an agent of peace and a guarantor of social stability[1] alongside other procedures such as criminal and administrative proceedings.[2]

The civil procedure did not come into being overnight. It is the fruit of a long historical process,[3] and was originally inspired by several sources, notably canon law and the laws of the Salian Franks.[4] Gradually, certain characteristics were established. However, the real impetus for its emergence can be traced back to the 1667 ordinance on civil procedure, drafted at the instigation of Colbert, a former minister of Louis XIV. This ordinance, also known as the Code Louis XIV, is the main foundation of contemporary French civil procedure.

At the dawn of the 21st century—and more precisely since the 2000—civil procedure has taken a new turning point in its history, namely its adaptation to the advent of digital technology and the promotion of amicable dispute resolution. Numerous normative provisions (laws, decrees, orders), reform projects and study reports bear unequivocal witness to the legislator's concern to make digital technology and amicable negotiation cardinal pillars of contemporary justice. The goal of this chapter is twofold. On the one hand, it takes

---

1 René Morel, *Traité élémentaire de procédure civile: organisation judiciaire, compétence, procédure*, Paris, 1949, 6 footnote 8; Paul Cuche, *Precis de procédure civile et commerciale*, Paris, 1951, 1.

2 Morel, *Traité élémentaire*, 2.

3 Ernest Desire Glasson, *Les Sources De La Procedure Civile Francaise*, Paris, 1882, 17 ff.

4 Serge Guinchard and Frédérique Ferrand and Cécile Chainais and Lucie Mayer, *Procédure civile*, Paris, 2021, 15 footnote 36.

 | DOI:10.1163/9789004736672_015

a retrospective look at the history of civil procedure[5] (I), without claiming to be exhaustive. Secondly, to analyze its adaptation to the digital age, and its orientation towards the amicable resolution of disputes (II).

1 Civil Procedure Confronted with Its Past

The history of civil procedure can be revisited through the Ordinance of 1667, which inspired the former Code of Civil Procedure of 1806, and through the new Code of Civil Procedure of 1975. French civil procedure certainly did not begin with the Ordinance of April 1667, since civil procedure already existed in the old law.[6] The ancient procedure also seemed rich, since it was the conciliation of various tendencies and drew inspiration from various sources.[7] A number of early legal texts were also concerned with procedural principles. These include the Montils-lès-Tours ordinance of 1453, which was seen as "the first Code of civil procedure of the Ancien Régime,"[8] and the Villers-Cotterêts ordinance of August 25, 1539, which substituted French for Latin as the language of procedure. Similarly, the ordinance drawn up by Chancellor Michel de Maurillac, also known as the "Code Michau," seems to have taken an interest in civil procedure.[9] However, the procedural contributions of the "Michau Code" are uncertain, since as Foyer points out, "[i]t is not clear whether it was actually implemented and applied."[10]

However, it was not until the 17th century, with the advent of the 1667 ordinance under the reign of Louis XIV, that the real foundations of civil procedure were laid. It was during this reign that "the ordinance of 1667 on civil procedure was prepared."[11] Work on this ordinance was carried out by Pussort and Lamoignon.[12] It was "one of the finest legislative works of the great reign;

---

5 For a detailed analysis of the history of civil procedure in its various dimensions, see *Itinéraires de l'histoire de la procédure civile*, vol. 1: *Regards Français*, Loïc Cadiet, Serge Dauchy, Jean-Louis Halpérin (eds.), Paris, 2014.

6 Cécile Chainais and Frédérique Ferrand and Serge Guinchard and Lucie Mayer, *Procédure civile. Droit commun et spécial du procès civil, MARD et arbitrage*, Paris, 2022, 8 f.; Loïc Cadiet and Emmanue Jeuland, *Droit judiciaire privé*, Paris, 2020, 21.

7 Chainais and Ferrand and Guinchard and Mayer, *Procédure civile*, 8 f.

8 Chainais and Ferrand and Guinchard and Mayer, *Procédure civile*, 9 footnote 12.

9 Jean Foyer, "Préface", in *1806–1976–2006. De la commémoration d'un code à l'autre: 200 ans de procédure civile en France*, Loïc Cadiet, Guy Canivet (eds.), Paris, 2006, xiii.

10 Foyer, "Préface", xiii.

11 Ernest Glasson, *Précis élémentaire de l'histoire du droit français*, Paris, 1904, 314.

12 Chainais and Ferrand and Guinchard and Mayer, *Procédure civile*, 10.

for the first time, it established procedural unity throughout the kingdom; it reduced costs, simplified acts and shortened delays. It was commented on by Jousse, Bornier, Boutaric, Serpillon, Rodier, Pothier and Pigeau."[13]

The Louis ordinance of 1667 was therefore the high point[14] in the evolution of civil procedure. This ordinance "remained in force until the promulgation of the Code [of 1806], except for an interruption of six years, from Year II to Year VIII."[15] It was applied for 140 years and inspired the 1806 Code of Civil Procedure, which came into force on January 1, 1807.[16]

The commission that drew up the 1806 Code was essentially made up of practitioners[17] already familiar with the 1667 ordinance and somewhat hostile to innovative procedural rules.[18] The various books of this Code were successively promulgated on April 24 and May 9, 1806.[19] Comprising 1,042 articles,[20] the Code of 1806 is often "presented as a simple adaptation of the Ordinance of 1667"[21] or even "a slavish copy" of the latter.[22] In reality, however, it was more than just a simple reworking of the 1667 ordinance, since it also contained elements of Roman and canon law.[23]

Due to the imperfections attributed to the Code of 1806, notably the absence of provisions relating to judicial[24] organization or to certain remedies such as the *pourvoi en cassation* (appeal to the Supreme Court), the "old Code of Civil Procedure" has been the subject of much criticism. For example, it has been described as a "Code of formalities" by Doyen Cuche and Morel,[25] a "Code for practitioners"[26] and a "nascent old Code."[27] However, despite these imperfections and the philippic of which it was the object,

13 Glasson, *Précis élémentaire*, 314.

14 Loïc Cadiet, "Ouverture—D'un code à l'autre: de fondations en refondation", in *1806–1976–2006*, 9.

15 Cuche, *Precis de procédure*, 7; Morel, *Traité élémentaire*, 5.

16 Cadiet, "Ouverture", 3.

17 Bernard Beignier, "Le nouveau Code de procédure civile: un droit de professeurs ?", in *1806–1976–2006*, 35.

18 Cuche, *Precis de procédure*, 7; Cadiet and Jeuland, *Droit judiciaire privé*, 22.

19 Cuche, *Precis de procédure*, 7.

20 Chainais and Ferrand and Guinchard and Mayer, *Procédure civile*, 12.

21 Cuche, *Precis de procédure*, 21.

22 Beignier, "Le nouveau Code", 36.

23 Chainais and Ferrand and Guinchard and Mayer, *Procédure civile*, 12.

24 Cuche, *Precis de procédure*, 8.

25 Morel, *Traité élémentaire de procédure civile*, 8.

26 Jean-Louis Halpérin, "Le Code de procédure civile de 1806: un code de praticie", in *1806–1976–2006*, 23–34.

27 Albert Tissier, "Le centenaire du code de procedure", *RTD civ.* (1906), 648.

the Code of 1806 benefited from a certain favorable reception from the doctrine of the time[28] and even remained in force for more than a century without undergoing a major substantial reform.[29] Reform projects undertaken in 1868 and 1894 failed.[30] However, this procedural work of 1806 eventually yielded to criticism.

2 Civil Procedure as Seen through the New Code of Civil Procedure of 1975

Faced with the ravaging of the Code of 1806 and the need to draw up a modern code of civil procedure, the project for a new Code of Civil Procedure (later on NCPC) was born in 1968 during a fruitful discussion at the Palais de Bourbon between Jean Foyer, who was chairman of the Law Commission, and René Capitant, the Keeper of the Seals at the time.[31] Much of the work on the NCPC was carried out by a sub-committee.[32] However, the entire Code was drafted by Doyen Gerard Cornu, who was its architect,[33] so that, according to Foyer, it could be called the "Cornu Code."[34]

The Decree no. 75-1123 of December 5, 1975, created the "new Code of Procedure," which incorporated several provisions of the Code of 1806. Article 3 of this decree set the Code's effective date at January 1, 1976. However, the NCPC did not come into force nationwide until January 1, 1977.[35] Creation of the new code required a huge effort, taking almost 18 years to draw up the final project.[36] While "three months were enough to assemble the elements of the Code of Judicial Organization, three months entirely devoted to the arid and tedious dissociation of the legislative part from the regulatory part."[37]

Continuing along this path, the new Code of Civil Procedure was designated purely and simply the "Code of Civil Procedure" by Law no. 2007-1787

28 Loïc Cadiet, "Le Code", in *Le nouveau code de procédure civile: 20 ans après—Actes du colloque des 11 et 12 décembre 1997*, Paris, 1998, 46.
29 Cuche, *Precis de procédure*, 7.
30 Cuche, *Precis de procédure*, 8.
31 Jean Foyer, "Synthése des travaux", in *Le nouveau code*, 323.
32 Foyer, "Synthése", 323.
33 Doyen Jean Carbonnier, "Président de séance", in *Le nouveau code*, 17.
34 Foyer, "Synthése", 323.
35 Cadiet, "Ouverture", 3.
36 Gérard Cornu, "L'élaboration du Code de procédure civile", in *La Codification*, Bernard Beignier (ed.), Paris, 1996, 71–80, 75.
37 Cornu, "L'élaboration", 75.

of December 20, 2007 on the simplification of the law, with effect from January 1, 2008. In 2008, the law of December 20, 2007, also repealed all existing regulatory provisions of the 1806 Code of Civil Procedure.[38]

Since 2008, the name of the Code of Civil Procedure has remained unchanged. But this is not the case for its content. The latter has never ceased to evolve, sometimes enriching itself with new rules, sometimes becoming more complex through provisions adopted under the guise of procedural simplification. Procedural challenges are thus perpetual, and some are already looming on the contemporary processual horizon.

3 Contemporary Challenges Facing Civil Procedure: "Digital Justice" and Amicable Procedures

Contemporary civil procedure faces two major challenges.[39] On the one hand, it is seeking to adapt to the trend towards dematerialization and digitalization of legal sphere. On the other, it regularly irrigates its veins with amicable procedures.

As early as 2005, the French legislature enshrined the "digital justice" by the use of electronic communication. Decree no. 2005-1678 of December 28, 2005 on civil procedure, certain civil enforcement procedures, and the procedure for the change of name established the legal framework for the use of electronic communication. Article 73 of this decree inserted into Book I of the Code of Civil Procedure (CPC) a Title XXI on communication by electronic means, comprising articles 748-1 to 748-6.[40] The legal framework derived from the 2005 decree has continued to evolve, but with little harmony or visibility.[41] In fact, several provisions in the form of technical decrees, professional agreements or laws and decrees have subsequently extended it.[42] De-

---

38 Cadiet and Jeuland, *Droit judiciaire privé*, 25.

39 *Droit et pratique de la procédure civile; droit interne et européen*, Serge Guinchard (ed.), Paris, 2021.

40 These provisions have been in force since January 1, 2009. Charles Brenner, in *La communication numérique. Un droit, des droits*, Bernard Teyssié (ed.), Paris, 2012, 447–463, 450; Chainais and Ferrand and Guinchard and Mayer, *Procédure civile*, 715.

41 Abdoul Yatera, *Notification of civil proceedings in the age of new technologies*, Paris, 2021, 49.

42 Natalie Fricero, "Les métamorphoses technologiques, synthèse", in *Actes de colloque: Les métamorphoses de la procédure civile, Gazette du Palais* 212 (2014), 45.

cree no. 2009-1524 of December 9, 2009, and Decree no. 2015-282 of March 11, 2015,[43] have largely completed this legal framework.

The use of electronic means in today's procedural landscape is a gradual process. Since 2012, the use of electronic notification has been extended to the acts of judicial commissioners (*commissaires de justice*—former bailiffs) through decree n°2012-366 of March 15, 2012.[44]

Since January 1, 2013,[45] all pleadings relating to the appeal procedure with representation must be sent to the court clerk's office electronically, in accordance with article 930-1 of the CPC. This obligation was strengthened by the Order of May 20, 2020,[46] amended by the Order of February 25, 2022, which put an end to the subtle distinction depending on whether the document is intended for the court itself or for the first president.[47] Before the order of May 20, 2020, only documents intended for the court of appeal itself[48] and not for the first president could be communicated electronically.[49]

---

43 The decree of December 9, 2009 created article 748-7 of the CPC, and that of March 11, 2015 created articles 748-8 and 748-9 of the CPC.

44 About this decree, see Gabriele Mecarelli, "Demain, la signification par voie électronique", *Droit et patrimoine* 7 (2012), 172–173.

45 Corrine Bléry, "Procédure avec représentation obligatoire devant les cours d'appel et communication par voie électronique: panorama des difficultés", *Revue des procédures* 10/4 (2013), 10.

46 Order of May 20, 2020 on electronic communication in civil matters before the courts of appeal, see Corrine Bléry in *Dalloz actualité from 2 juin 2020*.

47 Article 2 of this decree has enshrined electronic communication to the first president of procedural documents since September 1, 2020.

48 For example, a reference against an order of the Conseil de mise en état was already one of the acts that had to be formalized by electronic means under article 930-1, unless an extraneous cause was alleged., Cass. civ. 2e, June 1, 2017, n°16-18361, see Romain Laffly in *Dalloz actualité 23 juin 2017*.

49 On the basis of article 930-1 of the CPC, the Cour de cassation ruled in 2017 that: "only procedural documents intended for the court of appeal must be delivered electronically; the court of appeal therefore rightly accepted the validity of the delivery to the clerk's office of the request drawn up on paper asking the first president of the court of appeal to set the day on which the case will be called by priority, and consequently declared the appeal admissible": Cass. civ. 2e, 7 December 2017, n°16–19336, see Corrine Bléry in *Dalloz actualité from December 14, 2017*. Antérieurement, et toujours dans le même sens v. Cass. civ.2e, July 6, 2017, n°17–01.695, see Mehdi Kébir in *Dalloz actualité 20 juillet 2017*: "the application for recusal, which introduces an autonomous procedure falling within the remit of the first president of the court of appeal, was sent to the latter via the lawyers' virtual private network, without the technical procedures for recourse to electronic transmission having been defined by an order of the Minister of Justice for such a procedure; it follows that this application is inadmissible."

Article 796-1 of the CPC, created by the decree of May 6, 2017[50] and applicable to documents relating to proceedings commenced on or after September 1, 2019, and which became article 850 of the CPC with the decree of December 11, 2019, has stipulated since January 1, 2020:[51] "On pain of inadmissibility raised *ex officio*, in matters of ordinary written procedure and fixed-date procedure, procedural documents with the exception of the petition mentioned in article 840 are delivered to the court by electronic means."

The computerization of trials through the use of new technologies is making steady progress. Several reports bear witness to this trend. These include the report by the Montaigne Institute entitled, *Justice: faites entrer le numérique*,[52] as well as the reports on Improving and simplifying civil procedure and on the digital transformation devoted to the justice projects submitted to the Minister of Justice on January 15, 2018.[53] The report by the Reflection commission on the Court of Cassation 2030 also calls for a rapid and far-reaching strengthening of the High Court's IT resources in order to promote dematerialized data exchanges with the lower courts.[54] However, this move towards dematerialization sometimes comes into tension with certain procedural guarantees.

4 The Delicate Balance between Digital Trials and Traditional Procedural Guarantees

The dematerialization of procedures is not without its difficulties. Its articulation with certain procedural guarantees owed to litigants has sometimes proved so difficult that the European Court, in the so-called *Xavier Lucas*

50 Decree no. 2017-891 of May 6, 2017, on objections to jurisdiction and appeals in civil matters, J.O n°0109 from May 2017, text, n°113.

51 Corrine Bléry, "Les réformes de la communication par voie électroniqu", in *Nouvelles procédures civiles, nouvelles pratiques professionnelles ? Bilan et perspectives*, Natalie Fricero, Marie-Cécile Lasserre (eds.), Paris, 2020, 93–112, 99.

52 *Justice: faites entrer le numérique*, Institut Montaigne, Novembre 2017, available at: https://www.institutmontaigne.org/ressources/pdfs/publications/justice-faites-entrer-le-numerique-rapport.pdf.

53 Frédérique Agostini and Nicolas Molfessis, *Chantiers de la justice. Amélioration et simplification de la procédure civile: Ministère de la Justice; JPC G 2018.*

54 *Report of the Commission de réflexion sur la Cour de cassation de 2030*, available at: https://www.courdecassation.fr/IMG///Rapport%20Commission%20Cour%20de%20cassation%202030%20sans%20annexe.pdf, 73–77. See especially recommandations 25–29 of the report.

v. France case of June 9, 2022,[55] had to intervene to censure what it described as an excess of formalism imposed by the Cour de cassation in its ruling of September 26, 2019.[56] In this ruling, the French Supreme Court (Cour de cassation) ruled that an action for annulment of an arbitration award was inadmissible on the grounds of non-compliance with the use of the lawyers' private network (RPVA). This was despite the fact that the version of the e-barreau platform available at the time the action for annulment was lodged did not enable the parties to be identified, nor did it allow such an action to be regularized. Consequently, the Cour de cassation could not require the petitioner to regularize his appeal with an unsuitable IT tool without seeing his decision challenged as being contrary to the right of access to a court.

The European Court's review of formalities is infringing the right of access to the courts. By sanctioning excessive formalism in the Xavier Lucas case, on the basis of article 6§1 of the ECHR guaranteeing the right of access to the judge,[57] the European Court delivered a fundamental message: the substance of the trial must not be sacrificed for reasons of purely technical form.

The solution reached in the above-mentioned ruling is in the same vein as a previous ECHR ruling, *Lawyer Partners a.s v. Slovakia*, of June 16, 2009.[58] Although not handed down against France, in this judgment the ECHR ruled on a question involving the right of access to the courts and the use of new technologies. The ECHR had found a violation of article 6§1 of the ECHR against Slovakia when applicants were prevented from registering their legal claims on a CD, despite the fact that the State in question had imposed the use of electronic means to bring cases before the courts. The Strasbourg Court held that "before enshrining in domestic law the possibility of recourse to electronic means in procedural matters, the State must equip the courts and provide the necessary means to ensure the practical use of these new technologies."[59]

55 CEDH, June 9, 2022, n°15567/20, *Xavier Lucas c/ France*, obs. Corrine Bléry, *Dalloz actualité* 16 juni, 2022. On the adoption of this ECHR case law by the Cour de cassation, v. Cass. civ. April 1, 5, 2023, n°22-21.863, obs. Corrine Bléry, *Dalloz actualité* 20 avril 2023.

56 Cass. 2nd, civ., 26 September 2019, n°18-14.708.

57 On the right of access to a court or to a judicial remedy, see CEDH, February 21, 1975, *Golder c/ Royaume-Uni*, n°4451/70. Compare *Les grands arrêts de la Cour européenne des Droits de l'Homme*, Frédéric sudre (ed.), Paris, 2019, 317.

58 CEDH, June 16, 2009, *Lawyer Partners S.A c. Slovaquie*, n°54252/07, *Procédures* 2009, comm. 358, obs. N. Fricero.

59 On point, see Elsa Forey, "La dématérialisation de la justice et l'accès au juge", in *L'accès au juge, Recherche sur l'effectivité d'un droit*, Virginie Donier, Béatrice Lapérou (eds.), Bruxelles, 2013, 456–473, 460.

5 The Challenge of Amicability

Today's civil procedure is very open to amicable justice. Provisions on amicable justice have never been absent from civil trial law, because the 1806[60] Code of Civil Procedure preserved from "revolutionary law a few happy institutions" such as "conciliation."[61] However, it is undeniable that it is contemporary civil procedure that is strongly marked by the contractualization of social relations.[62] Numerous legislative initiatives have been launched to promote negotiated justice.[63] Thus, as early as 2012, through decree no. 2012-66 of January 20, 2012, a book was created within the Code of Civil Procedure devoted to amicable dispute resolution methods outside of legal proceedings. Book v of the Code of Civil Procedure is now dedicated to "the amicable resolution of disputes."[64]

Alternative dispute resolution (ADR) is defined as "a set of procedures aimed at resolving disputes, conflicts, or litigation in an amicable and negotiated manner, without judicial intervention, in particular through conciliation, mediation, a transaction or a participatory procedure agreement."[65] Book 5, which now houses amicable settlement procedures, was traditionally devoted to "enforcement procedures." These are now codified in a fall code since the ordinance of December 19, 2011[66] for the legislative part and a decree of May 30, 2012, relating to the regulatory part.[67]

60 "As far back as 1806, the drafters of the old Code of Civil Procedure had high hopes for conciliation in cases before the Civil Court and the Justice of the Peace...", Chainais and Ferrand and Guinchard and Mayer, *Procédure civile*, 1876, 2403.

61 Cuche, *Precis de procédure*, 7.

62 Loïc Cadiet and Thomas Clay, *Les modes alternatifs de règlement des conflits*, Paris, 2019, 5.

63 To illustrate the regulatory incentive to use MARD s, v. Decree no. 2022-245 of February 25, 2022, promoting the use of mediation, implementing the law on confidence in the judiciary and amending various provisions. For a detailed analysis of this decree, see Lucie Mayer, "Les aspects du décret n° 2022-245 du 25 février 2022 relatifs aux modes amiables de résolution des différends", *Gazette du Palais* 14 (2022).

64 Chainais and Ferrand and Guinchard and Mayer, *Procédure civile*, 1745 f.

65 Thierry Debard and Serge Guinchard, *Lexique des termes juridique*, Paris, 2023, 704.

66 Ordinance n°2011-1895 of December 19, 2011 relating to the legislative part of the Code of Civil Enforcement Procedures.

67 Decree no. 2012-783 of May 30, 2012, relating to the regulatory part of the code of civil enforcement procedures.

The legislator continues to instill amicable settlement by successive touches within the Code of Civil Procedure.[68] As Doyen Carbonnier predicted, today we are witnessing the development and encouragement of justice consisting not "in an exchange of rational argumentation and a thought of these arguments," but "in an exchange of kisses of peace at all costs."[69]

Do we head toward widespread use of alternative dispute resolution? A decisive step had been taken in the introduction of recourse to amicable dispute resolution. Article 750-1 of the CPC, as amended by Decree no. 2019-1333 of December 11, 2019, required the parties to precede any legal action, on pain of inadmissibility, with either an attempt at conciliation conducted by a court conciliator, or an attempt at mediation or a participatory procedure, where such action was for the payment of a sum not exceeding 5,000 euros, or where it related to one of the actions mentioned in articles R.211-3-4 and R.211-3-8 of the French Code of Judicial Organization (COJ).

However, in a decision dated September 22, 2022, the Conseil d'État annulled article 750-1 on the grounds that its content was imprecise. However, this annulment was short-lived, as decree no. 2023-357 of May 11, 2023, on the mandatory prior attempt at mediation, conciliation or participatory proceedings in civil matters reinstated article 750-1[70] of the CPC. The aforementioned decree attempted to clarify the notion of "legitimate reason,"[71] the justification of which may dispense with recourse to an ADR.

The general observation is that the impetus for amicable justice continues to gain ground and concerns various matters, including those relating to personal status. For example, the law of November 18, 2016, known as *J21*, introduced divorce by mutual consent into the French legislative corpus as of January 1, 2017.

The purposes of recourse to amicable dispute resolution methods, and the main reasons behind the growing use of alternative dispute resolution meth-

---

68 Soraya Amrani-Mekki, "La codification de l'amiable", in *Retrouvez Quarantième anniversaire du Code de procédure civile (1975–2015)*, Isabelle Pétel-Teyssié, Catherine Puigelier (eds.), Paris, 2016, 105.

69 Carbonnier, "Président de séance", 16.

70 On this point, see Géraldine Maugin, "L'extraordinaire histoire de l'article 750-1 du code de procédure civile: le rétablissement", in *Dalloz actualité 11 mai 2023*.

71 Under the terms of 3° of article 750-1 of the CPC: "If the absence of recourse to one of the amicable resolution mentioned in the first paragraph is justified by a legitimate reason relating either to urgency or to the circumstances of the case making such an attempt impossible or requiring that a decision be rendered non-adversarially, or to the unavailability of justice conciliators leading to the organization of the first conciliation meeting within a period of more than three months from the referral to a conciliator."

ods, to put it bluntly, are: to combat court congestion, to pacify social relations and to make the judge a last resort.[72] The legislator is therefore using the amicable settlement lever to considerably reduce the number of cases that the courts are called upon to judge, some of which are already overcrowded. The other reason for the rise of alternative dispute resolution is purely managerial,[73] namely to manage the financial shortage from which the judicial system is suffering.[74]

72 Soraya Amrani-Mekki, "Les modes amiables de résolution des différends dans la loi de modernisation de la justice du XXIe siècle", *Gazette du Palais* 5 (2017).

73 Loïc Cadiet, "Case management judiciaire et déformalisation de la procedure", *Revue français de droit administratif* 125/1 (2008), 133–150.

74 Amrani-Mekki, "La codification de l'amiable", 105.

CHAPTER 14

Civil Procedure in Poland of the Communist Era

Radosław Flejszar

1 Introduction

The current Code of Civil Procedure of November 17, 1964 (hereinafter: CCP),[1] which is largely based on the previous Code of Civil Procedure of November 29, 1930,[2] is one of the most extensive and most frequently amended legal acts in the Polish legal system. The purpose of this chapter is to trace the historical evolution of this code, conditioned by the political and socioeconomic transformations taking place in the post-1944 period, starting with the construction and strengthening of the socialist state, referring to the ideology of Marxist-Leninism (these transformations were reflected in the fundamental amendment of the previous code under the law of July 20, 1950, and then in the CCP, built on the foundations of the previous codification), through its gradual erosion up to 1989. The latter date is considered to be the beginning of the political transformation in Poland, which gradually led to the adoption of the concept of a democratic state ruled by law, based on patterns characteristic of European cultural circles. The presentation of the shape and evolution of Polish civil procedure in the communist era will allow an answer to the question of how much influence the solutions adopted in Soviet law had on Polish law.

After the end of the Second World War, Poland underwent fundamental changes of a social, economic and political nature. In these conditions, the old, prewar legal norms, maintained by the will of the new Polish legislature, became a constituent part of the new legal order, intended to protect the new social and political system,[3] which was essentially authoritarian in nature. Characterising the differences between the capitalist system and the socialist system, Marian Lisiewski stated that in the former regime civil law is classified as private law, as a result of which in a trial the parties are the hosts of the proceedings.[4] By contrast, in a socialist system, in which there is no division of

1 *Journal of Laws,* no. 43, item 296, as amended.

2 *Journal of Laws,* no. 83, item 651.

3 Jerzy Jodłowski, *Z zagadnień polskiego procesu cywilnego,* Warszawa, 1961, 26.

4 Marian Lisiewski, "Podstawowe problemy struktury nowego postępowania cywilnego", *Nowe Prawo* 3 (1957), 9.

 | DOI:10.1163/9789004736672_016

law into public and private, society is interested both in ensuring that civil rights are respected and that they are not abused. A consequence of society's attitude to civil law shaped in this way is that the principle of the discovery of objective truth is brought to the fore among the elements shaping the structure of the trial (which means a significant limitation of the rights of the parties in the trial).[5]

The principles and institutions regulated in the Code of Civil Procedure of 1930, which was "an excellent instrument for the protection of capitalist private property and all social relations based on that property,"[6] did not correspond to the assumption that in a socialist society the interests of the individual are not contrary to the interest of the whole. Referring to this account, Marian Waligórski stated that "socialist law, by abolishing the institution of capitalist private property and starting from the assumption that there can be no contradiction between the interests of the individual and the interests of the state, thus rejects the division of law into public and private, abolishes the domain of rights to which the state cannot interfere, and thus excludes the possibility of the existence of such a domain of law, the concretisation and realisation of which would depend solely on the initiative of the interested parties themselves."[7] It was therefore considered necessary to reconstruct Polish procedural law and base it on new principles "corresponding to the new balance of social forces, the new political and economic conditions and the new tasks of the judiciary."[8]

2 Transformation of Polish Civil Procedural Law after the Second World War (1944–1964)

In the course of the first six years after the end of the war, necessary changes in civil procedure were introduced, which did not cover its fundamentals. Włodzimierz Berutowicz refers to this period as "the first stage of the transformation of the law of civil procedure," which was followed by a "socialist reconstruction of the law of civil procedure."[9] One of the most important changes

5 Lisiewski, "Podstawowe problemy", 9.

6 Włodzimierz Berutowicz, *Zasada dyspozycyjności w postępowaniu cywilnym*, Warszawa, 1957, 69.

7 Marian Waligórski, *Odbicie ze Sprawozdań Polskiej Akademii Umiejętności*, vol. 52/3, Kraków, 1951, 181.

8 Jodłowski, *Z zagadnień*, 26.

9 Berutowicz, *Zasada dyspozycyjności*, 69–79

was the unification of noncontentious proceedings, combined with its reconstruction and expansion of its scope of application. Issued on July 18, 1945 (in the form of a decree), the Code of Noncontentious Proceedings[10] was based on completely different grounds than the 1930 Code of Civil Procedure. The noncontentious proceedings were dominated by the investigative principle and broadly defined official principle, manifested, inter alia, in the possibility for a court or other body representing the public interest (and in particular the public prosecutor) to initiate proceedings. In this way, guarantees were created for the discovery of material truth, thus ensuring the protection of the public interest.[11] The consequence of the increased powers of the court in non-contentious proceedings was a significant reduction in the scope of the parties' disposability. It primarily concerned formal disposition. However, due to the nature of the cases heard in non-contentious proceedings, it was often not possible to perform acts of material disposition either. Article 21 of the Code provided that a settlement agreement could only be concluded as regards the property claims involved in the proceedings. By contrast, in cases other than property, the public interest was usually involved, which precluded arbitrary disposition of rights and thus the possibility of settlement.

During this period, the Code of Civil Procedure was amended nine times. The most important amendments were made by the decrees of September 25, 1945 and January 22, 1946, containing provisions introducing (respectively) matrimonial law and family law,[12] and through the act of April 27, 1949 amending certain provisions of the code, bankruptcy law and provisions introducing matrimonial law.[13] The above decrees added new chapters to the Code of Civil Procedure regulating separate proceedings, i.e., matrimonial and parent-child proceedings. In these proceedings the courts were endowed with extensive powers designed to enable them to discover material truth. A significant expansion of the scope of the investigative principle was combined with a limitation by the legislator of the application of the dispositive and adversarial principle by taking away the legal significance of the acknowledgement of a claim and the admission of facts.[14] On the other hand, the act of April 27, 1949 laicised the judicial oath and abolished the derivative determination of the

10 *Journal of Laws*, no. 27, item 169.

11 Jodłowski, *Z zagadnień*, 28.

12 *Journal of Laws of 1945*, no. 48, item 271, and *Journal of Laws of 1946*, no. 6, item 53.

13 *Journal of Laws*, no. 32, item 240.

14 Jodłowski, *Z zagadnień*, 29.

local jurisdiction of a married woman depending on the place of residence of her husband.[15]

A fundamental reform of civil procedure was made by the act of July 20, 1950 on the amendment of the rules of procedure in civil cases[16], which passed simultaneously with the introduction of the new organisation of the judiciary. At that time there was a change in the structure of common courts, linked to the new regulation of the material jurisdiction of the court and the introduction of a social factor in the form of jurors, and the three-instance system was replaced by a two-instance system.[17] The reconstruction of the civil procedural law, made in July 1950, was an important stage in its evolution, the final completion of which was the enactment in 1964 of the Code of Civil Procedure, which is still in force today. The changes introduced by this law referred to the solutions adopted in Soviet law. The recourse to these solutions was due to the fact that Poland—formally an independent state—was in reality in the orbit of influence of the Soviet Union. The 1923 Code of Civil Procedure in force in the USSR was regarded as a model for the countries of the socialist camp.[18] The purpose of these solutions was to ensure the protection of the state's interest in civil cases, to create procedural guarantees for the protection of social property and the rights and interests of state and socialised institutions and enterprises, to ensure the protection of the personal and property interests of citizens insofar as they are pursued in accordance with the principles of social coexistence, and to create guarantees for the detection of material truth in a trial.[19] A consequence of these assumptions was that the public prosecutor was broadly allowed to participate in civil cases as an advocate of the broad public interest. The public prosecutor was given not only the right to intervene in pending proceedings but also to initiate a trial and collect trial material. Criticising such a position of the public prosecutor in civil proceedings, Lisiewski stated that the public prosecutor, by bringing an action, disposes of someone else's rights of investigation, which has nothing to do with the realisation of the principle of objective truth, but means interference with subjective rights. In the author's opinion, the prosecutor's participation in the trial should be limited to cases of particular social importance and be

15 Berutowicz, *Zasada dyspozycyjności*, 73.

16 *Journal of Laws*, no. 38, item 349.

17 For more on these changes, see Jodłowski, *Z zagadnień*, 34–47.

18 The solutions adopted in it were presented by Berutowicz, *Zasada dyspozycyjności*, 55–62, who formulated a definition of the "socialist dispositive principle."

19 Jodłowski, *Z zagadnień*, 32.

based on a specific provision of the law. The role of the prosecutor in the trial should be clearly defined, as he or she cannot be a kind of *tutelary spirit*.[20]

As a result of the reform, the guiding principles of the civil process were transformed. At the forefront was the principle of material truth, which took on "the significance of the supreme principle, dominating over all other procedural principles, which are formed under its influence and, to a greater or lesser extent, directly or indirectly serve its ultimate purpose."[21] The adoption of such an assumption entailed a very far-reaching restriction of both the dispositive and the adversarial principle. Włodzimierz Berutowicz stated that these principles—which are of fundamental importance for a civil trial —have been transformed, and their content "has been shaped on the basis of the compatibility of the interests of individual citizens with the social interest, thanks to which they serve today to achieve objective truth in the civil trial, and thus to give protection to the real right and not to its spectre, as in the bourgeois trial."[22] As a consequence of the new understanding of the nature and purposes of civil procedure, which under the new conditions could no longer be regarded as an institution serving only the protection of private legal interests, the dispositive principle was limited and given a new meaning, while being linked to the official principle.[23] The scope of the principle thus framed was as follows:

1) the initiation of a trial is in principle at the request of a party, but this right of a party is supplemented by the right of the prosecutor to bring an action in all cases (the court is not able to initiate a trial *ex officio*);
2) the scope of the requested legal protection is in principle determined by the party (it is its duty); however, the court is not bound by the scope of the plaintiff's demands (it may rule beyond the demands) in cases, where the plaintiff is the State Treasury or another entity subject to state economic arbitration and the amount of the claims has not been determined by agreement or special provisions, and where the subject of the action are claims deserving special protection for social reasons, i.e., claims for alimony, from an employment relationship or for compensation for damage caused by a tort (Article 329 § 2);
3) the effectiveness of the withdrawal of the claim and the waiver or limitation of the claim, as well as the conclusion of a settlement in cases of non-property rights, maintenance claims, claims from the employment

20 Lisiewski, "Podstawowe problemy", 12–13.

21 Jodłowski, *Z zagadnień*, 56.

22 Berutowicz, *Zasada dyspozycyjności*, 76–77.

23 Jodłowski, *Z zagadnień*, 57.

relationship and compensation for damage caused by a tort is subject to the court's consent; the court will grant this consent if the above dispositive actions are not contrary to the interest of the state or the interest of the entitled persons (Articles 209 § 3 and 231 § 2);

4) the court is not bound by the recognition of the claim, but may rely on it if it is justified by the circumstances of the case (Article 218 § 2);
5) the right to appeal a judgment of the court of first instance is in principle available to the interested party, but this right is supplemented by the right of the public prosecutor to appeal any judgment—both in cases initiated at his request and in cases in which the public prosecutor participates (Article 90);
6) the court hearing the revision is not bound by the limits of the revision in cases concerning non-property rights and property claims arising from family and employment relationships (Article 380 § 2); it may also hear the case ex officio against persons who have not appealed the decision, where there is substantive co-participation between the appellants and non-appellants (Articles 381 and 63 point 1);
7) the waiver of an appeal by a party does not per se cause the judgement to become final (this is a limitation of the dispositive principle in terms of the disposal of appeals);
8) it is not possible to exclude documentary and witness evidence in the event of consensual opposition by both parties (such a manifestation of the parties' disposition would be contrary to the principle of material truth).[24]

In fact, there has been a substitution of the dispositive principle for the official principle by excluding the disposition of the parties at all stages of the process, from the initiation of the action up to the moment of judgment and even revision.[25] At the same time, the scope of the investigative principle was extended. The court was given the possibility of practically unlimited interference in the evidence procedure. In addition to admitting evidence not called by the parties, it was obliged to order appropriate investigations to establish the actual facts of the case (Article 236, CCP). This brought the contentious proceedings closer to the noncontentious proceedings, and the adversarial principle was in practice supplanted by the investigative principle. In addition to the above-mentioned changes—signifying a de facto departure from the dispositive-adversarial model of civil trial towards the official-investigative

24 Jodłowski, *Z zagadnień*, 59–63.

25 Kamil Stefko, "Postępowanie dowodowe w polskim procesie cywilnym", *Przegląd Notarialny* 1–3 (1951), 17.

model, the amendment of the Code of Civil Procedure of July 1950 introduced regulations manifesting the tendency to deformalize proceedings, at the same time realizing the postulate of achieving procedural economy.[26] An example of such regulations was Article 220 (which allowed for the extension of the group of defendants in the event that not all persons against whom the case should be brought jointly were sued) and Article 206 § 1 (which allowed for the change of the claim during the first instance without any restrictions, subject only to the retention of the court's jurisdiction).

Referring to the regulations introduced by the amendment to the Code of Civil Procedure of 1950, Lisiewski stated that "limiting the right to dispose of the subject matter of the litigation by recognition, waiver and conclusion of a settlement is incompatible with the freedom to dispose of subjective rights recognized in substantive law" and that "this limitation is illusory, because it does not deprive the parties of the possibility to dispose of the rights covered by the litigation by acts taken outside a trial."[27] According to the author, these limitations (similarly to limiting the effectiveness of the award and limiting the plaintiff's right to withdraw the lawsuit in general) "are also unnecessary for the protection of the parties against harm, because in the absence of the risk of one party exploiting the other in a trial, a prohibition of abusing subjective rights and procedural actions should be sufficient."[28] The above position was not adopted during the work on the draft of the new Code of Civil Procedure. According to Zbigniew Resich, it is not correct, because "legal acts performed outside a trial are secured by the court's control in the event of a potential initiation of a trial, while acts performed in a trial would no longer have this control, thus undermining the authority of the court accepting such defective acts in the event of their defect."[29]

The reconstruction of the civil process, the first stage of which was the act of July 20, 1950, was continued in subsequent amendments to the Code of Civil Procedure and amendments to the Code of Noncontentious Procedure. Of particular importance was the decree of 23 April 1953 on the amendment of certain provisions of civil procedure[30], in which the legislator explicitly regu-

---

26 Jodłowski, *Z zagadnień*, 69–70.

27 Lisiewski, "Podstawowe problemy", 12–13.

28 Lisiewski, "Podstawowe problemy", 12–13.

29 Zbigniew Resich, "Drugie czytanie projektu k.p.c. i jego polityczne aspekty", *Nowe Prawo* 7–8 (1961), 843.

30 *Journal of Laws*, no. 23, item 90.

Commission for Civil Law Reform, established in 1986, but they were not realised until after 1989.

4 Closing Remarks

According to Zbigniew Resich the third stage of civil procedural law reform began with the establishment of the Civil Law Reform Commission (and, within it, the Civil Procedural Law Team) on September 6, 1986, with the aim of adapting the civil procedural law "to the current and prospective social and economic needs of the country, especially to the needs arising from the introduction of the economic reform."[48] In fact—while the separation of two stages of civil procedure reform in the period after the Second World War can be considered justified, as the new Civil Procedure Code enacted in 1964 consolidated and developed the assumptions adopted in the 1950 and 1953 amendments—it was the changes in civil proceedings after 1989 that were of a completely opposite nature and led to the restoration of the dispositive-adversarial model of civil procedure referring to the assumptions on which the Polish Code of Civil Procedure of 1930 in its prewar wording was based.

As a consequence of the political and socioeconomic transformation that began in 1989, it was necessary to adapt the provisions of substantive and procedural civil law and procedural law to the new situation. By the act of May 24, 1989 on the cognizance of commercial cases by courts[49], state commercial arbitration was abolished, commercial courts (being divisions of general courts) were established and separate proceedings in commercial cases were introduced into the code. In connection with the formation of a free market economy based on private property, by the act of July 13, 1990,[50] provisions were removed from the code on the protection of social property and regulations reflecting procedural privileges of socialised economy entities were removed from the code.[51] One of the repealed provisions was Article 194 § 4 of the Code of Civil Procedure, which allowed the court to make ex officio personal transformation of the claim if the protection of social property required it.

48 Resich, "Trzeci etap reformy", 5 ff.

49 *Journal of Laws*, no. 33, item 175.

50 Act of 13 July1990 on amending the Act—Code of Civil Procedure (*Journal of Laws*, no. 55, item 318).

51 In this regard, see Tadeusz Ereciński, "O potrzebie nowego kodeksu postępowania cywilnego", *Państwo i Prawo* 4 (2004), 3 ff.

4 Growing Complexity in Appellate Systems and the Constitutionalization of Civil Procedure

Under the same amendment of April 22, 2004, an additional extraordinary remedy was introduced alongside the existing cassation appeal and complaint for reopening proceedings already present in the 1930 Code of Civil Procedure. This new remedy took the form of a petition to declare a final judgment unlawful (*skarga o stwierdzenie niezgodności z prawem prawomocnego orzeczenia*). Its adoption as a means to enforce the right guaranteed under Article 77, Section 1 of the Constitution—to seek compensation for damage caused by unlawful actions of public authorities, including courts issuing final judgments in civil cases—is part of the phenomenon known as the *constitutionalisation* of Polish civil procedural law.[22]

This phenomenon entails adapting the norms and institutions of civil procedural law through legislation, decisions of the Constitutional Tribunal, and appropriate judicial interpretation and application to meet constitutional requirements and implement European standards for the protection of human rights and fundamental freedoms. These standards, particularly the right to a court and a fair trial under Article 6 of the European Convention on Human Rights,[23] are sometimes exceeded in implementation.

Notably, Article 190, Section 4 of the Constitution grants the right to reopen any proceedings concluded with a final court decision based on provisions later deemed inconsistent with the Constitution or other higher-ranking norms by the Constitutional Tribunal. This right was codified in Article 401^1 of the CCP under the Act on the Constitutional Tribunal of 1 August 1997,[24] which provided a new basis for petitioning to reopen proceedings ending with a final decision.[25] Subsequently, the aforementioned amendment to the CCP as of 22 December 2004 extended this right to reopen proceedings that not

---

22 For more on this phenomenon, see Paweł Grzegorczyk, "O konstytucjonalizacji prawa procesowego cywilnego", *Kwartalnik Prawa Prywatnego* 2 (2012), 293 ff., and the literature cited there, as well as a collection of dissertations in *Konstytucjonalizacja postępowania cywilnego*, Łukasz Błaszczak (ed.), Wrocław, 2015.

23 Convention for the Protection of Human Rights and Fundamental Freedoms made in Rome on November 4, 1950, subsequently amended by Protocols Nos. 3, 5 and 8 and supplemented by Protocol No. 2, *Journal of Laws of 1993*, no. 61, item 284, as amended, hereinafter referred to as "ECHR".

24 *Journal of Laws*, no. 102, item 643, as amended.

25 Pursuant to Art. 401^1, CCP one may also request the reopening of proceedings if the Constitutional Tribunal has ruled on the noncompliance of a normative act on the basis of which the judgment was issued with the Constitution, a ratified international agreement or with the statute.

cesses aim to improve access to the justice system in civil matters, enhancing its time and cost efficiency. Apart from the widely used electronic order for payment proceedings, which mass-claimants frequently use to pursue claims for payments from everyday contracts (such as gas and electricity bills, telecommunications service fees, and other basic services), it is also worth mentioning the full digitalization of registration procedures based on the National Court Register[51] and the bankruptcy and restructuring proceedings using the National Register of Debtors.[52] Both are integrated within the Portal of Court Registers, an ICT system of the Ministry of Justice used to provide court register services to citizens.

In 2009, pursuant to an amendment to the CCP as of December 5, 2008,[53] Polish civil proceedings permitted for the first time the taking of evidence using technical devices that enable remote activities. This includes two-way communication in real time, allowing the transmission of sound, or image and sound, between participants in specific procedural acts. Starting from July 1, 2010,[54] traditional written minutes of public court sessions, prepared by a

51 The National Court Register, which includes among other items, the Register of Commercial Companies, is kept by district courts (commercial courts) in an ICT system provided and maintained by the Ministry of Justice since the adoption of this register and its launch in 2001 on the basis of the Act of August 20, 1997, on the National Court Register, consolidated text *Journal of Laws of 2023*, item 685, as amended. However, only since January 1, 2007, it was allowed to submit applications for entry in this register electronically after providing them with a secure electronic signature, verified with a valid qualified certificate. Since July 1, 2021, applications regarding all entities subject to entry in the register of entrepreneurs are submitted mandatorily via the ICT system. Applications submitted in a form other than via the ICT system lack any legal effect and are subject to return without advanced notice with a call for correcting the deficiencies.

52 The National Register of Debtors has been kept by the Minister of Justice in an ICT system since the entry into force of the Act of December 6, 2018, on the National Register of Debtors, consolidated text *Journal of Laws of 2021*, item 1909, as amended, on December 1, 2021. From that day on, all pleadings and documents both in the bankruptcy and restructuring proceedings must be submitted via the ICT system under the pain of ineffectiveness.

53 Article 235 § 2, CCP, added pursuant to the Act of December 5, 2008, amending the Act—Code of Civil Procedure and certain other acts, *Journal of Laws*, no. 234, item 1571. For the critical assessment, see Anna Kościółek, "Informatyzacja czynności dowodowych w postępowaniu cywilnym", *Przegląd Prawa i Administracji* 82 (2010), 253 ff.

54 Article 157, CCP, as amended pursuant to the Act of April 29, 2010, amending the Act—Code of Civil Procedure, *Journal of Laws*, no. 108, item 684. In the literaturę, see e.g. Jacek Gołaczyński and Sylwia Kotecka and Anna Zalesińska, "Protokół w postaci zapisu dźwięku albo obrazu i dźwięku z posiedzenia jawnego w sprawach cywilnych", *Monitor Prawniczy* 18 (2010), 1045 ff.; Anna Łazarska, "Metoda protokołowania przebiegu rozprawy a gwarancje rzetelnego procesu cywilnego", in *Elektroniczny protokół a wymiar*

Ontario,[72] and Australia.[73] These jurisdictions, despite historically adhering to a strictly adversarial and availability-oriented approach, have increasingly recognized the necessity of positioning the court as an active participant in the dispute resolution process. This procedural model aims to achieve reliable, fair, and efficient resolution of civil matters, thereby maintaining a delicate balance between safeguarding private interests and serving the public interest in the proper functioning of the justice system. It acknowledges the finite nature of the resources allocated to the judiciary and seeks to optimize their utilization. Central to this management approach is the attribution of primary responsibility to the court, while also emphasizing the shared responsibility of the parties and their representatives. They are expected to engage in loyal cooperation, adhering to established procedural norms and good practices. The court is empowered to employ a wide array of procedural tools and instruments, guided by judicial discretion, to ensure the proceedings' proper conduct and alignment with their intended goals.

---

the Supreme Court of the United Kingdom, led the codification committee responsible for drafting the new rules of civil procedure (*Κανονισμοί Πολιτικής Δικονομίας*) for Cyprus. These rules were adopted by the Cypriot Supreme Court in May 2021 and came into effect in September 2023. They fully embraced the principles of the English CPR, particularly regarding the significance of the principle of proportionality in civil proceedings. For further details on the reform of Cypriot civil procedural law, refer to Nicolas Mouttotos, "Reform of civil procedure in Cyprus: Delivering justice in a more efficient and timely way", *Common Law World Review* 2 (2020), 99 ff; Nicolas Kyriakides, "Cyprus Civil Justice System Reform: Developing a National Identity", *The Cyprus Review* 1 (2019), 31 ff.

72 Pursuant to Rule 1.04(1) of the Ontario Rules of Civil Procedure (R.R.O. 1990, Reg. 194) which constitutes part of the Courts of Justice Act 1990 (R.S.O. 1990, c. C.43), the provisions of that Act shall be liberally construed to secure the just, most expeditious and least expensive determination of every civil proceeding on its merits. Pursuant to Rule 1.04 (1.1.), in applying these rules, the court shall make orders and give directions that are proportionate to the importance and complexity of the issues, and to the amount involved, in the proceeding. For more information on the principle of proportionality in Canadian civil procedural law, see Colleen M. Hanycz, "More Access to Less Justice: Efficiency, Proportionality and Costs in Canadian Civil Justice Reform", *Civil Justice Quarterly* 1 (2008), 98 ff; Catherine Piché, "Figures, Spaces and Procedural Proportionality", *International Journal of Procedural Law* 1–2 (2012), 145 ff; Catherine Piché, "The 'New Normal' of Civil Procedure in Canada: Technological Efficiency over Proportionality and Accuracy of Outcomes", in *Civil Courts Coping with Covid-19*, Bart Krans, Anna Nylund (eds.), Hague, 2021, 36 ff.

73 See Susan Campbell, "Proportionality in Australian civil procedures: a preliminary review", *Journal of Judicial Administration* 3 (2005), 144 ff; Hazel Genn, *Judging Civil Justice*, Cambridge, 2010, 61–62.

lated the relationship of contentious and noncontentious proceedings, recognising them as two separate modes of civil court proceedings.[31]

3 Polish Civil Procedure Law after the Entry into Force of the Code of Civil Procedure of 1964 and before the Political and Socioeconomic Transformation (1965–1988)

Despite the introduction of numerous amendments, the provisions of the 1930 Code of Civil Procedure did not correspond to the new "social needs" and were not adapted to the emerging new substantive law.[32] Therefore, work was undertaken to develop a new Code of Civil Procedure. The first draft of the new code was elaborated in 1955 by a team appointed by the minister of justice and headed by Seweryn Szer. Further work was carried out within the Codification Commission by the Civil Procedure Law Team, established at the end of 1956. The team of Civil Procedural Law consisted, among others, of Zbigniew Resich (chairman), Marian Lisiewski, Bronisław Dobrzański, Jerzy Jodłowski, Jan Korzonek, Władysław Siedlecki, Jan Gwiazdomorski and Stanisław Gross (members), and Henryk Trammer and Edmund Wengerek (appraisers). In the course of the work on the draft of the code, two monographs[33] on the proposed regulations were published, as well as numerous articles.[34] Proposed solutions were widely discussed. The materials from this public discus-

---

31 For more on this amendment, see Jerzy Jodłowski, "Nowy etap przebudowy polskiego procesu cywilnego", *Państwo i Prawo* 5–6, (1953), 689–715.

32 Zbigniew Resich, "Zasady opracowania nowego Kodeksu postępowania cywilnego", *Nowe Prawo* 12 (1965), 1355.

33 Władysław Siedlecki, *Podstawy rewizji cywilnej*, Warszawa, 1959; Zbigniew Resich, *Poznanie prawdy w procesie cywilnym*, Warszawa, 1958.

34 See, in particular, Władysław Siedlecki, "Realizacja zasady swobodnej oceny dowodów w polskim procesie cywilnym", *Nowe Prawo* 4 (1956); Władysław Siedlecki, "Z prac Komisji Kodyfikacyjnej nad nowym Kodeksem postępowania cywilnego PRL", in *Studia Cywilistyczne*, vol. 1, Kraków, 1961, 181 ff; Walery Masewicz, "Czy potrzebny jest udział prokuratora w procesie cywilnym?", *Nowe Prawo* 6 (1957); Zbigniew Resich, "Zasada dyspozycyjności i kontradyktoryjności w procesie cywilnym PRL", *Państwo i Prawo* 7–8 (1957); Zbigniew Resich, "Ochrona własności społecznej w projekcie kodeksu postępowania cywilnego", *Państwo i Prawo* 10 (1960); Stanisław Włodyka, "Udział prokuratora w postępowaniu cywilnym w projekcie kodeksu postępowania cywilnego PRL", *Państwo i Prawo* 8–9 (1960); Stanisław Włodyka, "*Zmiana* strony pozwanej w procesie cywilnym", *Nowe Prawo* 12 (1960); Marian Lisiewski, "Scalenie postępowania spornego i niespornego", *Zeszyty Naukowe UŁ — Prawo* 14 (1959); Marian Lisiewski, "Z warsztatu prac kodyfikacyjnych nad ogłoszonym projektem kodeksu postępowania cywilnego", *Nowe Prawo* 2 (1961).

sion formed the basis for further work during the second reading of the draft. After their completion the draft entered the deliberations of the Presidium of the Codification Committee, which introduced a number of significant changes (primarily in enforcement proceedings), and then it was subjected to inter-ministerial arrangements. The draft thus established—adopted by a resolution of the Council of Ministers—was sent to the Sejm, where further amendments were made in the course of legislative work. Finally, on November 17, 1964, the new Code of Civil Procedure was enacted.[35]

The 1964 Code of Civil Procedure, which came into force on January 1, 1965, was in its original formulation a piece of legislation fully in line with the political and socioeconomic realities of the time. The legislator retained many of the institutions from the former code but standardised them in accordance with new ideological assumptions, among which the pursuit of objective truth and the protection of social property were fundamental. In the doctrine and jurisprudence, it was commonly accepted that the principle of objective (material) truth is the chief procedural principle of overriding character in relation to other principles.[36] Most representatives of the doctrine also regarded the principle of protection of social property as the chief procedural principle.[37]

The enactment of the Code of Civil Procedure in 1964 was treated as the second stage of the reform of civil procedure, as "its codification assumptions were rooted in the legislative assumptions of 1950, as well as those of 1953, with their appropriate updating, being a consequence of the court jurisprudence, the voices of the doctrine and comparative legal research."[38] During the drafting of the code an assumption was made to consolidate the principles realised in the 1950 and 1953 amendments. Conclusions resulting from the long-term practice of applying solutions included in the above-mentioned legal acts were also taken into account.[39] In the draft of the new Code—depending on the needs of practice—either the supervision and control of the court over the parties' dispositional activities was maintained in the current

35 *Journal of Laws*, no. 43, item 296. For more on the work on the draft of the new Code of Civil Procedure and its key features, see Resich, *Zasady opracowania*, 1355–1363.

36 For more details, Jerzy Jodłowski, "Zasady naczelne socjalistycznego procesu cywilnego", in *Wstęp do systemu prawa procesowego cywilnego*, Jerzy Jodłowski (ed.), Wrocław, Warszawa, Kraków, Gdańsk, 1974, 75–79, and the literature cited therein.

37 See Jodłowski, "Zasady naczelne", 80.

38 Zbigniew Resich, "Trzeci etap reformy prawa procesowego cywilnego", in *Współczesne tendencje rozwoju procedury cywilnej w Europie. Materiały międzynarodowej konferencji naukowej Popowo 25–27 październik 1988*, Edward Warzocha (ed.), Warszawa, 1990, 4.

39 Lisiewski, "Z warsztatu prac", 166.

scope, or it was modified or expanded, and only slightly narrowed.[40] The proposals of the authors of the draft were adopted practically without changes in the 1964 Code of Civil Procedure (in its original wording). Consequently, in the Polish civil process—despite the different declarations of the authors of the new codification—the official-investigative elements continued to dominate. The relationship between the elements of the dispositive-adversarial model of civil trial towards the official-investigative model was as follows:

1) the initiation of a trial occurs in principle on the initiative of a party, but this right of a party is supplemented by the right to bring an action by the public prosecutor and by the social organisations of the working people; the powers of the public prosecutor in this respect have been limited in certain non-property cases (the rule is that he may request the initiation of proceedings in any case if, in his assessment, the protection of the rule of law, the rights of citizens, the social interest or social property requires it—art. 7 sentence 1, CCP), and social organisations may initiate proceedings only in cases provided by law for the protection of citizens' rights (Article 8, CCP);
2) a public prosecutor and social organizations may join the proceedings at any stage (Article 60 § 1 and Article 61 § 2, CCP, respectively);
3) the determination of the scope of the requested legal protection is in principle up to the party (Article 321 § 1, CCP); however, the court may rule on an object that was not covered by the request and award more than the request in cases where the plaintiff is a socialized economy unit and in cases concerning maintenance claims and redress for damage caused by a tort (Article 321 § 2, CCP), as well as in cases concerning employees' claims (Article 475 § 1, CCP);
4) the effectiveness of the withdrawal of the claim and the waiver or limitation of the claim, as well as the conclusion of a settlement in all cases, is dependent on the absence of the court's objection; the court shall consider each of the above actions as inadmissible if it is contrary to the law or the principles of social coexistence or grossly violates the justified interests of entitled persons (Article 203 § 4 and 223 § 2, CCP);
5) a public prosecutor bringing an action on behalf of a designated person may not independently dispose of the subject matter of the dispute (Article 56 § 2, CCP); this regulation applies mutatis mutandis to social organisations (Article 62, CCP);

---

40 Lisiewski, "Z warsztatu prac", 167.

6) the subject change of the claim is admissible if it does not affect the jurisdiction of the court (Article 193 § 1, CCP); the court's control over this dispositive action of the claimant takes place only if the modification of the claim may at the same time be deemed to be one of the actions listed in Article 203 § 4, CCP (i.e., withdrawal of the claim, limitation or renunciation of the claim);
7) the court is not bound by the recognition of the claim, but may rely on it if it is justified by the circumstances of the case (Article 213 § 2, CCP);
8) the right to appeal against a judgment of the court of first instance is in principle available to the parties, but it is supplemented by the right of the public prosecutor to appeal against any judgment against which there is an appeal (Article 60 § 2, CCP) and the right of a social organisation to appeal against a judgment in a case in which it has brought an action on behalf of a citizen or in a case in which it has joined (Article 62, CCP);
9) the court hearing the revision is not bound by the limits of the motions and grounds of revision in cases, in which the plaintiff is a unit of the social economy and in cases for non-property rights, alimony claims and tort damages (Article 381 § 2, CCP); it may also hear the case ex officio against persons who have not appealed the decision, where there is substantive co-participation between the appellants and non-appellants (Article 384 and Article 72 § 1 point 1, CCP);
10) the court has the right to review such dispositive acts of the parties as the withdrawal of an objection to a default judgment (Article 349 § 2, CCP), the withdrawal of a revision (Article 393 § 2, CCP), the withdrawal of a complaint (Article 393 § 2 in connection with Article 397 § 2, CCP) and the withdrawal of objections to a payment order issued in proceedings by writ of payment (Article 497 § 1, CCP);
11) the court has the right to act ex officio in the case of subjective change of the claim if the protection of social property so requires and there is a lack of passive legitimacy in the case (Article 194 § 1 and 4, CCP) or if it turns out that an action for the same claim may be brought against other persons who do not act as defendants in the case (Article 194 § 3 and 4, CCP); in other cases, an initiative of the party is required to carry out a subjective change of the claim.

Comparing the reconstruction of the civil procedural law, made in July 1950, to the solutions adopted in the 1964 Code of Civil Procedure (in its original formulation), outlined above, it should be noted that all solutions characteristic of countries remaining in the orbit of Soviet influence have been maintained. In particular, the possibility to bring action (Article 7, sentence 1, CCP, and

Article 8, CCP) and join the proceedings at any stage thereof (Article 60 § 1 and Article 61 § 2, CCP) by the prosecutor and social organisations has been retained, as well as the possibility for the court to rule on the subject matter, which was not covered by the demand, and to adjudicate beyond the demand in enumerated cases (Article 321 § 2, CPC, and Article 475 § 1, CPC). The possibility of making subject changes of the claim (Article 193 § 1 of the code) and personal transformations of the claim (Articles 194–198) has also been maintained. The legislator also did not abandon the court's control over the dispositive actions of the parties and even extended its scope. The following procedural actions of the parties were subject to such control: withdrawal of a statement of claim and waiver or limitation of a procedural claim (Article 203 § 4, CCP), conclusion of a settlement (Article 223 § 2, CCP), withdrawal of an objection against a default judgment (Article 349 § 2, CCP), withdrawal of a revision (Article 393 § 2, CCP), withdrawal of a complaint (Article 393 § 2 in connection with Article 397 § 2, CCP) and withdrawal of objections to a payment order issued in proceedings by writ of payment (Article 497 § 1, CCP). Thus, under the 1964 Code of Civil Procedure (in its original version), elements of the official-investigative model prevailed, while elements of the dispositive principle and the adversarial principle were in fact given a secondary character. This was a consequence of the foregrounding of the public interest, referred to as the "social interest" and manifested in the "principles of social coexistence," the realisation of which was to be served by both the broad powers of the court and the prosecutor in a civil trial.

Prior to the political breakthrough in 1989, the 1964 Code of Civil Procedure had been amended only a few times, and the changes introduced did not concern issues relevant to its basic premises and structure. Twenty years after the enactment of the code an assessment of its functioning was made. At that time it was concluded that the code "passed the test in practical operation" and that "there is no justified, substantive, legal and social need to create a new civil procedure."[41] It was concluded, however, that "it is necessary and justified to undertake work on making some changes to the regulation of certain institutions of civil procedure and to critically assess and modify the formulation and understanding of several of the main procedural principles."[42] The scope and understanding of the adversarial principle in civil proceedings, as well as its relation to other procedural principles (and above all to the principle of active court action and the dispositive principle) were consid-

41 Edward Warzocha, "Funkcjonowanie w praktyce Kodeksu postępowania cywilnego (Refleksje na tle konferencji naukowej w Popowie)", *Palestra* 3–4 (1985), 57.

42 Warzocha, "Funkcjonowanie w praktyce", 57.

ered the most important issues. According to the assumptions guiding the drafting of the 1964 Civil Procedure Code, the obligation to prove facts was not only imposed on the party but also on the court, which—according to the circumstances—was even obliged to conduct an investigation ex officio in order to establish the relevant evidence. In this way—through a harmonious interaction between the parties and the court, combining elements of the investigative principle and the adversarial principle—the aim was to establish objective truth with regard to the facts to be used as a basis for a judicial decision.[43] In practice, the elements of the investigative principle gained the upper hand altogether, and the essence of the "active" court model was reduced to an alleged duty of the court to assist the parties in their efforts to provide the court with knowledge of the facts constituting the basis of the dispute and to produce evidence in support of their assertions and claims.[44] As a consequence, a situation arose in which civil court proceedings in the field of evidence relied to an increasing extent on the court acting ex officio, and the activity of the parties systematically decreased.[45] Proposed amendments to the provisions of the Code of Civil Procedure aimed at activating the parties by strengthening the elements of the adversarial and dispositive principle and removing manifestations of unequal treatment of the parties (in the sense of unjustified privileging of social economy entities over natural persons).[46] At that time it was emphasised, inter alia, that the legislator should generally limit the principle of ex officio activity of the court (initiative) in favour of broadening the implementation of the dispositive principle in civil proceedings.[47] These postulates were considered right by the members of the

43 Warzocha, "Funkcjonowanie w praktyce", 57.

44 Gerard Bieniek and Edward Warzocha, "Funkcjonowanie przepisów Kodeksu postępowania cywilnego w praktyce sądów powszechnych", in *Zeszyty Naukowe IBPS*, no. 25, Warszawa, 2007, 83–85.

45 Warzocha, "Funkcjonowanie w praktyce", 57. The author noted that the litigants and participants in the nonprocedural proceedings and their attorneys quickly realised that the court had to establish the relevant facts ex officio anyway. In practice, there were often situations where the parties were not at all active in gathering the procedural material and then in their revision raised the allegation that the court of first instance had not fulfilled its obligations in this respect.

46 The need to change the basic assumptions of the code and to carry out a "deeper" revision has been recognised by, among others, Jerzy Jodłowski, "Kierunki reformy postępowania cywilnego", *Państwo i Prawo* 5 (1987), 3, and Warzocha, "Funkcjonowanie w praktyce", 58.

47 Kazimierz Lubiński, "Il principio dispositivo nel processo civile polacco", *Rivista di diritto processuale* 44/31990 (1990), 1006 ff.

The changes initiated a reconstruction of Polish civil proceedings in a direction corresponding to the assumptions of the democratic system and the needs of economic turnover.[52] In their essence, they came down to the rejection of those solutions that Poland had to introduce when it was a country in the orbit of influence of the Soviet Union. It should be emphasized that although the impact of the solutions adopted in the Soviet Union on Polish civil procedure was significant, the transition to the model of civil procedure functioning in democratic countries was facilitated by the fact that the current Code of Civil Procedure of November 17, 1964, is largely based on the previous Code of Civil Procedure of November 29, 1930. Certain procedural institutions characteristic of the socialist camp countries have remained in Polish civil proceedings to this day. Among them, it is worth mentioning, among others, the very broad possibility of the public prosecutor's participation in these proceedings and the possibility of making subjective change of the claim.

52 The issue is discussed in Chapter 15.

CHAPTER 15

Polish Code of Civil Procedure (*semper reformandus*): The Ongoing Evolution of Polish Civil Procedure

Future Insights from Three Decades of Never-Ending Reform

Andrzej Olaś

1 Setting the Scene

Since the fall of the communist regime in Poland which culminated in the partially free elections and establishment of a democratic government in 1989, the Polish Code of Civil Procedure of November 17, 1964 (hereinafter: the 1964 Code of Civil Procedure or CCP)[1] has undergone more than 200 amendments. This transformation process seems far from complete, as widespread criticism continues to highlight significant inefficiencies, delays, excessive formalities, and the irrational complexity of procedural rules. These deficiencies of the law governing civil procedure contribute significantly[2] to a civil justice system that fails to meet the needs and legitimate expectations of a modern EU member state, which should uphold the principles of the rule of law and adhere to international and European standards of access to justice and fair trial in civil and commercial matters.

The aforesaid period of the last 35 years has been marked by numerous hectic and somewhat disorderly processes, which can be categorized as follows: departure from the socialist civil procedure model and the restoration of the adversarial model based on the principles of party disposition and party

1 *Journal of Laws,* no. 43, item 296, as amended.

2 There is a growing consensus among Polish scholars and practitioners that improvements or modernizations of civil procedure law alone will not effectively address the excessive delays and inefficiencies of the civil justice system. An urgently needed overhaul of the organization and management of civil courts is required, along with ensuring an appropriate level of judicial staff. This includes properly remunerated, professional, and adequately numbered support staff, such as judges' clerks, assistants, and administrative employees in court secretariats and registrars. In this vein see e.g. Andrzej Olaś, "Czy dążenie do przyspieszenia postępowania może usprawiedliwiać ograniczenie konstytucyjnych gwarancji prawa do sądu? Uwagi na tle orzecznictwa Trybunału Konstytucyjnego", *Palestra* 4 (2024), 58.

 | DOI:10.1163/9789004736672_017

presentation; *constitutionalization* and *Europeanization* of civil procedure; diversification, decodification, or even disintegration; attempts to improve access to justice by simplifying and expediting proceedings as well as increasing the efficiency of civil procedure; promotion of the out-of-court dispute resolution methods, and finally deployment of modern ICT technologies and digitalization. It is important to note that most of these processes and phenomena, which will be discussed or at least touched upon in this chapter, are still ongoing and oftentimes far from over.

2 The Grand Reform of 1996: Restoring the Liberal Procedural Model

The most significant amendment to the CCP, widely regarded as the most substantial reform of civil court proceedings since 1950, was introduced by the act of March 1, 1996.[3] This reform aimed to align Polish civil procedure more closely with the standards prevalent among European Union countries.[4] It reinstated the adversarial principle and the principle of disposition in their classical forms into Polish law and reformed the system of appeals by drawing on solutions that were in place during the interwar period.[5] Notably, it repealed provisions that obligated the court to pursue objective truth, including the general Article 3 § 2 of the CCP, and removed the original Article 381 § 1 of the CCP, which addressed revision.

This led to a situation where the responsibility for presenting facts and evidence in the proceedings primarily rested with the parties, significantly limiting the court's role in this regard—specifically, its authority to admit evidence ex officio. It was the parties, not the court, who were to elucidate the relevant circumstances of the dispute. They could not remain passive nor rely on an appeal later in the process to claim that the court had failed to clarify the factual or legal relations.[6] The removal of elements of the investigative principle from Polish trials was accompanied by an expansion of the parties' autonomy, with the court's control over dispositive actions being significantly reduced.

3 The Act of March 1, 1996 amending the Code of Civil Procedure, the Orders of the President of the Republic—Bankruptcy Law and the Law on Arrangement Proceedings, the Code of Administrative Procedure, the Act on Court Costs in Civil Cases and certain other acts, *Journal of Laws*, no. 43, item 189.

4 Ereciński 2004, 4.

5 Karol Weitz, "Czy nowa kodyfikacja postępowania cywilnego?", *Państwo i Prawo* 3 (2007), 16.

6 Ereciński, "O potrzebie nowego kodeksu", 4.

As regards acknowledgment of a claim, a reverse rule was introduced (in Article 213 § 2, CCP), whereby the court was bound by the defendant's acknowledgment, subject to the same criteria for control as the plaintiff's dispositive actions (listed in Article 203 § 4, CCP). Concerning appeals, a new three-instance model was adopted, eliminating the extraordinary review and replacing it with an appeal while introducing cassation as the second appeal, available within the course of an instance. In this system of remedies, the second instance (appeal) served both a review and substantive function, while the third instance (cassation) had a purely review (control) function, limited to certain errors of law.[7]

3 Striving Forward amid Early Setbacks

Another significant development in the reconstruction of civil proceedings was the amendment to the Code of Civil Procedure on May 24, 2000,[8] which continued the direction of changes initiated in 1996. By introducing a new separate procedure in the form of simplified proceedings to handle minor and straightforward cases, this amendment marked the symbolic beginning of a new paradigm in civil procedure. This paradigm focused on streamlining, simplifying, and expediting civil proceedings, thereby enhancing access to justice and the efficiency of judicial protection.[9]

In subsequent years, this trend continued with the introduction of another accelerated procedure in the form of an electronic order for payment procedure (Act of January 9, 2009[10]), and the progressive expansion of the powers of court registrars (*referendarze sądowi*) through various statutes (particularly

7 Weitz, "Czy nowa kodyfikacja", 16.

8 The Act of May 24, 2000, amending the Act—Code of Civil Procedure, the act on registered pledges and the register of pledges, the act on court costs in civil cases and the act on court bailiffs and enforcement, *Journal of Laws*, no. 48, item 554, as amended.

9 For the critical assessment of this procedure and its development in the CCP since its adoption, see Andrzej Olaś, "Postępowanie uproszczone", in *System Prawa Procesowego Cywilnego*, vol. 2 part 4; *Postępowanie procesowe przed sądem pierwszej instancji. Postępowania odrębne. Postępowania przyspieszone*, Sławomir Cieślak (ed.), Warszawa, 2023, 872 ff.; see also Radosław Flejszar and Irina Izarova and Vigita Vebraite, "Access to justice in small claims procedure: comparative study of civil procedure in Lithuania, Poland and Ukraine", *International Journal of Procedural Law* 1 (2019), 97 ff.

10 The Act of January 9, 2009, amending the Act—Code of Civil Procedure and certain other acts, *Journal of Laws*, no. 26, item 156, as amended.

the Acts of December 22, 2004,[11] July 10, 2015,[12] and July 4, 2019[13]). These expansions affected both modes of civil case examination (contentious and non-contentious matters) as well as civil enforcement proceedings.[14]

This phenomenon, justified by the need to relieve judges of non-adjudicatory duties related to legal protection, has raised controversy regarding the respect for judicial monopoly in the administration of justice as provided for pursuant to the 1997 Constitution of the Republic of Poland.[15] This is especially contentious in the context of authorizing court registrars to issue orders for payment in the documentary writ of payment procedure, pursuant to the aforementioned amendment to the CCP, effective from July 4, 2019.

While the validity of the goals of reforms highlighted by the legislator, namely accelerating and streamlining proceedings, cannot be questioned, doubts arise regarding the manner of their implementation. This concerns the legitimacy of the new institutions introduced, the legislative correctness of the solutions implementing them, and maintaining a proper balance between the need for expeditious proceedings (without compromising procedural diligence) and their reliability. This includes upholding basic principles such as openness and immediacy, which have been increasingly limited by expanding grounds for closed sessions without adequate public hearings.[16] Furthermore, procedural guarantees, notably the principle of collegiality in second-instance proceedings, have been significantly reduced under the

11 The Act of December 22, 2004, amending the Act—Code of Civil Procedure and the Act —Law on the System of Common Courts, *Journal of Laws of 2005*, no. 13, item 98.

12 The Act of July 10, 2015, amending the Act—Civil Code, the Act—Code of Civil Procedure and certain other acts, *Journal of Laws*, item 1311, as amended.

13 The Act of July 4, 2019, amending the Act—Code of Civil Procedure and certain other acts, *Journal of Laws*, item 1469, as amended.

14 Only within the years 2005–2015 there were 13 amendments relating to the scope of competences of court registrars in civil proceedings; see Aneta Arkuszewska, "Zakres kognicji i pozycja referendarza sądowego w postępowaniu cywilnym", in *Podmioty w postępowaniu cywilnym*, Krystian Markiewicz, Andrzej Torbus (eds.), Warszawa, 2018, 88 ff.

15 Constitution of the Republic of Poland of April 2, 1997, *Journal of Laws*, no. 78, item 483, as amended, hereinafter referred to as "Constitution."

16 See Tadeusz Zembrzuski, "Ograniczenia jawności postępowania w sprawach cywilnych w dobie pandemii—potrzeba chwili czy trwałe rozwiązania?", *Forum Prawnicze* 3 (2021), 3 ff; Tadeusz Zembrzuski, "Przeciwdziałanie i zwalczanie epidemii COVID-19 w postępowaniu cywilnym, czyli pożegnanie z kolegialnością orzekania", *Polski Proces Cywilny* 1 (2022), 59 ff; Marcin Dziurda, "Czy nadchodzi zmierzch zasady ustności w postępowaniu cywilnym?", *Polski Proces Cywilny* 1 (2022), 125 ff.

amendment to the Code of Civil Procedure as of July 7, 2023,[17] becoming more of an exception to the rule of adjudicating in single-person panels.[18]

The fundamental reform of the appeals system in 1996 marked a significant intervention, yet it was not the final overhaul in this domain. Less than a decade later, through an amendment to the CCP on 22 December 2004,[19] another substantial change reshaped the entire structure of court proceedings. The three-instance procedure introduced in 1996 was replaced with a two-instance system, aligning with the minimal constitutional standard stipulated in Article 176, Section 1 of the Constitution.[20] This transformation redefined *cassation* (*kasacja*), previously a standard remedy against second-instance court judgments concluding cases, into a *cassation appeal* (*skarga kasacyjna*), now an extraordinary means of appeal.

The new regulations governing cassation appeals introduced stringent criteria for admitting them for consideration on their merits (Article 398^9 § 1 CCP). These changes emphasized limiting cassation review to purely legal issues, excluding factual and evidentiary matters (Article 398^3 § 3 and Article 398^{13} § 1 and 2 CCP), and tightened the formalism and rigor of cassation proceedings (Article 398^4 and Article 398^6 CCP). Furthermore, the competence to adjudicate on the substance of disputes in cassation proceedings (Article 398^{16} CCP) was minimized.

These adjustments returned the cassation appeal to its doctrinal origins, akin to the French cassation system introduced in Poland in the early 19th century and slightly altered in the CCP of 1930, as well as during the period from 1996 to 2004.[21] As a result, the cassation appeal has reemerged as a "pure" extraordinary remedy, serving primarily the public interest by ensuring the correctness and consistency of case law.

17 The Act of July 7, 2023, amending the Act—Code of Civil Procedure, the Act—Law on the Organization of Common Courts, the Act—Code of Criminal Procedure and certain other acts, *Journal of Laws*, item 1860.

18 See Olaś 2024b, 335 ff.

19 *Journal of Laws of 2005*, no. 13, item 98.

20 It sets forth that court proceedings involve at least two instances.

21 In this regard, in particular, see see Jacek Gudowski, "Skarga kasacyjna", in *System Prawa Procesowego Cywilnego*, Vol 3. *Środki zaskarżenia*, Tadeusz Ereciński, Jacek Gudowski (eds.), Warszawa, 2013, 902.

only concluded with a final judgment on the merits but also purely procedural decisions rendered, due to procedural obstacles (such as the inadmissibility of civil proceedings), barring resolution of the dispute in the substantive judgment.[26]

However, it must be acknowledged that the current system of appeals in the CCP, including extraordinary appeals against final judgments, is excessively extensive and complex. This complexity undermines the efficiency of proceedings and erodes confidence in the finality and stability of judgments, thereby impacting trust in the judicial process and the law itself.

5 Never Give Up: Persistence in Promoting Out-of-Court Dispute Resolution

On the other hand, the consistent efforts to promote consensual dispute resolution, including mediation in civil cases introduced in Articles 183^1-183^{15} of the CCP by the amendment to this code of July 28, 2005,[27] should be seen as a positive step toward the improvement and modernization of Polish civil procedural law. Mediation can be initiated and conducted either before the commencement of court proceedings or during ongoing proceedings, based on a mediation agreement between the parties or a court referral, provided the case is suitable for settlement by agreement. A settlement reached before a mediator, once approved by the court, holds the same legal weight as a court settlement and can be enforced through court execution.

---

26 See Art. 399 § 2, CCP, the adoption of which was preceded by the Constitutional Tribunal's judgment of October 27, 2004, SK 1/04, OTK-A 2004, no. 9, item 96, deciding that Art. 401^1, CCP, was unconstitutional thus far, as it precluded the admissibility of a reopening of proceedings ending with decisions other than a judgment on the merits of a dispute.

27 The Act of July 28, 2005, amending the Act—Code of Civil Procedure and certain other acts, *Journal of Laws*, no. 172, item 1438. By virtue of the same act, significant reform was effectuated to the Polish arbitration law. The preexisting provisions governing the arbitration were repelled (Part 3 of Book 1 of CCP), and the completely new one set of rules were adopted constituting Part 5 of CCP. The new Polish law on arbitration proceedings closely follows the 1980 UNCITRAL Model Law on International Commercial Arbitration, with relatively minor deviations and necessary additions concerning such issues as arbitrability, consumer protection and post-arbitral procedures. Since 2005 the most important reform of the arbitration law so far occurred in 2015, when setting aside as well as recognition and enforcement proceedings were limited to one instance, with a right of extraordinary recourse to Supreme Court on strictly limited grounds.

Significant enhancements to the normative framework of mediation in civil proceedings were implemented in 2016 through an amendment to the CCP as of October 10, 2015.[28] This amendment granted courts the authority to refer parties to mediation ex officio at any stage of proceedings in the court of first or second instance.[29] Previously, the court could only initiate such referral until the closure of the initial trial hearing. After this point, referral to mediation required the parties' joint request.[30]

Under this law, the court is now obligated to consider, before the first trial hearing, whether to refer the parties to mediation. To facilitate this assessment, the presiding judge may summon the parties to a closed session for personal appearances if deemed necessary.[31] Additionally, during the preliminary stage of proceedings, the presiding officer may invite the parties to attend an informational meeting on methods for amicably resolving disputes, particularly mediation.[32] This meeting may be conducted by a judge, court clerk, court official, judge's assistant, or a designated permanent mediator.

While mediation remains voluntary (parties may decline to participate at any time), the claimant is required to indicate in the statement of claim whether mediation or any other out-of-court dispute resolution methods were attempted. If no such attempts were made, the claimant must provide reasons for their omission.[33] Moreover, a blatantly unjustified refusal to engage in mediation (such as failing to attend a scheduled session without valid excuse after prior agreement) may lead to the party being ordered to reimburse the proceedings' costs, irrespective of the case's outcome.[34]

---

28 The Act of September 10, 2015 amending certain acts in connection with supporting amicable methods of resolving disputes, *Journal of Laws,* item 1595. For more in-depth analysis, see Aneta Arkuszewska, "Postępowanie mediacyjne—perspektywy (kilka uwag na tle ustawy z dnia 10 września 2015 r. o zmianie niektórych ustaw w związku ze wspieraniem polubownych metod rozwiązywania sporów)", in *Kodeks postępowania cywilnego z perspektywy pięćdziesięciolecia jego obowiązywania. Doświadczenia i perspektywy*, Elwira Marszałkowska-Krześ, Izabella Gil, Łukasz Błaszczak (eds.), Sopot, 2016, 303.

29 In this regard, see Art. 183^8 § 1, CCP.

30 Article 183^8 § 1, CCP, in force till 1 January 2016.

31 Article 183^8 § 4, CCP.

32 Article 183^8 § 5, CCP.

33 Article 187 § 1 point 3, CCP, added by the amendment of 10 July 2015.

34 Article 103 § 2 and § 3 point 2, CCP, as amended by the act of 4 July 2019.

6 When Skills and Competence Do Not Meet the Challenge: With a Little Wooden Sword against the Three-Headed Hydra of Civil Justice

The negative trend toward hastily introducing successive amendments to civil procedural law, often extensive and inadequately prepared from a legislative standpoint, intensified significantly following the Minister of Justice's dissolution of the Civil Law Codification Commission on December 17, 2015. These actions justified by the noble declaration of combating the "three-headed hydra" of civil justice system comprising delays, costs, and vexation/complexity,[35] paved the way for the progressive disintegration of the CCP from conceptual, editorial, and even linguistic perspectives. Concurrently, a phenomenon characterized in literature as legal or procedural "obscurantism" intensified.[36] This manifested in the revival of previously discarded solutions, either directly—such as the reinstatement, through the amendment of the CCP as of July 4, 2019, of procedural formalism and preclusion systems in commercial cases, previously abolished in the amendment of September 16, 2011[37]—or indirectly, disguised as changes in appellate proceedings through the same amendment of July 4, 2019, which indirectly referred to solutions annulled in 1996. Additionally, another extraordinary appeal mechanism, the "extraordinary complaint" (*skarga nadzwyczajna*),[38] resembling the former extraordi-

35 This nasty creature is in fact a notorious and perennial adversary of the justice system—manifested, over centuries and across various jurisdictions; see in that regard e.g. Jacob 1985, 226; Storme 2004 (introduction); Storme 2005, 96.

36 See Jacek Gudowski, "Kodeks postępowania cywilnego A.D. 2022. Esej o postmodernizmie, obskurantyzmie prawnym i niekompetencji", in *Non Omne Quod Licet Honestum Est. Studia z prawa cywilnego i handlowego w 50-lecie pracy naukowej Profesora Wojciecha Jana Katnera*, Szymon Byczko, et al. (eds.), Warszawa, 2022, 20 ff; Jacek Gudowski, "Tradycja, postęp i coś jeszcze. Czy Konstytucja uratuje Kodeks postępowania cywilnego?", in *Konstytucyjne aspekty procesu cywilnego*, Aleksandra Orzeł-Jakubowska, Tadeusz Zembrzuski (eds.), Warszawa, 2023, 17 ff; Andrzej Olaś, "Podstawa zarzutu potrącenia po nowelizacji Kodeksu postępowania cywilnego z 9.03.2023 r. jako *exemplum* prawnego obskurantyzmu w najnowszej praktyce polskiego prawodawcy", *Przegląd Sądowy* 9 (2023), 18 ff.

37 The Act of September 16, 2011, amending the Act—Code of Civil Procedure and certain other acts, *Journal of Laws*, no. 233, item 1381. In this regard, see Radosław Flejszar, "Standard ochrony procesowej w postępowaniu odrębnym w sprawach gospodarczych na gruncie poprzedniego i aktualnego stanu prawnego", *Gdańskie Studia Prawnicze* 1 (2023), 133 ff.

38 For the critical assessment of this new appellate measure, see Tadeusz Ereciński and Karol Weitz, "Skarga nadzwyczajna w sprawach cywilnych", *Przegląd Sądowy* 2 (2019), 3 ff.

nary revision abolished in 1996, was introduced within the framework of the new Supreme Court Act of December 8, 2017.[39] Moreover, viable solutions that, after overcoming initial challenges in their assimilation by legal professionals and the development of jurisprudential standards, were starting to function effectively, were abolished without offering a suitable alternative. Notably, the model of concentrated procedural material, universally applicable across proceedings and based on discretionary judicial power introduced by the September 16, 2011, amendment to the CCP, was replaced by a hybrid mechanism mixing disparate elements, proving rather dysfunctional.[40]

Concurrently, pursuant to the same amendment of the CCP of July 4, 2019, under the theme of streamlining and speeding up proceedings, some ostensibly modern and necessary solutions were introduced. However, in practice, these turned out to be largely dysfunctional due to faulty drafting of the implementing provisions and a lack of adequate organizational capacity within the judiciary. For instance, preparatory proceedings and organizational hearings, which were intended to significantly streamline the process by strengthening proactive judicial case management, largely remained theoretical.[41] Additionally, some changes were fundamentally misguided, as they significantly limited the procedural guarantees of the parties. An example is the introduction of a complaint to another panel of the same court, replacing the complaint to the second instance court for numerous procedural decisions issued by the first instance court.[42]

7 Poland's Accession to the Council of Europe and EU: Europeanization of Polish Civil Procedure

Having previously mentioned the *constitutionalization* of Polish civil procedural law, one cannot overlook its "Europeanisation," which is related to Po-

39 Consolidated text in *Journal of Laws of 2023*, item 1093, as amended.

40 In this regard, see in particular Andrzej Jakubecki, "Koncentracja materiału procesowego w postępowaniu cywilnym A.D. 2019—dyskrecjonalna władza sędziego czy prekluzja?", in *Praktyka wobec nowelizacji postępowania cywilnego. Konsekwencje zmian*, Marcin Dziurda, Tadeusz Zembrzuski (eds.), Warszawa, 2021, 27 ff.

41 Articles 205^{1}-205^{12}, CCP. In this regard, see in particular Marcin Dziurda, "W sądzie jak w arbitrażu—czy to się może udać?", in *Praktyka wobec nowelizacji postępowania cywilnego. Konsekwencje zmian*, M. Dziurda, T. Zembrzuski, Warszawa, 2021, 182 ff; Andrzej Olaś, "Zasada proporcjonalności w postępowaniu cywilnym", Warszawa, 2024, 210 ff.

42 Article 394^{1a}, CCP, as introduced pursuant to the amendment to the CCP as of July 4, 2019.

land's accession to the Council of Europe in 1991 and the European Union in 2004. Whereas the standards of right to court and fair trial envisaged in ECHR were integrated in the 1997 Constitution, joining EU brought another challenge obliging Poland to adopt the *acquis communautaire*, including in the area of judicial cooperation in civil matters, and to ensure compliance with the principles of primacy, equivalence, and effectiveness of EU law.[43] The dynamic development of European civil procedure in recent decades, including the case law of the EU Court of Justice, has triggered significant changes not only in numerous provisions of the CCP and their interpretation and application by competent courts but also in the introduction of supplementary and implementing provisions to EU regulations. These regulations establish autonomous European redress procedures such as the European order for payment procedure[44] and the European small claims procedure,[45] as well as some autonomous *albeit* auxiliary procedures such as proceedings on the European Account Preservation Order.[46] The main changes in these areas

43 Regarding the impact of EU law on the Polish civil procedure as well as the interplay between the notion of the procedural autonomy of the member states and the guiding principles of EU law, such as the principle of equivalence and effectiveness, see, in particular: Karol Weitz, "Wpływ prawa Unii Europejskiej na krajowe prawo procesowe cywilne", *Kwartalnik Prawa Prywatnego* 2 (2019), 207 ff. The author identifies three basic dimensions of influence of European Union law on the civil procedural law of the member states, including Poland: 1) the influence of primary law, with particular emphasis on the freedoms of the internal market, the general prohibition of discrimination and the EU concept of procedural fundamental rights; 2) the impact of secondary law, especially in the area of judicial cooperation in civil matters and within the sectoral harmonization of law at the EU level outside the framework of this cooperation; 3) application of EU law, especially in the area of private law (with particular emphasis on consumer protection law) by national courts and its impact on the civil procedural law of the member states. As Weitz rightly notes, in addition to *constitutionalisation*, digitization and ensuring the protection of collective interests, the impact of EU law on national civil procedural law is and will remain in the coming years one of the fundamental challenges in the Polish civil procedure.

44 Articles 505^{15}-505^{20}, CCP, supplementing and executing provisions of the Regulation (EC) No. 1896/2006 of the European Parliament and of the Council of December 12, 2006, creating a European order for payment procedure (OJ L 399, 30.12.2006, 1–32).

45 Articles 505^{21}-505^{27}, CCP, supplementing and executing provisions of Regulation (EC) No. 861/2007 of the European Parliament and of the Council of July 11, 2007, establishing a European Small Claims Procedure (OJ L 199, 31 July 7 2007, 1–22).

46 Articles 1144^{4}-1144^{13}, CCP supplementing and executing provisions of Regulation No 655/2014 of the European Parliament and Of The Council of 15 May, 2014 establishing a European Account Preservation Order procedure to facilitate cross-border debt recovery in civil and commercial matters (OJ L 189, 27 June 2014, 1–59).

were implemented pursuant to the amendment to the CCP of December 5, 2008.[47]

A significant step in adapting Polish procedural law to EU standards in recent years was the introduction, on July 1, 2020, of a new, separate procedure for intellectual property matters.[48] This change implemented the measures provided for in Directive 2004/48/EC of the European Parliament and Council of 29 April 2004 on the enforcement of intellectual property rights[49] in a unified manner. Additionally, the introduction of a separate procedure involving consumers,[50] by the amendment to the CCP on 4 July 2019, can be seen as an attempt—albeit somewhat awkward—to strengthen the legal and procedural protection of consumer rights guaranteed by European and Polish consumer protection laws.

8 Polish Civil Procedure Entering the Digital Age: Slowly but Steadily

An important area of change in Polish civil procedural law over the last 23 years is its successive computerization (already completed) and digitalization (still in progress), accompanied by the growing use of modern ICT technologies in the administration of justice, including civil proceedings. These pro-

47 The Act of December 5, 2008, amending the Act—Code of Civil Procedure and certain other acts, *Journal of Laws*, no. 234, item 1571.

48 Articles 479[89]-497[129], CCP. Previously, relevant provisions implementing Directive 2004/48/EC were scattered in several statutes regulating particular types of intellectual property rights, such as the Act on Copyright and Related Rights, the Act on Industrial Property Rights, the Act on the Protection of Plant Varieties and the Act on the Protection of Databases. This solution was subject to criticism for the lack of adequate harmonization and excessive complexity. Establishment of a new procedure dedicated to intellectual property cases in CCP came along with the introduction of special courts (namely the intellectual property divisions in the circuit courts in Gdańsk, Katowice, Lublin, Poznań and Warsaw and the intellectual property appellate divisions in the Court of Appeal in Warsaw and Poznań) specialising in intellectual property cases. On this new procedure, see Marcin Dziurda, "Postępowanie w sprawach własności intelektualnej z perspektywy systemowej", *Przegląd Sądowy* 10 (2020), 5 ff.

49 OJ L 157, 30 April 2004, 45–86.

50 Articles 458[14]-458[16], CCP. For the critical assessment of this new procedure, see Monika Strus-Wołos, "Postępowanie odrębne z udziałem konsumentów—czy potrzebne jest procesowe wzmocnienie ochrony konsumenta?", *Polski Proces Cywilny* 2 (2023), 285 ff; Katarzyna Gajda-Roszczynialska, "Czy potrzebne jest w polskim procesie cywilnym nowe postępowanie odrębne—'postępowanie z udziałem konsumentów'?", *Polski Proces Cywilny* 4 (2023), 641 ff; Tadeusz Zembrzuski, "Dokąd zmierza ochrona konsumenta w procesie cywilnym?", *Palestra* 8 (2023), 106 ff.

court reporter under the supervision of the chairman of the court, have been replaced by the so-called "e-minutes." These consist of two elements: the shortened written minutes and electronic recordings of the hearing using sound or image and sound recording devices.

In 2016, pursuant to an amendment to the CCP of July 10, 2015, the legal availability of holding remote court hearings was extended beyond taking evidence.[55] However, due to remaining restrictions (inadmissibility of participating in these activities from a place other than the courtroom of the court conducting the session or the courtroom of another court assisting in this activity), the actual use of this procedural tool was minimal for almost four years. The broad application of remote court hearings became a reality only in 2020 due to the COVID-19 pandemic, which necessitated the extensive use of modern technical solutions to maintain the continuity of the judiciary amid an unprecedented public health threat.[56]

The legal basis for the extensive use of remote court sessions using available videoconferencing applications (such as Zoom, MS Teams, Google Meet, Jitsi, Skype, and WhatsApp), allowing participation from a location of their own choice by parties, their representatives, and other participants (including witnesses or experts), was introduced through episodic provisions located outside the CCP.[57] These provisions were in force during the state of epidemic

---

sprawiedliwości. Materiały z konferencji Stowarzyszenia Sędziów Polskich 'Iustitia', Anna Łazarska (ed.), Warszawa, 2015, 35 ff. Critically, from the traditionalist persperctive, see Jacek Gudowski, "Protokół elektroniczny, czyli próba zamachu na Jana Gutenberga", in *Postępowanie rozpoznawcze w przyszłym Kodeksie postępowania cywilnego. Materiały Ogólnopolskiego Zjazdu Katedr i Zakładów Postępowania Cywilnego w Katowicach—Kocierzu (26–29 września 2013 r.)*, K. Markiewicz, A. Torbus (eds.), Warszawa, 2014, 767 ff.

55 Article 151 § 2, CCP, added pursuant to the Act of July 10, 2015, amending the Act—Civil Code, the Act—Code of Civil Procedure and certain other acts, *Journal of Laws,* item 1311, as amended. For the critical assessment, see Lucyna Łuczak-Noworolnik and Anna Żebrowska, "Przeprowadzenie rozprawy i postępowania dowodowego drogą elektroniczną—założenia, cele, przyjęte rozwiązania", *Polski Proces Cywilny* 3 (2018), 5 ff.

56 On the impact of the COVID-19 pandemic on the Polish civil procedure, see, in particular Piotr Rylski, "Transformation of Polish Civil Procedure in Light of Covid-19", in *Civil Courts Coping with Covid-19*, Bart Krans, Anna Nylund (eds.), Hague, 2021, 155 ff. For a broader perspective of the evaluation of the impact of COVID-19 pandemic on the justice system in Poland and beyond, see *Impact of the COVID-19 Pandemic on Justice Systems Reconstruction or Erosion of Justice Systems—Case Study and Suggested Solutions*, Katarzyna Gajda-Roszczynialska (ed.), Göttingen, 2023.

57 Article 15^1 of the Act of March 2, 2020, on special solutions related to the prevention, counteracting and combating of COVID-19, other infectious diseases and crisis situations caused by them, consolidated text: *Journal of Laws of 2023,* item 1327, as amended. For an in-depth analysis, see Jacek Gołaczyński and Sylwia Kotecka-Kral, „Protokół w postaci

threat, or the state of epidemic announced due to COVID-19, and for one year after the cancellation of the last of these states. There is no doubt, however, that remote (including hybrid) hearings have become a permanent element of Polish procedural reality. This is evidenced by the introduction to the CCP of extensive (though not comprehensive or entirely clear) regulations of these sessions under the amendment of July 7, 2023,[58] which replaced the episodic COVID regulations on March 14, 2024.[59]

A significant, although unfinished, element of the digitalization process in civil proceedings is the digitization of communication between the court and the participants in the proceedings. Currently, the court can deliver court documents (including summonses, notices, and copies of issued judgments) using the ICT system supporting court proceedings (*Portal Informacyjny*). From March 14, 2024, pursuant to the amendment to the CCP of July 7, 2023, this procedure became mandatory for parties represented by professional attorneys, who will be legally obliged to set up accounts in this system and use it in their interactions with the court.[60]

A substantial shortcoming in the digitalization of civil proceedings in Poland is the lack of digitization of court files. This, combined with deficiencies in the development of the ICT system supporting court proceedings, prevents full bidirectional digital communication between the court and the participants in the proceedings. To date, the existing legal and technical infrastructure does not allow participants to submit their pleadings or other documents to the court electronically. Consequently, all documents still must be prepared and submitted in traditional written form, which significantly impedes the digitization of court files.

The full digitization of court files, along with providing secure remote access to authorized individuals and entities, is crucial. This step would unlock the potential of modern technologies, including artificial intelligence, as tools

zapisu dźwięku albo obrazu i dźwięku z posiedzenia jawnego w sprawach cywilnych", *Monitor Prawniczy* 18 (2010), 637 ff.

58 Article 151, CCP, as amended by virtue of the Act of July 7, 2023, amending the Act—Code of Civil Procedure, the Act—Law on the Organization of Common Courts, the Act—Code of Criminal Procedure and certain other acts, *Journal of Laws*, item 1860.

59 In this regard see Andrzej Olaś, "Looking beyond Covid-19 pandemic: does Artificial Intelligence have a role to play in preparing the justice system for the next global pandemic or similar hardship? The European perspective", in *Impact of the COVID-19 Pandemic on Justice Systems Reconstruction or Erosion of Justice Systems—Case Study and Suggested Solutions*, Katarzyna Gajda-Roszczynialska (ed.), Göttingen, 2023, 250 ff.

60 Article 131[1a] § 1, CCP, added by virtue of the Act of July 7, 2023, *Journal of Laws*, item 1860, and associated changes made in the acts governing legal professions established to provide legal services, including representation in court proceedings.

to support judges and other judicial staff in data processing and case management.[61] Such advancements could greatly improve civil proceedings beyond the current capabilities.

9 *Quo vadis* CCP? The Need for Reflection, Harmonization, Modernization, and Embracing Best Practices and International Standards

The chaotic development of Polish civil procedure in recent years, or even decades, necessitates an urgent yet meticulous review of the numerous and extensive amendments to the CCP. Many of these amendments are often flawed in terms of legislative technique and highly questionable in substance.[62] More pressing, however, is the need to completely overhaul the standards of the legislative process in this area. Some hope in this regard comes from the establishment of the new Codification Committees for The Organization of Common Courts and the Prosecutor's Office, Penal Law, Civil Law, and Family Law by the Minister of Justice in April-May 2024. Lawmakers, practitioners (judges and members of other legal professions), academics, and other stakeholders should examine the CCP from the perspective of the requirements of a modern, European democratic state of law and, above all, the needs of its citizens. This approach also calls for careful observation and review of the changes occurring in civil proceedings worldwide, especially within EU member states, to identify and adopt the best normative patterns and practices.

In this context, it is impossible to ignore the joint achievements of the European Law Institute (ELI) and the International Institute for the Unifica-

61 In this regard, see Olaś, "Looking beyond Covid-19", 249 ff.

62 This includes gradual erosion of some basic principles securing the right to fair trial, such as openness (publicity of the proceedings), orality, the collegial composition of courts as well as immediacy, often justified with the need for accelerating and simplifying proceedings. These processes were strengthened during the COVID-19 pandemic by virtue of the episodic provisions adopted outside the CCP under the veil of the temporary need to tackle extraordinary situations but thereafter petrified in the CCP under its amendments of March 9, 2023 and July 7, 2023. For the critical assessment of these issues, see Tadeusz Zembrzuski, "Ograniczenia jawności postępowania w sprawach cywilnych w dobie pandemii—potrzeba chwili czy trwałe rozwiązania?", *Forum Prawnicze* 3 (2021), 3 ff.; Tadeusz Zembrzuski, "Przeciwdziałanie i zwalczanie epidemii COVID-19 w postępowaniu cywilnym, czyli pożegnanie z kolegialnością orzekania", *Polski Proces Cywilny* 1 (2022), 59 ff.; Marcin Dziurda, "Czy nadchodzi zmierzch zasady ustności w postępowaniu cywilnym?", *Polski Proces Cywilny* 1 (2022), 125 ff.

tion of Private Law (UNIDROIT) in the form of the ELI/UNIDROIT Model European Rules of Civil Procedure.[63] This model represents the culmination of many years of work by a team of approximately 50 outstanding experts in civil procedural law, representing most European jurisdictions, including Poland. Their focus was on developing model principles and rules that establish the foundations of a modern system of civil procedural law, aimed at providing effective legal protection in a fair, efficient, and proportionate manner in terms of time, resources, and costs involved in the proceedings.

In contrast to the MERCP, the CCP is marred by poor and often unintelligible wording, blatant casuistry, and formalism. Moreover, the CCP suffers from an enormous and largely unjustified diversification of proceedings in contentious matters. Currently, apart from the ordinary proceedings, there are about 20 separate procedures (mandatory, semi-mandatory, optional, and mixed) distinguished based on various criteria[64] plus procedure on the collective redress (group action) adopted in 2009 within by a separate statute.[65] These procedures intersect with each other, and due to the lack of clear and comprehensive collision rules, this leads to significant procedural complications and

---

63 The ELI/UNIDROIT Model European Rules of Civil Procedure Rules (hereinafter referred to as "MERCP"), accompanied by official comments and available both in English and in French, were approved by the ELI Council and Membership in summer 2020, as well the UNIDROIT Governing Council at the second meeting of its 99th session from September 23 to 25, 2020. Its final text was published by Oxford University Press in 2021 and is publicly available at https://doi.org/10.1093/oso/9780198866589.001.0001 (access 25.09.2023). As regards MERCP, see Astrid Stadler and Vincent Smith and Fernando Inchausti Gascón, *European Rules of Civil Procedure. A Commentary on the ELI/UNIDROIT Model Rules*, Cheltenham, 2023. On this act and its potential impact on the polish civil procedure, see Andrzej Olaś, "W stronę modelowego Europejskiego Kodeksu Postępowania Cywilnego: od Projektu Storme do Modelowych Europejskich Reguł Postępowania Cywilnego", *Przegląd Sądowy* 9 (2021), 7 ff.

64 On the dilemmas between unification and diversification of civil procedure and the optimal model of civil procedure, see in particular Andrzej Jakubecki, "Jednolitość czy różnorodność postępowania cywilnego? Optymalny model kodeksu postępowania cywilnego", *Gdańskie Studia Prawnicze* 5 (2022), 9 ff.; Andrzej Olaś, "*E pluribus unum*? O optymalny model procedury cywilnej w sprawach spornych—uwagi na tle Modelowych Europejskich Reguł Postępowania Cywilnego", *Gdańskie Studia Prawnicze* 5 (2022), 294 ff.

65 Act of December 17, 2009 on pursuing claims in group proceedings, consolidated text: *Journal of Laws of 2023*, item 1212. According to Art 24 Section 1 of this act, to the extent not regulated therein, the provisions of CCP are applicable (except those provisions expressly excluded by this provision). Currently this Act is subject to the pending legislative process aimed at its amendment so at to align the Polish collective redress mechanism with requirements of the Directive (EU) 2020/1828 of the European Parliament and of the Council of 25 November 2020 on representative actions for the protection of

interpretative doubts, adversely affecting the certainty and predictability of the entire process.[66]

Another crucial element of the MERCP that should serve as a model for the overhaul of the Polish civil procedure is its approach to guiding procedural principles. In addition to recognizing the *classical* principles that have formed the cornerstone of modern civil procedure since the great codifications of the 19th century—such as the principle of party disposition and the adversarial principle—it places special emphasis on somewhat more novel principles that are less universally recognized but fundamental for the proper functioning of the modern procedural system. These two intimately intertwined principles are: the principle of loyal cooperation between the parties, their lawyers, and the judge,[67] and the principle of proportionality.[68]

The principle of proportionality should be understood as a directive to shape the norms governing civil proceedings and to apply them in a way that favors a fair resolution of the case in fair proceedings. This principle emphasizes minimizing adverse effects on the rights and legitimate interests of the involved parties and third parties, conducting proceedings within a reasonable time (without unnecessary delay), avoiding excessive costs, and making optimal use of the limited public resources devoted to providing access to justice as a public service.

It is imperative to recognize the strong interconnections between the concept of proportionality and influential notions of justice, spanning from ancient to modern times, as well as rationality, in both pragmatic and axiological terms. Civil procedural law, designed to uphold the administration of justice and adhere to rationality, cannot concurrently flout the demands of proportionality or inadvertently foster disproportionate and abusive actions due to leniency or ineffective sanctioning of such behavior. As underscored by the Polish Constitutional Tribunal in one of its judgments, "the rule of law is premised on the legislature's rationality, and adherence to proportionality in the

---

the collective interests of consumers and repealing Directive 2009/22/EC (OJ L 409, 4.12.2020, p. 1–27).

66 On the relations between various proceedings within the Polish civil procedure system, including separate proceedings within the framework of examination proceedings (litigation) in contentious matters, see especially Sławomir Cieślak, *Powiązania wewnątrzsystemowe w postępowaniu cywilnym*, Warszawa, 2013, 1 ff.

67 Cornelius Hendrik (Remco) Van Rhee, "Towards Harmonised European Rules of Civil Procedure: Obligations of the Judge the Parties and their Lawyers", *Access to Justice in Eastern Europe* 1 (2020), 6 ff.

68 On this principle, see Wiebke Voß, "Proportionality in Civil Procedure: A Different Animal?", in *Proportionality in Private Law*, F. Bauer, B. Köhler (eds.), Tübingen, 2023, 181 ff.

legislative process is a necessary condition for fulfilling this premise. A rational legislature crafts just laws, thereby linking the principle of justice to the principle of proportionality."[69] In addition to this assertion, it can be inferred that the foundation of the rule of law also rests on the rationality, both praxeological and axiological, of the actions taken by other public authorities, including judicial bodies tasked with dispensing justice. Compliance with proportionality in the application of the law by these entities is a requisite for upholding this assumption. A rational court, in fulfilling its constitutional mandate to administer justice, applies the law equitably, thus reinforcing the principle that justice serves as the bedrock for the application of both substantive and procedural law.

To fortify the principle of proportionality within the doctrinal framework of civil procedural law, and potentially consider its explicit codification, especially in the context of drafting a new Code of Civil Procedure, it is essential to underscore its interconnections with active judicial case-management of proceedings. This approach has become prevalent in most modern legal systems, extending beyond civil law jurisdictions to encompass various common-law systems such as England and Wales,[70] Cyprus,[71] the Canadian province of

69 Judgment of the Constitutional Tribunal of January 31, 1996, K 9/95, OTK 1996, No 1, item 2.

70 The procedural dimension of the principle of proportionality should be associated with the developments during the reforms of English civil procedural law at the turn of the 20th and 21st centuries (Lord Woolf's reform leading to the adoption of the Civil Procedure Rules of 1998, and then Lord Jackson's reform resulting in the amendment of the CPR in 2013). This is the so-called "three-dimensional justice strategy." According to this strategy, the court must strive not only to achieve a fair resolution of the case but must do so within a reasonable time and with reasonable and proportionate use of available procedural resources. The justice system is undoubtedly one of the most priority public services, alongside ensuring external and internal security, education, healthcare, and minimum social security. However, the state resources that can be allocated to it are always limited. This approach represents a paradigm shift from the classical theory of justice, which assumes that the primary goal of legal conduct is to achieve a state of substantive justice, with the efficiency and effectiveness of the process being merely means to that end, rather than independent and equivalent values. According to the classical theory, excessive length of proceedings and unnecessary costs should be combated only to the extent that they do not hinder achieving fair decisions. In contrast, the three-dimensional justice strategy emphasizes balancing efficiency, effectiveness, and substantive justice. It recognizes that achieving justice involves not only the fairness of the decision itself but also the timeliness and cost-effectiveness of the process. This strategy, which can be identified with the new concept of proportional justice, aims to ensure an appropriate balance between these conflicting values and goals, making the process itself an integral component of justice; see John Sorabji, *English Civil Justice after the Woolf and Jackson Reforms: A Critical Analysis*, Cambridge, 2014, 1 *passim*.

71 The solutions outlined in the English CPR served as a benchmark for the recent reform of civil procedural law in the Republic of Cyprus. Notably, Lord Dyson, a former judge of

The principle of proportionality, alongside other fundamental procedural principles shaping the fairness of proceedings and enhancing the likelihood of a just outcome, serves as a crucial guiding principle for courts exercising discretionary powers. It provides a compass for courts to tailor their decisions appropriately to the specifics of each case, including the type of dispute, the interests at stake, the socio-economic significance, the complexity of facts and law, the conduct of the parties, the anticipated costs, and the caseload burden on the court. Given the increasing prominence of active judicial management of proceedings in Polish civil procedural law, which draws inspiration from, among others, British reforms such as those initiated by Woolf and Jackson, as well as practices from arbitration, it is prudent to intentionally align individual procedural tools with the overarching principle of proportionality. By employing a weighing approach, courts can ensure the rational and effective utilization of these tools while considering their impact on conflicting procedural principles and values. Therefore, a conscious and deliberate linkage between procedural instruments and the principle of proportionality enables courts to navigate the complexities of litigation and uphold the integrity of the judicial process, ensuring that justice is served efficiently and equitably in each case.

Undoubtedly, the necessity to maintain proportionality between means and objectives in civil proceedings has been underscored by the COVID-19 pandemic and the consequential changes in civil procedural law. Many of these changes, particularly the widespread adoption of remote hearings, have become integral components of the justice system in numerous jurisdiction.[74] It appears that in the "post-COVID" era, the imperative for a broad

74 On the experience of Council of Europe member states in this area, see Anne Sanders, "Video-Hearings in Europe Before, During and After the COVID-19 Pandemic", *International Journal for Court Administration* 2 (2021), 1 ff. See also in this respect Fernando Gascón Inchausti, "The impact of Covid-19 pandemic on Spanish civil justice: remote hearings as a new tool for the effectiveness of the system", in *Impact of the COVID-19 Pandemic on Justice Systems. Reconstruction or Erosion of Justice Systems—Case Study and Suggested Solutions*, K. Gajda-Roszczynialska (ed.), Göttingen, 2023, 199 ff.; Cornelius Hendrik (Remco) Van Rhee, "Covid-19 pandemic and the Role of Orality and Writing in Civil Litigation", in *Impact of the COVID-19 Pandemic on Justice Systems. Reconstruction or Erosion of Justice Systems—Case Study and Suggested Solutions*, K. Gajda-Roszczynialska (ed.), Göttingen, 2023, 284 ff. These solutions have been implemented to varying degrees in many countries for years. However, the COVID-19 pandemic acted as a catalyst for their widespread adoption, presenting challenges in maintaining continuity in the justice system while upholding fundamental rights and procedural guarantees, and safeguarding the health and safety of individuals involved in judicial proceedings to prevent the spread of the SARS-CoV-2 virus. Looking back, it can be assessed that

application of the principle of proportionality has not diminished but rather intensified, given the challenges and opportunities posed by the inevitable integration of modern digital advancements, such as artificial intelligence, into civil court proceedings. Despite advancements in science and technology aimed at resolving conflicts between values under legal protection while upholding fundamental principles and rights, no tool in jurisprudence has proven as effective and universal as the constitutional test of proportionality, reminiscent of the "age of coal and steel." Thoughtfully designed and properly implemented regulations and organizational strategies leveraging these innovations, while adhering to the requirements of proportionality, not only align with traditional procedural norms but also enhance the efficient realization of procedural objectives and functions. At times, these principles may necessitate reinterpretation, as evidenced by the adaptation of the principle of immediacy considering remote proceedings. However, such reinterpretations do not compromise the essence of these principles or their underlying values.

10 Closing Remarks

The author concurs with the position that the numerous amendments to the CCP in recent decades, combined with their poor quality, have led to the ex-

the option to conduct public hearings, including remote ones, emerged as a crucial tool in achieving these goals. The objective and universal advantages of remote hearings, regardless of pandemic-related issues, are evident in terms of streamlining and expediting proceedings, reducing costs, and minimizing the compromise to classic principles, guarantees, and procedural values such as transparency, oral nature, adversarial nature, and directness. This stands in contrast to alternative solutions like extending the written format of proceedings, resolving cases at closed sessions without a hearing, or extensive use of legal assistance in evidence-taking by designated judges or requested courts. Moreover, the relative advantages of remote hearings, such as eliminating geographical and communication barriers to accessing the court—especially for disabled and elderly individuals, facilitated by increasing internet accessibility—and reducing digital exclusion, suggest that this solution has undeniably become an integral aspect of modern civil procedure. Looking ahead, given the ongoing trend toward digitalization of public services, including the judicial system, it's foreseeable that remote hearings will become the default method of proceedings in many jurisdictions, especially for minor and simple cases. Traditional hearings, on the other hand, may remain prevalent in certain categories of civil cases, particularly those involving family and guardianship law, where physical interaction between the judge and participants could be crucial in achieving the case's objectives. In such cases, opting for traditional hearings would require justification based on weighing the values supporting this choice.

treme and arguably irreversible disintegration of this act.[75] This situation necessitates steps to develop a new, coherent, transparent, flexible, and as comprehensive and uniform as possible codification of civil proceedings tailored to the aspirations and needs of a modern democratic state within the political and legal framework of the European Union and the Council of Europe. Such a system must be based on the rule of law and the protection of fundamental human rights and freedoms.

Effective protection is unattainable without a properly designed civil procedure that allows for the correct implementation of the standards of the right to a fair trial as outlined in Article 6 of the ECHR, Article 47 of the Charter of Fundamental Rights of the European Union, and Article 45 of the Constitution. Drafting a new, future-oriented codification of civil procedure should involve a diligent analysis of past experiences, leveraging the best practices while avoiding the repetition of past mistakes. As an old Latin maxim states that *errare humanum est, sed perseverare diabolicum* ("to err is human but to persist is diabolical"). Despite the truth that *Panta rhei* ("everything flows"), we must remember that *historia magistra vitae est* ("history is the teacher of life"), a principle that also applies to legal history.

75 In recent years this opinion was expressed by many distinguished academics, pointing at the downfall and decomposition of the CCP both in terms of its structure, language and contents. In this regard, see, in particular Karol Weitz, "Współczesne problemy kodyfikacji prawa postępowania cywilnego", *Forum Prawnicze* 3 (2020), 34; Robert Kulski, "Upadek polskiego Kodeksu postępowania cywilnego", *Monitor Prawniczy* 8 (2023), 463 ff. Interestingly though, calls for a new code of civil procedure were formulated almost since the beginning of the 21st century. See in particular Ereciński, "O potrzebie nowego kodeksu", 3 ff.; Karol Weitz, "Czy nowa kodyfikacja", 13 ff. See also Andrzej Oklejak, "Co dalej z kodeksem postępowania cywilnego w czterdziestolecie jego istnienia?", in *Czterdziestolecie kodeksu postępowania cywilnego. Zjazd Katedr Postępowania Cywilnego w Zakopanem (7–9 X 2005 r.)*, Kraków, 2006, 7 ff.; Feliks Zedler, "Co dalej z kodeksem postępowania cywilnego?", in *Czterdziestolecie kodeksu postępowania cywilnego. Zjazd Katedr Postępowania Cywilnego w Zakopanem (7–9 X 2005 r.)*, Kraków, 2006, 309 ff. Conversely, pointing at the value of the continuation and limited changes in the existing CCP, see in particular Witold Broniewicz, "Czy potrzebny jest nowy kodeks postępowania cywilnego?", *Państwo i Prawo* 4 (2004), 11 ff.; Piotr Osowy, "Tradycja a współczesność w nowelizacji Kodeks postępowania cywilnego (refleksja ogólna)", in *Kodeks postępowania cywilnego z perspektywy pięćdziesięciolecia jego obowiązywania. Doświadczenia i perspektywy*, E. Marszałkowska-Krześ, I. Gil, Ł. Błaszczak (eds.), Sopot, 2014, 213 ff.

Afterword

Andrzej Dziadzio and Franciszek Longchamps de Bérier

In 1523, the codification of land court proceedings was carried out in the Crown of the Kingdom of Poland as part of the initiative undertaken by the king and the nobility at the turn of the 15th and 16th centuries to write down the law and initiate thorough legal reforms in the country. This was not a phenomenon uniquely confined to the Polish-Lithuanian lands. In the same era there was a pan-European trend to make efforts to organize and standardize the applicable law. Importantly, it was at this time that political and legal reforms were carried out in the German Reich. This was a direct consequence of the adoption of the *Ewiger Landfriede*—Perpetual Peace—in Worms, where, in 1495, the Imperial Chamber Court was established, its jurisprudence in civil matters being based on the achievements of Roman law and *ius commune*, with a form of proceedings that was determined by the principles of the Procedural Roman-Canonical law. And it was only a little later, in 1532, that, in the form of *Constitutio Criminalis Carolina*, the Reichstag adopted a penal codification for the entire German Reich.

Following models created within canon law, the German *Constitutio* introduced the inquisitorial process with regard to criminal cases and in this way court procedures in civil and criminal cases went their separate ways in Germany. The process of reforming judicial proceedings followed a similar course in France. The ordinance of 1539 issued in Villers-Cotterêts regulated court procedures in civil and criminal cases differently. The French civil trial was, of course, based on the tenets of the Roman-Canonical procedure, while in criminal cases patterns taken from the inquisitorial process were adopted. Civil procedure was addressed in the subsequent royal ordinances of 1566 and 1667, which regulate French court proceedings in civil cases.

The law codification movement of the Renaissance era, which impacted almost all of Europe, including the Polish-Lithuanian state, did not aim to completely eliminate the norms of customary law in favor of the validity of statutory law only. The movement sought first and foremost to create legal regulations that were stable and accessible to each of the parties to legal proceedings, and that ensured the most uniform possible application of these regulations. Therefore, the codes of this era did not through their regulations attempt to exhaust all issues related to the course of civil proceedings, and it was to this group of legal acts that the Polish codification of 1523 in particular belonged.

 | DOI:10.1163/9789004736672_018

The history of judicial proceedings in the Polish-Lithuanian Commonwealth took a different path than that in Western countries because in the former claims arising from both criminal and civil breaches of the law continued to be pursued under the same provisions. This was due to the great resistance in that territory of customary land law to the influence of *ius commune* and of the Procedural Roman-Canonical law widely promoted by the Church. It is for this reason that the basic principles of the old complaint process, i.e., the principle of orality, the principle of openness, and the adversarial principle, were maintained in the Crown of the Kingdom of Poland in modern times: they were perpetuated by the *Formula processus* of 1523.

However, land customary law did not exist in an axiological vacuum. Indeed, its application was determined by *maximae iuris*, that is, legal rules derived from canon law—*actor sequitur forum rei*, for example, i.e., the principle that the plaintiff should sue in the court of the defendant's domicile. It was also widely accepted that a case that has been finally adjudicated—*res iudicata*—should not be disturbed. Therefore, the complaint process under customary law could not remain completely free from the influence of patterns that were successfully applied in the practice of ecclesiastical courts. Elements of the Procedural Roman-Canonical law, such as a written summons with its components, types of procedural objections—*exceptions*—and, finally, the appeal as a means of challenging a judgment, also entered the land judicial process. Besides, the general divisions of the provisions of the *Formula processus* itself referred to the ecclesiastical legislative systematics.

After this epoch, no new period in the development of civil procedure in Europe was initiated until the French *Code de procédure civile* of 1806. This Napoleonic civil procedure was put into use in some German countries, such as the Kingdom of Westphalia and the Duchy of Berg, but also in the territory of the Polish lands in the Duchy of Warsaw and in the Free City of Kraków. In Poland, the French code met with the approval of the Polish landed gentry because its principles were in line with the openness and orality of the old Polish court proceedings. A public trial with the participation of an elected justice of the peace resembled the old tradition of an open and public trial presided over by a land judge who represented the local nobility. And it was not only in Poland that the French code was appreciated. It turned out to be the mother act for numerous codifications of civil procedural law in the second half of the 19th century which were carried out in central and eastern Europe, that is, in Germany, Austria, and Russia.

With regard to the German model of civil procedure, the turning point in determining the direction of changes was the Code of Civil Procedure of the Kingdom of Hanover of 1850. Subsequently, the solutions adopted in the Hanoverian procedure found both continuity and creative development in the German procedural law of 1877 as well as the Austrian one of 1895. Both of these statutes regulating civil procedure, despite drawing on the general assumptions of the jurisprudential framework of the Napoleonic procedure, chose to follow the Germanic tradition, which advocated an active role of the judge and a broader application of the investigative principle in civil court proceedings. This modern model of civil procedure as issued by Germanic legal culture significantly influenced the norms of the 1933 Polish Code of Civil Procedure. However, the Polish Code was not in thrall to the German model and made its own independent decisions. Its provisions contain admirable procedural constructions that are to this day a hallmark of the Polish civil process. The best example of this is the combination of cassation in appellate proceedings before the Supreme Court with a review judgment.

The historical picture of the development of civil procedure which our monograph has outlined justifies us in concluding that the European model of judicial procedure which has developed over the past centuries is clearly characterized by certain features—features which we have highlighted in the course of the work. Nevertheless, this does not imply that the process of development is at an end. On the contrary, our analysis of the course of civil procedure reforms in France and Poland at the turn of the 21st century gives the undeniable impression that the European model of court proceedings is still *in statu nascendi*. The modern legislator is once again looking for ways to speed up and simplify civil proceedings—this time through the use of modern information and communication technologies. The introduction of electronic forms of procedural activities makes it incumbent on modern reformers to reread the main principles of civil procedure, which in the European legal tradition play a primary guarantee role for the parties to the proceedings. The role of alternative forms of civil dispute resolution, such as arbitration, conciliation, and mediation, is also increasing in the current legislation, and these forms should not be abstracted from the jurisprudential achievements in the field of court proceedings, all in the name of justice and fairness, which the parties to every proceeding reasonably expect. Thus, the most important result of the analyses carried out in the monograph turns out to be findings regarding the course and content of civil procedure in various jurisdictions in Europe, i.e., transformations of the procedure over the centuries until we arrive at its shape today. And we see that the present shape of civil procedure on our continent is the result of a heritage that is either consciously accepted or consciously rejected.

Appendix: Perspectives on Civil Procedure at Law and in Equity in Old England

Honoring the Anniversaries of the Enactment of Formula Processus (*Poland, 1523*) *and the Judicature Acts* (*England, 1873*)

Vincent R. Johnson and Jan Halberda

The 500th anniversary of the enactment of *Formula Processus*, and thus of the fundamental Polish procedural codification, coincides with the 150th anniversary of the United Kingdom's judicial reforms of 1873. These, among other things, led to the merger of courts that up to then adjudicated cases according to either common law or equity law.

It is worth noting that for a number of centuries the most important English royal courts operated under different, only partly mutually respectful, legal orders. In simple terms: the Westminster courts applied common law while in the Court of Chancery equity principles were observed. Today's substantive law derives historically from either common law or equity law and it is useful to remember the fundamental importance of what procedure was followed by the respective courts in earlier days. In common law, adversarial procedure and formalism prevailed, and a framework of writs (forms of action) and associated evidentiary limitations were applied. The chancellor, on the other hand, acted inquisitorially, without the legal restrictions known to common law courts (both as to the subject of adjudication and the scope of circumstances and evidence considered).[1] The use of mechanisms derived from equity law, often referred to by the adjective "equitable", is most often discretionary: the court has a certain leeway, and the direction and content of the decision are not bound by precisely defined premises.[2] These were procedural differences that determined whether a court would be able to dispense justice to the parties. Again, it was the procedure that led plaintiffs' attempts to bring their case to a particular court. This, in turn, could lead to popularization of that version of substantive law that was applied in the most plaintiff-friendly court. Hence, the phenomenon of juris-

1 Michael Lobban, "Contractual Fraud in Law and Equity, c1750–c1850", *Oxford Journal of Legal Studies* 17 (1997), 443–446.

2 Rafal Zakrzewski, *Remedies Reclassified*, Oxford, 2005, 85 ff.

 | DOI:10.1163/9789004736672_019

dictional drift could occur: a given version of substantive law was gaining recognition not because of its merits but because it was applied by the court chosen by many litigants.[3] That is how adjective law impacted and still impacts substantive law.[4]

This chapter focuses on particular aspects of civil procedure in England between the 13th and 19th centuries which prompted the popularity of particular courts and which, in turn, have influenced the shape of procedure and substantive law today. It starts with setting the jurisdictional scene on which royal courts were to administer justice (part 1). What follows is a framework of original writs[5] that was the very cause of English law development (part 2). Before the appellate process is presented (part 4), the paper shows these phases of a first instance process (part 3), namely mesne process, pleadings, and evidence, whose shape resulted in no need for an appeal in medieval England.

It is a truism that remedies for challenging a judgment are crucial. This is why—due to an adoption of the appeal into Polish law in 1523—the anniversary of *Formula Processus* is so important. In English law, the modern appeal was only introduced with the reforms in the late 19th century. Earlier, as we shall soon appreciate, the need for an appeal was not foreseen. The pleadings phase of litigation was used to determine what was being disputed. If these were facts, supernatural assistance was sought to prove what really happened. If, on the other hand, a dispute was about the points of law and no consensus in this respect had been reached among lawyers, the matter was not resolved at all. The Gordian knot was not cut. There was therefore nothing to appeal against. It was the changes described in this paper concerning the drafting of an original writ, the phase of pleadings, the law of evidence, and the change in decision-making of courts, which opened the way to a place for a modern appeal.

---

3 On a different feature of the jurisdictional drift, see Jan Halberda, "Mistake of law and mistake of fact in English law of restitution", *Tijdschrift voor Rechtsgeschiedenis* 82 (2014), 281–283.

4 Joshua Getzler, "Legal History as Doctrinal History", in *The Oxford Handbook of Legal History*, Markus D. Dubber, Christopher Tomlins (eds.), Oxford, 2018, 174; Michael Lobban, "Contract", in *The Oxford History of the Laws of England. 1820–1914: Private Law*, William Cornish, et al. (eds.), vol. 12, Oxford, 2010, 321, 433–434; Reinhard Zimmermann, *The Law of Obligations. Roman Foundations of the Civilian Tradition*, Cape Town, 1990, 99.

5 Filing an original writ with a court was the very first step to start a case. Each writ initiated peculiar legal proceedings and thus terms *writ* and *action* are frequently applied interchangeably to refer both a basis of claim and a specific procedure that followed.

Both of these anniversaries—the 500th and the 150th—provide an excellent opportunity to undertake research on how a particular way of shaping adjective law in England has influenced substantive law there. In this article, authored by legal scholars from different legal cultures—continental civil law and American common law and statutory law—an attempt is made to present a course of proceedings at law and in equity against their historical background.

1 The Clash between Jurisdictions

1.1 *The Royal Courts*

From today's perspective, the common law, and the Westminster courts applying it, seem to be the most important law and courts in England—always and everywhere. Meanwhile, during the period treated as the dawn of English legal history, that is, in the 12th and 13th centuries, that law and these courts were only some among many other legal orders applied in England and among many other courts operating there.[6]

Common law was judge-made law developed in the royal courts of Westminster since that period. When these began to appear on the scene, they did not fill a jurisdictional vacuum. There were already other courts in place, i.e., local,[7] feudal,[8] ecclesiastical,[9] and others. The royal courts applied law in a context of a continuous competitive struggle over the business of the administration of justice.[10] These courts and sources of law had to fight for their places first with those other abovementioned courts acting "since time imme-

6 John H. Baker, *An Introduction to English Legal History*, Oxford 2019, 15ff.

7 Their jurisdiction covered most of the issues of the local community.

8 During the medieval period, at least in theory, the rule was that only before these courts could property ownership disputes be heard.

9 Nonperformance of a promise could be deemed not only a breach of law but also a sin and its punishment was within the Church's authority. On this basis, ecclesiastical courts resolved matrimonial and succession disputes, but also contract cases. See generally Robert E. Rodes, Jr., *Ecclesiastical Administration in Medieval England. The Anglo-Saxons to the Reformation*, Notre Dame, 1977, 129.

10 Vincent R. Johnson and Chenglin Liu, *Studies in American Tort Law*, Durham, 2022, 54–55: "Following the Norman conquest, justice in England was administered by many local courts. Gradually, the King began to permit some cases to come before his Council, usually for a fee ... Because the exercise of royal jurisdiction interfered with and impaired the income of local courts, it was strongly resisted. Writs were available to cover only a limited, though ever-expanding, number of situations" (citing Charles A. Keigwin, *Cases in Common Law Pleading*, Rochester, 1934, 1–10, 15–16).

morial." Later, on the flywheel of English legal history, there was a jurisdictional rivalry with the Court of Chancery and among the Westminster courts themselves. This contest came to an end only with the judicial reforms finalized in 1873.

At the outset, the royal judiciary was twofold and included, on the one hand, three Westminster courts dealing—respectively—with tax, criminal, and civil cases, and, on the other hand, those courts held in the countryside by special commissioners. The former emerged from *curia regis* and operated at the king's side. One of these, the Court of Exchequer, was responsible for solving disputes on royal revenues. Its name came from a pattern of a checkered cloth covering a table on which taxes collected were checked. While its jurisdiction was formally limited to fiscal matters only, in practice it expanded steadily because of plaintiff-friendly procedural rules (see: quo minus procedure).[11]

The Court of King's Bench[12] settled in Westminster as late as in the 14th and 15th centuries. Up to then it followed the monarch in his journeys around the country as the ruler himself presided over this court. This court heard *placita coronae* or *criminalia*, i.e., those matters in which the king had a personal interest: complaints against officials, significant criminal cases, and all those in which either a fine was demanded in favor of the king or a breach of the king's peace was alleged. Therefore, the rise of a writ of trespass was closely linked to this court's practice because that writ's formula treated even a slight injury as a breach of the peace.[13]

The necessity of filing lawsuits in a place where curia regis happened to be was extremely troublesome.[14] That is why the barons at Runnymede (1215)

11 Baker, *An Introduction*, 21ff, 44ff; Edward Coke, *The Institutes of the Laws of England*, London, 1809, vol. 2, 23, 551, vol. 4, 70–76, 98–119 (at 112: "it is foursquare and the carpet that sometime lay upon it had wrought in it the form of a cheffe board"). Since the Elizabeth I's reign and until the Court of Chancery Act 1841 (5 Victoria c. 5 s. 1) this court was entitled to decide cases on the basis of equity in particular circumstances.

12 During periods of the queen's rule, this court was referred to as the Court of Queen's Bench (or the Queen's Bench Division), while during the Commonwealth of England (1649–1660) it was called the Upper Bench.

13 See Petstede v. Marreys (1310; Y.B. 3 & 4 Edward II (S.S.) vol. 22, 29, 208), anon. 1313 (Y.B. 7 Edward II (S.S.) vol. 39, 14, C.P.), Rattlesdene v. Grunestone (1317; Y.B. 10 Edward II (S.S.) vol. 54, 141), Colan v. West (1367; K.B. 27/428 m. 56), anon. 1481 (Y.B. 21 Edward IV Pas. fo. 28 pl. 23)—quoted after John H. Baker and Stroud Milsom, *Sources of English Legal History. Private Law to 1750*, London, 1986, 298–304, 314–316).

14 In order to file a writ with a court, a plaintiff in Richard de Anesti v. Mabel de Francheville (1158–1163) (quoted after: David C. Douglas and George W. Greenaway, *English Historical Documents*, vol. 2, London, 1961, 456–457) had to travel to Normandy wherein

forced John Lackland to confirm that *communia placita*, i.e., these cases which did not affect the king directly, would be decided by a court having its seat in a settled place.[15] That led to the formation of the Court of Common Pleas. It adjudicated disputes brought under real actions and older personal actions. No other royal court was authorized to decide civil matters.

The Westminster judges did not operate in isolation. During the 14th century, a practice developed of discussing the most complex legal issues at informal meetings such as collective lunches of judges and attorneys. The goal was to reach a compromise to satisfy all stakeholders. A belief prevailed that courts lacked law-making authority and unanimity of judges guaranteed compliance with good old law. Therefore, if judges could not agree, they usually did not pass judgment at all. Symptomatic is the fact that for centuries the Westminster courts consisted of four judges each, which could lead to a stalemate—a 2:2 vote split. Because of this, a given case could remain unresolved. A change of approach regarding the power of the judiciary occurred only at the dawn of the Renaissance. At that time, majority judgments began to be issued.[16]

Because judges met informally in the Exchequer's chamber, the name of Court of Exchequer Chamber began to be used. Although no formal act establishing this body was ever passed, its authority was not questioned. Many significant decisions in the evolution of common law were made there.[17]

The king exercised his judicial powers also through special envoys dispatched to the country. These commissioners (ad omnia placita; justices in eyre) initially performed mainly fiscal functions. More judicial powers were given to them during Henry II's reign (1154–1189). Later on, custom developed, modified by the Statute of Westminster II (1285), of holding proceedings with

rex ambulans was present. See also Vincent R. Johnson, "The Ancient Magna Carta and the Modern Rule of Law: 1215 to 2015", *St. Mary's Law Journal* 47 (2015), 1, 33–34 (discussing the "problems of peripatetic justice" in medieval England).

15 Coke, *The Institutes*, vol. 2, 22.

16 John H. Baker, "English Law and the Renaissance", *Cambridge Law Journal* 44 (1985), 57–60.

17 The examples (in contract law) include Slade's case (1602) Coke Rep. IV 91–92a, Pynchon v. Legat (1611) Coke Rep. IX 86b–90b. Anon. (Trin. 1488) Caryll 10 pl. 15 (*Reports of Cases by John Caryll*, John H. Baker (ed.), London 1999–2000; "it was said in the Exchequer Chamber before All the justices and serjeants of England"). Coke, *The Institutes*, vol. 1, 71b. The practice of setting significant rules by the court itself has survived to this day. Judges have thus developed Rules of Court which are an equivalent of codes of judicial procedure (for example, Civil Procedure Rules 1998).

a jury (trial by jury) under the presidency of an assize judge who was commissioners' successor (*nisi prius* procedure).[18]

1.2 *Rivalry among the Courts*

Despite the king being considered the supreme judge and guardian of peace, the *curia regis*' authority to try cases was still not the rule, but only an exception. There was a rule granting general jurisdiction to local courts (until 1833).[19] The royal courts dealt with a short list of king's pleas, i.e., cases involving issues concerning the monarch himself.[20] The scope of these, however, steadily expanded. During the reign of Henry II, it began to be accepted that anyone who served a royal court with a particular writ would be able to demand justice there. On the other hand, a defendant was not required to appear before a court if a plaintiff did not present a writ.[21]

At the same time, the royal lobby pushed the principle that "false judgment is a king's plea." According to it, a royal court was to solve complaints about a refusal of judgment, or an issuance of an unjust one, by a local or feudal court. At the request of one of the parties to a dispute (which may not have belonged to the short list of king's pleas), the king could address a writ to the feudal senior of the petitioner ordering him to issue a just judgment. Disregard of the writ would lead to taking a dispute for adjudication by a royal court.[22]

The royal judiciary gained a dominant position as a result of the king's active policy. The means by which the law was modified were writs. These were orders given either by the king, a chancery, or a court. It was a catalog of writs issued by the chancery that set the limits of royal jurisdiction. The creation of new types of original writs meant, in practice, that the royal court extended legal protection to cases that had hitherto been legally irrelevant. Although reforms were procedural in nature, their results reached deep into the substantive law—in particular property law. In essence the formation of new types of writs came close to the introduction of legal regulations by force of statute. This is why barons protested.

18 Baker, *An Introduction*, 17 ff.; Coke, *The Institutes*, vol. 2, 422, vol. 4, 158–161.

19 Real Property Limitation Act 1833 (3 & 4 William IV c. 27).

20 These were cases regarding entitlements to royal property, disputes between the king's immediate vassals and the most serious crimes—those breaching the king's peace.

21 Henry Bracton, *On the Laws and Customs of England*, transl. by Samuel E. Thorne, Cambridge Mass., 1977, vol. 4, 286: "no one may sue without a writ, since without a writ the other is not bound to answer."

22 Portubus v. Merry (1204) Curia Regis Rolls, III, 133 (quoted after: Baker and Milsom, *Sources*, 31–32).

Crucial to the outcome of rivalry between courts were reforms carried out in the area of adjective law. This trump card of the royal judiciary became an efficient procedure. The Westminster courts guaranteed, to a much higher degree, the fair settlements of disputes. Among other things, these procedures could compel a defendant to appear before a court. The means of finding the facts were more rational, and therefore more reliable. The enforcement of judgment was effective as a sheriff was able to carry out executions from real estate. In addition, royal judges embodied a higher level of legal awareness than their counterparts in local and feudal courts. Therefore, by bringing a claim before a royal court, a plaintiff reduced the risk of losing a just case. Consequently, even if a local court had exclusive jurisdiction in a particular case, a plaintiff often tried to circumvent it.[23]

Royal judges had a reason to support royal reforms. They did not earn fixed salaries, but received a percentage of court fees collected.[24] It was therefore in the judges' interest to decide as many cases as possible. As they had to comply with jurisdictional rules, they did their best to find legal tricks for expanding the scope of their powers. In turn, providing a court with a significant influx of cases in the future depended on efficient handling of current proceedings. Therefore, judges introduced a number of procedural devices designed to induce plaintiffs to file cases with their particular court as the most efficient one.[25] That triggered not only the expansion of royal jurisdiction but also rivalry among the Westminster courts themselves.

In such circumstances, to some extent, a free market for judicial services emerged in England. Often a plaintiff had the option of choosing a court (and thus the jurisdiction and the applicable law) before which to litigate. Plaintiffs did their best to profit from forum shopping.[26]

Since the 14th century, the writ of quo minus began to be applied before the Court of Exchequer. As this court was empowered to hear tax cases, it was often unfriendly to defendants. It was possible to arrest defendants and the

---

23 Stroud Milsom, "Sale of Goods in the Fifteenth Century", *Law Quarterly Review* 77 (1961), 258–260. In 1494, a plaintiff claimed entitlement to payment of the price of 6 shillings for two full carts of hay and repayment of a (probably fictional) loan in the amount of 34 shillings only for the sake of meeting the threshold of 40 shillings, which allowed him to file a writ with a royal court. Anon. (C.P. Trin. 1494) Caryll 257–258 pl. 178.

24 On the greed of Polish judges that was to be overcome by the reform see Witold Maisel, "*Formula processus iudiciarii*—code polonais de procédure civile de 1523", *Právněhistorické studie* 19 (1975), 214, 226.

25 Baker, *An Introduction*, 48–50.

26 Joshua Getzler, "Patterns of Fusion", in *The Classification of Obligations*, Peter Birks (ed.), Oxford, 1997, 170.

wager of law[27] mechanism for resolving disputes was not available. Thus, filing a suit with this court, instead of any other, could increase a plaintiff's chances of winning. In addition, a legal fiction, referred to as quo minus, was developed. The plaintiff, wishing to collect a private debt, would declare that his debtor's default materially impaired his (plaintiff's) ability to pay taxes. The Court of Exchequer would launch proceedings against the actual debtor of the potential debtor of the Crown.[28]

The Court of King's Bench was particularly creative in finding legal ploys to increase the influx of cases. Its jurisdiction did not include civil cases, and these were indeed the primary source of lawyers' income. To lure numbers of plaintiffs, King's Bench took advantage of its know-how in the area of criminal law that forced defendants to appear before a court. Beginning in the 15th century, the following practice was common. A plaintiff would file a writ of trespass with the court, alleging that "by force and in breach of the king's peace" a defendant had committed a tort in Middlesex (the county where the court was seated). This would give a casual civil dispute at least an appearance of a criminal case. Even if that allegation was untrue, the court did not consider at all whether any tort had been committed. Nonetheless, the King's Bench—issuing the bill of Middlesex—ordered the defendant's detention. This allowed a plaintiff to file a bill indicating an actual legal basis for his claim (e.g., failure to pay a debt).[29]

As a result of the widespread use of a number of legal tricks, by the mid-17th century, all three Westminster courts had *de facto* equal jurisdiction. *De jure*, the rules of exclusive jurisdiction of particular courts still applied.[30]

---

27 A wager of law was a judicial oath, usually made by a defendant, allowing him to prove certain facts. See "Wager of Law", in *Black's Law Dictionary*, Bryan A. Garner (ed.), St. Paul, Minn. 2014: "A method of proof in which a person defends against a claim by swearing that the claim is groundless, and by enlisting others (compurgators) to swear to the defendant's credibility."

28 William Blackstone, *Commentaries on the Laws of England, A Facsimile of the First Edition of 1765–1769*, Chicago, London, 1979, vol. 3, 45–46. Differently, Coke, *The Institutes*, vol. 4, 110–115, who pointed out—perhaps contrary to a reality—that only the prosecution of a direct, and not an indirect, debtor of the Crown was permissible before this court.

29 According to Coke, *The Institutes*, vol. 2, 23, vol. 4, 71–72, 100, proceedings by bill could be started before any other royal court against "any that is in custodia mareschalli or any officer, minister, or clerk of the court." The principle of an exclusive jurisdiction of the Court of Common Pleas applied only to cases initiated by writ. On top of that a bill was less expensive than a writ.

30 Baker, *An Introduction*, 48–59; Blackstone, *Commentaries*, vol. 3, 285–286; Coke, *The Institutes*, vol. 2, 23, vol. 4, 71–72, 76, 100; John H. Langbein and Renee Lettow Lerner and Bruce P. Smith, *History of the Common Law. The Development of Anglo-American Legal Institutions*, New York, 2009, 250–251.

1.3 *Court of Chancery and Equity Law*

Little has been said so far about the Court of Chancery. It was already treated as equal in status to the Westminster courts in the second half of the 14th century. This Court developed from the chancery whose tasks (one of many) were to issue original writs by means of which proceedings before royal courts were initiated. If among ordinary writs there was none that could be applied to the particular facts of a case, the last resort was a petition to the monarch. Dealing with such petitions was, over time, transferred to a chancellor. He was to cope with difficult cases in which application of the common law led to unsatisfactory results. As a consequence, the office of chancery began, steadily, to perform judicial functions. The chancellor's jurisdictional powers consisted thus of two agendas. The first included issuance of original writs initiating a proceeding and in this matter common law was followed. The second agenda was to administer justice in those cases in which Westminster courts would fail.[31] A reference to the "Court of Chancery" is most often a reference to the latter form of the chancellor's business.

Until the 16th century, a chancellorship was always held by clergymen. Later on, lawyers familiar with common law began to be appointed to the office. Initially, the basis for the chancellor's decision was said to be good conscience (as he could resort to methods of discovering facts unknown to common law) which gave rise to complains of discretion. Having that in mind, Selden (in the mid-17th century) sarcastically claimed that the criterion for a chancellor's decision-making changed as often as the size of the feet of successive chancellors. When chancellors were no longer clergymen, but lay lawyers, the term "equity" began to be used instead of conscience.[32] The rules applied in the Court of Chancery were referred to as equity law and, gradually over the 17th and 18th centuries, took on the features of a system of law. Significant influence on the shape that equity law later achieved was exerted especially by chancellors Ellesmere (1603–1617), Bacon (1617–1621), Nottingham (1675–1682). Transformation of equity into a system of law resulted in its rules becoming rigid, strict and formalized. That was just what had happened earlier under common law, and just what was to be cured by equity principles.[33]

---

31 Coke, *The Institutes*, vol. 4, 77–84: "one oridinary, coram domino rege in cancellaria. (...) Another extraordinary according to the rule of equity, *secundum aequum et bonum*."

32 David Ibbetson, "A House Built on Sand: Equity in Early Modern English Law", in *Law & Equity. Approaches in Roman Law and Common Law*, Egbert Koops, Willem J. Zwalve (eds.), Leiden, 2014, 55; George Mousourakis, *Comparative Law and Legal Traditions Historical and Contemporary Perspectives*, Cham, 2019, 266–268.

33 Baker, *An Introduction*, 107, 114–119; Getzler, "Patterns of Fusion", 176, 185; Langbein and Lerner and Smith, *History of the Common Law*, 316; Frederic W. Maitland, *Equity, also the*

In theory the Court of Chancery was supposed to intervene only exceptionally.[34] In 1615 Chancellor Ellesmere defined the role of equity as follows: "to soften and mollify the extremity of the law." That is why it has been repeatedly said that equity law was contemplated as a "gloss" to the common law, and, therefore, English equity was compared—although with some reservations—to the Roman *ius honorarium*.[35]

Importantly, while common law could exist on its own, equity had no life without the former. The Court of Chancery was not intended to compete with other royal courts, but only to modify some of the overly strict and formalistic principles of common law which the Westminster courts could not avoid. It was designed to prevent mischiefs of other courts, for example, when administration of justice could not be dispensed in a particular country due to corruption, feudal wars, or peasant unrest.[36] In some instances this could lead to that court awarding a claim in favor of a plaintiff who would not be granted protection in the Westminster court because of lack of an original writ that could start procedure there. In a case decided in 1489, the chancellor noted: "no one departs from the Court of Chancery without remedy."[37] That quota-

Forms of Action at Common Law; Two Courses of Lectures, Cambridge, 1910, 28–29; Mousourakis, *Comparative Law*, 271; Peter Turner, "Fusion and Theories of Equity in Common Law Systems", in *Equity and Law: Fusion and Fission*, John Goldberg and Henry Smith, Peter Turner (eds.), Cambridge, 2019, 10.

34 Samuel Bray, "The System of Equitable Remedies", UCLA *Law Review* 63 (2016), 544–545, 581; James Edelman in *Snell's Equity*, John McGhee (ed.), London, 2010, 105–106 ("Equity follows the law", "Where there is equal equity, the law shall prevail"); Gareth Jones, "The Role of Equity in the English Law of Restitution", in *Unjust Enrichment. The Comparative Legal History of the Law of Restitution*, Eljto Schrage (ed.), Berlin, 1995, 151; Maitland, *Equity*, 23–27; Lord Neuberger of Abbotsbury, "The Stuffing of Minerva's Owl? Taxonomy and Taxidermy in Equity", *Cambridge Law Journal* 68 (2009), 538 ("But equity is not a sort of moral U.S. fifth cavalry riding to the rescue every time a claimant ..."); Turner, "Fusion and Theories", 11–12.

35 Baker, *An Introduction*, 119, 123; John Cartwright, "Equity's Connivance in the Evasion of Legal Formalities", in *Law & Equity*, 126–127; David Fox in *Snell's Equity*, 9; Getzler, "Patterns of Fusion", 176; Jones, "The Role of Equity", 151; Langbein and Lerner and Smith, *History of the Common Law*, 271, 278; Maurizio Lupoi, "English 'equity' and the civil law — a tale of two worlds", *Trusts & Trustees*, 26/2 (2020), 180 ("the parallel with the Roman praetor has no foundation"); Maitland, *Equity*, 37–38, 175; Mousourakis, *Comparative Law*, 265, 269–270. See: Jan Halberda, "Parallels between Roman Civil Law and English Common Law (Litigation, Obligations)", in *Acta Historico-Iuridica Pilsensia* (2009–2010), Plzen, 2011, 78 ff.

36 Macheid's case (C.P. 1617–1619) HLS MS. 2068, fo. 32v, pl. 2, quoted after William H. Bryson, *Cases concerning Equity and the Courts of Equity 1550–1660*, London, 2000–2001, 477.

37 Anon. 1489 (Y.B. 4 Hen. VII fol. 4 Hil. Pl. 8) (quoted after: Langbein and Lerner and Smith, *History of the Common Law*, 313–314). Edelman in *Snell's Equity*, 107, begins the list of

tion foreshadowed the path of future development. Invocation of equitable principles was resorted to with increasing frequency, and gradually that court took over cases hitherto decided at Westminster.

What caused concerns was that the Court of Chancery often engaged in disputes that had already been solved by other courts. For example, before the Court of Common Pleas, a payment could be sought on the basis of a deed, i.e., a sealed bond stating that a defendant owed a plaintiff a certain amount of money. Deeds were used in business as collateral if significant assets were being borrowed or if a piece of real estate was being sold. The rules of evidence applicable before the Westminster court did not allow an offer of any counter-evidence if a deed was presented. Thus, if a defendant had already repaid a loan or paid the price of goods, but did not recover a deed previously issued, then a plaintiff presenting the deed was certain to prevail. In such a case, an unfortunate defendant petitioned the Court of Chancery for an injunction forbidding the plaintiff from enforcing the Westminster judgment. The availability of the Court of Chancery intervention was pronounced by King James I in the Earl of Oxford case (1615), one of the most significant disputes in English legal history. There, deciding according to a political criterion, the king upheld the Court of Chancery's decision that prevented a former plaintiff from enforcement of the King's Bench decision.[38]

Where did this flexibility of the chancellor's equity come from? Its source was adjective law. There were rigid procedural rules at law: the process was set in motion only on the basis of a proper writ, and parties had to apply precise rules of pleading. They were allowed to focus only on one field of the dispute (a single issue). Strict rules of evidence applied, ruling out the possibility of providing counter-evidence in many cases. Finally, an award available was mostly based on payment of money. While many cases did not fit into this corset, the chancellor could, within certain limits, step outside the box: he didn't need a writ to begin with; he could resolve questions of law and fact at the same time; he could, to much greater extent than his colleagues, act like an inquisitorial judge and obtain evidence. Finally, he could thus determine what the facts really were while this knowledge was unavailable to judges at

maxims of equity with the following one: "Equity will not suffer a wrong to be without a remedy."

38 Earl of Oxford's Case (1615) Chan. Rep. 1, 21 ER 485 (quoted after: David Ibbetson, "The Earl of Oxford's case (1615)", in *Landmark Cases in Equity*, Charles Mitchell, Paul Mitchell (eds.), Oxford, Portland, 2012, 1). Getzler, "Patterns of Fusion", 182; Ibbetson, "A House Built", 56–60; Langbein and Lerner and Smith, *History of the Common Law*, 329–335; Maitland, *Equity*, 28; Zimmermann, *The Law of Obligations*, 97.

Westminster. This, in turn, made it possible for the chancellor to arrive at a more fair decision[39] — for example, to prohibit a creditor from seeking payment on the basis of a deed if an unfortunate debtor had already repaid the loan but neglected to recover the deed.

The tension between jurisdictions (Westminster and Chancery's) and legal orders (common law and equity law) was important for the development of English law. The Court of Chancery developed a number of legal doctrines that, over time, were more or less consciously recycled by Westminster judges. In the area of contract law this court began to allow parties to use charges of mistake, deceit, accident, and forgery,[40] as well as to protect simple executory contracts which were agreements concluded without resort to a solemn form of deed and not yet performed by any party. The parties to these disputes could not claim protection under medieval common law. However, the Court of Chancery forced an active policy on the Westminster courts, resulting in a significant transformation of English law in the 15th to 17th centuries.[41]

2 Original Writs

2.1 *Initiation of Proceedings*

As already alluded to, in order to start proceedings before a royal court, a plaintiff had to furnish an original writ (Latin: *breve*). It is difficult to overestimate the importance of writs for the evolution of English law. The prominent 19th-century legal historian Frederick W. Maitland equated the history of common law to the history of writs.[42] The key importance of writs was due to the principle according to which royal jurisdiction was not the rule, but only an exception (part 1.2). In view of this, the royal courts could dispense justice only under special royal authorization. It was given in the form of an

39 Fox in *Snell's Equity*, 6–7; Getzler, "Patterns of Fusion", 176–177, 191; Ibbetson, "A House Built", 60; Lobban, "Contract", 435 ff; Michael Lobban, "Mapping the Common Law: Some Lessons from History", *New Zealand Law Review* 21 (2014), 30–31; Mousourakis, *Comparative Law*, 267; Turner, "Fusion and Theories", 11–12.

40 It was not until the mid-19th century that the use of these defences was made available more widely in the common law. This happened under the Common Law Procedure Act 1854 (17 & 18 Victoria c. 125 ss. 83–86).

41 Skip v. Huey, Wilcox and Edwards (1744) Atkyns III 93. Baker, "English Law", 47; Baker, *An Introduction*, 107, 111–112, 267 ff, 309 ff; Blackstone, *Commentaries*, vol. 2, 442; Coke, *The Institutes*, vol. 4, 84; David Ibbetson, *A Historical Introduction to the Law of Obligations*, Oxford, 1999, 72–73; Jones, "The Role of Equity", 151–160; Zimmermann, *The Law of Obligations*, 662, 778.

42 Frederic W. Maitland, *The Forms of Action at Common Law*, Cambridge 1962, 10.

original writ issued by the chancellor. Therefore, it was the list of these that set the limits of the royal jurisdiction. Dozens of specific writs were developed. Each writ concerned a narrow category of cases with peculiar facts.

Each writ triggered its own specific proceeding, referred to as a form of action, which was designed to fit best the specific injury whose remedy was the goal of the proceedings. The form of action resulted in particular rules concerning the wording of a writ, ways of pleading (presentation of argumentation) and modes of proving the truth, as well as a remedy available in judgment.[43] There was no ordinary procedure that could be equated with a general pattern of proceedings to which only specific provisions provided particular exceptions. Instead, there were dozens of specific proceedings. The diversity of the proceedings initiated by various writs was justified by the different types of disputes, the types of legal interests at stake, and the potential injuries to be cured. By creation of a number of specific proceedings, a priori tailored to specific types of disputes, judges were equipped with rules of procedure from which they did not have to deviate. Otherwise, if only a general pattern of proceedings was in operation, a judge would be forced in each case—by making discretionary decisions—to shape the rules of procedure so that *in casu* purpose of proceedings would be achieved to the greatest extent possible. In England it was feared that it might cause a wave of abuse. A plaintiff was therefore equipped with an arsenal of types of specific proceedings, governed by formalized and highly detailed procedural rules. Deviations from these rules were strictly forbidden. Later, when some of the procedural doctrines began to be criticized, it was still feared that even the slightest change could cause the intricate construction of a procedural system to crash. Consequently, procedure remained the most irrational branch of English law until the reforms carried out in the 19th century.[44]

Edward Coke divided original writs into those pertaining to criminal cases (*placita criminalia*) and to civil cases (*placita communia, civilia*). Among the latter, he listed writs initiating litigation as to real property (real actions),

---

43 Frederic Pollock and Frederic W. Maitland, *The History of English Law Before the Time of Edward I*, vol. 2,Cambridge, 1968, 561–562 ("Our plaintiff is not merely choosing a writ, he is choosing an action, and every action has its own rules").

44 William Holdsworth, *A History of English Law*, London, 1903–1972, vol. 3, 626, quotes a perverse statement of Fortescue C.J.: "Sir, the law is as I say it is, and so it has been laid down ever since the law began; and we have several set forms which are held as law, and so held and used for good reason, though we cannot at present remember that reason" (anon. 1458, Y.B. 36 Henry VI pl. 21, 25–26).

against some person (personal actions) and mixed actions.[45] The classic example of a real action was a writ of right that could be used exclusively before the Court of Common Pleas to test legal title over a piece of real property. Personal writs, in turn, included older formulas, such as writs of debt, or detinue, and newer ones—a writ of trespass, action on the case, assumpsit.[46] Mixed actions included petty assizes. There was no clear criterion for the division of writs. In light of these qualification difficulties, the 19th-century legal scholars Maitland and Pollock indicated that an English student would most likely describe the majority of writs as mixed, and some of them as very mixed.[47]

Exceptionally it was possible to file a bill with a Westminster court instead of a writ. Compared to the latter, the advantage of the former was less formalism and lower costs. In contrast, proceedings in the Court of Chancery were always commenced by a bill. Only if the defendant did not appear the chancellor would address a writ of subpoena ordering him to come. As proceedings were not conducted according to particular writs but following a uniform bill, for this reason, different types of special proceedings did not develop before the Court of Chancery.[48]

2.2 *The Nominalism of Writs*

When a case did not correspond to any of the ordinary writs, the only hope left was to persuade chancery clerks to issue a writ irrespectively. These clerks were entitled to slightly modify the writ in such a way that it could be applied *in casu*.[49] Lacking a proper writ a plaintiff could not count on royal justice but had to sue in other courts (e.g., local, feudal or even ecclesiastical). Later on, support for a plaintiff's claims could possibly be sought in the Court of Chancery (part 1.3). Nevertheless, desperate plaintiffs attempted to file their cases with the Westminster court. More often than not, however, they lost.

---

45 Coke, *The Institutes*, vol. 1, 284b, vol. 2, 22, 40: "Common or civil pleas are divided into reall, personall, and mixt."

46 Debt and detinue were forms of action used in claims for a liquidated sum of money due to payment of debt or value of goods. Trespass was applied in case of torts involving direct use of force. Action on the case and assumpsit were its derivatives referred to—respectively—in event of (other) torts or contracts.

47 Pollock and Maitland, *The History*, vol. 2, 570–572.

48 Baker, *An Introduction*, 111; Coke, *The Institutes*, vol. 4, 109; Stroud Milsom, *Historical Foundations of the Common Law*, London, 1981, 34, 54.

49 Coke, *The Institutes*, vol. 4, 82: "originall writs according to law, which are not of course; whereupon such are called in our ancient authors brevia magistralia."

According to Bracton if a proper writ was missing, a new one would simply be drafted without delay.[50] Thus, the number of writs grew rapidly: while around fifty were known at the beginning of the 13th century, by its end there were already more than half a thousand.[51] Nevertheless, since the time of Henry II, the opposite position began to gain support. The creation of new writs was repeatedly opposed by the barons in Merton (1236) and Oxford (1258), who argued that the good old laws should not be changed. It was pointed out that only those who presented their claim within the framework of already known writs deserved protection of a royal court. Consequently, the right to obtain justice before a royal court became conditional on availability of a procedural remedy—the writ. The petrification of law in this respect was facilitated by a listing of all writs in an official register of writs under Henry III. After his death in 1272, no new writs were created. The principle of nominalism held sway.[52] This led to the Latin maxim *ubi remedium ibi ius*—"wherever there is a remedy, (only) there is a right."[53] The list of writs was henceforth to be a closed catalogue that set limits of royal courts and royal power. English judges shied away from formulating general rules of substantive law. It seems that these would be superfluous, since an analysis of a legal situation of an individual party was carried out through the prism of the application in his case of a specific form of action governed by a set of rules of conduct specific to it. The nominalism of writs as found in the adjective law resulted in substantive law nominalism as well. For example, isolated doctrines of particular torts had emerged from the Westminster courts' judge-made law. The case law set conditions for obtaining an original writ that fit the specific injury. Partic-

---

50 Bracton, *On the Laws and Customs of England*, vol. 4, 286: „there will be as many formulas for writs as there are kinds of actions."

51 See Percy H. Winfield, "The Foundation of Liability in Tort", *Columbia Law Review* 27 (1927), 5: "Torts of a specific character have increased steadily in number throughout our legal history, and the courts can even now, if they think fit, enlarge the list. … [At times, the willingness of English courts to recognize new remedies was so great that it] was more difficult for jurists to state this branch of the law scientifically than for judges to make the law itself. Writers on the law were like map-makers whose rulers conquer territory so rapidly that the bounds of their realms cannot be traced."

52 Baker, *An Introduction*, 62–63; Coke, *The Institutes*, vol. 1, 74a, vol. 2, 94–96; Langbein and Lerner and Smith, *History of the Common Law*, 105, 272; Maitland, *The Forms of Action*, 6.

53 Compare translation of *ubi ius ibi remedium* in Aaron x. Fellmeth, Maurice Horwitz, *Guide to Latin in International Law*, Oxford, 2009, 281; see also Robert E. Rodes, Jr., *The Legal Enterprise*, Port Washington, N.Y., 1976, 93: "The problem is this: Does the law apply because someone in authority has discerned a right, or does it speak of a right because someone in authority has resolved on applying a remedy? Will the sheriff put you off my land because it is mine? Or do we say it is mine because the sheriff will put you off."

ular rules of substantive law were a reflection of procedural rules. Thus, the development of the former took place through the evolution of the latter.[54]

2.3 *Wrong Choice*

A plaintiff's use of an improper writ was fatal.[55] For this reason, matching the facts of a case to one of the writ formulas was the most important skill of a lawyer.[56] Until the 19th century it entailed a loss of the case (meaning the defeat of the claim) and could expose a plaintiff to criminal penalties for perjury.

Significantly, a defendant could allege that an improper writ was chosen even as late as in error proceedings. However, it is not clear whether a plaintiff could have taken the case to a court again, using a proper original writ this time. Probably he could have another try. Still, in some cases dismissal of a claim under a particular writ could de facto deprive a plaintiff of legal protection. To give just one practical example: plaintiffs attempted to resort to an action on the case to avoid using a writ of debt. If a suit was dismissed due to choice of an improper writ, the only alternative was to sue with a writ of debt. This form of action, however, allowed a defendant to "wage his law" (i.e., to swear that the claim is not based on truth) what in a majority of cases had led to the plaintiff's defeat. Thus, the dismissal of a writ, although not formally blocking the path to justice, could in practice have very similar effect.[57]

2.4 *Abolition of Writs*

From the late 13th century until the reforms carried out in the 19th century, the nominalism of writs was one of the cornerstones of common law. The plaintiff was given effective protection provided that a proper writ was resorted to. Successive attempts to covertly circumvent this principle mark the milestones

---

54 As a result of the medieval framework of the original writs, English law of torts has not formulated a general basis of liability similar to that expressed in the Article 1240 (former Article 1382) of the French Civil Code of 1804 or Article 415 of the Polish Civil Code of 1964. The English law of torts comprises some seventy separate legal regimes. A similar situation exists in the field of the law of unjust enrichment. Zimmermann, *The Law of Obligations*, 913–914.

55 Coke, *The Institutes*, vol. 1, 303a.

56 Getzler, "Legal History", 171, 173. Pollock and Maitland, *The History*, vol. 2, 561–562, compare the chancery issuing the writs to an arsenal, where a plaintiff procures an appropriate armour for the dispute in question.

57 Maitland, *The Forms of Action*, 4, pointed out to definite consequences of a choice of an improper writ, while Holdsworth, *A History*, vol. 2, 250, merely procedural (transitional) ones. He quoted Bracton: "Litigants who sued by the wrong form of action were in mercy for a false claim and must purchase another writ."

of English legal history. Lawyers pushed to broaden the scope of writs' application. Over the centuries, however, the principle itself was not openly contested.

The call to abolish forms of action was put on the agenda only in the 19th century. Gradual changes were introduced in stages. First, in 1832, particular personal actions were replaced by a uniform writ of summons. Nevertheless, even while using a writ of summons, a plaintiff had to present a claim within a framework of formulas that were copies of the old writs. Therefore, the forms of action remained intact and an improper choice of a procedural formula resulted in a loss.

Another piece of legislation passed in 1833 abolished almost all real and mixed actions. The following reforms, as late as 1852, deprived a defendant of a right to raise objections based on impropriety of procedural formula. Despite the changes that were taking place, it was still worthwhile to invoke a proper writ. Indeed, that party often prevailed who convincingly based his arguments on principles governing the use of an old, formally no longer applicable, writ. This was due to the fact that old precedents relating to specific (procedural) writs were closely linked to particular (substantive law) doctrines. A further step was the judicial reform of 1873. From then on, a statement of claim had to be presented in an application without being framed by a writ formula.[58]

3 First Instance Process

3.1 *Mesne Process*

The phase of litigation aimed at forcing an unwilling defendant to appear before a court was referred to as the mesne process. While, initially, summoning a defendant constituted a private act of a plaintiff, later on, this became the responsibility of a sheriff. The defendant's default might result in the sheriff's imposing fines and securing his movables (by attachment). If further de-

58 Uniformity of Process Act 1832 (2 & 3 William IV c. 39 s. 1), Real Property Limitation Act 1833 (3 & 4 William IV c. 27 s. 36), Common Law Procedure Act 1852 (15 & 16 Victoria c. 76 ss. 3, 9, 34, 42 ff), Common Law Procedure Act 1860 (23 & 24 Victoria c. 126 ss. 26–27), Judicature Act 1873 (36 & 37 Victoria c. 66). Baker, *An Introduction*, 74–76, 98–99, 230; Getzler, "Patterns of Fusion", 173; Lobban, "Contract", 313 ff; Maitland, *The Forms of Action*, 2, 7–9, 81 ("The forms of action we have buried, but they still rule us from their graves").

fault occurred, movables might be confiscated (distraint) and land seized.[59] The consequences depended on the peculiarities of a specific writ.

However, the course of mesne process was extremely protracted. The defendant had a number of procedural means at his disposal to effectively delay it. He could "prove" by a judicial oath (wager of law) that he was not duly summoned.[60] Then, he could excuse his absence resorting to a series of dilations (essoins). A broader range of them were applicable in real actions, in which a title to land was decided. Significantly, for a long time, a judgment by default was in principle not allowed.[61]

While court proceedings were extremely slow, it was not until later that delays became controversial and began to be criticized.[62] Proceedings were conducted at the pace of life at the time. In many instances, it was assumed that there was no need for speed. For example, if the ownership of a piece of land was disputed, there was no risk that the subject matter of the contest would be somehow hidden or taken away by a dishonest defendant. The protractedness of proceedings was certainly influenced by a limited number of court days (*dies iuridici*) on which procedural actions before the Westminster court could take place. That was due to a calendar of farm work and of church holidays. In the 16th century, there were only about a hundred court days in the entire calendar year. Fortescue pointed out that before English courts there were no "frivolous and unfruitful delays. (…) For judgment often mature in deliberation, but never in hasty procedure." Several centuries later Pollock and Maitland concluded that in the Middle Ages "law must be slow in order

59 Coke, *The Institutes*, vol. 2, 252.

60 See: anon. (C.P. Trin. 1504) Caryll 422 pl. 287, anon. (C.P. Mich. 1504) Caryll 431 pl. 300.

61 Coke, *The Institutes*, vol. 2, 122–126; John Fortescue, *De Laudibus Legum Angliae*, Stanley Chrimes (ed.), Cambridge, 1942, 135.

62 Criticism of protractedness has found expression in the 17th century's theatre piece authored by Thomas Middleton: "the best course is to bring thy eiectione firmae, and in Seaven yeare thou mayst shove him out by the Law." When it turned out that a plaintiff is very time-sensitive: "then my advice is thou must set fire ath house & so get him out", Thomas Middleton, *Michaelmas Term and A Trick to catch the Old One. A critical edition*, George B. Price (ed.), The Hague, Paris, 1976, act IV, stage V, line 123–125, 129–130. See Maisel, "*Formula processus iudiciarii*", 214, 220, on overgrowth of formalism and protractedness of Polish procedure in the eve of reform that led to *Formula Processus* enactment. That the process had to be made swifter shows the emphasis put by this statute drafters on mesne process and essoins in particular, Stanisław Kutrzeba, *Dawne polskie prawo sadowe w zarysie*, Lwów, Warszawa, Kraków, 1927, 67, 82–83; Maisel, "*Formula processus iudiciarii*", 218.

that it may be fair."[63] Significantly, the competing Court of Chancery received parties throughout the year.[64]

In view of the ineffectiveness of mesne process, legal devices to expedite the proceedings became very important. One of these was to cause defendant's appearance before a court by making him subject to arrest. Such practices were available before the Court of Chancery, as well as if an action was initiated with resort to the bill of Middlesex or quo minus procedure (part 1.2). If a defendant was not found and therefore not arrested, he became an outlaw. Significantly, as Coke pointed out, an outlaw could not invoke a wager of law.[65] A defendant could avoid arrest or outlawry as long as he promptly provided security for his appearance in a form of either a surety or a bond. While in medieval England surety's liability was taken extremely seriously (he was even risking his head if a defendant defaulted), in later times, another legal fiction was created. Indeed, suretyship by two non-existent persons—John Doe and Richard Roe—was considered sufficient. Importantly, such surety allowed a plaintiff to conduct proceedings even in cases of a defendant's non-appearance.[66]

The complicated and ineffective mesne process was extensively reformed in the 19th century. In 1832 and 1852 it was further allowed to proceed in the absence of a defendant and to issue judgment by default.[67]

3.2 *Pleading*

After securing the defendant's presence, a phase of presentation of arguments followed (pleadings). The goal of pleadings was to clarify what indeed was being disputed by both parties. The subject matter of an argument was referred to by the term "issue" (from Latin *exitus* meaning the end of that phase). While the golden age of pleading was considered to be the era of Edward III, the tradition of teaching the proper way to plead was still praised by Coke.[68]

---

63 Fortescue, *De Laudibus*, 131–135; Pollock and Maitland, *The History*, vol. 2, 591.

64 Coke, *The Institutes*, vol. 2, 264–265, vol. 4, 81.

65 Statute of Westminster II (1285; 13 Edward I c. 11), statutes of 1352 (25 Edward III st. 5 c. 17) and of 1504 (19 Henry VII c. 9). Baker, *An Introduction*, 71–72; Coke, *The Institutes*, vol. 1, 295a, vol. 2, 378–379.

66 Baker, *An Introduction*, 53.

67 Uniformity of Process Act 1832 (2 & 3 William IV c. 39 s. 16); Judgments Act 1838 (1 & 2 Victoria c. 110 s. 1); Common Law Procedure Act 1852 (15 & 16 Victoria c.7 6 ss. 27 ff). Baker, *An Introduction*, 75.

68 Coke, *The Institutes*, vol. 1, 126a, 303a: "Issue, exitus, a single, certaine, and materiall point issuing out of allegations or pleas of the plaintife and defendant, consisting regularly

Pleadings had an informative and evidentiary function. Since original writs were created according to a predetermined pattern, from which no deviations were accepted, these could not present accurate information about an actual dispute.[69] Therefore, it was only during the pleadings that all stakeholders, including a court, got acquainted with what the parties were fighting for. At the same time, parties' statements could be accompanied by the assertions of transaction witnesses or the production of a deed. Finally, pleadings also fulfilled an extremely important delimiting function. In a common law proceeding, a court's task was exclusively to resolve questions of law. It was not, however, competent to determine questions of fact. The pleadings made it possible to determine whether a key issue should be dealt with either by a court or by a jury. An offshoot of this function was inadmissibility of simultaneous pleas of fact and law.[70]

A plaintiff presented his claim first (declaration, count). Then arguments were presented by a defendant. He could either make dilatory pleas or address a dispute on its merits (pleas in bar, peremptory pleas). According to rigid rules of pleading, allegations had to be made in a fixed order. Once a "further" plea had been made, a defendant could no longer "return" to a plea that should have been made earlier. The various rules of pleading differed depending on a chosen writ. In the newer formulas, the rules of pleading were not as strict as in the proceedings initiated by the older writs. In practice, this was very important, as a breach of procedural rules could often impact the outcome of the case.[71]

In addressing a dispute on its merits (answer), a defendant had four schemes of defense at his disposal. He could deny all of plaintiff's claims (general traverse) or only one of these, but one that was crucial to the case (special traverse). A defendant could confirm facts presented by a plaintiff and either

upon an affirmative and negative to be tried by twelve men." Coke pointed out that in order for a legal issue to arise, the interaction of two parties is necessary, and therefore analogous to a natural issue, that is … a child. Baker, *An Introduction*, 83–84, 94; Matthew Hale, *The History of the Common Law of England and an Analysis of the civil part of the law*, London, 1820, 198–199.

69 On the other hand, see that *Formula Processus* article 3 required that statement of claim should show what is the case ("for the defendant to find out why the plaintiff has summoned him before the court"), Jakub Sawicki, *Wybór tekstów źródłowych z historii państwa i prawa polskiego*, vol 1 part 1, Warszawa, 1952, 118–119.

70 The prohibition of double pleading was in force from the 14th century until the statute of 1705 (4 & 5 Anne c. 16, R.C. c. 3). John H. Baker, *The Law's Two Bodies. Some Evidential Problems in English Legal History*, Oxford, 2001, 11–12; Coke, *The Institutes*, vol. 1, 71b; Holdsworth, *A History*, vol. 3, 632 ("He must not use two sticks to defend himself").

71 Coke, *The Institutes*, vol. 1, 125b, 303a.

draw attention to additional facts (confession and avoidance) or deny legal consequences alleged by a plaintiff (demurrer). In the first two scenarios, the end of pleading followed because as a result of a defendant's response, it was already known which facts were disputed and which were confirmed. Thus, it was already established which facts had to be "proved" (by either wager of law or trial by jury). In the third case, the situation was reversed—it was now up to a plaintiff to answer a defendant's allegation in one of the four ways indicated. A defendant's use of a plea of demurrer (the fourth alternative) led to a court deciding a legal issue. A denial of all plaintiff's submissions was referred to as a general issue while the other three defenses were treated as a special issue or a special plea.[72]

Certain circumstances could not be invoked unless these were expressly emphasized in the form of a special plea. Sometimes an application of a general issue could result in a defendant losing his case. A plea of special issue was available to a defendant in limited cases: only if a general issue could mislead a jury. The list of these cases—crucial for success—was determined by the court's practice. It included, inter alia, acting by a defendant in a state of necessity, or a deed being forged. These did not include the infliction of damage by accident.[73] If any facts appeared in a medieval yearbook, it was often in the context of whether a proper plea was raised. However, more often than not, defendants resorted to a general issue, which, in result, limited the development of substantive law. Indeed, the task of deciding complex questions of substantive law, such as the basis and extent of liability for damage, remained the jury's province. The jury, in turn, did not give reasons for its verdicts, nor were these disseminated via yearbooks or reports.

Defendant's questioning of facts (issue of fact) led to a jury deciding a case. If, on the other hand, a defendant applied the fourth alternative (demurrer), proceedings focused on a legal dispute (issue of law) and it was entirely for the Westminster court to decide it. In such a case, a jury was not convened at all. As medieval judges were reluctant to take on the burden of resolving difficult legal disputes, it was usual for a party to demur tentatively. This led to lawyers entering into an informal discussion that allowed a defendant to check judges' opinions. If, on the other hand, the demurrer had been put firmly, it would have meant accepting the facts presented by a plaintiff.[74] In complicated cases, other Westminster judges were asked to join. If, despite this, no com-

72 Baker, *An Introduction*, 84–85.

73 Baker, *An Introduction*, 87–89; Coke, *The Institutes*, vol. 1, 303a.

74 Milsom, *Historical Foundations*, 73–75, 296.

promise was reached, the hearing was usually adjourned. It was often pointed out that a case could not be solved because there was no relevant legal rule.

Initially, pleadings were oral and were recorded very succinctly in a plea roll. Then evolution toward a written pleading occurred. From the 15th century onward, texts of pleadings provided by lawyers were attached to a plea roll. Over the next two hundred years, rules of (written) pleading became more precise and rigid. Deviations from established formulas were not allowed, and a mistake in pleadings led to losing a case. Among most frequent mistakes were those concerning the person involved. According to Dyer's account, a spelling mistake in a juror's name made it necessary to start trial by jury anew (1563). Also, an omission of certain words in a writ formula could cause the failure of a claim. This was true in a 1727 case in which an unfortunate plaintiff lost because his lawyer omitted the very word assumpsit. The defendant made this formal plea after a jury had already passed a verdict for the plaintiff. Many problems were caused by use of Latin. In 1703, a mistake in a double negation resulted in another plaintiff losing his case. Two years later, the consequences of using improper grammatical tenses were considered. However, judgment was given in favor of the plaintiff. In earlier times, many courts were not so liberal.[75]

Formal rules of pleading seemed to be an obstacle to the administration of justice and thus attempts were made to limit these obstructions. From the 14th century onward, pieces of legislation known as statutes of jeofail were issued by the Parliament. Through their use, it was possible to disregard obvious mistakes that in earlier days were fatal to a claim.[76] The reduction of formalism was also sought by some judges, as reflected in 17th- and 18th-century case law. Thorough reforms of pleadings were carried out in the 19th century. The changes led to a deformalization and simplification of

75 Drope's case (C.P. Trin. 1563) Dyer Note. 87, pl. 128 (*Reports from the lost Notebooks of sir James Dyer*, John H. Baker (ed.), London 1993–1994), Dillon v. Harper (1703) Salkeld I 328, Moverly v. Lee (1705) Raymond II 1223, Lea v. Welch (1727) Raymond II 1516–1517. Baker, *An Introduction*, 94–95; Holdsworth, *A History*, vol. 2, 251 ("A mistake in a name, or syllable, or letter was fatal"). *Formula Processus* in article 5 pointed out that omission of party's name or title in a statement of claim was to result in plaintiff's losing his case. Note that he could still file a suit anew. Maisel, "*Formula processus iudiciarii*", 219.

76 E.g., statute of 1340 (14 Edward III st.1 c.6) "no Process shall be anulled, or discontinued, by mistaking in Writing one Syllabe, or one Letter too much or too little." See *Formula Processus* article 1 which probably had also a goal of limiting number of clerical errors that could entail if a plaintiff were to refer precisely to all royal titles. Kutrzeba, *Dawne polskie*, 81; Maisel, "*Formula processus iudiciarii*", 219.

that phase of litigation. In particular, the need to distinguish between general pleading and special pleading was abolished.[77]

The rules of pleading had an important impact on substantive law. Because general pleading prevailed, principles of substantive law could not emerge. The key issues such as the basis and extent of liability were decided by local juries. Justice was administered in casu according to extra-legal norms and intuition of fellow-neighbors. Again, a jury did not give reasons for its verdict, and jurors' deliberations were not documented, which prevented dissemination of the reasons that guided individual juries. Consequently, viewed from a *de facto* perspective, counties may have followed different rules in disputes involving, say, contract law. Thus, the scope of widespread common law principles may have been limited to adjective law.[78]

3.3 *Evidence*

Once the issue had been established, a court would pass judgment. However, it did not address the merits of a case. The court merely decided how a particular dispute would be resolved: whether it be by an ordeal, trial by battle, wager of law, or trial by jury. Thus, a judgment preceded the taking of evidence. If, on the other hand, the dispute related to law rather than facts, it was entirely up to the court to decide.[79]

In the medieval judicial process, (procedural) truth was most often established with assistance of divine intervention by such means as an ordeal, trial by battle, or wager of law. Written evidence (such as a deed) was a complete rarity. Rational means of evidence like witness statements were not known. An important reform was the introduction, by Henry II, of a trial by jury.[80]

---

77 Civil Procedure Act 1833 (3 & 4 William IV c. 42), Common Law Procedure Acts 1852 (15 & 16 Victoria c. 76, ss. 42 ff, 49), 1854 (17 & 18 Victoria c. 125), and 1860 (23 & 24 Victoria c. 126), Judicature Act 1873 (36 & 37 Victoria c. 66). Baker, *An Introduction*, 97–98. John Baker, "The Three Languages of the Common Law", *McGill Law Journal* 43 (1997–1998), 13–14, suggests that perhaps writs containing minor spelling errors were rejected not so much for formal reasons, but for meritorious ones—if circumstances spoke against a plaintiff, and a better argument was lacking, a court, passing judgment against him, used the only available, albeit flimsy, reasoning. Interestingly, such case might become a (bad) precedent followed by other courts which will dismiss plaintiff's claims focusing on formal reasons and disregarding meritorious ones. That jurisdictional drift has been referred to by Halberda, "Mistake of law", 281–283.

78 Baker, *The Law's Two Bodies*, 62–64; Ibbetson, *A Historical Introduction*, 57.

79 Baker, *An Introduction*, 8; S. Milsom, *Historical Foundations*, 49.

80 Johnson, "The Ancient Magna Carta", 17–21 (discussing divergent views about whether the Magna Carta was the origin of trial by jury).

3.3.1 Wager of Law

After ordeal[81] and trial by battle[82] were no longer used, wager of law and trial by jury became the most important ways to prove facts. Wager of law (compurgation, Latin: *vadiare legem*) also invoked divine intervention. The court's evidentiary judgment indicated that a litigant was entitled to take an oath and specified the content of the oath and number of oath-helpers. Issues about oaths almost always related to defendants. From the 15th century onward, the Court of Chancery granted protection to plaintiffs who lost a case as a result of a defendant waging his law. It was assumed that at law such plaintiffs no longer had any means of protecting their rights.[83]

The oath was taken primarily in actions initiated with older writs, such as a writ of debt or of detinue. When a jury was introduced into English legal proceedings, the scope of the wager of law's application was determined by reference to the knowledge available to jurors. They were presumed to know land in their neighborhood as well as be acquainted with crimes committed nearby. That's why a wager of law could not be invoked in disputes concerned with land tenure (such as payment of rent) or in tort cases initiated by a writ of trespass. At the same time, it was assumed that jurors were not aware of agreements which might be concluded secretly. If, therefore, payment of a price or repayment of a loan was demanded on the basis of a writ of debt, recourse to a wager of law was in place.[84] After all, a wager of law could not be used if an opponent proved his case with the assistance of a deed or a royal judgment.

---

81 As in continental Europe, the use of ordeals came to an end with the Fourth Lateran Council (1215). Since that time, clergy were forbidden to consecrate objects used during ordeals. Interestingly, the custom of floating witches remained until the 19th century.

82 As duels in civil cases were not fatal, there were the hired knights (champions) who took part in it. After Henry II's reforms the trial by battle fell into oblivion and was mentioned as an antiquarian curiosity. Still, as late as in 1571, one of disputes was settled by a duel. However, when it was put into practice again, which happened surprisingly in 1818, the Parliament immediately abolished it. Lowe and Kyne v. Paramore (East. 1571, C.P. 40/1291, m. 108) Dyer Note. 212 pl. 293. Ashford v. Thornton (1818) 3 B. & Ad. 405. Appeal of Murder, etc. Act 1819 (59 George III c. 46). Baker, *An Introduction*, 80–81; Coke, *The Institutes*, vol. 1, 294b, vol. 2, 246–247; Hale, *The History*, 125, 145.

83 Baker, *An Introduction*, 348; Coke, *The Institutes*, vol. 1, 295a; David Ibbetson, "Sixteenth Century Contract Law: Slade's Case in Context", *Oxford Journal of Legal Studies* 4 (1984), 313; William M. McGovern Jr., "Contract in Medieval England: Wager of Law and the Effect of Death", *Iowa Law Review* 54 (1968–1969), 26–27.

84 Anon. 1310 (Y.B. 2 & 3 Edward II (S.S.) vol. 19 195 C.P.; quoted after: Baker and Milsom, *Sources*, 265), Cheyny v. Fairfax (Hil. 1598) Richard Powle's Reports (quoted after: Bryson, *Cases*, 219), Mood v. The Mayor of London (1701) Salkeld II 683–684, Thorneton v. Bernard (1703) Raymond II 991–992. Blackstone, *Commentaries*, vol. 3, 151–154; Coke, *The Institutes*, vol. 1, 295a; McGovern Jr., "Contract", 20 ff.

Likewise, recourse to a wager of law against the Crown was unacceptable. For this reason, it did not take place in any proceedings before the Court of Exchequer, particularly if the action began with a writ of quo minus.[85]

It seems that in the Middle Ages, wager of law could effectively lead to finding the truth. If a defendant did not have a good reputation in the vicinity, he could hardly ever persuade a sufficient number of oath-helpers to swear for him.[86] After all, nobody wanted to risk eternal damnation. There have also been cases where a court denied a defendant a right to wage his law because of his questionable reputation. In modern times, however, this doctrine has ceased to perform its function. There were agents, who, for a small fee, were in charge of hiring oath-helpers. Therefore, plaintiffs sought to reduce the risk of a defendant resorting to an oath. For centuries, painstaking attempts were made to persuade judges that it was legitimate to use an action on the case in circumstances where a writ of debt had hitherto been used. The plaintiffs were making these efforts out of fear that, despite the merits, they might lose their case as a result of a defendant's compurgation. The idea was to set in motion proceedings that did not allow any litigant to take an oath. The last time a case was put to an end by a defendant successfully waging his law occurred in 1824. Few years later—in 1833—wager of law was abolished by statute.[87]

3.3.2 Trial by Jury

Henry II's introduction of trial by jury opened a new chapter in the history of the common law.[88] Since a jury was to be a royal prerogative, this mode of trial was allowed only before a royal court. That is why plaintiffs were often willing to file their case with a royal court instead of a local or feudal one. Initially, a type of trial by jury in the form of an assize was used to settle land disputes. "Twelve free and lawful men of the neighborhood", referred to as a petty assize, were to test recent dispossession of land. The grand assize was to try seisin (the title) to land in proceedings initiated by a writ of

85 Blackstone, *Commentaries*, vol. 3, 154; Coke, *The Institutes*, vol. 1, 295a.

86 This still happened in Cristy v. Sparks (1680) Sir Francis North's CJ reports (quoted after: Baker and Milsom, *Sources*, 223–224).

87 King v. Williams (1824) 2 B. & C. 538. Civil Procedure Act 1833 (3 & 4 William IV c. 42 s. 13). Coke, *The Institutes*, vol. 1, 295a; Holdsworth, *A History*, vol. 2, 108; Ibbetson, "Sixteenth Century", 308–309; Maitland, *The Forms of Action*, 17, 63 ("a long chapter in that history might be entitled 'Dodges to evade Wager of Battle', a still longer chapter, 'Dodges to evade Wager of Law'"); McGovern Jr., "Contract", 28; Milsom, *Historical Foundations*, 67, 245–248.

88 The subject of further consideration will be a civil jury and not a criminal one.

right.[89] The grand assize was engaged in solving questions arising out of the original writ (and not as a result of pleadings) and these could either concern facts or law. Significantly, in a trial by jury, issues to be settled were limited to facts only, but included also factual disputes that were raised as late as during pleadings. If, as a result of pleadings, it turned out that a dispute related to law rather than to fact, a jury was not convened at all. Over the 13th century, a trial by jury replaced ordeals, trial by battle, and began to compete with wager of law.[90]

The settlement of disputes by a jury presented certain practical problems. A court was seated in Westminster while a jury was to be convened in the place where land was located or a tort was committed. A practice known as *nisi prius* proceedings thus developed for conducting pleadings and resolving legal issues in Westminster, while proving facts in a certain county. The Westminster court (known as the court in banc) summoned a sheriff to order jurors to come to Westminster on a specified date unless before that day (Latin: *nisi prius*) an assize judge did arrive in their county. Dates were set deliberately in such a way that a jury actually had time to assemble earlier—during a periodic visit of an assize judge whose cooperation with a jury was referred to as the court *nisi prius*. A verdict rendered by a jury was sent back to the Westminster court, which then passed judgment.[91]

Medieval English law was essentially ignorant of the law of evidence. A jury's verdict was based on its own knowledge gathered privately by jurors. They were supposed to know who occupied a piece of land or who committed a tort.

As already mentioned, a jury decided disputes of fact, which was sometimes referred to by the maxim *de facto respondent iuratores, de iure iudices*. Similarly, Coke pointed out: *veredictum, quasi dictum veritatis, as iudicium est quasi iuris dictum*. The jurors' task was to say what is the truth and hence, their ruling was called a verdict (Latin: *veritas*—truth). Since there is only

89 Foliot v. Selvein (1205) Curia Regis Rolls IV 58, Brackley v. Blois (1212–1214) Curia Regis Rolls VI 241 (both quoted after Baker and Milsom, *Sources*, 15 ff). Grand assize has been abolished only in Real Property Limitation Act 1833 (3 & 4 William IV c. 27 s. 36). Due to the volume of this paper, we are unable to devote attention to the doctrine of seisin.

90 Baker, *An Introduction*, 79 ff; Coke, *The Institutes*, vol. 2, 399–400, vol. 4, 158; Hale, *The History*, 149, 174, 339.

91 Baker, *An Introduction*, 25 ff; Coke, *The Institutes*, vol. 2, 24, 422, vol. 4, 158; James Oldham, *English Common Law in the Age of Mansfield*, Chapel Hill 2004, 52–53.

one truth, the leading case of 1367 provided that the verdict should be unanimous.[92]

In practice, the line between questions of fact and of law was not clearly drawn. For this reason, there were often doubts as to whether a dispute should be decided by a jury or by a court in banc. The attribution of a given issue to either a sphere of fact or law was important from the point of view of the development of English law.[93] For example, questions critical to recognition of civil liability such as sufficient causation between defendant's act and plaintiff's damage, as well as the latter one's contribution to it were treated as pertaining to fact and were solved by lay jurors and not by lawyers in Westminster whose argumentation would be recorded for later analysis. It seems to have been the understanding of English lawyers of the time that legal issues to be decided at Westminster were merely questions of procedure.

A party dissatisfied with a verdict could challenge it. A special proceeding was then conducted as a result of a writ of attaint. Jurors, fearing that an erroneous verdict would be handed down, sometimes resorted to a conditional verdict (a special verdict). While stating certain facts, jurors drew attention to the need for a court in banc to decide on legal consequences of those facts.[94]

An important transformation of the jury took place in the 15th to 16th centuries. Then, it ceased to consist of jurors who knew the case from their own experience (self-informed jury). Laymen began to be appointed to it, for whom the trial was their very first contact with a particular dispute. It therefore became necessary to conduct an entire parade of evidence before them. The law of evidence was steadily created, mainly so that jurors would not be subjected to manipulation by either side, and so that they would focus on the issue in question. The trial by jury was reformed in the 19th century. The relevant law was consolidated into a single statute (1825) and, gradually, availability of a trial by jury was significantly narrowed (1846, 1854, and 1873). Litigants were authorized to dispense with a jury and leave factual findings to the judge. In the 20th century, juries were involved only in cases of fraud, seduction, breach of engagement, or defamation. Some of the reforms of the law of evi-

92 Baker, *An Introduction*, 82–83 (anon. 1367; Y.B. Mich. 41 Edward III fo. 31 pl. 36); Coke, *The Institutes*, vol. 1, 155b, 226a; Fortescue, *De Laudibus*, 61; Hale, *The History*, 150, 348.

93 Baker, *An Introduction*, 365, 429; Ibbetson, *A Historical Introduction*, 57–61; Oldham, *English Common Law*, 79.

94 Coke, *The Institutes*, vol. 1, 226b, vol. 2, 425–426; Hale, *The History*, 351. In Brainton v. Pinn (1290; quoted after: Baker and Milsom, *Sources*, 320–321) a jury determined facts (in case: how fire occurred), assessed scope of damage, but left it to a judge to decide whether it was a defendant who was to be held liable.

dence were a reception of procedural solutions long known in the Court of Chancery. In 1854, the possibility of ordering either an opponent or a third party to give written evidence under oath (affidavit) or to produce documents needed to resolve the dispute was introduced.[95]

The need to assess written evidence materialized rarely. If a party produced a sealed deed its verification could take place in a trial by jury with participation of transaction witnesses who could join jurors to reach a verdict. Common law was reluctant to involve other witnesses in a trial. Eventually trial witnesses testifying under oath began to appear in Westminster in the 15th century, and even earlier in commercial and ecclesiastical courts. According to Coke, witnesses could "always" testify (but probably only in a written form) before the Court of Chancery. Since the mid-16th century, it was possible to order a witness to appear before a court even if he was not willing to do it, as well as to conduct a cross-examination, i.e., to ask questions to another party's witnesses. It is worth noting that until the mid-19th century, the common law did not allow a party itself to give evidence as it was feared that it could lead to perjury. From 1851 to 1853 onward, however, parties and their spouses could be heard at trial.[96]

3.4 *Judgment*

After a verdict was rendered by a jury during a *nisi prius* session, an assize judge sent it to the court in banc sitting in Westminster. Most often, that court did not have to take any further action.[97]

At this stage of the proceedings, however, a litigant could file a motion in banc (motions after trial). In the Middle Ages, such supplication could relate to a formal mistake made by an opponent (for example, regarding a choice of an improper writ). In early modern period, however, an important change took place, as motions relating to questions of substantive law also began to be

95 An Act for consolidating and amending the Laws relative to Jurors and Juries 1825 (6 George IV c. 50); County Courts Act 1846 (9 & 10 Victoria c. 95); Common Law Procedure Act 1854 (17 & 18 Victoria c. 125, ss. 1, 50); Judicature Act 1873 (36 & 37 Victoria c. 66 ss. 56 ff). Baker, *An Introduction*, 100 ff, 122–124; Getzler, "Patterns of Fusion", 188; Jones, "The Role of Equity", 168–169; Langbein and Lerner and Smith, *History of the Common Law*, 450 ff; Lobban, "Contract", 320–321; Milsom, *Historical Foundations*, 68.

96 Statute of 1563 (5 Elizabeth c. 9); Evidence Act 1851 (14 & 15 Victoria c. 99 ss. 2–4); Evidence Amendment Act 1853 (16 & 17 Victoria c. 83 ss. 1–3); Evidence Further Amendment Act 1869 (32 & 33 Victoria c. 68 ss. 1–3). Baker, *An Introduction*, 99; Coke, *The Institutes*, vol. 2, 662, vol. 4, 278–279; Langbein and Lerner and Smith, *History of the Common Law*, 246–247; Lobban, "Contract", 321; McGovern Jr., "Contract", 23 ff.

97 Coke, *The Institutes*, vol. 2, 424.

submitted and taken into consideration. These motions in banc played an important role in the development of the common law because these made it possible for parties to engage first in a dispute as to facts and only then, once a verdict had been rendered, to discuss substantive law issues. A consequence of prohibition of double pleading, this was not possible in earlier times.

Motions after trial were available to both the plaintiff and the defendant. The latter, using a motion in arrest of judgment, was able to admit that it accepted the jury's verdict while denying that any claim arose from the facts found. Similarly, by filing a motion *non obstante veredicto*, a plaintiff could infer that although a verdict spoke in favor of a defendant, this did not affect the validity of his claim. A motion for a new trial, which to a limited extent fulfilled the role of an appeal, was extremely important. Motions of this kind could result in a case being transferred to the Court of Exchequer Chamber where an informal discussion involving all Westminster judges would ensue. Motions thus assisted the rise of debate focusing on substantive law. However, these also impacted development of the law of evidence.

In the 18th century, Lord Mansfield disseminated yet another technique—a special case. If a judge present at a *nisi prius* session was in doubt about a proper disposition of a case, he would introduce the key issue to all judges of the court concerned.[98]

What remedies were adjudicated to a successful plaintiff? In case proceedings initiated by a real or mixed action, the award would amount to restitution in kind of a particular piece of land (and an additional compensation would follow in a mixed action). Finally, a plaintiff in a personal action was seeking payment. A characteristic feature of the common law since the 14th century was the lack of legal remedies for recovery in kind of movable personal property. In view of this, a defendant ordered by a Westminster court to surrender goods could simply keep them and only pay their value.[99] In proceedings under older personal actions (e.g., debt, or detinue), a plaintiff sought surrender of a liquidated amount of money actually belonging to him (due to the payment of the price or value of goods). The certain quota had to be determined at a stage of filing a writ and a following judgment was passed on an all-

98 Special case should not be identified with another procedural device applied by Lord Mansfield: a special jury composed of merchants and assessing facts in commercial cases, Getzler, "Patterns of Fusion", 187–188; Oldham, *English Common Law*, 52–53, 104–105.

99 Baker, *An Introduction*, 403. Cases in which restitution of movables was granted were quoted by Blackstone, *Commentaries*, vol. 3, 145, 152, and Holdsworth, *A History*, vol. 7, 438 (in the 18th c.). Perhaps these were only exceptions to the rule.

or-nothing basis. If, therefore, a plaintiff proved his claim only in part, he would be defeated. This harsh rule did not apply if damages were claimed under new personal actions (for example, trespass or assumpsit). Damage suffered by a plaintiff and a proper compensation for it (damages) were determined by a jury in a course of proceedings. It was, however, not permitted to award damages in excess of what a plaintiff requested.[100]

Therefore, a particular advantage of the Court of Chancery was a power to order (specific performance) or prohibit (injunction) a defendant to behave in a particular way. These powers were illustrated and justified by maxims of equity: "equity looks on that as done which ought to be done" and "equity acts *in personam*."[101] The sanction for ignoring such judgment was imprisonment for contempt of court. Thus, the Court of Chancery could order a party to a contract to effectively perform it in kind.[102] The resulting benefit for a plaintiff referred primarily to disputes over land, since in a case of movable property it was assumed that it could usually be purchased on a market.[103] According to the medieval standpoint these powers of the Court of Chancery were beneficial especially to a defendant who could be thus saved from posthumous punishment.[104] The Court of Chancery could also prohibit (injunct) a defendant from behaving in a certain way: for example, from enforcing a judgment already given by the Westminster court.[105] On the other hand, however, before the Court of Chancery a plaintiff could not seek an award of monetary damages. These were awarded in this court quite exceptionally.[106] In the mid-19th century, statutory reforms were made in this respect and, henceforth, the Westminster courts could order specific performance (1852–1854), while in the Court of Chancery it became possible to award damages (1858). Thus, one of the serious defects of English law was removed.[107]

---

100 Coke, *The Institutes*, vol. 2, 289.

101 Edelman in *Snell's Equity*, 105–106.

102 Zimmermann, *The Law of Obligations*, 776–781.

103 See: Buxton v. Lister and Cooper (1746) Atkyns III 383–384. Lobban, "Contract", 550 ff.

104 Anon. (1489) Y.B. 4 Hen. VII fol. 4 Hil. Pl. 8 (quoted after Langbein and Lerner and Smith, *History of the Common Law*, 313–314).

105 Note (c. 1629) BL MS Hargr. 30, fo. 119, pl. 1 in Turnour's Reports (quoted after Bryson, *Cases*, 595).

106 Maplesden v. Rastall (Ch. 1605) Herts. R.O. MS. Verulam XII.A.30, fo. 56, pl. 1, Longman v. Hopgood (Ch. 1628) Herts. R.O.MS. Verulam XII.A.50, fo. [76v], pl. 1 (both quoted after: Bryson, *Cases*, 343, 548), City of London v. Nash (1747) Atkyns III 512–517.

107 Common Law Procedure Act 1852 (15 & 16 Victoria c. 76 s. 126), Common Law Procedure Act 1854 (17 & 18 Victoria c. 125 ss. 78, 79), Chancery Amendment Act 1858 (21 & 22 Victoria c. 27 s. 2).

What were the consequences of a judgment? The principle of res judicata had been known to some extent since the early 13th century, and from the mid-14th century a plea of estoppel by record was also recognized. These devices made it possible for a defendant to overcome a claim that contradicted a previous judgment. Nevertheless, English law has not developed clear rules on the effect of judgments. Coke explained that a plaintiff's loss of a case could mean either nonsuit or *retraxit*. While a *retraxit* was peremptory, a nonsuit did not, in principle, preclude a plaintiff from re-starting the proceedings anew. The difficulty in understanding how a plea of res judicata was applied is perhaps rooted in the lack of clear rules binding at that time. Lawyers did not distinguish between decisions dismissing a plaintiff's claim on a formal basis and those dismissals that were founded on the merits.[108] Holdsworth, on the other hand, pointed out that res judicata applied in real actions while a judgment issued in a personal action did not deprive a losing party of a chance to defeat his opponent in a new litigation.[109]

Considerations as to the plea of res judicata were also carried out in relation to incidents where a defendant had waged his law. Could a plaintiff, in such circumstances, trigger new proceedings, this time on the basis of a writ not allowing an oath to be taken? While Coke and Style denied such availability ("the plaintiff is barred forever"), there were others, among them Powell, proposing alternative answers.[110]

Powell's standpoint could be regarded as theoretically correct.[111] Coke's position, on the other hand, was probably more reflective of practice, particularly in a field of contract law. If a defendant waged his law in a suit initiated by a writ of debt, he thereby prevented a plaintiff from re-litigating the dispute

108 In *Bass v. Firmen* (1701) Raymond I 697 it was stated that a nonsuit not addressing the merits is not an obstacle to a subsequent proceeding.

109 Coke, *The Institutes*, vol. 1, 139a. Holdsworth, *A History*, vol. 5, 323, vol. 7, 16–17, points out to Ferrer's case (1599) Coke Rep. VI f. 7b (*res iudicata* in *real actions*) and Keene on the Demise of Angel v. Angel and Another (1796) T.R. VI 740–741. Coke in his report of Ferrer's case emphasizes twice the maxim *interest reipublicae ut sit finis litium* (7a, 9a). Nevertheless, analysis of this case is not easy, and thus it is difficult to assess Holdsworth's opinion. *Formula Processus* in article 5 was explicit that if a plaintiff lost due to an omission of party's name or title in a statement of claim, he could still file a suit anew.

110 Coke, *The Institutes*, vol. 1, 295a; William Style, *Practical register* (1694). Differently: Thomas Powell, *The attourney's accademie* (1623, 130–131) (both quoted after: Baker and Milsom, *Sources*, 223 ff): "the plaintiff may be non-suit, pay the defendant his costs, and be at liberty to begin anew again at another time, and to lay his action so (in some cases) that no wager of law shall lie therein."

111 Robert Millar, "Historical Relation of Estoppel by Record to Res Judicata", *Illinois Law Review* 35 (1940–1941), 49–50.

using an action of assumpsit, with which contractual obligations were claimed in Coke's time. This was because, in both disputes, the claim's justification was a defendant's debt. A plaintiff, on the other hand, most often did not have an option of using yet another writ.

4 Appellate Process

While the introduction of appeal into Polish adjective law was a cornerstone of *Formula Processus* (article 39),[112] English law did not know an appeal for many centuries. Despite that fact, it seems that this omission was not noticed at all by common law lawyers. If litigants could not agree what is the law, tentative pleadings occurred. Often, if reservations of points of law were raised, a case was moved to the Court of Exchequer Chamber. If no settlement was reached as a result of an informal discussion between judges and attorneys, a court took no further action at all. In cases involving such stalemates there was nothing to appeal against.

If a dispute was about facts, medieval means of proving the truth resorted to God's intervention and thus there was no higher instance to which to appeal. Later, these measures (an ordeal, trial by battle, wager of law) were replaced by trial by jury. However, a jury's verdict was not based on an evaluation of evidence, but was a categorical statement of the truth based on a jury's own knowledge. An erroneous verdict equaled perjury.

The robust development of remedies did not arise until the dawn of modern times. Note that in the Middle Ages the most important stage of a trial was pleadings, which sought to determine the issue in the case. In modern times, the burden has shifted to a later stage of the proceedings—the phase of assessing the outcome of the presentation of evidence. Thanks to new practices (motions in banc, special case), judges were able to control the line between fact and law. This also opened up possibilities for development of substantive law. The courts also began to issue majority decisions, i.e., rulings to which not all judges subscribed. At the same time, they became aware that jurors often lacked sufficient knowledge of relevant facts. Gradually, additional evidence began to be introduced, and a growing possibility of mistake or manipulation at this stage of litigation supplied reasons for providing parties with an opportunity to contest courts' decisions. Common law practice developed legal remedies that, to some extent, fulfilled the function of appeal. These remedies

112 Kutrzeba, *Dawne polskie*, 112.

included writ of error, writ of false judgment, writ of attaint, and motion for a new trial.[113]

Writ of error could be resorted to if a litigant alleged that a court made a formal mistake as to the points of law. This procedure applied only to judgments of the courts of record, which included royal courts. The Court of Exchequer Chamber was authorized to conduct proceedings under a writ of error from judgments given by the Court of Exchequer (from the mid-14th century), the Court of the King's Bench (under the statutes of 1585 and 1589), and finally by the Court of Common Pleas (since 1830). Up to that latter date the King's Bench dealt with writs of error regarding judgments of the Common Pleas. A writ of error against a decision issued by the Court of Exchequer Chamber was to be heard in the House of Lords.[114]

Proceedings conducted as a result of a writ of error did not constitute a modern appeal. It concerned only violations of adjective law, as found in a record. It did not, however, pertain to determinations of facts and substantive law. A party who lost the initial proceedings (plaintiff in error) could file a writ of error only with the permission of a court that issued the challenged judgment. In a new proceeding (process in error), a court (in error) reviewed the formal record and could alter the lower court's judgment. In this way, the wording of an original writ, pleadings, as well as relationship between the issue and the decision were examined. Even the omission of the words *vi et armis* in a writ of trespass could cause the first judgment to be overturned. However, a court record did not reflect the entire course of the legal proceedings. In particular, it omitted events occurring at a *nisi prius* session when trial by jury was taking place. Therefore, procedural errors committed at this stage of the proceedings, such as dismissal of proof filed by a party, could not justify a writ of error. Any doubts relating to the facts and the legal consequences to be drawn from them remained outside the record. For obvious reasons, a jury's findings on substantive law (for example, the causation) could not be challenged in error.[115] Steps toward a modern appeal involving a rehearing by

---

113 Baker, *An Introduction*, 91–93, 145 ff; Langbein and Lerner and Smith, *History of the Common Law*, 250–251, 439–449; Milsom, *Historical Foundations*, 73–80; Oldham, *English Common Law*, 73–74.

114 Statutes of 1585 (27 Elizabeth c. 8) and of 1589 (31 Elizabeth c. 1), Law Terms Act 1830 (11 George IV & 1 William IV c. 70 s. 8). Baker, *An Introduction*, 146–148; Coke, *The Institutes*, vol. 2, 23, vol. 4, 71–72, 110.

115 Statute of Westminster II (1285; 13 Edward I 1 c. 31). Coke, *The Institutes*, vol. 2, 426–428; Hale, *The History*, 344; S. Milsom, *Historical Foundations*, 58.

the second instance court were the reforms carried out in 1852 and 1873. At that time (1873), the Court of Appeals also began to function.[116]

While a writ of error was applicable to contest a judgment of a court of record, in the case of other courts, such as feudal courts, it was possible to file a writ of false judgment. A party dissatisfied with a decision, by submitting this writ, accused judges of deliberate issuance of an unjust judgment. The rule of "false judgment is a king's plea", in effect, resulted in a possibility of bringing such a complaint to the Westminster court.

One could also demand a new trial based on an allegation that a jury's verdict was manifestly inconsistent with known facts (*contra manifestam evidentiam*). A procedural remedy used in such cases was a writ of attaint, known to common law since the reign of Henry II and applicable until 1825. This writ was also used in cases of unauthorized influence by a litigant on jurors' selection, or deliberate misleading of the jury. As a result of bringing it, a new jury was convened that consisted not of twelve, but of twenty-four jurors. If the verdicts of the two juries differed, members of the first one risked severe punishment for perjury. According to belief of that time a difference between both verdicts was unacceptable. Since the truth was one, it followed that the existence of two conflicting verdicts meant that one of the juries had rendered an untrue, false verdict. In order to bypass this risk, in more difficult cases a jury would pass a special verdict. When a jury ceased to be perceived as a self-informed body, it was recognized that, despite acting in good faith, it could commit mistakes. Having that in mind, a jury operating in a writ of attaint proceeding rarely rendered a verdict exposing the first jury to risk of punishment.[117] For similar reasons, a legal measure of *nagana sędziego* (attaint of judge) in old Polish procedure was arguably an ineffective measure.

In practice, the writ of error ceased to be used in the second half of the 17th century. At that time, a new measure aimed at verifying proceedings involving jurors began to be used: motion for a new trial, which belonged to motions in banc. The grounds for that motion included, among others: issuance of a ver-

116 Common Law Procedure Act 1852 (15 & 16 Victoria c. 76 ss. 148–149), Judicature Act 1873 (36 & 37 Victoria c. 66 ss.18–20, 45). Baker, *An Introduction*, 145–153; Patrick Hodge, "The Scope of Judicial Law-Making in the Common Law Tradition", *Rabels Zeitschrift für ausländisches und internationales Privatrecht* 84/2 (2020), 214–215.

117 An Act for consolidating and amending the Laws relative to Jurors and Juries 1825 (6 George IV c. 50). For an example of a 24-person jury see: Burton v. Valoines (1212) Curia Regis Rolls VI 335 (quoted after: Baker and Milsom, *Sources*, 32). Baker, *An Introduction*, 146; Coke, *The Institutes*, vol. 1, 294b; Fortescue, *De Laudibus*, 61, 63.

dict that contradicted evidence gathered in a case,[118] misleading of a jury by a judge during a *nisi prius* session, award of an abnormally high compensation by a jury. The first known case of such motion that proved successful was Wood v. Gunston (1655).[119]

5 Final Process

Reform of final process was key for *Formula Processus* drafters as the bulk of its provisions referred to that stage.[120] In England, the enforcement of a judgment was, at the outset, a plaintiff's task. Only in later times a sheriff, as a royal official, began to deal with the execution of royal court judgments. If a court passed a judgment on the basis of a real action, a sheriff would forcibly put a plaintiff in possession of the disputed property. In case of personal actions, the execution was conducted primarily against the person of a defendant. Imprisonment was possible, initially in proceedings initiated by a writ of trespass, and later also by a writ of debt or detinue (1352), or by an action on the case (1504). Arrest for debt as an enforcement measure was abolished as late as in 1869. While an enforcement of a royal court judgment could also be aimed against a defendant's property, this was a significant advantage, since judgments issued by non-royal courts gave a possibility of execution against a defendant's person only.[121]

6 Conclusion

The period of dualism of courts acting either at law or in equity ended with Parliament passing the Judicature Act 1873. Under this statute, all English superior courts, including the Westminster courts, and the Court of Chancery, were transformed into the Supreme Court of Judicature consisting of the High Court of Justice and the Court of Appeal. The jurisdiction of abolished courts was taken over by the High Court of Justice that embraced five divisions: the

118 Granting a judge the power to overturn—at a request of a party—a jury verdict demonstrates an abandonment of a belief in jury self-knowledge.

119 Wood v. Gunston (1655) Style 466. Langbein and Lerner and Smith, *History of the Common Law*, 439.

120 Kutrzeba, *Dawne polskie*, 107; Maisel, "*Formula processus iudiciarii*", 218.

121 Statute of Westminster II (1285; 13 Edward I c. 11), statutes of 1352 (25 Edward III 5 c. 17) and of 1504 (19 Henry VII c. 9), Debtors Act 1869 (32 & 33 Victoria c. 62 ss. 4 ff). Baker, *An Introduction*, 73–74; Coke, *The Institutes*, vol. 1, 47a, 289a–b, vol. 2, 393–397.

Queen's Bench, the Common Pleas, and the Exchequer, which were in 1881 united into one—the Queen's Bench Division, the Chancery Division, and the Probate, Divorce and Admiralty Division.[122] The Court of Appeals was to perform appellate functions. The apex court was the House of Lords to which parties could further appeal (since 1876).[123] This state of affairs has changed only as a result of the Constitutional Reform Act 2005, when the Supreme Court of the United Kingdom was created and (as of 2009) took over the House of Lords' judicial functions.[124]

The courts established in 1870s were authorized to decide cases on the basis of common law and equity law. A kind of symbiosis between both systems had already developed by then.[125] In the event of a conflict between these orders, equity law was to prevail over common law.[126] Despite the passage of almost 150 years since the reforms were carried out in England, the dissimilarities in the operation of doctrines once developed in common law and in equity law are still apparent.[127] There has been merger of the courts and procedure but not in substantive law.[128]

Similar reforms were initiated in other common law jurisdictions. They started in the state of New York in 1848 (Field Code) and have since extended to almost all American states.[129] Under U.S. law, the consequence of division between law and equity is still visible in adjective law. This is because the

122 Commonly referred to as „Wills, Wrecks and Wives."

123 Judicature Act 1873 (36 & 37 Victoria c. 66 ss. 1–4, 16 ff, 31); Supreme Court of Judicature Act 1875 (38 & 39 Victoria c. 77); Appellate Jurisdiction Act 1876 (39 & 40 Victoria c. 59); Supreme Court of Judicature Act 1881 (44 & 45 Victoria c. 68). Significantly, from the mid-19th century onward, judicial functions within the House of Lords were carried out exclusively by law lords. In turn, the highest appellate authority for cases outside the metropolis was the Judicial Committee of the Privy Council.

124 Constitutional Reform Act 2005 c. 4, ss. 23, 40.

125 Getzler, "Patterns of Fusion", 178, 183–184; Matthew Harding, "Equity and the Rule of Law", *Law Quarterly Review* 132 (2016), 302; Maitland, *Equity*, 36, 175.

126 Judicature Act 1873 (36 & 37 Victoria c. 66, ss. 25, 11). That provision is now to be found in the Senior Courts Act 1981 c. 54, s. 49(1). Baker, *An Introduction*, 59–61, 107–110, 131–133; Fox in *Snell's Equity*, 7, 12–13.

127 See split between common law torts and equitable wrongs. Peter Birks, "Equity in the Modern Law: An Exercise in Taxonomy", *Western Australian Law Review* 26 (1996), 25–29, 53; Andrew Burrows, "We Do This at Common Law But That in Equity", *Oxford Journal of Legal Studies* 22 (2002), 1 ff.

128 Bray, "The System", 539, 590–591; Burrows, "We Do This", 1 ff; Getzler, "Patterns of Fusion", 191, Mousourakis, *Comparative Law*, 273, Irit Samet, *Equity: Conscience Goes to Market*, Oxford, 2018, 194; Turner, "Fusion and Theories", 18, 27.

129 Karen Funk, "The Union of Law and Equity. The United States, 1800–1938", in *Equity and Law*, 46 ff; Mousourakis, *Comparative Law*, 272; Kevin M. Teeven, *A History of the Anglo-*

Seventh Amendment to the U.S. Constitution, which guarantees the participation of a jury, literally refers to claims arising under the law, that is, that part of the legal order developed through the jurisprudence of the Westminster courts. If a party claims under equitable doctrine then he cannot demand that his case be tried by a jury.[130]

Throughout this paper the authors have attempted to show that there were very similar problems in the area of adjective law, although there were significant differences between Poland and England in the structure of state government, the organization of the judiciary, as well as the administration of the law. The essence of these challenges were issues of tension between formalism and flexibility. Whether every formal error will make a claim fatal? How to bring a defendant to appear before a court so that the trial can proceed? Whether there is an opportunity for appeal? What purposes it is supposed to serve? Whether the enforcement stage of legal process is effective? These, indeed, are the evergreen issues of adjective law in any given jurisdiction.

American Common Law of Contract, New York, 1990, 197–202; Turner, "Fusion and Theories", 1.

130 C&K Engineering Contractors v. Amber Steel Co Inc (1978) (California) 23 Cal.3d 1, 151 Cal.Rptr. 323, 587 P.2d 1136 (quoted after E. Allan Farnsworth, William F. Young, *Cases and Materials on Contracts*, New York, 1988, 96). Bray, "The System", 542–543, 548; Funk, "The Union", 69; Teeven, *A History of the Anglo-American*, 253.

Index of Names

Prepared by Mateusz Mataniak

www.ingramcontent.com/pod-product-compliance
Lightning Source LLC
Chambersburg PA
CBHW051401240926
51852CB00002B/79
9789004736665